PRAISE FOR *OVERTURNING A*

In the increasingly crowded field of scholarship on Aboriginal legal issues,
Overturning aqua nullius *makes a significant break-through in our understanding of Indigenous water rights in Australia, a subject that has received insufficient attention. Dr Marshall's excellent book cements her reputation as a pioneering scholar charting new ground in this important field of law.*

Professor Benjamin Richardson, Professor of Environmental Law,
University of Tasmania

A powerful book of global relevance for why and how law must be reformed.

An outstanding contribution to why we must all listen intently to Indigenous peoples for Indigenous solutions for local, national and global issues. This is a book for us all but especially law and policy makers to make happen the necessary and reasonable proposed legal reform. Read with urgency.

Professor Jacinta Ruru, University of Otago and Co-Director Ngā Pae o te
Māramatanga New Zealand's Māori Centre of Research Excellence

Our water rights and interests of Aboriginal people have been ignored by government and powerful stakeholders, who together have carved up the water market in Australia.

Aboriginal communities have been left with inadequate water infrastructure and often with poor quality water that impacts their health and welfare. Our economic interests in water are not even considered. Overturning aqua nullius *is an important contribution to the debate on Aboriginal water rights.*

Anthony Watson
Chairman, Kimberley Land Council

OVERTURNING AQUA NULLIUS:

SECURING ABORIGINAL WATER RIGHTS

Virginia Marshall

ABORIGINAL
STUDIES PRESS

First published in 2017 by Aboriginal Studies Press

Aboriginal Studies Press
is the publishing arm of the
Australian Institute of Aboriginal
and Torres Strait Islander Studies
GPO Box 553, Canberra, ACT 2601
Phone: (61 2) 6246 1883
Fax: (61 2) 6261 4288
Email: asp@aiatsis.gov.au
Web: aiatsis.gov.au/asp

National Library of Australia
Cataloguing-in-Publication data:

Author: Virginia Marshall
Title: Overcoming Aqua Nullius
ISBN: 9781922059093
Subjects: Native Title (Australia)- Water law and legislation- Water rights

Front cover: Annie Milgin 'Water Dreaming'
Cover design: Sprout Design
Printed in Australia by SOS Print and Design

FOREWORD

The Hon. Michael Kirby AC CMG[1]

In this important work, Dr Virginia Marshall quotes the United Nations World Water Development report of 2006 as making the self-evident comment that 'Water is power, and those who control the flow of water in time and space can exercise this power in various ways'.[2] The recognition of this fact provides part of the explanation as to why this book is important to the law and justice in Australia. However, the importance long precedes the work of the United Nations, and the adoption of universal human rights law to safeguard the basic entitlement of people everywhere (and indigenous peoples in particular) to have access to, and use of, water. Water is one of the essential elements: a precondition to human and other life forms, to the existence of planet Earth, and to the very beginnings of the universe itself.

Scientists tell us that water is a by-product of the formation of stars. Long millennia before the beginnings of human society on Earth, water emerged from the fusion of hydrogen and oxygen to create gigantic clouds of water vapour that exist in the universe, not only in our galaxy but inferentially in galaxies beyond our imagination.

Without water, life in its myriad forms could not exist. Liquid water covers more than 70 per cent of the Earth's surface. Two planets, Earth and Mars, have or have had significant oceans. When humans peer into the universe at celestial bodies, they are constantly searching for evidence of water. Without water, human beings, with their developed brains and consciousness, could not survive. Water constitutes up to 75 per cent of the human body. Some water is ingested through food. Humans can live for a time without food. But without water, we quickly die. We need a lot of it. Much of the effort of the global community since the Millennium Development

Goals of 2000 has been directed to ensuring reliable and ready daily access to safe drinking water, which has, until now, been denied to billions of human beings.

Water is not only essential to the lives of individual human beings. It is crucial to human society. It is necessary to washing and purification, transport, the growth of agriculture, recreation, and the development of enterprise and industry. Water is thus a chief ingredient to the survival and prosperity of the communities that allow humans to live together in relative peace and with access to water.

We know all these facts in a general way in Australia because our continental country is all too often subject to drought and severe water shortages. The first words of this book begin with reminders of the claims by political leaders, media and others that a particular drought is the 'worst for a hundred years' or the 'worst in living memory'. This recurring issue is important for us all. But most of us live in a relatively narrow strip of land not far from the coastline of our huge country. The Indigenous people, especially Australian Aboriginal people, live, and have lived for millennia, in remote dry areas of the country rarely visited by their fellow citizens. This is the Australia that is rarely seen, except from a seat of an aeroplane traversing the Red Centre on the way to more hospitable places, where drinkable and safe water flows freely at the turn of a tap.

The mention at the outset of this book of the great droughts to which Australia is prone affords an immediate metaphor for a drought of a different kind. I refer to the gaps in the law of Australia that have afflicted Indigenous peoples, especially the Aboriginal people, ever since the beginnings of European settlement. For nearly 150 years after the establishment of the British penal colony in Sydney in 1788, the law of Australia did not recognise, or acknowledge in any way, rights in law belonging to the people native to the land.[3] Neither to land nor to water. In 1847 the Supreme Court of New South Wales stated 'that [title to] the wastelands of this Colony are, and ever have been, from the time of its first settlement in 1788, in the Crown'.[4]

This title of the Crown was originally held to be 'inconsistent with any interest of the ancient owners ... the aboriginal inhabitants'.[5] Quite quickly, every colony in Australia went on to develop institutions involving various forms of democracy, a by-product of the lessons learned by the British Government from the loss of the American settlements following their revolution of 1776. It is a sombre reflection on the limitations of legislative democracy, as it has operated in Australia, that none of the elected parliaments, colonial, state or federal, saw fit, during the long drought of the law, to repair and correct fully the fundamental legal principle that stood in the way, like a mighty dam, to enforce the hypothesis of terra nullius.

None released the healing waters of reform to the parched lands below. That action was taken, in the end, not by elected parliaments of the Australian nation. It was taken by a majority of Justices of the High Court of Australia[6] in *Mabo v Queensland [No. 2]*.[7]

In order to comprehend the dimensions of the change in the understanding of the common law of Australia on this subject, it is essential to appreciate the foundations for the change. The first was the acceptance that a *factual* mistake had been made by the earlier judges in assigning the 'indigenous inhabitants of the Australian colonies as people too low in the scale of social organization to be acknowledged as possessing rights and interests in lands'.[8] The second was a *legal* conclusion that withdrawing recognition of such rights could now be seen as an 'unjust and discriminatory doctrine of [a] kind that could no longer be accepted'.[9] Important for the thesis that Dr Marshall advances in this book was the way in which Justice Brennan founded this legal conclusion in the developing notions of the law of the civilised international order, respecting universal human rights.[10] What the judges in 1847 had declared, the judges in 1992 could revise and re-declare. Which is what they did. And although the new declaration was expressed in terms of 'land', to the extent that evidence, and factual analysis, demonstrated that the same considerations were true, in at least some cases, of 'water', the same conclusions would necessarily follow as a simple matter of logic and consistent principle.

The *Mabo* decision was extremely controversial at the time. The judges in the majority were attacked as exceeding their function and altering a basic premise of the law on property rights in Australia, without democratic legitimacy. Attempts were quickly made by powerful interests to head off the impact and the reach of the *Mabo* principle. This resulted in further litigation before the High Court of Australia and other courts. Even before *Wik Peoples v Queensland*,[11] particular challenges arose in respect of claims to water rights in or over or near water, including offshore sea rights.[12]

However, the first substantial challenge before the High Court was rejected, repelling the substantial effort to turn the clock back. The survival of 'native title' in land, subject to state pastoral leases, was upheld in *Wik*. The majority on that occasion was smaller.[13] But having been decided, a series of further cases followed. They endorsed and applied the *Mabo* principle. Where the source of any proposed extinguishment of native title was said to be an Australian statute, it would not be given that meaning unless no other meaning was open in the circumstances.[14] Conceptually, the developing jurisprudence was not limited to interests in land as such. It extended (where it could be proved) to interests in water, including seawater, offshore water, rivers, streams and other water sources.

To bring greater order and justice into the developing statutory and case law, particular issues have been referred to, and reported upon, by the Australian Law Reform Commission (ALRC).[15] The focus of this book is upon how the Australian legal system should introduce into its developing principles on this topic logical concepts derived from common Aboriginal and Indigenous notions about water policy and law. In considering how this might be done, the author has afforded access both to the actual way, factually, that Indigenous (and especially Aboriginal) communities have traditionally addressed water rights and interests and how international human rights law often provides criteria for a framework for legal developments addressed to rights in water, its management, use and access.

A great strength of Dr Marshall's work is that it goes beyond purely factual (anthropological and social) descriptions, although these are examined. Dr Marshall deliberately restricts her recommendations to the law impacting Aboriginal peoples. She does not examine water rights and interests affecting Torres Strait Islander peoples. Dr Marshall, as herself Aboriginal, offers insights and guidance in respect of her own community. She defers to other Indigenous peoples and groups to speak for themselves. But much of what she has written will be relevant and helpful to the rights and interests of other Australian indigenes.

Dr Marshall's research confirms the nexus that exists between Aboriginal health and wellbeing and access to water. Health improves when economic development and cultural rights are exercised by Aboriginal communities. It is on this footing that she argues that a 'reserved water right' would ensure legal and economic certainty for Aboriginal communities, given that native title rights to water, as such, will often be of non-economic value.

Many of Dr Marshall's recommendations[16] call on Australian governments to introduce statutory regimes, to review current laws and to implement informed public policies. Given the state of the present Australian statutes, laws and policies impinging on water rights, these are inevitable proposals. This book should stimulate public enquiries and effective follow-up in the federal, state and territory legislatures. However, the abiding lesson of the great legal drought in Australia that preceded the decision in the *Mabo* case of 1992, and of the instances of injustice in legislation since that decision, render the outcome of legislation in Australia problematic. Certainly, it is a subject lacking the sense of urgency that this book seeks to promote.

Years ago, in the ALRC, I engaged with an early project to consider Aboriginal customary law.[17] The Commissioner of the ALRC in charge of that report, at the time it was delivered, was Professor James Crawford. A lawyer of the greatest distinction, he now serves as a Judge of the International Court of Justice. His report described the slow and only partial approaches to the recognition of land and like rights at that time, essential to the economic empowerment of Aboriginal Australians. An addendum in the report recorded that in March 1986, the federal Minister for Aboriginal Affairs had announced[18] the decision of the Hawke Labor government that it had abandoned the earlier declared proposal to introduce a federal statute for the recognition of such rights, based on the new constitutional power of the federal parliament to enact special laws for the people of any race (including the Aboriginal race).[19] Substantially the legislation proposed by the ALRC report has also not been enacted.

Nevertheless, of all the many important reports of the ALRC, the one on Aboriginal customary law[20] receives the most visits on the Commission's website. It is the most frequently downloaded. Immediately following its delivery, it began to influence civic discourse in the Australian Indigenous, legal and general communities. It raised a level of appreciation of the injustice of the then state of the law. It compelled the urgent need to address that injustice. It affected the Zeitgeist of the nation on this topic. I believe that it had an influence on the thinking of the High Court Justices when they came to write their reasons in the *Mabo* decision six years later.

Law reform in Australia sometimes works in mysterious ways. In this case, the ALRC report demonstrated injustices, and gaps, in the law. These affronted a basic tenet of our national make up, as well as our human sense of rationality and order. Just as the ALRC report of 1986 may have expedited the arrival of land rights for Australia's Indigenous peoples, so I believe Dr Marshall's book will influence the future of water rights as they affect Aboriginal and other Indigenous peoples in Australia. Looked at from the perspective of history, we are definitely on a path to correct the injustices and silences of the past. Dr Marshall can be proud of the contribution she has made to the rights of her people by writing this book. Its impact is now a challenge before all Australians. We can only be proud of ourselves if we accept the challenge and act upon it.

Michael Kirby
Sydney
22 June 2016

CONTENTS

LIST OF ACRONYMS & ABBREVIATIONS

ACT	Australian Capital Territory
AIATSIS	Australian Institute of Aboriginal and Torres Strait Islander Studies
ALRC	Australian Law Reform Commission
ARMCANZ	Agriculture and Resource Management Council of Australia and New Zealand
ATSIC	Aboriginal and Torres Strait Islander Commission
CEDAW	Convention on the Elimination of All Forms of Discrimination Against Women
CERD	Convention on the Elimination of All Forms of Racial Discrimination
COAG	Council of Australian Governments
CRC	Convention on the Rights of the Child
CSIRO	Commonwealth Scientific and Industrial Research Organisation
FPWEC	First Peoples' Water Engagement Council
HREOC	Human Rights and Equal Opportunity Commission
ICCPR	International Covenant on Civil and Political Rights 1976
ICESCR	International Covenant on Economic Social and Cultural Rights
ILUA	Indigenous Land Use Agreement
ILC	Indigenous Land Corporation
NAILSMA	North Australian Indigenous Land and Sea Management Alliance
NSW	New South Wales
NT	Northern Territory
NWI	National Water Initiative
NZ	New Zealand
OECD	Organisation for Economic Co-operation and Development
Qld	Queensland
QYAC	Quandamooka Yoolooburrabee Aboriginal Corporation
RIWR	Reserved Indigenous Water Rights
SA	South Australia
SDL	Sustainable Diversion Limit
Tas	Tasmania
TEK	Traditional Ecological Knowledge
UNDRIP	United Nations Declaration on the Rights of Indigenous Peoples
UNESCO	United Nations Educational, Scientific and Cultural Organization
Vic	Victoria
WA	Western Australia
WAL	water access licences

PREFACE

Water has and always will play a significant role in my life. As a young child I swam and went fishing. I remember swimming through the ocean waves far from the shoreline and then wiping the beads of saltwater off my skin. The freedom of being surrounded by glistening water, either in the river or the ocean, is an important part of my being.

Since embarking upon my research I am more acutely aware of the integral spiritual relationship water conveys in Aboriginal society and within my own family. My identity is central to this research and the Aboriginal perspective of this book. Many books are written about Aboriginal communities and not by Aboriginal peoples.

In 2005, the first year of my doctoral studies, Australia was in the midst of a devastating drought and a great number of Australians experienced the personal and economic impact of water scarcity. Public commentary in the media regularly debated the state of Australia's water management and the need for governments to advocate and secure water access and use for industry, farmers and irrigators. The experiences of Aboriginal communities were barely written or spoken about. From my daily reading and research, the silence of the media on Aboriginal water rights was telling. Why was there no interest in the First Australians?

The national dialogue on Australia's 'drought of the century' omitted generations of Aboriginal water knowledge – an intimate knowledge of seasonal weather cycles and hundreds and thousands of years in drought. Drought is the cyclical condition inherent to the Australian landscape and the lived experience of the First Australians. Australian society failed to recognise that this ancient knowledge was the result of thousands of generations of Aboriginal habitation, observation, experiment and adherence to the Aboriginal rule of law.

Australia's short timeline of European invasion and occupation virtually ignored Aboriginal water rights and interests. Aboriginal water knowledge would have been instructive for Australian society during this 'hundred year drought' – for example in evaluating the human and cultural relationships of water, how to maintain water access and water quality, to identify the parameters of water use during cyclical conditions of drought and appreciate the significance of Aboriginal water creation stories to understand Australia's ecological environment.

It's taken many years for Australian society to value Aboriginal knowledge such as fire management practices, bush medicines, bush tucker and traditional ecological knowledge. Some sectors of the broader community accept this knowledge as Aboriginal science — a systematic approach to understanding the environment and our relationship with the land, the waters and the ecological systems that depend on them. Recognising the value of Aboriginal water use practices is critical if we are serious in responding to Australia's future water needs. There is a universal benefit in applying Aboriginal knowledge to the Aboriginal environment — Australia's ancient cultural creation is unique and Aboriginal water knowledge is the key to future water planning.

It was timely to receive the Stanner Prize because it provided national recognition for Aboriginal water rights and why there is an urgent need to prioritise major policy and law reform on these issues. It is well overdue to overturn the myth of *aqua nullius* that exists in Australia's constitutional and legal framework — and remedy the wrongs. My desire is to share this research with a wider audience — not just an academic work for the few but a conversation that we all need to have.

This book explores Aboriginal water rights and interests in Australia. In the early drafts of my research I wrote about the experience of common law countries in Canada, New Zealand and the USA and how they addressed water resource regimes with Indigenous communities. Sadly, this material was cut to meet the academic word limit.

My doctoral work examines the general failure of the Australian legal system to formalise Aboriginal peoples' ownership of water as an Aboriginal property right and why this failure affects Aboriginal peoples' rights. In particular for Aboriginal communities to make decisions on the use and management of water resources. The chapters explain why Australia's marginalisation of the water rights of Aboriginal peoples impacts upon the living standards of Aboriginal communities and compounds intergenerational poverty.

The water interests of the Torres Strait are not addressed because I believe this research is better instructed by Torres Strait Islander peoples, who are innately connected to the cultural knowledge and interpretative water dialogue of their communities.

About the author

I am a Wiradjuri Nyemba woman. Wiradjuri Country is generally accepted as 'extending from Coonabarabran, the Great Dividing Range to the Murray River and western NSW'. As long as I can remember I have loved water. Swimming past the surfers and riding the waves back to shore. Childhood memories of throwing a line in - eating freshly caught mullet and pippies. Just sitting on a beach and watching the sunset is enough. My boys love fishing and eating what they catch. Horses have been a lifelong passion and my daughter is a fearsome rider. As long as I can remember music was always played in the house – on the piano, the ukulele or the accordion.

The idea of university came years later. With four years of high school and four young children I applied to TAFE College because I wanted to join the police force. It was hard to believe that a year at TAFE opened other doors to under-graduate studies. My study load with three concurrent degrees in arts, education and law was challenging. Education offered my family the prospect of a better life. There was always a sacrifice — studying when I wanted to play with the kids, leaving early to lectures and home late for evening tutorials and working in-between. When I was admitted as a practising lawyer in Sydney I looked over to see the smile on my daughter's face. We made it!

I started legal practice as a criminal defence lawyer in 2003 before taking up a research and associate position in the Federal Court of Australia under Justices Wilcox and Branson. In 2005 I led the Aboriginal Water Trust of the NSW Department of Natural Resources to establish, administer and implement an increased level of Aboriginal participation in the water market. This opened my eyes to the bureaucracy in water management and the poor level of support for the water needs of Aboriginal communities.

I was invited to attend the inaugural Indigenous Water Summit established by the National Water Commission and was commissioned by the Western Austral-ian Government's Department of Water to review and make recommendations on Indigenous water policy for the Water Resources Management Bill. Since 2013 I have been principal solicitor of Triple BL Legal specialising in intellectual property and Indigenous Traditional Knowledge, commercial law and pro bono work with remote Aboriginal communities.

My role as Executive Officer of the first Aboriginal Water Trust in Australia gave me a deeper understanding of the legal and political issues surrounding water resources — and the government's position with state water policy, water planning and enterprise development. At the time I was Virginia Falk changing my name to Virginia Marshall on my marriage in 2010.

ACKNOWLEDGMENTS

The Australian Institute of Aboriginal and Torres Strait Islander Studies WEH Stanner Prize, with the ongoing support of Mrs Stanner, is recognised as a significant acknowledgement of Indigenous academic scholarship. Winning the Stanner Prize as a 'unanimous decision by the judges' has been a life-changing experience for me– a national acknowledgement of the importance of law reform on Aboriginal water rights. Thank you to the exceptional staff of AIATSIS, the judges and my publisher, Aboriginal Studies Press.

This book originated from my 2014 doctoral thesis, 'A Web of Aboriginal Water Rights: Examining the competing Aboriginal claim for water property rights and interests in Australia', which sought to open a new paradigm in water rights discourse, not as a 'special' interest group but as the First Peoples of Australia. The generosity and support of the Black Women's Education Action Foundation (now the Roberta Sykes Indigenous Education Foundation) allowed me to complete a Master in Laws at the Australian National University. The awarding of the Macquarie University PhD Law Scholarship was crucial to the development of this body of work.

My participation with Nyoongar* Traditional Owner David Collard in championing the water rights of Aboriginal peoples in Western Australia involved emails which were included in the thesis doctoral research – David gave permission for their inclusion, as these were important to understand the context of water policy development. I also refer to my sent emails. For the purpose of research, study and education, portions of other emails, where I am the recipient, are included to provide background and context to issues I explore in water management.

Dedication

This book is dedicated to my children Alecx, Natasha, Duncan and Stewart, and my husband Paul for their inspiration, guidance and support during my university studies and doctoral research. It is also a timely recognition of the generations of Indigenous peoples who fought to protect their rights to water, lands and laws.

* Please note that the spelling of Aboriginal words will vary according to the primary and secondary sources used throughout the book.

PART A

THE INTERCONNECTED WATERSCAPE

Chapter 1

INTRODUCTION — THE WEB OF WATER RIGHTS

Yoongoorrookooni yamoo Woonyoombooni mardoowarra yirramanamirri banoo yamoo koolarrkoordany. Marloo walaninada mardoowarra yoolbooroo. Woonyoombooni yinmany kinya mardoowarra. Nyardoo ningarra Bookarrakarrayoonoo.[1]

The snake and Woonyoomboo created the Fitzroy River, running upstream from Mijirrikan through the waterholes from Nookanbah and up to Fitzroy Crossing. Before that there was no river. Woonyoomboo made that river.[2]

An Aboriginal person from Nyikina Country in the Kimberley region of Western Australia, in describing his or her relationship to the land and waters and all things tangible and intangible, might begin with this story. Aboriginal water values date from the timeline of Aboriginal sovereignty, well before British contact with Australia. The spiritual relationships of Aboriginal peoples to waterscapes and between land and water are inseparable:

In Aboriginal culture in Australia, there is no clinical distinction between land and water, either of water that flows over the land, rests upon it or flows beneath it. Land and water interface as equal components of country.[3]

Aboriginal peoples' relationship to watercourses is tied to the spiritual creation of the lands and waters, and understood as a relationship to an animate object. Aboriginal customary property rights to land and water are bound by birthright, in a familial connection that includes the concept of ownership. In the southern Gulf of Carpentaria, for example, the Waanyi and Ganggalidda peoples hold primary interests in the Gregory River.[4] The Mingindda and Garawa peoples have secondary rights to this region of the river:[5]

Waanyi, and Ganggalidda people are closely related to each other through territorial association, ceremonial relationships ... there are close historical ties with the Lardil and Kaiadilt people of the Wellesley Islands. Rules of Kinship and social

organisation undoubtedly determined access to land and water ... A consequence
of close social and ceremonial ties with Northern Territory based language groups
... is also used to describe land interests.[6]

Water landscapes hold meaning and purpose under Aboriginal laws. After
thousands of years, the spiritual relationship of being part of Country remains
integral, and despite the significant political and social change heaved upon the
lives of Aboriginal communities the sacredness of water shapes the identity and
values of Aboriginal peoples.

The creation story that opens this chapter recognises the relationship of
Nyikina peoples to the river system, the land and the *liyan* (spirit) in its peoples
and all things on Nyikina Country.[7] Nyikina peoples have a name for the river,
mardoowarra (the Fitzroy River), and *yimardoowarra* means Nyikina peoples
'belong'[8] to the lower part of the *mardoowarra*.[9] Underground water, which travels
through neighbouring Aboriginal land, creates a joint responsibility.[10]

Aboriginal water management, as discussed in a Northern Territory study of
water values and interests in the Katherine Region, represents a complex web
of relationships:

> Every aspect of water as a phenomena and physical resource as well as the hydro
> morphological features it creates is represented and expressed in the languages
> of local Aboriginal cultures: mist, clouds, rain, hail, seasonal patterns of precip-
> itation, floods and floodwater, river flows, rivers, creeks, waterholes, billabongs,
> springs, soaks, groundwater and aquifers, and the oceans (saltwater).[11]

The inherent relationships of Aboriginal peoples with land and water are regulated
by traditional knowledge. For generations Aboriginal peoples have developed
significant water knowledge for resource use. Aboriginal water knowledge, traditional sharing practices, climate and seasonal weather knowledge underpin water
use knowledge. Aboriginal customary water use cannot be decoupled from the
relationship with the environment and water resources because Aboriginal water
concepts are central to community and kinship relationships. Unlike Western
legal concepts, water cannot be separated from the land because Aboriginal
creation stories have laid the foundations for Aboriginal water values.

The Western commercial value of Aboriginal knowledge systems – such
as water knowledge, Aboriginal foods and the use of medicinal plants – has
attracted significant interest from institutions and corporations because of the
commercial research value of Aboriginal knowledge. I have worked, and continue

to work, in this area on a pro bono basis for Traditional Owners and Aboriginal representative organisations in the Kimberley region of Western Australia. This includes volunteer work with my husband Paul and commercial lawyer Mark Allen, negotiating and developing various stages of the 'Mudjala Aboriginal Medicine Research and Development Project', to ensure its unique Aboriginal knowledge use and international patent rights of community are defended. My husband Paul was employed as administrator/manager in the early days of the Kimberley Land Council (KLC) when John Watson was the KLC Chair. Our community work with the Jarlmadangah Burru Aboriginal Community and other Kimberley Aboriginal organisations is focussed on strategic capacity building, community skills training and enterprise development on country.

I lived in Derby, Western Australia, and through my marriage, I have kinship with Nyikina Mangala peoples and have been given a skin name to ensure the marriage is 'straight' (correct kinship marriage). My husband's skin is Tjangala and my skin is Nangarrayi. A skin name is the kinship (group) to which one belongs. This familial relationship has opened my eyes to the significant water issues faced by Aboriginal peoples in the Kimberley region and commonalities with other Aboriginal peoples in Australia on water rights and interests.

Like Aboriginal plant and medicine knowledge, Aboriginal water knowledge can be vulnerable to unfettered exploitation by others if such knowledge has weak legal protection. Aboriginal water knowledge has the potential for commercialisation but also exploitation by non-community organisations and individuals, for instance in the way Aboriginal knowledge in Aboriginal bush foods and Aboriginal art have often been exploited.

Aboriginal language is a conduit for water knowledge – language misinterpreted by poor translation into the English language can seriously misrepresent the nature of Aboriginal water rights and interests. The variation of spellings in writing Aboriginal language is common.

The interface of Aboriginal water knowledge and water values present challenges for governments and water authorities in drafting policy and legislative instruments because these values are not understood. The water needs of Aboriginal communities are treated as just another interest group. If government is to address those challenges it should consult with Aboriginal peoples widely *prior* to drafting policy and legislative instruments and also ensure that Aboriginal peoples within their respective agencies and community are engaged in the drafting process. Australia's national water reform process clearly lacked this involvement.

The creation stories of Aboriginal peoples across Australia have often been interpreted by non-Aboriginal writers as simple child-like narratives. During the early to mid-1900s many non-Aboriginal writers were fascinated by what was generally referred to as Aboriginal mythology.[12] But Aboriginal knowledge is complex and encoded within ceremony, creation story and is replete with cultural subtleties.[13] Problems arise in transferring these values into Western concepts. An Aboriginal creation story interpreted by Charles P Mountford entitled the 'Salt Lakes of Kiti' illustrates a reconstruction of Aboriginal knowledge:

> Gumuduk was a tall, thin, medicine man, who belonged to the hills country. He owned a magical bone of such power that he could use it to make rain fall in season, the trees bear much fruit, the animals increase, and the fish multiply. Because of such good fortune the hills people always had plenty of food.

> However, the tribe that lived on the fertile plain below the Kiti range captured the medicine man and his bone, convinced that they, too, would in future have more food.

> But instead of bringing them prosperity, the theft resulted in a calamity which totally destroyed their country. For the medicine man escaped, and was so angry over the indignity he had suffered that, plunging his magical bone into the ground, Gumuduk decreed that wherever he walked in the country of his enemies salt water would rise in his footsteps.

> Those waters not only contaminated the rivers and lagoons, but completely inundated the tribal lands. And when these waters dried up, the whole area was changed to an inhospitable desert of salt lakes, useless to both creatures and the aborigines.[14]

Mountford uses words such as 'magical' to describe the 'bone' belonging to the 'medicine man'. The reference to the 'medicine man' conjures up powerful symbolism of Aboriginal primitive powers. However, the reconstruction of Aboriginal story and knowledge through a Western interpretation of values, beliefs and practices is often inaccurate, and the 'ethnographic writing of frontier settlers, colonial writers and diarists, is founded upon the writer's preoccupation, prejudice and assumptions about Aboriginal peoples'.[15]

Lawyers and policy drafters in the same way often deconstruct Aboriginal laws and practices, to then reconstruct them into less complex Western legal concepts. This approach fails because it seeks simplistic Western concepts which compartmentalise the diverse social and cultural experiences of Aboriginal peoples.

Aboriginal wellbeing is integral in the development of water policy and achieves positive outcomes in Aboriginal health and self-determination as well as maximising the potential for Aboriginal economic development. Although not all Aboriginal communities seek to exploit water rights through commercial opportunities or seek to trade water rights for financial gain, wealth creation through Aboriginal water ownership would become a reality when national and state water reforms are initiated.

The complexity of the interplay between Aboriginal and Western perspectives demands the examination of a broad range of interconnected themes because the Australian legal system has developed, over time, distinct non-Aboriginal legal concepts that are at odds with Aboriginal water use. Arguments in water management and water use in this book are presented through the lens of Aboriginal ontology or put simply how Aboriginal peoples view the world and the universe, and not from the other perspectives, or beliefs and interpretations of Aboriginal water rights. To unbundle the many layers of Aboriginal meaning in water resources requires a particular emphasis on developing an Aboriginal voice and Aboriginal narrative.

The Aboriginal perspective of this book examines concepts and values of water and shows that values exist as ancestral rights which should be formally incorporated within the body of Australian law. Although ancestral water use and contemporary use represent different ideological concepts, cultural and economic water requirements of Aboriginal communities across Australia must be viewed as primary water rights.

This perspective establishes a new understanding of the significance of water to Aboriginal peoples — a value that is inextricably connected to, and informed by, a wider system of laws and customs that govern its use and protection. Aboriginal peoples continue to maintain their cultural rights to water in Australia. This requires national recognition to harmonise Aboriginal water rights and interests throughout the commonwealth, states and territories; unlike the hotchpotch of Australia's Aboriginal heritage laws. The widespread legal destruction of Aboriginal heritage sites is testament to the low worth placed on Aboriginal values, as is the unregulated sale of Aboriginal artefacts on the internet. The continued devaluation of Aboriginal ways of understanding and relating to an Aboriginal environment impedes reconciling past injustice.

Nuances of Aboriginal language are critical to understanding Aboriginal water resource use and the relationship of Aboriginal peoples within their Aboriginal environment. This book uses Aboriginal narratives to explain Aboriginal values because Aboriginal peoples are better placed to tell their own stories. Aboriginal narratives depict the care and protection for water landscapes within 'country' as a legal obligation and a cultural expectation to abide by Aboriginal laws on country.

The purpose of this book is to cultivate a new understanding of Aboriginal water rights and interests by looking at key features such as Aboriginal water concepts, Aboriginal water management and Aboriginal water policy development. Because research in this area is an emerging jurisprudence, it requires an interdisciplinary approach to identify the range of Aboriginal issues that interface with Australian water management, such as international human rights.

This book is divided into three parts. Part A, 'The interconnected waterscape', examines the history, culture and stories of water of Aboriginal peoples in Australia and focuses on Aboriginal perspectives of water and how it is distinguished from Western and European perspectives in water values, use and management.

Part B, 'Trading water — the disconnect in water values' considers Aboriginal water values in relation to the Western ideologies, policies and laws that have led Australia to its current situation. These first two parts are brought together in Part C, 'A paradigm shift for Aboriginal water rights', which proposes solutions to address the rights and interests of Aboriginal peoples by formally incorporating robust human rights within Australian water law and policy.

This book demonstrates that when the unique Aboriginal concept of water resources, and their value and purpose, is interpreted in legislation and in common law definitions, it should be evaluated from the perspective of the Aboriginal community – which is to say, the community that holds the knowledge. There is an inherent danger in defining and interpreting Aboriginal water concepts through Euro-Australian frameworks. This often reconstructs Aboriginal concepts or cultural interpretations incorrectly and diminishes the nature of Aboriginal property rights. The federal amendments to native title legislation and its interpretation provide ample examples of diminishing Aboriginal human rights.

A changing waterscape — cultural identity in contemporary Australia

In contemporary Australia, Aboriginal identity can be a synthesis of Aboriginal and Western social constructs. Aboriginal peoples may seek to maintain Aboriginal customary practice – for example, in their spiritual attachment to water sources to exercise cultural obligations, recognising familial relationships to place, and pursuing economic rights to water while respecting cultural values. However, Aboriginal peoples are generally expected to remain static in exercising traditional customs, law and practices, and when Aboriginal peoples adapt to Western influence and revitalize traditional laws, customs and practices they are generally excluded from exercising their inherent rights or interests. The credulous reasons given in the High Court decision of *Yorta Yorta Community v Victoria*[16] that all Aboriginal peoples should remain in a time warp prior to British invasion/settlement hit hard. Aboriginal communities cannot be expected to live in a colonial vacuum.

> [A]boriginal rights are not frozen in time. Aboriginal culture is inherently dynamic and adaptive and should not be bound to archaic constructs of what practices encompassed traditional life in the pre-historic past. Although Aboriginal rights are identified in a western timeframe, they are not doomed to a static existence.[17]

The Australian Law Reform Commission in its important inquiry into 'The Recognition of Aboriginal Customary Laws' (1986) acknowledged that Aboriginal communities should be allowed to adapt their customs and practices to the changing environment:

> [c]hanges or adaptions in traditional rules or customs, to cope with the drastic difficulties European settlement has posed for Aborigines, may produce something which could be described as synthetic. It is hardly surprising that Aboriginals have attempted to synthesise these new elements along with their own beliefs, traditions and world view. All legal and cultural systems with a long history are likely to be synthetic in this sense. But that does not mean that they are less real or important to those whom they affect.[18]

Jackson, Storrs and Morrison (2005) in 'Recognition of Aboriginal Rights, Interests and Values in River Research and Management', note the importance of the waterscape for Aboriginal communities:

> Aboriginal people have managed their water bodies and riparian areas for millennia. They rely heavily on these nationally and internationally significant wetlands for food, for cultural values, and, increasingly, for economic independence. The need for external advice or assistance has arisen chiefly from relatively recent changes driven by European settlement and other land management practices.[19]

Aboriginal communities are inherently connected to tangible and intangible Aboriginal values, and practices and customs that connect to Aboriginal identity, both as individuals and collectively. A holistic set of Aboriginal water values exists within all types of water because Aboriginal identity is characteristic of water kinship. To culturally identify as an Aboriginal person is important for the individual and the community, and resonates with a unique Aboriginal perspective in defining values, beliefs and practices. Historian Jackie Huggins, a Bidjara and Birri-Gubba Juru woman, described her Aboriginal identity like this:

> Foremostly I detest the imposition that anyone who is non-Aboriginal can define my Aboriginality for me and my race. Neither do I accept any definition of Aboriginality by non-Aborigines as it insults my intelligence, spirit and soul, and negates my heritage. The reincarnate anthropologists have made a stunning career out of a continuous 'Daisy Bates' serial. There are no books written by non-Aboriginals that can tell me what it is like to be Black as it is a fiction and an ethnocentric presumption to do so. I would never presume to know what it is to be white (except when I dine at the Hilton).[20]

It has been suggested in Australia that Aboriginal culture has been weakened because of the import of Western values and beliefs:[21]

> The Dreaming is a set of doctrines and values – the value of everything – which were determined once-for-all in the past. The things of the Market – money, prices, exchange values, saving, the maintenance and building of capital – which so sharply characterises our civilisation.[22]

Aboriginal ownership to water and land is held, from an Aboriginal perspective, by an Aboriginal title that is passed on by kinship succession planning when there are members of a group no longer alive to care for country. The Western notion that Aboriginal law is unstructured and random is baseless.

In his award winning book *Dark emu black seeds*, Bruce Pascoe unearthed archival materials in drawings of permanent dwellings and agricultural use of the land by Aboriginal peoples which contradicts the notion of Aboriginal peoples as nomadic 'hunters and gathers'.[23] Aboriginal customary values and beliefs are regulated by rules under Aboriginal laws that have operated for thousands of years. Australia's emerging colonies and plans for economic development saw governments demand unfettered possession of the land: '[p]re-European Aboriginal *country* was a set of complex and changing rights over land which does not translate into British real estate land subdivision'.[24]

Aboriginal peoples in Australia have experienced economic competing rights for their lands and waters since the introduction of common law and the concepts of English property law. These two distinct legal systems continue to be in dispute because of the increased demands on the use of and access to water, and demands for land and resource development. The 'bundle of rights' concept used in court judgements on determinations of native title compartmentalises cultural or legal rights as unconnected and separate rights (see Chapter 6).

Most notably, since the Commonwealth *Native Title Act (1992)* Aboriginal peoples have sought to assert their ownership of the land and the waters under the Australian legal system, and court decisions have not always met the expectations of Aboriginal communities.

> The culture of the common law has imposed a conceptual grid over both space and time which divides, parcels, registers, and bounds people and places in a way that is often inconsistent with Indigenous participation and environmental integrity.[25]

Professor Craig Arnold, an internationally recognised scholar on issues of land use, water, property, and the environment, argues that 'property concepts applied to understand human being's relationship with an object of property such as private property rights or the concept of the property right require a new metaphor' – that rights in property should be seen as a 'web of interests' in order to explain how everything is interconnected.[26]

Professor Arnold's concept of understanding the wider relationships between the owner of the property and the property itself struck me as a concept that could provide a better understanding for others to appreciate Aboriginal concepts and values of water. Aboriginal water values are not simple generic concepts that represent all Aboriginal peoples, as nuances exist. The development of a metaphor for Aboriginal relationships to water may be challenging because of the diversity which underpins community knowledge and community groups.

Australian society has defended the right to progress and to capitalise the development of the lands and waters, whilst available water resources such as groundwater and soaks held for millennia by Aboriginal groups have been marginalised by the establishment of the Australian colonies and the federation of Australia's states. Western values in property ownership underpin the control of the land and waters by non-Aboriginal interests and gives advantage to property owners in water. Exclusive ownership in water provides a legal expectation to fully participate in policy development.

> In the development of Australian capitalism other forms of ownership have become important, but the value accorded [to] land ownership has not diminished and,

quintessentially represented in pastoral property, it continues to confer social and economic power.[27]

The dialogue on water rights and property rights is similar to the issues surrounding native title and Aboriginal freehold land because Australia's hierarchy of rights and interests favours dominant Australian societal values.

> Labelling indigenous property rights as different from or non-analogous to common law interests in land … is an assertion of the cultural superiority of Western legal schemes over those of Aboriginal peoples … The continuance of such stereotypes makes it easier to assume the inferiority of Aboriginal property rights …[28]

Dominant values reside where Australia's legal concepts such as native title laws expressly state that the common law must prevail above Aboriginal rights.

Challenging the myth of *aqua nullius*

Gleeson CJ has argued that 'the next legal battleground for Australia will be water'.[29] There are transboundary water conflicts in various parts of the world and water scarcity is a major policy issue for developed countries and, according to the World Health Organisation, more so for developing nations. Clean water is vital for all peoples no matter where they live on this earth. Many communities do not have adequate clean water and services, including Aboriginal peoples living in remote areas of Australia. In the same way *terra nullius* was used by foreign powers and governments to seek to extinguish Aboriginal peoples ownership over Australia, there remains an intransigent myth of *aqua nullius*. Both fresh and marine waters, as well as submerged land, occupied and used by Aboriginal peoples, require urgent attention. Aboriginal communities' desire to exercise their traditional fishing rights across Australia are over regulated and a prime example of flawed government policy.

When the common law arrived with the First Fleet it brought Western views on water use and a failure to understand that Aboriginal country was unlike England or Europe. History records numerous examples of the British Empire and Government colonising the occupied lands of Indigenous peoples in countries such as Australia, the USA, Canada, New Zealand, parts of Africa and various island communities. The British plan to colonise the Indigenous-held lands and waters of Australia was backed up by hundreds of years of British experience and knowledge of interacting with Indigenous peoples.

The economic value of water in Australia today is highly prized. From an Aboriginal cultural perspective, however, water equates to much more than a water utility, aesthetic water value and drinking water, and is characterised through many layers of customary knowledge.

> Australians use more than 14,600 million cubic metres of water a year – the equivalent of 30 times the capacity of Sydney Harbour … [It] is the basis of one of our largest industries; it accounts for $90 billion worth of infrastructure investment; it contributes about $6 billion to annual revenues through irrigated agricultural production in New South Wales.[30]

The European four seasons of autumn, winter, spring and summer are not the seasonal cycles of Aboriginal peoples in Australia. Prior to British contact and the staggered stages of colonisation, Aboriginal communities applied laws within their respective countries to manage and resolve land or water issues.

Aboriginal water rights today should be regarded in a similar manner as Aboriginal land rights were when they were legally recognised by the High Court *Mabo* decision which formally acknowledged that Aboriginal title survived. Aboriginal peoples will always tell you that their sovereignty exists, yesterday, today and tomorrow. In the same way that Eddie Mabo and others changed the way Australian society understood *terra nullius* and challenged the fiction that British colonial settlement extinguished Aboriginal rights to land, water and resources, we also need to challenge the prevailing fiction of *aqua nullius*.[31]

Aboriginal communities relate to and contemplate value in the environment as integral to Aboriginal identity in a way that articulates both communal and individual belonging to country. The land, the waters and the creation stories are the essence of Aboriginal identity, where 'sacredness' particularises an inherent relationship to the environment unique to Aboriginal peoples. There is nothing English about an Aboriginal environment.

The landmark decision in *Mabo v Queensland [No 2] 1992* (Cth)[32] reformed the national dialogue on the concept of common law and statutory property rights. The *Mabo* decision did change the way all Australians had been conditioned to understand *terra nullius* and the notion that British colonial settlement had extinguished Aboriginal rights to land, water and resources.[33] Strangely enough, around the time of Australia's recognition of native title the Council of Australian Governments (COAG) was planning radical structural legal reform for water resources, which did not include reflecting upon the importance of Indigenous water rights and interests.

In the early 1990s when COAG decided to establish a national water reform framework, our peak Australian human rights agencies, Aboriginal organisations and Aboriginal Local Land Councils advocated for Aboriginal water rights to be included in the national discussion. Little interest was shown for First Peoples' water rights. In 2004 COAG agreed to implement the 'National Water Initiative' and the states entered into a legal agreement (the Intergovernmental Agreement) to advance a blueprint for national water reform.

Among other things, it meant that separating water from the land introduces water as new category of property right. The question of interests and rights to water became more complex for all stakeholders under these reforms. This was particularly so for Aboriginal communities because federal, state and territory laws had, prior to the introduction of national water reform, virtually ignored the water rights and interests of Aboriginal peoples.

A new understanding of the multiple issues involved with incorporating Aboriginal water rights and interests is overdue. An examination of the breadth of legal issues and social determinants affecting Aboriginal water access and use in Australia has not been previously attempted from an Aboriginal perspective, nor has a legal textbook been dedicated to articulate the themes discussed in this book.

The importance of research being undertaken by Aboriginal peoples on water issues is crucial to inform policy and law reform, and over time incrementally increases the critical mass of Aboriginal legal researchers and academics. In the words of Valerie Cooms, an Aboriginal Judge of the National Native Title Tribunal and Traditional Owner of the Nunukul people of North Stradbroke Island, 'unless there are more Indigenous people writing and publishing, there's not a lot for other scholars to hang their theory on'.[34]

An informed national discussion between Aboriginal communities and other water users is a priority, in particular how national policy and legislative water reform will be guided and based upon foundational Aboriginal concepts and values about, and relationships with, water that prioritise traditional Aboriginal knowledge. It is important to recognise the diversity of the Aboriginal values in water and the rich dialogue held in Aboriginal language. This recognition will create the paradigm shift needed to position Aboriginal water rights as Australia's priority.

Chapter 2

'WE BELONG TO WATER' — ABORIGINAL IDENTITY AND CULTURAL AUTHORITY

Aboriginal social, cultural, spiritual and economic water values are interwoven, as spiritually-linked concepts and values held within Aboriginal kinship, among all water resources.

According to Gagudju, a Senior Lawman of the Bunitj, the distinct cultural identity of Aboriginal people intrinsically exists as an inseparable part of the environment:

> If you feel sore …
> headache, sore body,
> that mean somebody killing tree or grass.
> You feel because your body in that tree or earth.
> Nobody can tell you,
> You got to feel it yourself.[1]

Western social constructs struggle to accommodate Aboriginal water values – which permeate the relationship of Aboriginal peoples' connection to country. Jackson and Morrison (2007) suggest that 'the characteristics of Aboriginal water use warrants further consideration of the broad landscape perspectives in assessing impacts and engaging Indigenous communities'.[2]

In Australia, Aboriginal peoples recognise a unique cultural identity within the water landscape through familial connections,[3] recognising kinship values and identity through such descriptors as saltwater, freshwater and bitterwater, which are especially relevant when travelling across traditional trade routes and boundaries.[4] In 2006 we went to Narooma for a family fishing holiday and called in to see Lionel Mongta, a Traditional Owner of Gulaga Mountain in the south coast of New South Wales. In conversation he explained that 'saltwater refers to Aboriginal coastal communities, freshwater to communities from inland river areas and bitterwater to communities where saltwater meets the freshwater'.[5]

Marcia Langton (2005) wrote in her doctoral thesis that the distinct cultural identity of Aboriginal peoples lies within definitions of fresh and coastal water and that the 'distinction between freshwater and saltwater is critical in the cultural construction of places in the environment and environmental and economic knowledge of place',[6] and the construction of cultural identity. This demonstrates commonalities with other Aboriginal communities: 'Freshwater and saltwater domains are distinct and separate, and rules that apply to the use of resources in each domain emphasize that distinctiveness in daily life'.[7]

The use of certain types of water has inherent cultural value, such as the preparation of traditional medicines:

> Salt water was used as an emetic, and various mixtures of earth and mud as a protective and haemastatic application to wounds. Bathing in mineral springs is also reported among Central Australians. Sand and mud baths were prescribed for feverish disorders in Western Australia.[8]

Aboriginality has an inherent connection with all tangible and intangible water landscapes,[9] and ancestral creation-based values under Aboriginal laws restrict usage within a gendered environment of land, water and other things. Aboriginal sites represent a balance in animal and plant life because of the gendered environment.

> The *Ngurru-nanggal Rom* is the First Creation Law of the Yolngu. Creation in Arnhem Land is cleft in twain: two halves called Dhuwa and Yirritja. This distinction is as fundamental as up and down, left and right, male and female, north and south.[10]

Aboriginal water management practice incorporates more than notions of utility about the use of water.[11]

> Cultural practices relating to water … include talking to country, 'watering' strangers and others, restrictions on behaviour and activities, protecting others from harm and management and protection of sites. These practices are a consequence of more recent remembered and unremembered ancestors, or 'old people', returned to their countries as spirits. The animating spirits that become children are also believed to enter their mothers from water … rivers and creeks, and their associated features, including gorges, waterfalls, plunge pools, waterholes, billabongs and springs … groundwater-base flows … seasonally inundated swampy areas.[12]

A Western Australian State Government Committee pointed to the emergence of the 'utilisation of Traditional Ecological Knowledge (TEK) as a valid mainstream management tool'.[13] Western knowledge systems should 'recognise diversity in and between Indigenous communities in the process of applying Indigenous knowledge and traditions'.[14]

Aboriginal customary use was also critical in Aboriginal trade along permanent water courses. The Genaren Creek was

> part of a trade route and a source of permanent water and game. Wiradjuri people who commanded country that took in the headwaters and mid-reaches of what are now the Murrumbidgee, Lachlan and Bogan Rivers … [and the] Murray-Darling Basin facilitated trade within and between clans and tribes …[15]

The D'harawal-Bidjigal groups, referred to as 'the D'harawal of the five rivers', are the Traditional Owners of the Hawkesbury (Worondirri), the Parramatta, Georges (Kaimia), Woronora and Shoalhaven river regions.[16] These rivers were surrounded by culturally significant swamps, from Sydney to the southern highlands, and the Goulburn region of New South Wales.[17] Paddy's River (which flows into the Wollondilly River near Goulburn) provided food, ceremonial and initiation areas, meeting places between groups, trade gatherings and medicine for use for Aboriginal communities.[18]

Both access to and use of traditional water landscapes relied on observing seasonal changes in the environment. Aboriginal peoples adapted to the natural ebb and flow of seasonal change and predicted change by traditional weather forecast methods. In contrast to the construct of four European weather seasons, Aboriginal seasonal cycles vary from six to ten cycles across Australia. The Bureau of Meteorology recognises and utilises a number of Aboriginal weather cycles such as D'harawal and Nyoongar.[19]

In Western Australia, the Nyoongar seasonal cycles are based upon an intimate relationship with the environment:

> The sensitivity to the natural environment led Nyoongar to see the world in six seasons. All seasonal changes and patterns of life were part of a group's collected knowledge, and portrayed in ritual, mime and lore. Participation in special ceremonies ensured that the cycle of life continued.[20]

The Nyoongar seasons are indicated by

> *Bunuru* for hot easterly and north winds from February to March, *Djeran* as becoming cooler with winds from the south-west in April to May, *Makuru* as cold

and wet with westerly gales from June to July, *Djilba* in becoming warmer from August to September, *Kambarang* in rain decreasing from October to November and *Birak* in hot and dry with easterly winds during the day and south west sea breezes in the late afternoon from December to January.[21]

Similarly, the climatic cycles for the D'harawal peoples in New South Wales identify

> *Talara* as the time of ice, *Ganabi* as the time of fire, *Gadalung Burara* as the hot and dry, *Murayung Murrai* as getting cooler, *Tugara Murrai* as cold and wet, *Goray Murrai* as getting warmer and wet, *Gadalung Murrai* as hot and wet, *Murayung Burara* as getting cooler and drier, *Tugara Burara* as cold and dry and *Goray Burara* as getting warmer and drier, ending with the appearance of the Aurora Australis in the sky.[22]

Donna Craig (2005) suggests that Aboriginal cultural water rights share common characteristics among Aboriginal communities: 'of law relating to water sites and common throughout Australia'.[23]

Teresa Crowley (2003) argued that interpreting Aboriginal culture is not a simple exercise to embark upon because the concept of culture for Aboriginal peoples in Australia maintains cultural relationships.

> Culture defines stewardship for land and community and these attributes are reinforced to ensure societal continuity. Culture extends to stories and songs of creation, ritual and ceremonial dances, painting and the use of natural materials including feathers, bone, wood, bark, ochres, pigments, leather, clay, stone and water, to express community events and important issues and to preserve indigenous knowledge.[24]

Matthew Rigney, a Ngarrindjeri of the Murray Lower Darling River Indigenous Nations, expressed the inherent Aboriginal connection with water in simple terms:

> [w]e belong to water … we represent 'country'.[25]

The Western notion that water is a utility and separate from human relationships is fanciful among Aboriginal belief systems.

The sacredness of country

Through thousands of years, the spiritual relationship of being part of country has remained integral to Aboriginal peoples.

The notion of country from a regional Aboriginal perspective is inclusive of fresh water, a form of inclusiveness that goes well beyond the western notion … to include all surface and ground water. While from a legal perspective land and water can be separated as distinct forms of property … from a customary Aboriginal perspective the term 'country' actually incorporates water and land.[26]

A notion of sacredness of country remains a challenge for Western value systems:

The abstraction of rights and interests and resulting fragmentation is at odds with the view of country that many Indigenous Australians continue to hold: that the country is not in some sense external to them; they *are* instantiations of country, which is consequently inalienable from them.[27]

Aboriginal concepts in defining the boundaries of country are also difficult to define through Western property tenure concepts, such as boundary marking trees which define territory or funeral areas, among lakes, along riverbanks and sand dunes, to designate the use of the water landscape under Aboriginal laws and hold highly sensitive cultural significance.[28] When I was talking with Leela Watson she recounted that her father could close his eyes, with his pen on paper, and draw every twist and turn of the Nyikina boundary area.[29] Leela said that native title made the traditional boundary lines of country into straight ones.[30]

A Nyoongar witness during the *Bennell*[31] proceedings gave evidence that country was distinguished by 'boundaries of trees amongst the landscape, and this identified country':

Boundaries are marked by landscape … on the other side of Southern Cross they have different trees. They have Gimlett trees … This is Gubran country. The trees in my country, Nyoongar country, are the white gum tree, the Yorgum trees and the jam gum trees. In Wongai country they have mallee trees. Boundaries are also marked by the hills and the names of hills. There might be a hill that you're not allowed to go past.[32]

An Aboriginal water landscape is projected into topographic features dominated by 'sea to mountain, and river to river'[33] and divided by ridge lines to mark Aboriginal boundaries to country.[34] Nyikina Elder Lucy Marshall explains the boundaries on her country:

Aunty's grandmother come from saltwater country. We don't talk about that country. They gotta talk about it, people from that side. We only meet them half way. People from riverside, that's yimardoowarra people, they meet and go back. They don't go over.[35]

Nyikina people's relationship and kinship connection, since time immemorial, is based upon a Nyikina value system. Water values on Nyikina country encompass seasonal cycles and water availability, the location of the water, water quality and the type of water (such as rivers and springs).[36] During the wet season the floods cleanse the waters and provide food sources,[37] and bush medicines, which have been formed by ancestral beings, such as the Nyikina story of the mudjala tree (*Barringtonia acutangula*) that grows on the river banks.[38]

Aboriginal laws are central to traditional and contemporary water management to access and control such things as introduced pests and exotic plant species as well as Aboriginal fire burning to refresh country. Aboriginal customs and practices in land and water management are integral to maintaining the standard of health of the environment.

Aboriginal laws

The *Milirrpum v Nabalco Pty. Ltd. (1971)* case occurred well before the recognition of native title in Australia, where the court rejected the notion of Aboriginal proprietary rights because Australian law had not legally recognised these rights as surviving. Milirrpum, a member of the Rirratjingu peoples, in the north-east corner of the Northern Territory,[39] asserted that 'his people had been unlawfully invaded by Nabalco mining activities which were granted by lease from the Commonwealth'.[40] Milirrpum asserted his proprietary rights to his ancestral lands and waters[41] as communal rights;[42] shared with the Gumatj people of Arnhem Land.[43]

Blackburn J in the *Milirrpum* decision acknowledged the existence of a 'system of Aboriginal laws' and said[44]

> the evidence shows a subtle and elaborate system highly adapted to the country in which the people led their lives, which provided a stable order of society and was remarkably free from the vagaries of personal whim or influence. If ever a system could be called 'a government of laws and not of men', it is that shown in the evidence before me.[45]

The traditional knowledge of Senior Law men and women holds the key to the comprehension and implementation of Aboriginal laws. Water is sacred and regulated by these laws.

Indigenous peoples in Australia hold unique and complex belief systems in the creation of water, and these cultural values are linked to a system of laws that require observance for the purposes of ensuring environmental health of the water, the land and communities. The body of Aboriginal creation stories is essential in understanding the web of interests and law relationships of Aboriginal peoples.

From an Aboriginal perspective, the importance of characterising water through contextual layers of creation stories remains paramount to understanding traditional law obligations – for example, in relation to particular meanings in Aboriginal use or maintaining the quality of a water-hole.

Aboriginal laws articulate the rights and interests of Aboriginal communities as they have always existed in the creation narrative. An ancestral creation story of the Ngarrindjeri explains the relationship of its peoples to the Creator:

> The creation figure Ngarrindjeri pursued his two wives down the River Murray. They had eaten the bream fish, prohibited to women, and were escaping punishment. They travelled to the sea and ran over the land bridge to Kangaroo Island. Ngurunderi called the waters to rise. He flooded the land bridge and drowned his wives, whose bodies became the rocky islands known as The Pages, just off the eastern tip of the island.[46]

An Aboriginal Senior Lawman explains that Aboriginal laws, and the values and beliefs that attach to it remain unchanged:

> Aboriginal law never change
> Old people tell us …
> You gotta keep it'
> It always stay.
> Never change.[47]

Aboriginal customary laws to exclude or not to exclude other Aboriginal groups were clearly taught from early childhood, as well as communal obligations and rights:

> We had our own rules – we couldn't go anywhere and camp. Wilcannia mob when we came down for picking camped on 'The Hill' on the Fletchers Lake Road – that was our camp, a bit away from old Victor Pottom's hut. When we found a job and met up with some of our other relations we might find a place closer in. We couldn't just go and camp, say where the Smiths were, but other Ngiyampaa people would go there.[48]

The traditional knowledge of Senior Law men and women safeguarded the comprehension and implementation of Aboriginal laws – these water laws and values are a dimension apart from how water is regarded in Australian society.

Aboriginal cultural obligations and cultural practice are steeped in layers of traditional and revitalized knowledge. Walmajarri Senior Lawman Joe Brown explains the laws for water:

> If the jila [water found in soaks] is dry we know the proper way to dig them out. And when we take the sand and clay out we know the right story to sing as we dig and how to do it properly. This has saved a lot of people's lives. It was our knowledge of jila that allowed guddeyus [white people] to live in this country. Water is the basis for our songs and our culture. We have been looking after our waterholes and rivers for thousands of years. We have respect because we know that if you don't treat it right many things can happen. This is the lesson that we need to make other people learn. People see water just as a thing that can be drunk or used. They don't see it as part of everything. They think they can own it. We know better. Many things fail because people don't understand this.[49]

A Pitjantjatjara Traditional Owner explains the vast intellectual divide that exists between Aboriginal and non-Aboriginal law concepts:

> There are two lines kuwari [now], two lines ngaranyi [two sets of laws in place]. Anangu Tjukurrpa [Aboriginal law] and government rules. Government rules are like this thing here, written on paper …[50]

> Our law is in the front …

> Should open up and from Terra Nullius to every person's land – A perspective from legal history give you freehold title. Not give you a tjitji one …

> Government law is on paper. Anaguku Law is held in our head and kurunpa [spirit]. You can't put Aboriginal Law on paper; it's the rules that our grandfathers and grandmothers and that fathers and mothers gave us to use, that we hold in our hearts and in our heads.

> Government might try and give you a flat tyre. Don't compromise your Law for a flat tyre.[51]

The Anangu law narrative suggests that Australian law holds a weaker right than Aboriginal laws. The Traditional Owner explains that 'Anaguku Law is not written', but 'held in the heart as spiritual and cultural rules'.[52] Early English laws were also unwritten and valued.

The following narrative of a Senior knowledge holder of the Bunitj[53] instructs on the importance of maintaining Aboriginal law.

Law never change …
always stay same.
Maybe it hard,
but proper one for all people.
Not like white European law
always changing.
If you don't like it, you can change.
Aboriginal law never change.
Old people tell us,
You got to keep it.
It always stays.[54]
Water is your blood.
Water … you can't go without water.
No matter no food for 2 days, 3 day, 4 day if you got water.
If no water … little bit weak … getting hard.
Water important.[55]

The Aboriginal inter-connective cultural relationship to the environment is repeatedly expressed by Senior Law men and women. Aboriginal values in the land, the waters and all things are centred upon this sacred relationship:

Rock stays
I die and put my bones in cave or earth
Soon my bones become earth …
My mother.
Our story is in the land …
It is written in those sacred places.[56]

An essay by the eminent anthropologist Ronald Berndt (1979) recognises the consequence of dismissing the significance of Aboriginal cultural values:

Land, and what it means in socio-personal terms, continues to remain significant. When land is alienated, its natural resources depleted, its physiographic features destroyed, this irrevocably harms not only the trappings of belief but, without doubt, traditional religion as such … Whilst ownership was thrown into doubt from the earliest European settlement, there was no doubt among the Aborigines themselves.[57]

As lawyers around the world recognise that the rule of law must be observed within a democracy, it is on similar terms that Aboriginal laws must be observed on country.

Language and the communication divide

If you ask an Aboriginal traditional owner or Senior Law-man or Law-woman to identify their country and the relationships and obligations it creates, it is carefully recounted. When native title claimants give oral and written evidence in the Australian court system it becomes abundantly clear that there is a language and communication divide. The long-accepted legal method of 'question and answer' in cross examination is problematic because of the cultural, language and communication misperceptions. The result of several law reform inquiries and public submissions into the operation of the law of evidence included a review of the problems for Aboriginal and Torres Strait Islander witnesses.[58] The intention of the original *Native Title Act 1993* (Cth) for legal proceedings was that it was not bound by legal technicalities and the rules of evidence but this was changed by Parliament in 1998.[59]

In *Commonwealth v Yarmirr*[60] the Aboriginal claimants said that 'no essential difference between land and sea country' exists under cultural belief.[61] Aboriginal stories 'often begin out at sea' then proceed towards the land.[62]

Harvey Murray, a Traditional Owner and Yilka native title holder describes a cultural obligation to care for water sites:

> Asked whether there are things I must do for my ngurra [country to which one belongs by birth and skin group], I say that sometimes we go around cleaning the rockholes so that we can have fresh clean water. We can hunt on my ngurra.[63]

Johnny Jango through an interpreter gave evidence in *Jango v Northern Territory*[64] about the ancient story of country that was passed down orally for generations within the Docker River Elders from grandfather to grandfather.[65] He recalled that 'ancestral stories were passed on from knowledge kept in their head, without the use of pencils and books'.[66]

Aboriginal water landscapes retain their purpose and meaning through Aboriginal language. The following demonstrates that place is regulated through customary law.

> The men's place, Pirlpirr is really important. Another name for it is Minnie Creek. Only wati, initiated men, know the story for that place that only wati can look after it.[67]

Reggie Uluru, a Senior Lawman, provided oral evidence on country of the significance of water for Traditional Owners.[68] Mr Uluru was questioned about the relationship of the Yulara Waterhole and responded that numerous waterholes in the area required regular cleaning under Tjukurrpa (law). Men, women and children drank at the waterhole 'many, many years ago' and today the 'Tjukurrpa story' is for men only.[69] He described what it means to care for the Aboriginal use of water-holes near Uluru:

> The family got their water from Ininti waterhole. They walked out to Kata Tjurta to hunt for meat and gather food (mai) and obtained water from the waterholes in the area, including Yulara Purlka. They were walking around this area being taught by my father about all the waterholes, and stories about when he used to live in the area. They were also taught how to dig out waterholes and clean them by taking out the dead animals.[70]

This narrative explains the concept of Aboriginal knowledge and the cultural restrictions on sharing the resources for water sites underpinned by Tjukurrpa.

Johnny Jango relates Aboriginal water values and its use under Anangu laws that underpin water quality knowledge:

> During the rainy time they would get water from the rock holes in the Ranges and the rocks all around. He learnt where to find water following the old people, who would know where to get water when it ran out. They were taught to swim in muddy waterholes, but not clear ones, as they were used for drinking.[71]

An Aboriginal claimant in the *De Rose*[72] case provided testimony for the criteria of the relationship of the Nguraritja (Traditional Owner) to water sources on country, and said:

> [a] claimant had been born of the claim area ... the claimant had a long-term physical association with the claim area ... his or her ancestors had been born on the claim area; or the claimants had a geographical and religious knowledge of the claim area ... the claimant is recognised as Nguraritja for the claim area by the other Nguraritja.[73]

The role of Nguraritja for Yuta (De Rose Hill Station) is that,

> [a] person could be Nguraritja for a creek, or part of a creek [or for] the karu-karu (watercourse) at Apu Maru, which was said to be the path that the Malu (kangaroo), Kanyala and Tjurki took as they travelled across the landscape.[74]

In *Bennell v Western Australia*[75] Nyoongar peoples equated boundaries in country with the traditional exclusivity for waterways. The Court held, Nyoongar still asserted and exercised their rights and interests such as hunting for turtles in the local swamps, the protection of sacred sites[76] and in their belief of the Wagyl, the carpet snake that created the rivers, rock holes and waterways on country[77] – who 'brings rain and ensures water would come'.[78]

In *Gumana v Northern Territory* (2005)[79] ('*Blue Mud Bay Case*'), the Yolngu peoples sought to exclude all others from fishing their traditional land and waters.[80] The Court acknowledged, among other things, that 'it was clear from the evidence that Yolngu law provided for the succession of rights and obligations between clans'.[81]

Gawirrin Gumana gave evidence that under Yolngu law he is entitled to speak for country, and explained succession rights for the Manatja and the Dhupuditj:[82]

Datjirri ... is a gutharra for Manatja country – his actual mari was a member of the Manatja clan. There are no living members of the Manatja clan. My father told me that members of this clan were killed in the Gangan massacre ... Manatja is Yirritja country. Within the claim area, there is an area of Manatja country known as Dhurrwanmirriwuy ... associated with Birrkuda, the Yirritja honey ancestor. I know and look after songs, dances and patterns for Manatja country. My father taught me these.[83]

These narratives succinctly describe how Aboriginal laws order the distinct relationship on country, as well as identifying the fundamental ideology that underpins Aboriginal beliefs. However, the narrative style of Aboriginal witnesses recounting and justifying their claim to country should be better understood by the court system. Today, native title legislation is more complex than the original intention of the Native Title Bill. Since the 1998 amendments to native title laws, where Parliament sought to create balance, instead it has diminished Aboriginal native title claimants' exercise of their customs, laws and practices. The 1998 amendments have impacted poorly on Aboriginal peoples' rights to water under the future act process of the *Native Title Act 1992* (Cth).

Anthropological and historical reports

Anthropological reports in native title claims can inform the context and dynamics of Aboriginal water values. From the early settlement of the colonies and during the federation of the states, countless documents were found to have recorded the inherent and cultural connection of Aboriginal peoples to their land and waters. The Paakantji of the Lake Victoria area and the Walbunga peoples, have substantial material documented since the 1800s and cite the cultural significance and connection of Aboriginal groups on country. The Paakantji and Walbunga anthropological reports include works from AW Howitt (1898), RH Mathews (1900) and Norman Tindale (1940).

Although the observations and analyses of ethnographers are written through a Western lens and value system, they provide insight of Aboriginal values, beliefs and traditional practices. Written colonial observations also demonstrate how Aboriginal peoples hold possession to water as exclusive and non-exclusive property rights. The explorer Thomas Mitchell commented in 1848 that 'the Paakantji occupied different portions of the river and owned the resources and the section of the river'.[84]

During the establishment of the Western Australian colony, an observation under the heading of 'Measures affecting the Swan River and other New Australian Colonies,' dated 19 August 1835, notes that Aboriginal peoples held ownership of the lands and waters because settlers advised the government to '[m]ake treaties with the natives before proceeding farther'.[85]

In 1959 Beckett documents how ownership is held by Aboriginal peoples to the land and the waters — describing when a right to access is allowed and where the use of water requires payment:

> Every man owned a series of swamps, all of which would be adjacent to one another. He shouted their names as he came onto ceremonial ground … He was not the sole owner but he had the right to hunt in them and to give others permission to do so, whereas hunting in another man's swamp necessitated giving the owner half the kill.[86]

The 1878 ethnographic record of Smyth of the Port Philip Aboriginal Protectorate in Victoria describes Aboriginal peoples' spiritual relationship to water:[87]

> [a]ccording to the Woiwurrung people, *Bunjil,* the creator spirit, made the earth and formed the creeks and rivers by cutting the earth with the large knife he always carried … rivers were the homes of Aboriginal people in their 'original' condition in Victoria. Merri Creek provided the Woiwurrung with a diverse range of aquatic resources, especially plant foods such as murrnong … eels, fish, mussels, and waterfowl.[88]

In Sarah Martin's (1997) 'Lake Victoria Report', the traditional marriage patterns of the Aboriginal communities of the Lower and Upper Murray-Darling Rivers are evidenced by reference to the anthropological research of the Berndts, who write:

Marriages between the Lower Murray people and the people they called walkendi-woni from further upstream than usual became more common after contact. The Lower Murray people called those areas other than the Murray River or Lower Darling River 'strangers' and they were not regarded as suitable partners.[89]

A reference in Martin's report includes further comment by the Berndts that 'the Murray River is an important route for trade and exchange of ceremonies and songs, and marriage partners'.[90] The documenting of genealogy in anthropological reports provides remarkable research material and an invaluable insight into the use of Aboriginal water resources.

The significance of Aboriginal water management also extends to the cultural values held in preserving Aboriginal burial sites and to ensure the correct flow of water for burial preservation.

> [A]boriginal peoples believe that it is quite acceptable for some lower burials, such as those along levee banks ... to be covered for short periods of time by natural floodwaters ... covering most of the burials for long periods of time by artificially high water is an unnatural interference ... our people didn't put them under water.[91]

The importance of water sites for Aboriginal peoples in their daily lives is acknowledged in a 1988 Western Australian Aboriginal site report that identified that[92] Aboriginal archaeological artefacts 'are likely to be located within 350m of a potential water source, including swamps, creeks, rivers, lakes, surface water, springs and soaks'.[93] When my family has been engaged to undertake archaeological field work to identify and record Aboriginal heritage sites, the departmental form measures artefacts by a significance rating of low, medium or high – to indicate social, historic, scientific and aesthetic values. This archaeological rating system has the real potential to ignore the connectivity of Aboriginal peoples to the land and water landscape, trading practices and the Aboriginal economy as well as land management practices.

The cultural landscape

A contemporary understanding of Aboriginal peoples' association in the use of the land and waters is evident in research reports, oral stories and other tangible and intangible sources. These associations express the personal and familial relationships to water resources and engage with Aboriginal land management and resource stewardship in catchment areas. The Balladong Noongar Working

Group documented the significance of Noongar country and how 'spiritual beings created the rivers, the rocks, the trees, the animals' and how 'the land was formed later, then man and woman, where the Law was handed to both to obey'.[94]

Cultural landscape is a contemporary term used in heritage management and archaeology to define both the material and non-material and the tangible and intangible environment: 'a cultural landscape consists of the fabric of the land and its natural resources, traditional sites and other evidence of material together with sites of ceremonial and spiritual significance'.[95] Wiradjuri water resources within this cultural landscape include 'billabongs, swamps, lakes, flood plains and tributary creeks',[96] and 'freshwater springs to [support] seasonal Wiradjuri occupation'.[97] Lagoons play an integral role in supplying fish, where the rising waters came from the river end and Wiradjuri men would trap the river water with a tree log to control fish movements.[98]

The International Council on Monuments and Sites (1996) defines an Aboriginal cultural landscape as:

> [a] place or area valued by an Aboriginal group (or groups) because of their long and complex relationship with that land. It expresses their unity with the natural and spiritual environment. It embodies their traditional knowledge of spirits, places, land uses and ecology.[99]

A 1998 research project on behalf of the Wiradjuri Regional Aboriginal Land Council analysed the Aboriginal association with three river systems, the Murrumbidgee, the Lachlan and the Macquarie, including an examination of the Warangesda Mission and Aboriginal reserves, and the significance of non-Aboriginal impact events.[100]

The value of these resources and oral and written testimony from Aboriginal peoples clearly recognises different perspectives on the creation of the lands and waters. It also establishes evidence of an inherent connection and obligation under Aboriginal laws. The oral histories of the Noongar peoples in the southern part of Western Australia are documented in *Ngulak Ngarnk Nidja Booja (Our Mother, This Land)* in the same manner as the Wiradjuri oral history. Kathy Yarran, a Noongar-Kija Elder, explained her meaning of Aboriginal values for belonging to country:

> My memory of the land is of something that we owned. We have always owned the land because we have always been here on this land. It is a beautiful feeling to walk on the land as our ancestors have always done before us. We ran free.[101]

The strength of Aboriginal oral story particularises how multi-faceted the layers of water values are, and how the environment is framed within a holistic relationship to all things.

Research reports inform the co-management of national parks with Aboriginal peoples and their descendants, such as the Biamanga and Gulaga National Parks management project. For some Aboriginal peoples consequences from colonisation include physical interference with maintaining cultural linkages on country. Aboriginal communities across Australia are revitalising their connection to traditional lands and waters:

> [u]nder the pressures of assimilation policy in the immediate post-war period, [Aboriginal peoples] left for places like Sydney to seek work or better paying positions. As these people have reached mid-life or later, some have returned to live in their cultural area. Frequently their absence may be used against them in public, or behind their backs, when issues to do with rights to resources come up.[102]

The Wiradjuri Heritage Study (2001) reported on the historical context of Aboriginal sites and areas of significance, identifying land use history and places of contemporary significance.[103] The Wiradjuri Study tells an oral story about the creation of the Murrumbidgee River (Bila Murrumbidya),[104] how the river was formed by the actions of the female goannas and 'the flood of water rushing down the valley into the Murray River'.[105] Creation story reveals the attachment of the Wiradjuri to Bila Murrumbidya and their connection to the Murray River.

Concepts of Aboriginal identity

The complexity of Western values and legal concepts in water are defended and defined by governments and interest groups. However, the inherent and indisputable rights of Aboriginal peoples have often had to conform to Western values and conceptual norms in order to have their Aboriginality recognised under Australian law. Racial conformity included the introduction of exemption certificates in the *Aborigines Protection (Amendment) Act 1943* by the Aborigines Welfare Board in New South Wales. In an application to the court an Aboriginal person could show how they would assimilate and cease to be Aboriginal. Which meant no further contact with Aboriginal family members once the application was granted— to live as a 'white person'.

Prominent Australian corporate chief Gerry Harvey expressed his view on Aboriginal identity:

[H]ow do you solve the black problem? Australia's got nowhere with solving it. You've got all these righteous people over the years, politicians and do-gooders, all going to solve the black problem – and it gets worse every year. They don't solve it, they're getting nowhere. Then you've got the black fellow who stands up and wants all the land in Australia. And he's only half a black fellow, so is he a white fellow or is he a black fellow? In fact if he's got a tenth or an eighth of black fellow in him he says he's a black fellow. Bullshit! He's a white fellow. All right, so if he's half-black half-white, is he a black fellow or a white fellow? He's half each. He's no bloody different to you or me? Most Australians think like that.[106]

Germaine Greer in her essay 'Whitefella Jump Up: The Shortest Way to Nation-hood' (2003) explained that the way Aboriginal peoples are defined is based upon skewed Western concepts of Aboriginality:[107]

Defining the Aborigine as irrevocably Other has resulted in the creation of non-viable pockets of Aboriginality, human zoos or living museums, in which Aboriginals are considered to be living 'unchanged'. But Aboriginality is the elaboration of the art of survival and survival demands adaptability. To rethink Aboriginality as inclusive rather than exclusive would not involve the assump-tion of a phoney ethnicity or the appropriation of the history of any particular Aboriginal people. The owners of specific dreamings would continue to be so still, and would continue to pass them on according to their law as it applies to those concerned.[108]

Aboriginal peoples' claim to exercise their rights and interests is challenged by Western conceptual norms – often posited in questions about when Aboriginal customs and practices are no longer traditional.

Olney J held in the *Yorta Yorta*[109] decision, that 'the traditional connection of the Yorta Yorta no longer existed because of the diary entries by squatter Edward Curr'.[110] The judge observed that 'the tide of history has indeed washed away any real acknowledgement of their traditional laws and any real observance of their traditional customs'.[111] Black J dissented in the Full Court decision in *Yorta Yorta*[112] on what characterised Aboriginal tradition, saying:[113]

[i]t can be readily appreciated how less physical or tangible manifestations of traditional laws and customs can be seen to be rooted in the past and to be tradi-tional customs in the adapted form currently observed. Adaptations of this nature may manifest themselves in many ways including, to take one possible example, changed leadership structures within modern Aboriginal society.[114]

Lametti (2003) argued that values hold a range of social meanings in land and water that are not restricted to legal and economic concepts: 'Value is a critical concept, the way in which we assign value focuses on use and exchange of particular resources'. The common method of valuation in Western market society is the exchange mechanism.[115] Lametti notes that 'social values central to a Western market society are ones of economic and aesthetic utility'.[116] The Aboriginal economy does not reflect these dominant societal values because kinship relationships within family groups and communities inform the value and meaning, such as the nature of reciprocity and cultural obligations among family.

Former Prime Minister John Howard said:

> There's no such thing as a nation without a dominant culture ... We have a dominant culture ... We have a dominant Anglo-Saxon culture. It's our language, our literature, our institutions ... You can be a part of the mainstream culture and still have a place in your life and your heart for your home country.[117]

Aboriginal values, customary rights and interests *were* the dominant culture for thousands of years, apart from the short time span of one or two hundred years of British occupation – which depends on when first contact occurred. Not every Australian embraces the historic fact that Indigenous culture is first in Australia's timeline. The dominant features of Australia's water and land *are* Indigenous. Aboriginal creation stories provide evidence of this. The difficulty in asserting an Australian dominant cultural perspective under Australian law is that it fails to recognise that Indigenous peoples have adapted to the impact of settlement/invasion. The revitalization of cultural customs and practices by Aboriginal communities is viewed by some as not genuine – a similar approach is formed by conceptualising the parameters of Aboriginal identity. International law recognises cultural revitalization as a legal norm.

> There is tension between the acceptance that the common law remedies are available to protect rights and interests in land held under traditional law, and the assertion that there is no room for a parallel system of Indigenous governance ... As the Court held in *Yorta Yorta*, native title can only continue to be recognised where the Indigenous people continue to acknowledge and observe traditional laws and customs.[118]

Robert Blowes, a Senior Barrister, pointed to the conceptual differences in the control and ownership of national parks between government and Aboriginal peoples.[119]

[i]t was argued that Aborigines should not own or otherwise be in a position to influence the control of national parks. Ownership and control, it was said should be in the hands of government as the elected representative of all Australians. The assumption implicit in this argument is that an elected body dominated by persons of European and capitalist traditions would more likely be able and responsible in preserving the intrinsic values of country and its attendant cultural features than if Aborigines had any real and significant influence.[120]

The dominance of sectional interests in Australia has significantly impacted upon Aboriginal peoples' ability to exercise their customary laws and practices, and assert Aboriginal ownership in water. The voices of Aboriginal peoples are often excluded in the development of national policy because of the limited interest in Aboriginal issues within Australian society. Recognition in the social benefits for increasing Aboriginal ownership in water is overdue. Both Labor and Liberal governments have pushed to increase long-term township leases (a minimum of 40 years and a maximum of 99 years),[121] converting Aboriginal communal lands to market-based freehold that require surrendering or extinguishing native title. Water property rights are just as vulnerable as freehold title because they can be purchased and sold on the open market – to anyone.

Giblett (2005) suggests that the quintessence of Aboriginal water values requires the inclusion of Aboriginal water rights:

> By excluding water rights from native title John Howard was not only dealing a cruel and savage blow to reconciliation. He was also demonstrating his ignorance that water and land cannot really be separated out in this way for both Anglo and Indigenous Australian cultures. Water is the life-blood of land, and land is people.[122]

As Meyers (1994) explains, 'Indigenous Australians value the spiritual connection and relationship with the land and resources rather than Eurocentric notions of native title laws'.[123] The social and economic development of Australian society and the progress of Aboriginal policy are often at odds in the allocation of water rights and interests because of divergent cultural, social and economic values.

> A key feature of the relationship between government and Indigenous peoples is its inequality. Instead of a government-to-government style of negotiation of needs, priorities and resources with Indigenous peoples, Australia has always had a top-down approach whereby the various Commonwealth, State and Territory government agencies … decide the functional areas and guidelines for expenditure.[124]

The Australian Government established the Royal Commission into Aboriginal Deaths in Custody because of public concern that the rate of Aboriginal and Torres Strait Islander people dying in custody was unacceptable.[125] Ninety-nine Indigenous Australians died in institutions — eighty-eight men and eleven women — between 1 January 1980 and 31 May 1989.[126] Commissioner Elliott Johnston QC wrote in his report on Aboriginal Deaths in Custody acknowledging the historic circumstances of Aboriginal Australians:

> I say very frankly that when I started upon my work in the Commission I had some knowledge of the way in which broad policy had evolved to the detriment of Aboriginal people and some ideas of the consequences. But, until I examined the files of the people who died and the other material which has come before the Commission and listened to Aboriginal people speaking, I had no conception of the degree of pin-pricking domination, abuse of personal power, utter paternalism, open contempt and total indifference with which so many Aboriginal people were visited on a day to day basis.[127]

Noel Pearson (2002) expresses many of the methods applied in Australia's plan to assimilate Aboriginal peoples into Western society:

> During the frontier phase Aboriginal people were dragged into the colonial economy for purposes of exploitation, which was only partially ameliorated during the protection phase when the State, in collaboration with the Christian churches, created the isolated institutions of the Aboriginal Reserves, and a modern form of subsistence economy was developed in these institutions.[128]

It is important to acknowledge the symbolic context of reconciliation as a process of education in Aboriginal history. Sadly, as a substantive policy response by government, the formal reconciliation process has not assisted Aboriginal peoples to exercise their rights to water as First Peoples. The recognition of Aboriginal customary rights and interests has only advanced because of *Mabo v Queensland [No 2]* and through the recognition of international conventions, not by national reconciliation activities. Marcia Langton put it this way:

> The rhetoric of reconciliation is a powerful drawcard, like a bearded woman at the old sideshow. It is a seductive, pornographic idea, designed for punters accustomed to viewing Aborigines as freaks. It almost allows 'the native' some agency and a future. I say almost because in the end, 'the native' is not allowed out of the show, forever condemned to perform to attract crowds.[129]

Indigenous Australians were strongly encouraged to forget past injustices – including the theft of land, water, resources, identity and the forced removal of children. National reconciliation was a theatrical event. A decade of distractions – and missed opportunities to embrace a shared history.

The Garma Conference and water rights

The Garma Conference on Indigenous Water Knowledge was held in August of 2008 in north-east Arnhem Land in the Northern Territory. I was invited to participate in acknowledgement of my doctoral research on Aboriginal water rights and professional experience as the Executive Officer of the NSW Aboriginal Water Trust. Garma was an opportunity to exchange knowledge with other Indigenous and non-Indigenous water experts from Australia and overseas – highlighting our particular water issues.[130] Discussions included water trading and water property rights, the United Nations Permanent Forum meetings on water and submissions to the United Nations Educational Scientific and Cultural Organization's Water and Culture Database.[131] The database is used to disseminate a comprehensive data on global surface water resources for agricultural, domestic and industrial purposes.

Garma also provided an opportunity to exchange our experience with water expertise and attend workshops on significant advocacy issues in Indigenous water rights such as the privatization of water resources, Indigenous water governance and the future security of freshwater.[132] We discussed increasing the recognition by Western science of Indigenous water knowledge, emerging global water issues, and the selection of delegates to draft an Indigenous water declaration for the 2009 Water Forum in Turkey.[133]

I was selected to assist with the draft but the water declaration proved challenging. Our small group was comprised of experts from very different backgrounds and local experiences. Reaching a consensus on the language of the declaration was difficult because the objective was to produce a generic framework using accepted definitions of international instruments. In the process I believe we suppressed the voice of Aboriginal peoples in Australia. From my perspective, the cultural, political and economic position of our lived experience in Australia was being poorly represented. In essence substance was being sacrificed for consensus.

What were the positive achievements from Garma? Well, we documented a comprehensive list of key issues for Indigenous water rights dialogue which included: adoption of the *United Nations Declaration on the Rights of Indigenous*

Peoples into Australian law; and recognition by the Nation States that Indigenous Intellectual Knowledge should remain the property of Indigenous Knowledge Holders.[134]

Carlos Batzin, a Kaqchikel Maya, and an advisor to the Central American Indigenous Council, delivered a heartfelt presentation at the Conference on behalf of the Indigenous peoples of Central America:

> Water is powerful … modern development for consumption is a problem that has created problems in the modern world … national laws to make water dearer, the rise of privatisation and the exploitation of our resources by others has affected our spiritual relationship and access to water. Governments have conceptualised water as a public good … they look at water in isolation. Consumerism is our destruction … we all use water.[135]

Sir Tipene O'Regan, a Māori Chief and treaty negotiator in Māori fishing rights, expressed that 'from their belief, God owns the water and the fish'. The Aboriginal water experts and Traditional Owners from various common law countries agreed in consensus that 'Indigenous peoples throughout the globe hold common themes in the value and use of water' and we reaffirmed the fundamental tenet that water *is* sacred.[136]

This chapter has examined why Aboriginal values in water, whether freshwater or marine, have inherent connection to Aboriginal identity and the complex relationships within an Aboriginal environment. Values are held in Aboriginal language – language that signals the seasonal weather cycles, water quality and its particular use and much more. Water cannot be regarded as a mere utility. The chapter demonstrates that Aboriginal laws embed rights and obligations that are more than feelings of the 'spiritual' – that creation stories explain the 'belonging' to country Aboriginal peoples have with water, the connection to land and the cultural authority to act on behalf of country.

Chapter 3

ABORIGINAL PROPERTY AND WESTERN VALUES — CONCEPTS OF OWNERSHIP

Aboriginal ownership of water is central to cultural identity. Aboriginal value systems, such as those relating to water resources and Aboriginal narratives, include an understanding of ownership:

> There is a difference between having an interest in a country and claiming it. I might marry a woman whose country is around Jamieson, live on her land for years, learn the business for country, but I still will not claim that country.[1]

Aboriginal law does not separate the land from the water, nor can Aboriginal laws allow unrestricted economic exploitation of the land or waters without compromising customary cultural values and obligations. The Western notion of the excision of Aboriginal sites into *in situ* or disconnected areas from the whole of the Aboriginal environment is ridiculous. Some Australian states legislate this approach in Aboriginal heritage. Equally, to advance an Aboriginal economy on the values and beliefs relevant to a Western economy model fragments the nature of Aboriginal water rights and interests. Aboriginal ownership rights exist beyond death, in contrast to Western concepts:

> Cultural heritage is the term used to refer to qualities and attributes possessed by places that have aesthetic, historic, scientific or social value for past, present and future generations … There has been an artificial separation of indigenous and non-indigenous interests for a place … the significance of indigenous places is defined by indigenous communities themselves … For many Aboriginal people natural heritage is a meaningless distinction – they are interested in totality with the land …[2]

Aboriginal laws regulate the Aboriginal environment, and the water rights and interests recognised in Aboriginal ownership express Aboriginal values and concepts, whereby Aboriginal spiritual beliefs embody both the tangible and intangible environments – and Aboriginal peoples' narrative of relationships.

> The relationship of Aboriginal peoples to land is particularised; each group is related to certain lands, bounded by physical features and meted [out] by religious ceremony and cultural heritage ... the land is not a lifeless, inanimate commodity to be used and disposed of, it is alive and has religious as well as economic value.[3]

European observations made in 1836 recognised the notion of Aboriginal ownership under Aboriginal laws:

> The land appeared apportioned to different families ... beyond doubt an inheritable property among them, and they boast of having received it from their father's father to an unknown period way back.[4]

To understand how Aboriginal water rights and interests can be recognised in national policies and laws it is important to discuss concepts of Aboriginal property. The national dialogue on transitioning to new types of water rights was a water policy response to the overuse of water by farmers, irrigators and pastoralists. These sector interests were given water on a nominal or no cost basis.

Langton (2005), in describing the property relationship of Pama customary land owners in Far North Queensland, said:

> Property relations are structured by the places as events, and by memories that spring up in a person's mind about that place. Landscapes are perceived not just as geographical places but as metaphorical entities laden with spiritual and moral agency. The property-object of Pama relations is not merely the land estate *qua* geographical space, but the confluent spatiality, temporality and sociality of the landscape, the people and the ancestral beings.[5]

An Aboriginal paradigm of water property rights presents a clear challenge to Western concepts in Australia. The categorisation of tangible and intangible Aboriginal water values brings out a conceptual difference between Aboriginal and Western property relationships. The Aboriginal spatial concepts of 'spiritual and moral agency' described by Langton (2005) represent unique relationships with water and land that have no common thread with Western water values.

An articulation of what defines Aboriginal water property rights in Western terms remains value-laden with social, cultural, economic and Western legal constructs that generally diminish the nature of Aboriginal rights and interests. The overarching framework of Western property rights:

[e]xist to facilitate the acquisition, control, and exchange of assets. While many definitions of property rights are similar, the literature shows disagreement as to the source and origin of property rights, particularly the role that the state plays in originating, specifying and developing these rights.[6]

However, Aboriginal communities' authority over property is governed by Aboriginal laws and the water values that attach to a relationship with land and water.

> In Australia, Aboriginal cultural values are generally regarded as subservient to the economic progress of the nation. Where any public purpose or planning requirement is proposed, the value of Aboriginal sites is doomed … Natural waterways continue to succumb to the urgency of improving and expanding the 'frontier'.[7]

There is a clear understanding from Langton's description of Pama relationships that these ancient 'property relationships' are unable to be severed from the landscape or the Pama community.

The virtual absence of Aboriginal water rights and interests in state water policy plans highlights the power of governments to regulate, at their absolute discretion, Aboriginal communities' participation in the use of and access to water. Robert Nicholson, a former Federal Court Judge, has suggested that Aboriginal law is not sufficiently valued in Australian society:

> It is a further concern of historians that culturally different approaches between that of the law and Aboriginal custom may be insufficiently appreciated and certainly need to be understood.[8]

Australian governments fail to appreciate the difference in approach in Aboriginal water management. The commercialisation of water resources in Australia has obscured the inherent water rights and interests of Aboriginal peoples and undermined progress on Aboriginal water policy development.

> Many Australian cultural attitudes, as well as government policies, remain the ones that have caused damage in the past and are still continuing to cause it … among political obstacles to a reform of water policies are obstacles arising from a market of water licences. The purchasers of those licences understandably feel that they actually own the water …[9]

The 'cultural attitudes' of the Australian Government was a clear sign in the return to colonial style values in the portfolio change by the Turnbull Government in September 2015 to move water resources from the environment portfolio to the Department of Agriculture.

The competition for water – colonial settlement and exploitation

The disputed ownership between Aboriginal customary law and British law has centred upon two very different authorities, those of Aboriginal peoples and the Crown. The introduction of the colonial use of the land, waters and natural resources for exploitation was not compatible with Aboriginal resource use. British colonisation imposed British values that were antithetical to Aboriginal laws and values. Subsequent fierce competition over time disempowered Aboriginal peoples from exercising their customary rights and interests.

The encroaching growth of the British settlement from Sydney to the outer regions led to contention over the new colonial settlement and the demarcation of extant ancient Aboriginal boundaries.

An organised Aboriginal society was 'observed' and recorded in government archives as land was surveyed for settlement purposes. Howitt and Mathews, both anthropologists, wrote from their studies about Aboriginal 'identifiable groups and communities, that Aboriginal peoples had maintained traditional law, custom and rights'.[10] An early account noted by a settler informed of:

> [o]bservations of constructed ceremony grounds, and of ceremonies involving participants performing particular roles, indicative of the existence of an organised society.[11]

The commencement of the British colony in Australia introduced not only a new legal system, but imposed upon Aboriginal peoples a new regime of social and political beliefs which bore no similarity to Aboriginal laws and customs. In the expansion of the Sydney region towards the Hawkesbury, Parramatta, the Southern Highlands and Goulburn regions of the first colony of New South Wales, colonial plans impacted upon the exclusive Aboriginal use of water and land – and their resources.

Colonial settler conflict occurred whenever a new settlement was formed. The disruption to pre-colonial Aboriginal boundaries and the pressure of Imperial Government orders to expand and exploit Australia's natural resources were some of the dramatic changes which caused displacement of Aboriginal communities' kinship areas.

Water resources were a central commodity in colonial Australia, and the necessity to secure water for the townships of Sydney and Melbourne was paramount in further developing these areas. Sydney's first fifty years relied upon water supplied by private wells and holding tanks.[12] After 1791, when the Tank Stream was excavated on the site of Sydney's Hunter and Pitt Streets, barrels were carted from there and from neighbouring swamps.[13] Some 12,000 feet of tunnel water was conveyed from the Lachlan Swamp, now known as the Moore Park Showground, through the use of water carts.[14]

From the 1830s Melbourne townspeople pumped their water near the present day Flinders Street Railway Station and fresh water was drawn from the Yarra River falls. Melbourne's Water Works Company supplied water from a well at the present day Flinders and Elizabeth Streets, in water barrels for retail consumption.[15]

The water supply for the New South Wales colony was improved by Busby's bore completed in 1837.[16] From 1844 the use of reticulated pipes fed colonial water supplies into public fountains. For nearly 100 years little was done by any of the respective government authorities to conserve water, except for the needs of the goldfields, and by the provision of tanks along stock routes.[17]

The Tank Stream in Sydney assured the survival for colonial settlement and underpinned future town planning.[18] Reliable access to water sources fulfilled colonial water requirements and provided settlers with unfettered access to harbours, major rivers and estuaries. But water exploitation alienated Aboriginal peoples, interfered with their water rights, and interrupted Aboriginal cultural business.[19]

The colonies managed water resources in an ad hoc fashion until the introduction of irrigation which commenced in the late 1880s in New South Wales, South Australia and Victoria; fifty years later the use of artesian bores was advanced.[20]

Alfred Deakin reported to the Victorian Parliament on his investigation as Royal Commissioner to the United States to assess the viability of American irrigation schemes for use in Australia. These irrigation schemes were lauded and supported by Parliament – the *Irrigation Act 1886* (Victoria) on its assent vested all riparian rights in the Crown.[21] Riparian rights are beneficial rights of the landowner whose property adjoins a body of water, where the property owner can use the water for drinking, domestic use and fishing. This changed when common law riparian rights were abolished in Australia and replaced with a new class of water rights under national water reforms.[22]

The Western concept of exploiting the natural environment was underpinned by Western values:

Land is described in Western contexts as 'an area of the surface of the earth together with the water, soil, rocks, minerals and hydrocarbons beneath or upon it and the air above it'. 'It embraces all things which are related to a fixed area or point of the surface of earth'.[23]

The private and government interest for a growing economy in Australia was controlled by a majority of wealthy landholders, who were also members of the Legislative Council of New South Wales, the judiciary, the banks and the pioneer pastoral fraternity.[24] William Macarthur and the signatories of forty-one magistrates in 1838 sought the support of the New South Wales Government and the British Government to supply the pastoral economy with additional free labour.[25] This bolstered future land sales and other resources.[26] Economic development in Australia was influenced by the abolition of convict transportation. Although convict transportation halted, the pastoral economy rapidly expanded throughout the Australian colonies. The economic exploitation of natural resources and the push for future land sales by major colonial landholders imposed restrictions on the amount of accessible land and water available for Aboriginal communities.

The utility demand for water resources and the government's control over land supported this expansion. The Western subdivision of land holdings often resulted in Aboriginal communities being expelled from their country:

In the early attempts of the Sydney settlers to farm in European methods their crops failed and when farming became more fruitful an expansion to the fertile riverbanks of the Hawkesbury and the Nepean Rivers were targeted for the colony, and Aboriginal owners repelled.[27]

In colonial Victoria Aboriginal groups were in direct competition for land and resources because of the pastoral economic goals of settlers and government town planning.[28] The pastoral industry became the backbone of the burgeoning colonial economy, and provided 90 per cent of the colony's exports.[29] Many members of the first New South Wales Parliament were squatters or had direct financial interests in expanding the industry for personal gain.[30]

The policy to expand land and water use was at the heart of frontier violence in Tasmania, and underpinned the near eradication of Aboriginal communities.[31] Government records show 'settler support for genocide policy to protect natural resources in order to secure colonial wealth creation during the 1800s'.[32] This human eradication policy was referred to by Tasmanian settlers as 'the destruction of black crows'.[33] Pastoralists flocked to Tasmania in the 1800s to farm sheep and to secure large land grants at little or no cost, where the impact upon Aboriginal communal land and water was not considered relevant.[34] My first visit to the Tasmanian Museum in Hobart confirmed this ugly history, where in one section of the room an inscribed timeline of Tasmania for 1826 had these words 'two pounds for children and five pounds for adults' describing the bounty placed on Aboriginal peoples.

In Queensland, the Darling Downs and the Brisbane Valley were alive with frontier hostility towards Aboriginal communities, which continued into central Queensland.[35] By the late nineteenth century Aboriginal peoples had established fringe camps on the outskirts of practically every town in the colony, as Aboriginal peoples were discouraged from entering town borders.[36] Eugene Bargo, a Goreng Kubbi Traditional Owner, pointed out during a trip to Brisbane (Queensland) that Boundary Street was the 'boundary line where Aboriginal peoples were not allowed to enter into the settlement outside daylight hours'[37] – these identifiers are common to other towns in Australia.

The South Australian colony was established in 1836 by the British on the River Torrens, on the lands of the Kaurna peoples.[38] The Kaurna were forced to move away from their communal lands because of frontier violence.[39] Advice from the Colonial Office in London stated that, 'the colony of South Australia could be established if the land was acquired from Aboriginal peoples on fair terms'.[40] The proclamation of the King of England of 1836 (the Letters Patent) was ignored.[41] Around 1880, the settlers in South Australia were demanding the release of more land for pastoral agriculture, and this exerted more pressure on Aboriginal communities to move further away from their traditional lands into neighbouring lands.[42]

Western Australia, invaded by the British in 1829, saw Aboriginal lands subdivided into 98 colonial blocs, and the Western Desert was the last area to experience the impact of pastoral advancement.[43] Such advancement depended on the exploitation of Aboriginal men, women and children in many roles such as stockmen, fencers, trackers, domestic labour and midwives. There is archival material and vividly told recorded oral stories of the massacres and brutality against Aboriginal communities – just place your finger anywhere on a map in Western Australia.

The Swan River Colony commenced a series of violent contacts between Aboriginal and settler groups.[44] Records of government inquiries into the inhumane treatment of Aboriginal people, including the methods of punishment, dispersal, murder and rape of Aboriginal people is found in many inquiries such as the Roth Inquiry (1904), Troy Inquiry (1908), and the Canning Stock Route Inquiry (1908).[45] Surveyor Ruddall gave evidence to the Canning Stock Route Inquiry that his 'method was to run Aboriginal men down on horseback to force them to find water'[46] – an accepted method by many.[47]

The Northern Territory had a similar history of frontier violence and dispossession. In the Territory, Aboriginal peoples of both sexes were exploited as a non-cash employment source under the frontier motto, 'work or be shot'.[48] Aboriginal peoples outnumbered Europeans for many years in the Northern Territory and remained relatively ignored for decades because governments believed that the Territory was 'uneconomic and difficult to irrigate or develop'.[49] However, British Lord Vestey, with the support of the Northern Territory Government, acquired '1950 leases over 10 and a half million acres for less than $10,000'[50] such as the Wave Hill cattle station in the Northern Territory. The famous Wave Hill strike[51] in 1966 by the Gurindji stockmen sought better conditions and wages, and revealed the shocking work conditions for Aboriginal women on the station.[52]

The emerging creation of State and Territory boundaries effected a national disenfranchisement of Aboriginal peoples and further marginalised their access to land and water resources. The eminent Australian historian Manning Clark argues that the Australian land use policy adopted between 1788 and the 1850s was based upon a land monopoly, almost exclusively for the benefit of the pastoral industry.[53]

> The origin and basis of our colonial prosperity has been pastoral occupation of the waste lands … it answered excellently its purpose of creating a valuable export, and spreading civilisation over the interior.[54]

In the 'Official Record of the Debates of the Australasian Federal Convention' in 1891, Mr John Forrest, representing the interests of Western Australia, highlighted the haphazard boundaries relating to the Murray River in the Australian colonies:

> [t]he boundary between Victoria and New South Wales is the river Murray a most unsuitable division. No line of division is so unsuitable as a river. The people living on each side of it marry, and become virtually the same people but they are divided by artificial boundaries …[55]

During the constitutional debates the colonial governments did not concern themselves with the interests or rights of Indigenous peoples as constituting part of the federation framework. The modern recognition of native title rights, the legal rights of Indigenous peoples or the significant influence of international law upon Australia's law-making was not contemplated in the creation of Federation. Sir Henry Parkes, father of the Federation, declared to the delegates of the National Australasian Convention on a Federal Constitution that,

> Australia, shall be free – free on the borders, free everywhere – in its trade and intercourse between its own people; that there shall be no impediment of any kind – that there shall be no barrier of any kind between one section of the Australian people and another …[56]

Indigenous peoples, the First Australians, were not recognised as citizens in their own country. Indigenous peoples were not free.

Unlike Canada, the United States of America and New Zealand, there were no federal treaties signed by the Crown with Aboriginal peoples. Subsequently, constitutional recognition in Australia's founding document does not seek to protect Aboriginal property, Aboriginal customary laws and practices, Aboriginal rights to water resources or ownership rights to mineral resources. Australia's recent national discussion on constitutional reform proposes to formally recognise Indigenous peoples as First Peoples through a referendum and amend the federal constitution to insert a non-legal effect clause. This symbolic gesture aligns with Australia's states that sought to amend their constitutions to include the recognition of First Peoples. Historically, Indigenous peoples in Australia were not legally recognised as 'self-governing nations', which would have allowed Indigenous peoples to retain their own laws and to assert Indigenous sovereignty where a claim for possession by a foreign government resulted.[57] From an Aboriginal perspective, Aboriginal sovereignty has not been relinquished. Aboriginal laws continue to be exercised by its peoples.

> Both 'sovereignty' and 'ownership' are terms that denote ideas of relative authority, and the incidents and recognisable interests that will be protected under those rubrics.[58]

The boundaries to the ownership and control of water and other resources inherent to Indigenous peoples have, since post-contact, been defined by the Crown. Governments of Australia, even after the federation of the colonies, still resisted the inclusion of the rights and interests of Indigenous peoples' to water. The exercise of Aboriginal water rights has continued to operate historically on the political will of governments and this has impeded legal certainty for Aboriginal peoples. The politics in the development of water policy and water law continues to marginalise the First Australians.

Opposing water values and the impact of Western concepts

The contestation for water rights and interests by Aboriginal communities, and their efforts to reclaim cultural property rights to water landscapes, is tied to a series of historic and modern events. The historical impact of the development of an expanding colonial settlement undermined Aboriginal peoples' familial cultural connection to country.

Inevitably, Western values regarding water have laid the foundation for modern concepts of water use in Australian society, and in the exploitation of water resources. This section demonstrates that Western water concepts have always been at odds with customary Aboriginal water values because of their antithetical and vastly different world views. There are more than conceptual differences underlying the clash of cultural traditions. At the heart of the disjunct is the fabric of British colonisation. The British Establishment and it's government viewed the world in terms of expanding military power and economic development. Indigenous peoples sought only to exercise and maintain their own communal sovereignty and to self-determine the compliance and adaption of their laws for social and familial cohesion within their own groups. Colonising other nations is not an Indigenous social concept.

I remember talking with a legal academic in the corridor of the Australian National University about the belief by some, that the British Government had little notion of how to deal with Indigenous peoples in Australia. We agreed that it was ridiculous to assume the British arrived in 1788 with little knowledge or understanding of Indigenous peoples. Towards the end of the conversation I explained that the strategies of British colonisation used on Indigenous peoples were not a series of hit and miss events across the globe. I emphasised that a suite of well-honed tactics were imposed to dispossess sovereign peoples – 'tried and tested' in South America, the USA, Canada and a long list of island-dwelling peoples such as Haiti and Hawaii. The academic responded that this was a fair assessment.

Former Prime Minister of Australia, Gough Whitlam, remarked on the dispossession of Aboriginal peoples from their customary ownership of the land and waters:

[i]n the 1990s, after *Mabo*, there was an attempt to argue that the squatters who spearheaded the spread of our occupation did not really understand that they were dispossessing anybody in *terra nullius*. The truth is that they understood it very well. All the contemporary documents, official, press, and private, show abundantly that everybody understood that they were engaged in one of the largest land appropriations in history and that everybody understood the consequences of what we were doing.[59]

The historical 'common thread of abuse'[60] experienced by Aboriginal peoples in Australia has significantly impacted Aboriginal peoples' ability to maintain an unbroken cultural association to land and water in each and every Aboriginal community. The Royal Commission Report into Aboriginal Deaths in Custody exposed the extent of polices and laws which underpins Aboriginal dispossession.

[A]boriginal people were dispossessed of their land without benefit of treaty, agreement or compensation is generally known … little known is the amount of brutality and bloodshed that was involved in enforcing on the ground what was pronounced by the law. Aboriginal people were deprived of their land and if they showed resistance they were summarily dealt with. The loss of land meant the destruction of the Aboriginal economy which everywhere was based upon hunting and fishing … the loss of the land threatened the Aboriginal culture which all over Australia was based upon land and relationship to the land. These were the most dramatic effects of European colonization supplemented by the decimating effects of introduced disease to which the Aboriginal people had no resistance.[61]

Dr Larissa Behrendt (2003) explains that 'the method of Aboriginal land use was always incongruent with British and European values and concepts of Western property'.[62] Behrendt does not make any distinction between British, European or Western value systems:

Despite claims that there were no Indigenous property rights, the British saw themselves from the earliest days of the colony as being in competition with Indigenous people for land.[63]

The conceptual frameworks that represent Western ideological constructs lie within the disciplines of social science and Western philosophy. The impact of Western concepts on water rights and their respective property values is connected to how they are valued by their society.

Aboriginal and non-Aboriginal values in water are based upon differing value systems and of themselves present a range of issues to address. The word 'Western' in this book captures the meaning of words, concepts and perspectives that are derived from English, Australian or other European origins and that are not concepts of Aboriginal peoples of Australia. Anthony Giddens (1993) proposes that the concept of ideology is useful for analysing relationships of power between different societies:

> [t]he interrelations of conflict and consensus is that of *ideology* – values and beliefs which help secure the position of more powerful groups at the expense of less powerful ones. Power, ideology and conflict are always closely connected. Many conflicts are *about* power, because of the rewards it can bring. Those who hold most power may depend mainly on the influence of ideology to retain their dominance, but are usually able to use force if necessary.[64]

Western ideology and Aboriginal ideology incorporate disparate values and beliefs and because of these disparate value systems there is a direct and indirect impact upon Aboriginal peoples' claims to exercise their rights and interests in water. Any attempt to define Aboriginal water paradigms through Western ideology is unreasonable because customary Aboriginal law has evolved from a non-related set of beliefs, values and law systems.

Aboriginal water rights to country are represented in the spiritual ancestral creation of the environmental landscape, the familial totems and oral knowledge which define the parameters of Aboriginal water use under Aboriginal laws.

Property rights in water

Australia's water rights rest upon the English legal system of common law riparian water rights held by the landowner. Under this system the property in water running through the land was defined in these terms.

> Property in water is naturally vested in the possession of the land, upon which, for the time being it lies. Whether falling as rain, or running from springs at the surface, or being drawn from the wells under the earth, the water belongs to the landowner, who has exclusive disposal of it, so long as it remains upon his land … The rain-water that falls on private land may be impounded and utilized in any way the proprietor may deem fit.[65]

Since the thirteenth century England recognised the importance of controlling its water resources, not only to advance economic development but to advance particular areas of industry, transport and urbanisation in the late 1700s to the mid-1800s.[66] Water doctrines were derived from Roman law and civil concepts of common goods and rights of ownership.[67] Australia's historic approach to the control and conceptualisation of water use has evolved from the British common law system.

The history of common law water rights, which preceded statutory law, commenced with the legal commentary of Bracton and with Roman jurisprudence, which influenced the development of modern water law.[68] Bracton formulated the user-rights principles based upon the broader civilian concepts of property.[69]

Bracton's classification of property rights to water, which have been cited in judgements and treatises for over 600 years, recognised that user-rights over land held by the property owner were natural rights inherent in land ownership – and recognised running water as a common good.[70] John Locke used the concept of water ownership to illustrate his theory on property rights.[71] Because of Australia's colonial settlement, these common law concepts of water 'ran with the land' where ownership of the land was held.

The nature of water was articulated by Blackstone: 'whatever moveables were found on or below the land or in the sea and unclaimed by any owner was said to be abandoned'.[72] Blackstone said that 'the transient nature of water could not be owned in the same way as land but it could be occupied by a first use'.[73] His theory expounds the general principles of Western ideological values that positions humankind's dominion over the natural environment:

> The earth and all things therein were the general property of mankind from the immediate gift of the Creator. Not that the communion of goods seems ever to have been applicable, even in the earliest ages … the substance of the thing; nor could be extended to the use of it. For, by the law of nature and reason, he who first began to use it acquired therein a kind of transient property that lasted so long as he was using it, and no longer … the right of possession continued for the same time only that the act of possession lasted. Thus the ground was in common, and no part was the permanent property of any man in particular … but the instance that he quitted the use or occupation of it, another might seize it without injustice.[74]

Western property concepts hold value through ownership and the right to exclude others. The common good principle changed when water resources became significant for the development of the Industrial Revolution, raw material production, agricultural expansion and urbanisation.[75]

> The truth is private property is central to political and economic freedom. We
> don't talk about this much, partly because it's such a basic premise of our civilisa-
> tion and partly because it slips between economics and law.[76]

In contrast to definitions of English water concepts, the framework of Aboriginal
values in water rights is based on a holistic creation-based belief that water was
created by ancestors. Where waters have been formed and particular kinship obligations apply to maintain water quality – some water sources are taboo because of
their creation stories. In the same way that Aboriginal traditional owners respect-
fully ask tourists not to climb Uluru, it is about respecting the law. The first laws
of this land are Aboriginal.

Aboriginal water knowledge – a comparative with Aotearoa

The complexity of Aboriginal knowledge systems is far-reaching on country.
The familial obligation to care for water holes, rivers or other water resources
encapsulates a unique cultural Aboriginal paradigm. Water resources are not
effectively described through a Western value system or rights discourse. Western
and Aboriginal concepts of water are distinct. Western cultures generally adopt
market-based economic methods to measure the value of the waters and the land
in Australian society. Aboriginal spiritual philosophy does not.

> The interpenetration of 'material' and 'spiritual' in Indigenous traditions confounds
> liberal philosophy's differentiation between religious and civil interests. Indige-
> nous traditions are likely to see much less distinction between religious and other
> dimensions of existence. Ritual practice and spiritual traditions help to define and
> produce economic and social relations.[77]

An understanding of Aboriginal concepts of water and landscapes is derived from
a cultural matrix of Aboriginal knowledge that is distinct from Western values
of ownership. There are commonalities that exist with other Indigenous peoples
across the globe:

> First Nation peoples carry maps of their homelands in their heads. For most
> people, these mental images are embroidered with intricate detail and knowledge,
> based on the community's oral history and the individual's direct relationship to
> the traditional territory and its resources.[78]

The definition of consumptive (the use of water for private benefit purposes including commercial use for irrigation, industry and urban areas and stock and domestic use) and non-consumptive (water that is diverted or used for purposes such as water for the environment, hydro-electric power stations and non-commercial) are not well suited to Aboriginal concepts because Aboriginal laws and customs relate to relationships to land and water. Western water management concepts seek to separate and compartmentalise water resources, whereas under Aboriginal water and land concepts, water is valued holistically and water and land are inseparable from one another. Klempton and Kleer (2003) say that 'all Aboriginal rights are based upon inherency' and are 'not dependent on acts of government to prove Aboriginal rights'.[79]

> Inherent indigenous rights are derived from existence (being here) and custom (adaption of a way of life to perpetuate existence or survival as peoples). Custom (or customary law) is in turn derived from the relationship with the Creator and the understanding why and for what purposes the Creator put a people here (in their own place in the universe).[80]

Culture, in the ordinary meaning of the word, is 'the total of the inherited ideas, beliefs, values and knowledge, which constitute the shared bases of social action'.[81] The literal meaning of culture is not adequate for interpreting an Aboriginal world view. The rigidity of Western property concepts is evident in Australia's legal system when Aboriginal peoples exercise their claim to water rights and interests under native title and Aboriginal access and use of customary water resources. Legal parameters exist within native title definitions, for example in domestic and international boundaries of high and low water marks. Such Western water boundaries are unnatural and artificial.

The research on customary marine tenure conducted by Peterson and Rigsby (1998) points out that Aboriginal water relationships have 'rich layers of law dimensions that dwarf the narrow descriptors of Australian water policy'.[82] Peterson and Rigsby argue that:

> Indigenous interest in the sea encompasses a great deal more than subsistence, as the anthropological literature makes clear ... The social construction of the seascapes is ... complex and varied.[83]

Advocating for Indigenous water rights as 'customary property' has been an ongoing issue for Indigenous communities. New Zealand highlights the difficulties experienced by Māori groups in communicating to the courts and governments about how Māori conceptualise customary meaning and relationships within European constructs of heritage. The New Zealand Court of Appeal in deciding *Ngati Apa v Attorney-General* [2003] NZCA 117 raises relevant and important issues on how the ownership of land and water can be advanced.

From the 1840 Waitangi Treaty (*Tiriti o Waitangi*) Māori claims were lodged and heard in the Native Land Court (established in 1862) on customary property rights to land and water. There were a number of claims on whether the Crown or the Māori claimants held the property rights in the foreshore. Of these claims the landmark case was decided in 1963 before Chief Judge Morison of the Māori Land Court (formerly the Native Land Court) in favour of the applicant.[84] The Court of Appeal decision in *re Ninety Mile Beach [1963]* NZLR 461 determined that the legal recognition of Māori customary law in land extended to the foreshore.

Since this case there have been a number of appeals in relation to *re Ninety Mile Beach* in the Māori Appellate Court, Supreme and the High Courts[85] of New Zealand on rights to the foreshore and seabed. The rights to water have been a contentious issue for the Crown. A summary of these matters is explained briefly.

On substantial questions of law the decision was challenged in the Supreme Court[86] of New Zealand (the final court of appeal). Judge Turner held that the Māori Land Court did not have the power to exercise jurisdiction over a Crown Grant, and that the Grant extinguished Māori customary title to the foreshore. The decision was that the seabed below the low water mark is owned by the Crown in common law. The Māori claimants applied to have their case heard by the Court of Appeal, however this was dismissed.

Eight iwi (tribes) in 1997, the claimants of the northern South Island of the Marlborough Sounds applied to the Māori Land Court on whether the land below the mean of the high water mark in the Marlborough Sounds to the territorial sea was included – in the definition of land under the *Te Ture Whenua Māori Act 1993 (Maori Land Act)*. The Court of Appeal unanimously decided that the Māori Land Court had jurisdiction under the *Te Ture Whenua Māori Act* to determine whether the foreshore and seabed had the status of Māori customary land. Judge Hingston in hearing the matter decided that Māori customary rights over the foreshore and seabed had not been extinguished.

In 2003 the Court of Appeal held in *Attorney-General v Ngāti Apa*[87] that 'the Crown was wrong to contend that certain statutes affecting the foreshore and seabed extinguished Māori customary title', further stating that, the 'Māori Land

Court under *Te Ture Whenua Māori* and the *Māori Land Act 1993* had jurisdiction to hear and determine foreshore and seabed issues on Māori customary land matters'.[88] While it affirmed the Māori Land Court's jurisdiction, the court noted that this decision did not actually constitute a ruling on the *Ngāti Apa* claim. Māori customary land was statutorily defined as 'land held in accordance with tikanga Māori (customary values and practices)'.[89] The Court rejected the Crown's argument that the Māori Land Court's jurisdiction did not extend to the seabed.

Elias CJ in *Ngāti Apa* ('*Marlborough Sounds Case*')[90] in rejecting the extinguishment argument to the foreshore (the intertidal zone, an area between high water and low water mark) and seabed in the northern part of the South Island in *re Ninety-Mile Beach*[91] said:

> [t]he common law as received in New Zealand was modified by recognised Maori customary property interests. If any such custom is shown to give interests in foreshore and seabed, there is no room for a contrary presumption derived from English law. The common law of New Zealand is different.[92]

The Clark Government in 2004 enacted the *Foreshore and Seabed Act* to override the New Zealand Court of Appeal decision of 19 June 2003 in the *Ngāti Apa* case and subsequently repealed this Act and replaced it with the *Marine and Coastal Area (Takutai Moana) Act 2011*.

Australian and New Zealand governments have struggled with relinquishing the Crown's power to Indigenous peoples – governments have preferred to bolt the door to stem the floodgates. These antics make a mockery of any attempt to 'reconcile' Australia's past acts of injustice with Indigenous Australians. Australian governments, just like the Clark Government, sought legislative amendments to end the recognition of Indigenous rights to water and land, such as the Howard Government's 'Ten Point Plan' in response to the High Court's *Wik* decision. The Australian Federal Parliament applied retrospective laws to overrule the 1996 decision in *Wik v Queensland*[93] that held native title could co-exist with pastoral leaseholders.

Australia's federal and state parliaments are reluctant to amend the definition of water to recognise Aboriginal water rights and land rights as economic 'customary property' rights. However, there may be a game changer for Indigenous traditional owners because the Abbott and Turnbull Federal Governments' focus on developing northern Australia's land and resources requires the 'full cooperation of Indigenous land owners who own the land'.[94]

Aboriginal native title claims that are centred upon contesting Western legal concepts of ownership to reclaim have not always met the Aboriginal community's expectations:

> The right to fish under traditional laws has not translated into commercial fishing rights; the native title right to take flora and fauna is not able to be used to sell bush foods or native wildlife as of right. The traditional use of minerals has not become a native title right to exploit minerals such as through mining enterprises … Native title rights are limited in law to anachronistic, domestic, non-commercial rights.[95]

Aboriginal and non-Aboriginal societies have distinct legal systems based on differing values, societal governance and relationships with the environment. The distinct common thread between Aboriginal laws and Australian law is that both legal systems seek to establish legal authority.

> Aboriginal title is subject to the various judicially crafted constraints of inalienability, communality, and undefined restrictions to its use … these restrictions will have commercial and economic implications, impairing the economic and commercial value of Aboriginal lands.[96]

Aboriginal laws, as they relate to water resources, are a conundrum for Western legal frameworks. Determining Aboriginal water values and land as inseparable has far-reaching implications for Western concepts in native title and water management because government policy and legislation would need to reflect these values. The core principle of Aboriginal property rights is the ongoing obligation to country acquired by birthright, whether those claiming property rights are recognised by governments or the courts as traditional owners or not.

This chapter has examined how the nature of water rights in Australia has posed many challenges for Aboriginal peoples to remain connected to country. There are two distinct world views after British-European contact in 1788 – settlement or invasion? As the chapter demonstrates there is less debate about the impact of establishing a British colony upon an already inhabited and occupied land of sovereign Aboriginal peoples – inevitably wars resulted in exercising a right to property. The challenge for Australian society is to fully accept the pre-existing rights of the First Australians. The next chapter explains the human cost of these opposing worldviews in terms of Aboriginal health, wealth and water.

Chapter 4

HEALTH, WEALTH AND WATER RIGHTS

The interconnection between natural resources, such as water and land, and the enjoyment of good health among Aboriginal communities is directly related to a range of benefits that can be derived from ownership of water. However the concept of self-determination is rarely discussed in the context of national water policy, or in relation to how Aboriginal water rights can contribute to *'Closing the Gap'* targets[1] and for the Australian Government's Indigenous Advancement Strategy[2] (IAS).

This chapter examines how the opportunities and barriers relating to Aboriginal peoples' access to water affect Aboriginal health. It also addresses how the inability to exercise self-determination through the customary use and economic development of water rights and interests impacts upon Aboriginal health. The chapter highlights ways to improve the state of Aboriginal health by providing cultural and economic certainty through establishing reserved allocations of water for Aboriginal communities, as 'first use rights' in the hierarchy of water rights. Lastly, the chapter identifies the consequences that may follow if water resources are not managed by Aboriginal communities. Some common themes in Indigenous policy acknowledge the social and cultural values of Aboriginal self-determination, Aboriginal sovereignty and self-governance which are directly linked to Aboriginal ontological concepts of water.

I assert that establishing a Reserved Indigenous Water Rights (RIWR) regime across Australia is critical to improving national Aboriginal health outcomes. Improving the health status of Aboriginal peoples is connected with economic prosperity and cultural certainty. RIWR should be entrenched in federal and state water policy and laws. After several hundred years of colonisation Aboriginal water rights have been virtually ignored, and consequently 'it is the great Australian paradox that the traditional owners of the land are the poorest people living on it'.[3]

Aboriginal health is integral to any national dialogue on water rights and interests. It is true that unemployment, the lack of education and low incomes are linked to poor health outcomes for all Australians, and the life expectancy and living standards for Indigenous Australians are that of a developing nation. Australia has an ageing population but Indigenous Australians do not.

> Indigenous Australians experience substantial social and economic disadvantages which are linked to poorer health ... Indigenous health disadvantage is shaped by the accumulated life experiences of social, economic and cultural inequality. Key periods in the life course are critical for determining future life opportunities and health and wellbeing.[4]

The social and cultural determinants of health are 'the conditions people are born, grow, live and age through'[5] – it is an evidence-based measure to indicate and address health priorities.[6] There are numerous government and non-government organisation reports, as well as media documentaries and academic research publications which overwhelmingly recognise the dire living standards of the majority of Indigenous communities in Australia.

The Australian Medical Association (AMA) highlighted in its AMA 2015 Report on Indigenous Health 'the stark difference in Indigenous imprisonment rates and the health and life expectancy gap of Indigenous peoples'[7] who come into contact with the criminal justice system at a young age.[8]

The 'Review of the 1994 Water Report' (2001) by the Human Rights and Equal Opportunity Commission (HREOC) noted the nexus between the right to water and the right to health:

> [a]s satisfactory health is a precondition of the full enjoyment of almost all human rights and fundamental freedoms, water is crucial in a chain of factors affecting the fulfilment of other human rights, and the right to water is implied throughout many of the more wide ranging provisions of the various instruments.[9]

The HREOC Review raised concerns from the Australian Health and Water Research Consortium, that 'water development in Aboriginal communities lacked a coherent strategy and service levels lacked clear priorities'.[10] The case for prioritising water requirements for Indigenous Australians was again highlighted in the 1994 Water Report by the Federal Race Discrimination Commissioner, Irene Moss.[11] The Commissioner noted that an investigation into the provision and sanitation of water supply in Indigenous communities required 'exploration of all the complex factors involved in providing water so as to assess whether their human rights had been protected'.[12]

In 1987 an earlier public inquiry was conducted into the Aboriginal settlement of Toomelah, on the NSW and Queensland borders, which recognised the impact of water supply, exposing a 'lack of access to adequate and reliable water' and identifying the 'serious health problems that resulted from water rationing'.[13] The issues for Indigenous communities addressed in HREOCs 1994 Water Report included the traditional and cultural use of water, the type of water sources and the impact of the contamination of water by mining and other activities.[14]

The centrality of water rights

The lack of Aboriginal economic empowerment has a nexus to poverty and the endemic health problems experienced by Aboriginal communities. Indigenous peoples are over-represented in prison and about 40 per cent of Indigenous children aged 10 to 17 years old are held in detention centres.[15] The evidence shows that Indigenous women are 'more likely to be victims of family violence'[16] and 'die due to an assault'.[17] The wellbeing of Indigenous communities is widely recognised through social and economic empowerment – where the impact of colonisation needs to be addressed.[18] Australia's post-contact history in relation to taking possession of water from Indigenous peoples with acts of violence and marginalisation is documented, notably by non-Indigenous individuals.

Both land and water ownership comprise of potential assets in building community capacity for Aboriginal peoples. The vesting of Aboriginal ownership rights in water would ensure that Aboriginal communities enjoy a higher standard of human rights in Australian society because they would have the economic base to fully participate in water economies.

Senator Aden Ridgeway argued that Aboriginal freehold title would provide economic capacity:

> [t]he findings of the 1998 Reeves Review of the Northern Territory Aboriginal Land Rights Act concluded that the most appropriate form of title for Aboriginal land was inalienable title … the inalienability of Aboriginal freehold does not significantly restrict the capacity of Aboriginal Territorians to raise capital for business ventures … Aboriginal title is most likely to protect the interests of Aboriginal people. [19]

The work of CK Meek in *Land Law and Custom in the Colonies*[20] explains that alienable 'freehold title belongs to the very essence of colonization'[21] and that, 'in order to protect the interests of the natives it is necessary to maintain systems of tenure that do not permit the full exploitation of land'.[22] Meek also notes that 'communal land holding ensures social stability'.[23]

Professor Jon Altman, during the Australian Government's '2020 Summit' in Canberra, spoke on the importance of recognising Indigenous property rights:

> [o]ne mechanism to close the gap of indigenous life expectancy in Australia should consider amending the law to provide Aboriginal land owners with legal property rights over resources, which occurs in the United States of America and most Canadian provinces … we need to start thinking about bestowing some commercially valuable resources and rights on indigenous groups.[24]

There is a lack of capacity for Aboriginal people to participate in water resource management. Aboriginal peoples' right to control and manage customary water would facilitate social, cultural and economic certainty. Oppressive discrimination and lack of self-determination have been hallmarks of government policy towards Aboriginal peoples.

> Although hundreds of Indigenous people served in the Australian armed forces, especially in the Second World War, it was not until 1962 that Indigenous people had the right to vote, and not until 1967 that a national referendum recognised them as 'people of their own country' and included them in the national census.[25]

The low incomes reported among Aboriginal communities eliminates the potential for communities to purchase water under federal and state water legislation, either as water licences, water trading or to maintain drinking water requirements. The Australian Government does not offer a national plan for Indigenous peoples to develop economic wealth through water assets.[26] Indigenous Business Australia in its *Indigenous Investment Principles* document recognises that 'investment opportunities will be defined by the income Indigenous communities receive from land, water and commercial agreements'.[27]

The negligible degree of Aboriginal ownership in water access indicates a serious threat to Aboriginal living standards and health conditions because no economic development in water is permitted.[28]

The state of Aboriginal health is linked to the average income of Aboriginal peoples. The Department of Aboriginal Affairs 'Two Ways Together Report' (2005) found that the average earnings for Aboriginal males were between $120 and $190 per week, and for Aboriginal females it was between $200 and $399 per week.[29] For non-Indigenous households the average weekly income was between $1500 and $1999.[30] In 2015 the incomes for Indigenous men and women remained well behind that of non-Indigenous Australians: Indigenous incomes were on average around $23,700 per year and for Indigenous people who were unemployed it was around $10,000 per year.[31] According to various reports, the health status of Aboriginal peoples links to the level of poverty experienced in communities.

> Mortality statistics released last week by the Australian Bureau of Statistics said the median age of death for Aboriginal men in Western Australia has dropped from 52.8 years in 2005 to 47.9 years in 2014...[32]

The life expectancy of Aboriginal peoples is approximately 20 years less than that of other Australians and the earning capacity of Aboriginal peoples are significantly lower. The potential for asset accumulation in Aboriginal communities is very low. This chapter argues that because of these statistics Aboriginal communities require legal certainty with respect to water allocations. Establishing Aboriginal water ownership and tradeable water licences would ensure economic certainty in the water market for Aboriginal communities, particularly in remote areas of Australia.

The poor earning capacity of Aboriginal peoples suggests that the poor socio-economic status of Aboriginal peoples is a significant barrier for Aboriginal communities. In order to realise economic self-determination and achieve the health standards of other Australians, a national reform in government water policy for Aboriginal peoples is required.

> In Australia, the degree of wealth inequality across households is much larger than the inequality in income alone ... Lack of policy attention to the economic implications of Indigenous premature mortality and to the savings implications of Indigenous employment conditions is symptomatic ... a key structural difference between the Indigenous and non-Indigenous populations [is that] ... most Indigenous people barely reach retirement age.[33]

In Western Australia, Nyungar peoples raised their concerns about the South West Water Plan during a conference organised by the Department of Water.[34] Nyungar participants emphasised the link between health, self-determination and Aboriginal water rights and interests:

> Nyungar people maintain that the ecological health of these systems is pivotal in maintaining Nyungar culture. Without a healthy environment, Nyungar

people cannot maintain their use of the waterways as a place to collect food and recreate and as a place to maintain their spiritual and cultural connection with the land and particularly as places with which to transmit their values and knowledge to the coming generations.[35]

The Nyungar community suggested that the government neglected opportunities for any meaningful engagement with their community. Nyungar participants cited

[t]he lack of Aboriginal consultation of Nyungar water management, the uncertain legal rights to water under native title policy, the barrier for Nyungar people's access to waterways and water sites under legislation, the lack of engagement of Nyungar people prior [to] and during planning projects and not post-planning and the payment of royalties for use of waterways that are held by Native Title Claimants.[36]

Sue Jackson, a former CSIRO researcher, noted that Australia's water management policy failed to achieve outcomes for Indigenous water rights and interests and, in particular, has failed to view Aboriginal water rights as property rights:

[l]ittle guidance is provided to water resource managers and regional bodies seeking to meet the objectives relating to Indigenous access and involvement. Researchers, Indigenous groups and policy makers will need to collaborate to overcome several key challenges that may impede progress in this area; namely, limited knowledge of the means of addressing Indigenous water requirements.[37]

Addressing Aboriginal rights through self-determination

Self-determination is considered by many Indigenous peoples to be the corner-stone of providing community capacity. Nicolas Peterson (1985) argues that land rights were implemented as a welfare measure:[38]

[t]he fact that in essence land rights are a welfare measure and not the act of compensatory justice they appear to be. In Australia, an interventionist welfare state has had little problem creating long term, distinctive rights, since it recog-nises it is a long term problem and it would presumably feel obliged to intervene should gross inequities result in the future.[39]

Australian governments clearly prioritise commercial water rights of industry and pastoral stakeholders, even at the risk to environmental water and Aborig-inal cultural flows. The ability of Aboriginal communities to exercise their full enjoyment of water rights and interests is undervalued in the national agenda.

> Within Australia as a whole, Indigenous peoples hold a special status as the first peoples of this land. Their status as first sovereigns necessitates that they be distinguished from other minorities by virtue of their distinct histories as political entities. At its heart, the call for recognition of the right to self-determination concerns the nature of engagement between Indigenous peoples and government.[40]

The principles of self-determination progressed in Australia's policy development under the 'guiding principles of Aboriginal Affairs were established by the federal government in 1973'.[41] After decades of protectionist and assimilation policies, opportunities for self-determination were encouraged by the 'management of Aboriginal policy controlled by Aboriginal peoples and who sought to improve community outcomes' through Aboriginal governance.[42]

During the National Inquiry into the Stolen Generations the concept of self-determination was discussed in relation to the forced separation of Aboriginal children from their families.

> Self-determination is a collective right of peoples to determine and control their own destiny. It is a right to exercise autonomy about their affairs and a right to make their own decisions.[43]

Mick Dodson, a former Aboriginal and Torres Strait Islander Social Justice Commissioner, acknowledged the importance of self-determination, saying that

> [e]very issue concerning the historical and present status, entitlements, treatment and aspirations of Aboriginal and Torres Strait Islander peoples is implicated in the concept of self determination.[44]

Mark Bennett (2004) reasons that the innate cultural and political difference between non-Aboriginal and Aboriginal communities lies within the notion of autonomy:

> Indigenous autonomy is different from general ethnic autonomy. Ethnic autonomy argues for exceptions to equal citizenship; indigenous autonomy appeals to the equality of nations … indigenous autonomy is not merely about the distribution of resources and rights among citizens within the state, but is rooted in the question of how indigenous peoples, as polities, political groups, or 'nations', were incorporated into the wider state.[45]

Mason Durie, a Māori academic, has articulated the idea that the autonomy sought by Māori communities incorporates various meanings for Māori governance:

> Maori aspiration for greater control over their destinies and resources is variously described as a search for sovereignty, autonomy, independence, self-governance, self-determination, *tino rangatiratanga*, and *mana motuhake*.[46]

The notion of Aboriginal autonomy appears to highlight some common themes among Indigenous peoples in other parts of the world. Shin Imai (2003) explains that the 'Canadian Court's position to seek a balance on negotiating Aboriginal rights in relation to the rights of others is problematic for Aboriginal sovereignty'.[47] This seems to be the case in Australia, where governments to date have not sought to recognise the existence of Aboriginal sovereignty in law. The superior court's interpretation of Aboriginal sovereignty is limited to commentary on these issues, thus preserving the notion of a 'skeletal frame' within Australia's legal system (see chapter 5). Imai (2003) commenting on Canada's treatment of Aboriginal sovereignty, said:

> The Court has approached this problem by attempting to balance recognition of Aboriginal and treaty rights required by the constitution against the unknown consequences of too broad an articulation of those rights.[48]

Identifying the parameters for Indigenous legal rights within the Western legal system are, as Imai (2003) suggests, not straightforward. McLachlin CJ of Canada emphasised the importance of 'reconciling Aboriginal rights with the Western legal system in order to repudiate prior injustices':

> Canadian jurisprudence on Aboriginal rights has emphasized the twin tasks of recognition and reconciliation. The goal of reconciliation requires us to abandon an all-or-nothing perspective, and to seek principled compromises based on a shared will to live together in a modern, multicultural society.[49]

Wilcox J in *Bennell v Western Australia*[50] ('*Single Noongar Case*') reasoned for a similar jurisprudential perspective on Aboriginal rights in Australia, in seeking to reconcile the impact of Australia's settlement upon Aboriginal peoples and the rule of law. The Bennell decision also acknowledged and accepted the revitaliza-tion of Aboriginal customs, laws and practices. Wilcox J was of the view that

> [t]he impact of European settlement has resulted in modifications to traditional law which must be accepted by the courts because these modifications are within the parameters of acceptable change and adaptation.[51]

The Commonwealth Government report 'Engagement of Indigenous Australians' (2007) found that Aboriginal autonomy is generally restricted by Western frameworks.

> The discussion of Indigenous governance and self-determination is dominated by the complexities of both internal and external accountability and capacity building that relate to such devolution of power [among Indigenous communities].[52]

If the legal recognition of self-determination for Aboriginal peoples is to eventuate, then issues about Aboriginal ownership of resources, land and water should rank as key factors in future policy development. In 1982 the New South Wales Department of Aboriginal Affairs raised their concerns about the unfettered exploitation of land and resources.

> The major concerns centred on the lack of provision of ownership and control of Aboriginal sites or for ownership of the entire subsurface (rights to gold, silver, coal and petroleum were excluded) … It gave Aboriginal people no real protection and no real control.[53]

Dr James Crawford, Commissioner for the Australian Law Reform's inquiry into the 'Recognition of Aboriginal Customary Laws' pointed out that the 'proclamation of British sovereignty over Australia is wrong as a matter of fact' and under 'modern standards of international law it is wrong'.[54] Dr Crawford notes that international law establishes the right to self-determination.

> The first general treaty provision on the subject was Art 27 of the Civil and Political Rights Covenant of 1966. Article 1 of the Covenant also refers to the right of self-determination of peoples. Advocates for ethnic, indigenous or linguistic minorities sometimes rely upon the principle or right of self-determination in international law as a basis for claims to political or legal recognition.[55]

Dr Larissa Behrendt (1995) analysed the socio-economic status of Aboriginal peoples in Australia, and identified a lack of social and economic power to control or manage their affairs.

> The Aboriginal community has a low socio-economic position in Australia. This lack of social and economic power coupled with the small Aboriginal population means that its political power within the non-Aboriginal community is minimal. This lack of power should be noted in relation to the ability of Aboriginal people to have resources to deal with government, mining and pastoral interests.[56]

The Australian Government report 'The Engagement of Indigenous Australians in Natural Resource Management' (2007) identified the 'nexus between land, water and human health of Indigenous peoples'. Land, water and human health are intimately integrated in Indigenous Australia and research is now trying to understand and even quantify the nexus'.[58]

Recommendations put forward by the Working Group for Advancing Indigenous Reconciliation in Primary Industries and Natural Resource Management confirmed the nexus between health and other policy frameworks:

Employment is one of a number of key elements that need to be addressed … improved health and housing, a safe family environment, law and order, and education. These major issues cannot be addressed effectively in isolation, as to do so will not provide the holistic framework for policy, service and project implementation that is required to reduce Indigenous disadvantage …[59]

The Ministerial Councils for Natural Resource Management and Primary Industries acknowledged the significance of land ownership in building the capacity of Aboriginal communities. 'Hand-back of land, whether co-managed or freehold, makes a significant contribution to investing in Indigenous community initiatives'.[60]

The lack of tangible benefits flowing to Aboriginal communities from the exploitation of land and resources by governments and industry remains unsatisfactory.

Despite living on the doorstep of this enormous development, there exists a stark disparity between the vast development and wealth being generated and the significant level of disadvantage in which Aboriginal people in these regions are living.[61]

The late Peter Cullen, a member of the Wentworth Group of Concerned Scientists, noted that the water reform policy of COAG provides 'irrigators with a greater involvement than Indigenous interests'.[62] A lack of inclusion of the water rights and interests of Aboriginal peoples reduces the level of opportunity for incorporating Aboriginal concepts and values in water. The nature of Aboriginal rights and interests in trading *things* is limited by Western concepts and values in the way the characteristics of an economy are defined:

The trade of [goods such as ochre] followed the dreaming tracks that connected waters of the intermittent waters … plentiful supplies of food allowed people to congregate at exchange centres at feast and trade … trading events were associated with the migrations of bogong moths … eels in Victoria, fish on the Darling River, and the ripening of bunya nuts in Queensland … Maccassan seafarers made annual journeys to Australia's northern shores [trading] trepang and turtle shells, out-rigger canoes, sails and tobacco.[63]

Senator Aden Ridgeway, delivering the Mabo Lecture for 2005, highlighted that a comparison of COAGs 'National Framework Principles for Government Service Delivery to Indigenous Australians' (2004) and its 'National Commitment Principles' (1992) shows that policy inconsistencies exist.[64] Senator Ridgeway added that the National Commitment Principles of self-determination, self-management, economic independence and equity-based Aboriginal social and cultural values were not included in the national policy outcomes.[65]

The Indigenous Engagement Report (2007) noted that governments considered that Indigenous governance mechanisms were preferable to Indigenous self-determination.[66] However, the omission of self-determination principles in Indigenous policy impacts upon securing certainty over resource rights and interests. Aboriginal communities lack the economic influence of non-Aboriginal stakeholders such as that wielded by industry, pastoralists and the agricultural sector. The incorporation of Indigenous self-determination principles in national and state policy would enable Aboriginal communities to exercise economic and cultural rights. Western models of governance are light on relevance for Aboriginal peoples.

> The use of surrogate governance is a predominant model for engaging with Aboriginal communities and needs to be reviewed. The critical question is whether the use of surrogate models negates the need to engage with communities and therefore undermines the opportunity for Aboriginal peoples to play an active role in their own governance.[67]

In contrast to Australia, the USA has validated the recognition of Native American sovereignty – that exists through the exercise of tribal government authority.[68] Jill Byrnes (1990) comments on the absence of a formal treaty process for Indigenous Australians:

> No treaties have been signed in Australia, but in Canada treaties were signed with many of the First Nations. The First Nations did not initiate the treaty process, or exert much influence over the terms or even understand them clearly. They were coerced to agree with them, usually under the constraint of starvation and with

the promise of food and other necessities, and in the obvious imminent, or actual, settlement on their land by Europeans.[69]

The Boomanulla Report (2002) resulted from a conference where Aboriginal peoples in many government departments sought to advance the protection of country. The Report recognised the general powerlessness of Aboriginal communities to secure their rights and interests in Australia:

> Aboriginal people have received few real benefits from the use (and often misuse) of the land and rivers.[70]

The Aboriginal and Torres Strait Islander Commission (ATSIC) was established by the Hawke Federal Government under the *Aboriginal and Torres Strait Islander Commission Act 1989* (Cth) to advocate on behalf of Indigenous Australians and promote self-determination.[71] Indigenous economic, social and cultural development remained far from being realised during the Commission's operation, for various political reasons.[72]

> The notion that the existence of the Commission rested on 'special laws', which would only benefit Aboriginal peoples is erroneous, and this has been well documented. The enactment of 'special laws' does not implement Aboriginal governance. It should also be noted that such laws are far removed from grass-roots Aboriginal processes and decision-making.[73]

In 2005 the Howard Federal Government dismantled ATSIC and then established the National Indigenous Council which was to provide advice to the government on Indigenous policy issues.[74] The National Indigenous Council was not elected by Aboriginal communities, and anecdotal evidence from communities deemed the Indigenous Council to be ineffective and powerless.[75] The Rudd Federal Government in 2008 disbanded the National Indigenous Council[76] and thereafter the Gillard Federal Government did not reinstate the ATSIC model.[77] Both the Abbott and Turnbull Federal Governments have remained with a government-appointed Indigenous Council. The nationally recognised and Indigenous elected organisation, the National Congress of Australia's First Peoples, has been treated with indifference by governments.

Water is power

Gough Whitlam, former Prime Minister of Australia, argued that human rights are central to Australian society:

It is unfair and absurd that universally proclaimed human rights are not available in some Australian States and are differently expressed in those Australian States where they are available … Human rights are more important than States' rights.[78]

The polarisation of Aboriginal policy in state and federal politics indicates that addressing the Aboriginal water rights and interests will be extremely challenging, in spite of Australia's human rights legislation. H C Coombs (1993) explained that 'the requirement of federation was to allay the conflict and metropolis-rural dichotomies between the States and the Commonwealth where Aboriginal people can be forgotten'.[79]

Social welfare provided by government since the 1970s produces a revolutionary change in the Aboriginal economy … Aboriginal people withdrew from participation in the real economy. Participation at the low end of the real economy was replaced by passive welfare. People came back home to work nominally in the institutional economy of the mission – an economy which was becoming more and more dependent on government funding.[80]

Australia is a signatory to human rights treaties, for instance the *Convention on the Rights of the Child* (CRC).[81] The Australian Human Rights Commission recommended that 'the Australian Government should incorporate the *Declaration on the Rights of Indigenous Peoples* (UNDRIP) into Australia's Human Rights Framework as one of the core instruments'.[82] The incorporation of UNDRIP into Australian laws would recognise the right to water. The United Nations Water Development Report (2006) recognised that 'governance systems control the management and allocation of water'.[83]

Water is power, and those who control the flow of water in time and space can exercise this power in various ways.[84]

The United Nations articulates a concept of water resources which is governed by four dimensions: the social dimension is the equitable use of water and its distribution over the various sectors of society; the economic dimension is the efficient use of water resources and its role in overall economic growth; the political empowerment dimension is the application of democratic opportunities to influence and monitor political processes and outcomes; and the environmental sustainability dimension, where an improved water governance is achieved, by increasing the quality of water flow to ecosystems, services, aquifers, wetlands and other habitats.[85]

The quality of water for Indigenous peoples has been sustained on country by Indigenous land management practices, well before the arrival of the First Fleet. Now however, the poor quality of drinking water for many Aboriginal communities in Australia has highlighted the ineffective water management practices of the states.[86]

The New South Wales Aboriginal Working Group in its annual report on Aboriginal Community Water (2006) identified that 'many Aboriginal communities have poor quality drinking water and deteriorated sewerage and water service infrastructure'.[87] The Working Group's report highlighted the consistent presence of *E. coli* bacteria in the drinking water systems in Aboriginal discrete communities.[88]

> In Australia, water is vested in governments that allow other parties to access and use water for a variety of purposes. ... The 1994 Council of Australian Governments' water reform framework and subsequent initiatives recognised that better management of Australia's water resources is a national issue.[89]

The Report on Aboriginal Community Water Supply and Sewerage Systems in New South Wales observed that 'the nature of water and sewerage provision was poor in discrete communities'.[90] It also highlighted the 'limited scope for community contribution to water and sewerage service costs due to the low socio-economic status of Aboriginal communities'.[91]

The Department of Aboriginal Affairs (NSW) has a statutory responsibility for the Aboriginal Communities Development Program, whereby the department addresses water and sewerage provision to Aboriginal communities across New South Wales.[92] The NSW Aboriginal Community Water and Sewerage Working Group Report (2006) highlighted the lack of financial and technical capacity within Aboriginal communities to effectively manage water servicing and operational maintenance,[93] and a lack which extends to Aboriginal Land Councils in rural, discrete and remote areas.[94]

The NSW Working Group Report makes the assumption that providing land and water ownership, of itself, enhances the opportunities for Aboriginal peoples, however this is not the case. When governments fail to deliver basic services it is essential for Aboriginal communities to be afforded the economic and social capacity to protect, develop and sustain continued ownership and management of their land, waters and resources. The development of Aboriginal communities' technical and operational capacities should be a national priority. Training and education must be consistent with Aboriginal values and Aboriginal ontological concepts of land and water management.

> A significant number of our land councils are non-compliant largely because of lack of capacity in the towns. About 50 per cent would probably fall into the unfunded category because of non-compliance … we inherited also the lack of facilities: water, power and sewerage.[95]

Local Aboriginal Land Councils hold statutory responsibility for the infrastructure on their land; however, Aboriginal communities often lack the resources and skills to maintain water operation systems over the long term. Many Aboriginal communities have small populations and cannot generate sufficient income to sustain essential water and sewerage systems.[96] The Guidelines for Assessing the Impacts of Water Sharing Plans on Aboriginal Peoples (2001) recognise that inclusion of Aboriginal values is important:

> [d]omestic, town, and environmental [water] may overlap and parallel the interests of Aboriginal peoples. However, it is important that Aboriginal interests and values are not subsumed under these other interests. Aboriginal interests and values need to be recognised independently.[97]

The New South Wales Water Sharing Guidelines (2001) highlight the government's lack of social inclusion of Aboriginal peoples during the consultation process:

> Historically, Aboriginal communities have been excluded from decision-making that affects communities and 'country' and have often suffered significant negative impacts as a result of natural resource management decisions.[98]

The Human Rights and Equal Opportunity Commission notes that social justice policy underpins appropriate living standards and is linked to health outcomes:

> Social justice is grounded in the practical, day-to-day realities of life. It's about waking up in a house with running water and proper sanitation; offering one's children an education that helps them develop their potential and respect their culture. It is the prospect of satisfying employment and good health.[99]

Under Australia's national water reforms, higher water prices present significant problems for Aboriginal communities, especially where government cost recovery methods are implemented in water servicing. The poverty experienced by Aboriginal communities strongly indicates that Australia has failed to meet its obligations under various human rights instruments.

The Environmental Health Needs Survey (2004) analysed water use among discrete Aboriginal communities in Western Australia.[100] The Survey data indicates that of the 274 Aboriginal communities surveyed only 42 were connected to town water, 200 relied on bore water and 4300 Aboriginal people lived with unsatisfactory water quality and supply.[101]

The Survey (2004) also found that one in every five Aboriginal persons living in discrete communities did not benefit from adequate sewerage treatment or have the use of a disposal system.[102] In view of the national water reforms, the Western Australian Government has failed to take into account basic human rights in delivering water requirements for Aboriginal communities.

The Western Australian Government report, Water Services in Discrete Indigenous Communities (2006), confirmed that improving government standards of water service delivery and water supply is integral to improving the health status of Aboriginal peoples.[103] Further, the Report notes that the discontinuation of the programs run by the Aboriginal and Torres Strait Islander Commission resulted in an acute reduction in the state's contribution to Aboriginal water supply and service delivery.[104]

> There is currently a lack of consistency between jurisdictions with regard to policy and practices around Indigenous cultural access to Country and natural resources
> … There is currently a skill shortage in water resource management in Indigenous communities, which can contribute to the lack of potable water.[105]

The Western Australian Government report, Implementation Plan for the National Water Initiative (2006),[106] indicates that the government would 'provide a framework for future reductions in the availability of water for consumptive use',[107] though 'no process is in place to resume sustainable limits'.[108] The WA report also expresses concern for the future health of Aboriginal communities; however, the government intends to limit water availability in the consumptive pool and reclaim any unallocated water.[109]

The significant health and economic issues facing Aboriginal communities in Western Australia were recognised in a set of recommendations to the Minister of Water Resources (2006).[110]

> [These included] the affordability of water to people on low incomes and appropriate methods of cost recovery … and whether these are consistent with international conventions and declarations on human rights and non-legally binding resolutions, such as Principle 4 of the Dublin Statement … "it is vital to recognize first the basic right of all human beings to have access to clean water and sanitation at an affordable price".[111]

In the Western Australian Auditor General's 2015 report on 'Delivering Essential Services to Remote Aboriginal Communities' it clearly states that the Western Australian Government still doesn't meet the Australian Drinking Water Standards for remote Aboriginal communities.[112] Australia's water reform strategies have failed to meet the most basic human needs of Aboriginal communities. Australian governments should have prioritised access and use of water resources in its *'Closing the Gap'* strategies and linked these to mandatory Key Performance Indicators to the states and territories under the national water policy framework. There is an overall failure to also focus on Aboriginal water rights ownership as a means for wealth generation.

Collings (2002) notes the nexus in water rights and a broad range of human rights entitlements among Indigenous communities:

> The on-going cultural attachment of Aboriginal and Torres Strait Islander peoples to water is recognised as creating a right or entitlement to continue this affiliation, and the social, political and economic foundations that exist. The entitlement of Aboriginal and Torres Strait Islander peoples to practice their cultural traditions affiliated with water includes other indivisible rights for sustenance of the community as a whole.[113]

A significant recognition of those rights and entitlements was gained through the native title recognition of Indigenous property rights, as the next chapter explores.

Aboriginal and Torres Strait Islander Social Justice Commissioner reports

The Aboriginal and Torres Strait Islander Social Justice Commissioner reports annually to the Federal Attorney-General via the Social Justice and Native Title Reports. The Commissioner monitors a range of national and state Indigenous issues such as discrimination, native title, water rights, human rights and international perspectives in Indigenous policy and evaluates the performance of Indigenous community programs.[114] The 2008 Native Title Report[115] was the first to include a dedicated chapter on Aboriginal water rights and interests.

These reports provide an annual analysis of the progress and development of Indigenous rights, and examine whether the human rights of Indigenous peoples in Australia are exercised under international standards such as the *United Nations Declaration on the Rights of Indigenous Peoples*.[116]

> Human rights are not just abstract concepts that exist in documents such as treaties, conventions and declarations alone. They become meaningful only when they are able to be exercised.[117]

In 2001 the Race Discrimination Commissioner of the Australian Human Rights Commission undertook a review of the 1994 Water Report[118] and made findings as to whether improvements had occurred for Indigenous communities in the provision of water supply and water quality.[119] The Report examined the status of Aboriginal health in relation to the Australian Government's national water reform agenda and how these reforms would address the interrelated issues of the dire living standards among Indigenous peoples and the inadequate water servicing in rural and remote Australia.[120] The Report indicates that the international literature in this area has 'abandoned targeting health in isolation and instead identifies human development and the alleviation of poverty as critical responses to these issues'.[121] It noted, 'in small remote Indigenous communities there are limitations with a competition model for service delivery'.[122]

The Social Justice Report 2008 cautioned on the use of general statistics alone to represent the experience of all Indigenous peoples in Australia:

> Statistics on Indigenous peoples are subject to a range of data quality concerns. In addition to cultural considerations in relation to statistical matters (such as concepts, definitions, collection practices), data quality issues arise from the relatively small size of the Indigenous population in comparison with the total population, the dispersion of the Indigenous population, particularly across remotes areas of Australia, and the way in which Indigenous persons are identified in statistical collections.[123]

Aboriginal peoples were only first counted as citizens in the 1971 Census[124] so the lack of information about Australia's Indigenous population, since Federation, and the depth of national research, is limited. The identification of community trends and the impact of various indicators such as health, housing and exercising cultural activities are central to improving Aboriginal health policy.[125]

> Most states and territories have been slow to enter into partnerships with Indigenous peoples, despite the 1992 National Commitment. It is only in the past five years that they have begun to enter into partnership agreements with the Aboriginal and Torres Strait Islander Commission on behalf of Indigenous peoples on issues such as housing and infrastructure, health and law and justice.[126]

The Australian Government pursued a social justice philosophy through the establishment of the Council for Aboriginal Reconciliation[127] to address 'Aboriginal disadvantage in land, housing, law and justice, cultural heritage, education, employment, health, infrastructure, economic development and other matters'.[128] Aboriginal water rights and interests were not included in the Reconciliation Council's 1994 report and did not feature in the campaign for reconciling Australia's past injustices.

The Native Title Report 2005 points to a review by the Productivity Commission Report, 'Overcoming Indigenous Disadvantage: Key Indicators 2005', which indicated that Indigenous peoples' access to traditional lands, and ownership and control of land creates positive socio-economic factors to alleviate disadvantage.[129] According to the National Survey on Land, Sea and Economic Development in 2006 by the Human Rights and Equal Opportunity Commission, 'cultural heritage protection of land and sea was the highest priority identified by traditional owners'.[130]

The Native Title Report 2007 argues that 'the native title system is not delivering substantial recognition and protection of native title, essentially, the system was not meeting the objects of the native title legislation'.[131] The Native Title Report 2008 highlighted that 'Indigenous water rights were not adequately recognised in Australia'[132] and noted that legislation is often silent on such issues as Indigenous water rights, access to water entitlements and water allocations.[133]

The Native Title Reports recognise the complexity of native title jurisprudence and the determination of Aboriginal claims to traditional lands and waters. Such rights to inland waters in Australia are recognised as exclusive possession and non-exclusive rights, for example, 'where non-exclusive rights to take water hold pre-existing interests determined by statutory legislation'.[134] Exclusive rights to 'flowing and subterranean waters for native title holders were determined, but limited in scope'.[135]

The Native Title Report 2008 notes that some procedural rights for Indigenous peoples in relation to leases, licences and permits which regulate the management of water have been weakened under the *Native Title Act 1993* (Cth). For example, to waive an obligation in order to comply with the common law rules of procedural fairness.[136] The *Native Title Act 1993* (Cth) held that native title holders had a procedural right to negotiate in future development activity on lands and waters, and for the ownership and use of natural resources.[137]

After the 1998 native title amendments the *Act* only allowed a 'right to comment' to the relevant representative body, prescribed body corporate and registered native title claimants before activities could be carried out.[138] This amendment excludes native title holders from the development of water management plans and the protection of cultural rights to water.[139]

The Native Title Report 2010 argued strongly that the native title system has continued to fail Indigenous peoples in realising the exercise and enjoyment of their legal and human rights, in particular the burden of proof required to meet the evidential standards of an Aboriginal claim.[140] The introduction of the *Native Title Amendment Act [No 1] 2010* (Cth) created a new future act process[141] which operates to circumvent agreement processes with Indigenous peoples and their rights to exercise self-determination, thus hindering the participation of Indigenous peoples in the decision-making process and developing strategies to protect their lands and resources.[142]

The Commissioner's reports clearly identify significant changes in the objects and the purpose of the *Native Title Act 1993* (Cth) since its introduction. The importance of the reports should not be undervalued in researching the context and underlying history that challenges the human rights of Indigenous peoples in Australia – every day of their lives.

Chapter 5

'LITTLE MORE THAN A SENSE OF JUSTICE': MABO AND NATIVE TITLE

The introduction of native title into the Australian legal system was a remarkable event, when the development of native title case law slowly recognised what Aboriginal and Torres Strait Islander peoples have always known— their legal right to land and water. Conceptualising Aboriginal traditions, laws and customs within the framework of native title, itself a creature of Australian law and distinct from the creation of Aboriginal laws, advanced an understanding of Aboriginal title.

Years later it was clear that the interpretation of Aboriginal practices and customs within the native title system complicated and reconstructed Aboriginal concepts of water and land rights. The impact of colonisation has left Aboriginal society with traditional customs and practices and revitalized traditions. Some view the decision to adapt tradition into contemporary norms as too progressive.

Aboriginal rights to water were not seriously considered until the *Mabo v Queensland [No 2]* decision. Twenty-one years before *Mabo* the Yolgnu peoples defended their sovereign rights to veto mining on country in *Milirrpum v Nabalco* – and lost. The *Mabo* decision restored Indigenous Australians' faith in the legal system, for a time. *Mabo* formally recognised that Indigenous peoples had not forfeited their rights to country. As Aboriginal people say – Always was, always will be Aboriginal land.

As I discussed in the introduction, the landmark decision changed the way Australia understood *terra nullius* and overturned the notion that British colonial settlement had extinguished Aboriginal rights to land, water and some resources.[1] Overturning the fiction of *aqua nullius* remains the next challenge for Australia.

This chapter explores native title in relation to water rights and argues that the Australian legal system has added to the complexity of understanding in Aboriginal peoples' relationship to land and waters. I argue that governments have been reluctant to adopt Aboriginal legal concepts of ownership to express how Aboriginal peoples understand the concept of Aboriginal title. This diminishes Aboriginal property rights.

Former High Court judge Mary Gaudron indicates the immense difficulty in unpacking the customary rights of Aboriginal peoples under the Western legal system.

> To embark on an analysis of native title law is to begin with the strange and unfamiliar ... with the notion of rights which owe their existence, not to our laws which are strange enough, but to customs and traditions in respect of which we have contrived ... to describe that framework as 'exceedingly complex' ... is, perhaps, a masterful understatement.[2]

Because of the Western ownership paradigm, Aboriginal values, practices and beliefs are in conflict with Western perspectives and values regarding property ownership. Aboriginal and Western conceptions of water rights and interests, as with land rights, are opposing ideologies. The High Court decision in *Mabo v Queensland [No 2]*[3] held that:

> [E]nglish land law in 1879 and to the present, whereby an estate in fee simple on a person in possession of land enforceable against all the world was the basis for common law except where a person could prove a better claim.[4]

The non-legal recognition of Aboriginal land ownership was considered by Lionel Murphy QC:

> [t]he aborigines did not give up their lands peacefully; they were killed or removed forcibly from the lands by United Kingdom forces or the European colonists in what amounted to attempted (and in Tasmania almost complete) genocide. The statement by the Privy Council may be regarded either as having been made in ignorance or as a convenient falsehood to justify the taking of aborigines' land.[5]

Brennan CJ in *Mabo v Queensland [No 2]*[6] considered the common law reasoning in relation to Aboriginal title in *Milirrpum v Nabalco*[7] that,

> [i]ndividual members of a community who enjoy only usufructuary rights that are not proprietary in nature are no impediment to the recognition of a proprietary community title.[8]

The concept of a usufructuary or beneficial right poses no threat to the land tenure system – essentially it allows for co-existence. Brennan CJ acknowledged that the recognition of Aboriginal laws under native title is limited because of an adherence to the 'skeletal frame' concept of the common law.

> [t]he common law is not to be frozen in an age of discrimination [and] ... the Court is not free to adopt rules that accord with contemporary notions of justice and human rights if their adoption would fracture the skeleton of principle which gives the body of our law its shape and internal consistency.[9]

In *Mabo v Queensland [No 2]*[10] the plaintiffs challenged the English concept of possession and property law as alien to Indigenous inhabitants.[11] *Mabo* recognised that the Australian law could accommodate Aboriginal rights to land and waters, and that it would not fracture the skeletal frame'[12] of Australia's legal system – for Aboriginal laws must be recognisable and compatible with the common law. As former High Court judge, Michael Kirby explained, 'it was the judiciary's increasing acceptance that human rights could resolve ambiguities in legislation and fill the gaps in the common law'.[13]

Generally, Aboriginal communities in Australia welcomed the landmark judgment as an opportunity to reclaim the ownership of traditional land. However, Aboriginal communities have had difficulty in reaching successful claims in the ownership of water because this involves the recognition of property rights.

Western legal concepts restrict the correct interpretation of Aboriginal concepts. The implication for Aboriginal water rights and interests when Aboriginal water is quantified by volume is that formidable barriers are created for Aboriginal peoples to claim water. For example, Aboriginal customary transition areas with land, which are shared by more than one traditional Aboriginal owner where traditional boundary lines overlap, are not accepted concepts under native title.

> Native title must *fit within* the existing system of Australian property rights. Therefore native title, and in particular its spatial dimensions, may bear little resemblance to the system of Indigenous laws and customs upon which it is based. To find a place with the taxonomy of property rights, native title must be presented in a form that can be located alongside and compared with other forms of estates and land tenures.[14]

The Australian Government accepted the High Court decision in *Mabo [No 2]* and this paved the way for discussions to draft the appropriate legislation, with the consultation of Indigenous representatives. In the Preamble of the Native

Title Bill 1993, presented to Parliament for the first time, it confirmed the status of Indigenous peoples as the first inhabitants of Australia – the Bill was to 'rectify the consequences of past injustices' and for Indigenous peoples to 'receive full recognition and status within the Australian nation'.[15] By including these words, 'the Australian Government recognised international standards for the protection of universal human rights and fundamental freedoms' when ratified – such as the *Racial Discrimination Act 1975*.[16] Section 10 of the *Racial Discrimination Act 1975* 'was critical in asserting native title'.[17]

Former Prime Minister Paul Keating addressed the reluctance of the Parliament and the Australian Courts to legally recognise traditional laws, customs and practices of Indigenous peoples. Mr Keating in his Second Reading speech on the Native Title Bill (1993) said:

> The Government has always recognised that despite its historic significance, the Mabo decision gives little more than a sense of justice to those Aboriginal communities whose native title has been extinguished or lost without consultation, negotiation or compensation. Their dispossession has been total, their loss has been complete.[18]

In Australia, the *Native Title Act 1993* (Cth) defines the waters as 'sea and freshwater'.[19] Section 208(1) of the Act describes the concept for the 'expression of native title rights and interests of Indigenous peoples to land or waters'.[20] Section 211 of the Act preserves the right of native title holders to fish and to engage in traditional activities, whereby s 212 confirms the Crown's right to use and control the flow of water.[21]

The primary definition of common law native title is found in s 223 of the *Native Title Act 1993* (Cth):

Common law rights and interests

(1) The expression native title or native title rights and interests means the communal, group or individual rights and interests of Aboriginal peoples or Torres Strait Islanders in relation to land or waters, where

(a) the rights and interests are possessed under the traditional laws acknowledged, and the traditional customs observed, by the Aboriginal peoples or Torres Strait Islanders; and

(b) the Aboriginal peoples or Torres Strait Islanders, by those laws and customs, have a connection with the land or waters; and

(c) the rights and interests are recognised by the common law of Australia.

Hunting, gathering and fishing covered in the Act
(2) Without limiting subsection (1), rights and interests in that subsection includes hunting, gathering, or fishing, rights and interests.

Statutory rights and interests in the Act
(3) Subject to subsections (3A) and (4), if native title rights and interests as defined by subsection (1) are, or have been at any time in the past, compulsorily converted into, or replaced by, statutory rights and interests in relation to the same land or waters that are held by or on behalf of Aboriginal peoples or Torres Strait Islanders, those statutory rights and interests are also covered by the expression native title or native title rights and interests. Subsection (3) cannot have any operation resulting from a future act that purports to convert or replace native title rights and interests unless the act is a valid future act. Subsection (3) does not apply to statutory access rights. (3A) Subsection (3) does not apply to rights and interests conferred by Subdivision Q of Division 3 of Part 2 of this Act (which deals with statutory access rights for native title claimants).[22]

The statutory framework for the definition of native title legislation is drawn from the interpretation of Brennan J in *Mabo v Queensland [No 2]* (1992) – this interpretation by the Court is considered to be a very narrow concept in comparison to the majority judgement.[23]

Under s 223(1)(a) to (c) of the *Native Title Act 1993* (Cth) the recent development of case law shows that s 223(1)(a) and (b) are not interpreted in a legal vacuum. The interpretation of the common law native title definition has been conceptualised by the courts and in many cases has narrowed the native title rights and interests of Indigenous claimants. For example, 'native title or native title rights and interests of communal, group or individual rights and interests, to land or waters' under s 223(1)(a) of the *Native Title Act 1993* (Cth) are strictly focused on 'traditional laws and the traditional customs observed by Indigenous peoples' but give insufficient weight to revitalized laws, customs and practices.

In s 223(1)(b) of the *Native Title Act 1993* (Cth) Indigenous peoples must show evidence of their 'laws and customs' in order to prove they have a 'connection with the land or waters'. The uneasy interrelationship between the common law definition of native title and the *Native Title Act 1993* (Cth) has resulted in ambiguity whereby the Federal Court has applied a textual interpretation to the proof requirements in s 223(1).[24] The Courts have significantly influenced 'setting the context in how native title legislation operates'[25] and by 'interpreting the words and legal concepts within the law'.[26] Aboriginal claimants and those working in the native title system recognize the doctrinal limitations of native title.[27]

In *Yarmirr*[28] the High Court held that international principles are a more persuasive source in a decision, as to whether or not, certain exclusive rights in the determination area may be recognised by the common law.[29] This view articulates that native title cases be interpreted under international human rights principles, which was the spirit and intent of the Native Title Bill.

The Native Title Act

> cannot be construed to allow the common law to operate in a discriminatory way preventing the recognition of traditional rights to the sea ... in making a determi-nation of native title rights and interests, the assertion of such rights be considered in the context of the relevant traditional laws and customs rather than applying English common law notions of exclusion.[30]

Contested notions in water resources

The High Court decision in *Mabo v Queensland [No 1]* (1988)[31] provided the foundation for *Mabo v Queensland [No 2]*.[32] Blackburn J in *Milirrpum v Nabalco*[33] remarked upon the dissimilar nature of Aboriginal law and Australian law that

> [t]here is so little resemblance between property, as our law, or what I know of any other law ....[34]

Interpreting the meaning of the ancient water rights of Aboriginal peoples is an ongoing challenge for the legal system. Applying Western meaning to explain Aboriginal values and concepts can often lead to the misrepresentation of Aborig-inal rights and interests and distort the concepts of traditional ownership.

The High Court decision in *Western Australia v Ward*[35] illustrates the miscon-ception of Aboriginal peoples 'speaking for country' as mirroring the concept in the Crown's right:

> [I]f it was correct that native title rights flowed from a 'right to speak for country', then, by parity of reasoning, because the Crown undoubtedly has 'spoken' for the land since the first non-indigenous settlement, that would be evidence of extin-guishment of native title, for two authorities could not in practical terms speak for the land.[36]

Speaking for country cannot be translated into literal English because Aboriginal law is an unequivocal authority for decisions by the Traditional Owner on country. The Crown as a Western common law concept has several meanings, such as 'the monarch of England' or 'the cluster of political institutions held within the concept of the State'.[37] Under the modern concept of the Crown in the Australian Constitution the meaning is more symbolic in nature.[38] The analogy adopted by the Court in *Western Australia v Ward*[39] was deficient because the authority of the Crown, under any of the above definitions, does equate to Aboriginal rights, obligations and birthright to speak for country. The right in speaking for country cannot be challenged and is not diminished by other interests.

A customary right to speak is, for example, held by a Senior Lawman or woman who holds intimate knowledge of sites under Aboriginal laws and has the only authority over any those issues for that area. The kinship authority to speak for country is an ancestral right from the Creation, where a person from a different kinship and community cannot speak for others. In the early concept of the Crown, the monarchs' powers were absolute and for all;[40] in a similar manner Traditional Owners command authority.

Kinship and community for Aboriginal peoples are tied to a range of activities on the land and waters. Scott Hawkins in 'Caught, Hook, Line and Sinker' (1992) examined communal sharing of Aboriginal fishing rights in New South Wales and highlighted the communal relationships and purpose of fishing:

> The purpose of continuing these practices is not only a practical answer to supplementing food and nutritional sources because of economic pressures or availability considerations, but also as a means of continuing traditional and cultural practices. These include communal sharing and trading for both subsistence and ceremonial and cultural purposes as well as the passing on of knowledge and custom from one generation to the next through these activities. Fishing and its associated activities form a major part of many Aboriginal people's lives.[41]

Djambawa Marawilli, in the Blue Mud Bay claim, declared that he was assured victory at court as seen in his dream, which affirmed that Yolngu ownership continues on out to sea:

> I was in my home in Baniyala, paddling into the sea, as far as I could go. My canoe was just about getting drowned. So I had to turn it around and paddle back. That was the point that told me how much of the sea belongs for indigenous people.[42]

The intrinsic nature of Aboriginal customary property rights in water resources, for example in salt, freshwater or groundwater, requires a paradigm shift in order to understand and recognise that the Aboriginal characterisation of water sits uneasily with the Western legal system. Therefore neither understanding nor legally recognising Aboriginal water rights and interests can be resolved adequately within the existing framework of the Australian legal system, or by using generic Western definitions which attempt to interpret or explain them.

Resolving this impasse will require a more nuanced approach to evaluating Aboriginal water rights than merely applying Australian law and using definitions that are too simple to explain Aboriginal laws. Aboriginal ownership has a unique conceptual framework that has complex cultural characteristics for determining the types of rights and interests which exist in water. Aboriginal law is central to how communal or individual rights are exercised and for deciding who has authority to speak for any activity on the land or waters.

The Western Australian Government, in reaction to the *Mabo v Queensland [No 2]*[43] judgment, passed the *Western Australian Land (Titles and Traditional Usage) Act 1993* to challenge the constitutional validity of the *Native Title Act 1993* (Cth) and if successful provide a blanket extinguishment of native title:

> [The Act] purports to validate all grants of title to land made in Western Australia between the 31 October 1975 and 2 December 1993 … to extinguish all native title in Western Australia existing immediately before the commencement of the Act and to create a substitute 'rights of traditional usage.[44]

In the High Court *Western Australia v Commonwealth 1995*[45] decision, the Commonwealth asserted that the Western Australian Act was inconsistent with both s10 of the *Racial Discrimination Act 1975* (Cth) and Article 5 of the *International Convention on the Elimination of All Forms of Racial Discrimination.*[46]

> Genuine equality incorporates the notion of justice and the proposition that equality requires those in the same circumstances to be treated the same and those in relevantly different circumstances to be treated differently … genuine equality, rather than being a project of eliminating difference, requires uniqueness to be preserved.[47]

The High Court rejected the argument submitted by the Western Australian Government. The Australian Government incorporated articles from the

International Convention on the Elimination of All Forms of Racial Discrimination in the *Racial Discrimination Act 1975* (Cth) to entrench human rights and prohibit racial discrimination.[48] However, there is nothing that would protect Indigenous rights if the Australian Government were to decide to legislate on the basis of race to the detriment of Indigenous peoples, for example in the Howard Federal Government's response to the *Wik* decision in the *Native Title Amendment Act 1998* (Cth).[49]

Mabo v Queensland [No 2][50] has advanced the cultural recognition of Aboriginal water rights and interests; however, it is arguable whether native title law has been an effective system for Aboriginal peoples to reclaim ownership in water. In effect, in order to establish their customary ownership rights, Indigenous peoples of Australia have had to engage with the native title system, which has become an onerous burden for the majority of Aboriginal claimants.

> *Mabo* itself demonstrates that the development of the common law to recognise a new right may conflict with pre-existing understandings of the common law, even contained in precedent.[51]

The High Court decision in *Wilson v Anderson*[52] clearly indicates how unworkable the processes of proving native title are and the barriers for Aboriginal claimants, Kirby J observed:

> The legal advance that commenced with *Mabo v Queensland [No 2]*, or perhaps earlier, has now attracted such difficulties that the benefits intended for Australia's indigenous peoples in relation to native title to land and waters are being channelled into costs of administration and litigation that leave everyone dissatisfied and many disappointed.[53]

Professor Patton (2000) argues that the legal recognition of the existence of Aboriginal law has been long overdue:[54]

> Australia is a special case in the modern history of colonization in that neither treaty nor conquest played any part in its acquisition by the British Crown ... indigenous inhabitants were considered incapable of being sovereigns over their territories ... without law ... [and] too low in the hierarchy of civilized races.[55]

Patton (2000) explains that

> [i]n parallel with the official account of the legal acquisition of the Australian territories, and despite many examples of legal pluralism in other parts of the British

Empire, the domestic law of the new colonies persistently refused any recognition of Aboriginal law and custom.[56]

The concept of legal pluralism is shaped by various political and legal constructs of colonisation to acquire land, water or resources, and generally exercised in the subordination of Indigenous groups by aggression or in some cases, in retaining some elements of Indigenous laws or practices within the imposed colonial legal system to ensure social order.[57] The central role of legal pluralism was to control the political economy, establish colonial institutions to enforce colonial laws and to regulate access to property interests.[58] At the point of British settlement Aboriginal groups in Australia were socially and politically reconstructed as 'non-inhabitants' and in the early 1800s Aboriginal peoples were redefined as 'colonial legal subjects'[59] not as independent self-governing groups or nations as in the United States.

Dr Lisa Strelein (2002) argues that 'it is inconsistent to deny Indigenous peoples the right to develop their economic and cultural independence under native title'.[60]

> The potential gap between the aspirations of Indigenous peoples and the capacity of common law native title to fulfil those expectations is enormous. The interpretation of the requirements of proof, and in particular the meaning attributed to the concept of 'traditional', form a significant part of that gulf.[61]

In *Commonwealth v Yarmirr* Olney J referred to the reasoning of Brennan and Toohey JJ in *Mabo v Queensland [No 2]* on the question of defining Indigenous 'ownership':[62]

> Brennan J thought that it may be confusing to describe the title of the Meriam people as conferring 'ownership', a term which connotes an estate in fee simple or at least an estate in freehold. It would be equally confusing to ascribe the right of ownership to an area of sea and sea-bed. To understand 'ownership' in the present context it will be necessary to consider in detail what Toohey J described in *Mabo [No 2]* as 'the abstract bundle of rights that are said to be enjoyed by reason of the connection of ownership'.[63]

There is a distinct gap between Western concepts in Australian law and Aboriginal definitions to exercise legal rights to water under traditional or customary laws. The courts have conceptualised Aboriginal ownership by various philosophical concepts such as the skeletal frame – as well as narrow definitions of native title law. The use of the word 'traditional' implies a Western concept that frames native title with a 'frozen in time' approach to Aboriginal laws.

The 2006 Native Title Report makes the point that Aboriginal peoples should be allowed to adapt their customary practices to Western concepts of tenure and use:

> Traditional owner rights to land are limited to the same customary activities as those that were practiced centuries ago and recorded by the 'first contact' non-indigenous colonisers. The claimable land that exists under the native title regime includes unallocated Crown lands, some reserves and park lands, and some leases such as non-exclusive pastoral and agricultural leases, depending on the state or territory legislation under which they were issued.[64]

The Australian Law Reform Commission in its inquiry on the *Native Title Act 1993* points out that, 'the interpretation of traditional has been criticised as restrictive and technical'.[65] These Western constructs fail to adequately express the nature of Aboriginal laws. The legal conceptualisation of native title as a 'bundle of rights' as adopted in the High Court decision in *Western Australia v Ward*[66] misconstrues the relationships of Aboriginal laws to traditional rights and interests in land, water and resources.

The concept of Aboriginal ownership was ignored because it did not bear any resemblance to British legal concepts of property.

> Upon European settlement, Australian governments proceeded on the basis that the indigenous people had no settled law and therefore nobody owned the land with the result that it all vested in governments to use as they saw fit.[67]

As discussed in this chapter, *Mabo v Queensland [No 2]*[68] the Court held that Australia was acquired under radical title in an 'act of state doctrine', where settlement commenced under an untruth on the basis that 'indigenous people were without laws or a sovereign, and presented a primitive social organisation'.[69] The majority in *Mabo v Queensland [No 2]*[70] were clear that the doctrine of native title formed part of Australia's laws, in relation to Australia's colonisation.[71] Since *Mabo v Queensland [No 2]*[72] the Court recognised that, Australian society has moved well beyond the reasoning in the *Mirrilpum v Nabalco*.[73] The rigid parameters of the Western legal system had undermined the Aboriginal concept of property in land and waters for far too long.

Kirby J in the High Court decision in *Wik Peoples v Queensland*[74] held that the recognition of property rights is central to domestic stability:[75]

[p]roperty rights of any kind are not fictional. They concern the interests of individuals. Where they involve estates or interests in land, their recognition and protection by the legal system is important to the social and economic stability and peace which is the function of the sovereign to protect and enforce.[76]

Kirby J explains that the law-makers in Australia had not anticipated the future changes to the law resulting from the *Mabo v Queensland [No 2][77]* – and the *Wik v Queensland[78]* decision:[79]

[as] *Mabo [No 2]* and *Wik Peoples v Queensland* demonstrate … Australian law at this time is in the process of a measure of readjustment, arising out of the appreciation, both by parliaments and the courts of this country, of injustices which statute and common law earlier occasioned to Australia's indigenous peoples.[80]

Kirby J in *Western Australia v Ward[81]* made the point that the 'inextricable linkage' of Aboriginal peoples to country warranted legal protection:[82]

It has been accepted that the connection between Aboriginal Australians and 'country' is inherently spiritual and that the cultural knowledge belonging to Aboriginal people is, by indigenous accounts, inextricably linked with their land and waters, that is, with their 'country'. If this cultural knowledge, as exhibited in ceremony, performance, artistic creation and narrative, is inherently related to the land according to Aboriginal beliefs, it follows logically that the right to protect such knowledge is therefore related to the land for the purposes of the *Native Title Act 1993* (Cth).[83]

Olney J in *Yarmirr v Northern Territory[84]* did not recognise the Croker Islanders' exclusive possession of the marine seas, on grounds of a 'public right to fish as against the private right to land'.[85] The Aboriginal claimants argued that their marine territories were held under three principles: as territories in joint or common property ownership, to exclude by an inherited right and to exercise responsibilities over others as the sea was handed down in law to them by ancestral figures under Aboriginal law.[86]

The Aboriginal claimants in *Commonwealth v Yarmirr[87]* claimed an exclusive right of possession, occupation, and use and enjoyment of their land and the sea. Olney J held:

There was nothing in the evidence to explain what the claimant group understood 'the connection of ownership' to encompass unless it be the aggregation of separate rights which are asserted in respect of the claimed area; and that the term 'ownership' was first used by counsel, and not by a witness.[88]

Australian judicial decisions in native title law on the one hand had reinforced a continuing relationship of Aboriginal peoples to the land and the waters, and on the other has a strong reluctance to formally recognise Aboriginal rights and interests *if* such a decision would fracture the skeletal frame of the common law. Legal concepts such as this embed the restrictive nature of the Australian legal system.

> Ethnographically speaking, the fact that much recent work on tenure has been carried out for sea closures and native title applications means there has been a pervasiveness of legal discourse in the ethnography of marine tenureship just as there has recently been for land tenure. This tends to alienate Aboriginal people from their own experience and practice at the same time as it makes those experiences and practices recognisable by the state.[89]

The significant cultural anthologies of the Yolngu peoples of the Northern Territory clearly outlined legal relationships to land and waters, as reported by anthropologists for the applicants in the *Milirrpum v Nabalco*[90] case.

However, for many Aboriginal peoples, the determination of native title still remains a pipe dream in providing certainty for Aboriginal claimant's rights and interests.[91] In many cases this occurs from the continuous events of the colonisation process – such as colonially sanctioned war on Aboriginal peoples, assimilation, segregation policies and unfettered vigilante violence.

Kirby J dissenting in *Western Australia v Ward* (2000)[92] said:

> When evaluating native title rights and interests, a court should start by accepting the pressures that existed in relation to Aboriginal laws and customs to adjust and change after British sovereignty was asserted over Australia. In my opinion, it would be a mistake to ignore the possibility of new aspects of traditional rights and interests developing as part of Aboriginal customs not envisaged, or even imagined, in the times preceding settlement.[93]

The courts have shown a reluctance to enter legal argument on the existence of Aboriginal sovereignty.

> Understanding the development of the law requires [an] understanding both of the contemporary Australian context in which potentially competing interests in land and resources occurs, and the unique Australian historical context which is largely about the denial of Indigenous land rights, including rights to self-government, land and resource management; which arise out of a proper conception of native

title that views Aboriginal title as inherent, with an acknowledgement of prior Indigenous sovereignty.[94]

The majority in the High Court decision *Yorta Yorta v Victoria*[95] held that native title rights were 'frozen in time at the moment of the acquisition of Australian sovereignty, which conceptualises native title into a relic of Australian law'.[96]

> Rights associated with laws and customs came into being at the intersection of two normative systems. That intersection occurred when the common law entered Australia and recognized rights and interests derived from traditional laws and customs. The common law continues to recognize those rights and interests to the extent that they continue to exist … the acquisition of sovereignty is simply a point of the transition of power.[97]

Dissenting in *Western Australia v Ward*,[98] Kirby J argued that the current evaluation of Aboriginal traditional rights required a human rights approach to interpret the law. He remarked:

> Because the statutory concepts of 'recognition' and 'extinguishment' are themselves ambiguous or informed by the approach of the common law, this Court should adopt, and consistently apply, several interpretative principles … First … in any case of ambiguity, the interpretation of the statutory text should be preferred that upholds fundamental human rights rather than one that denies those rights and enforcement.[99]

However, in *Western Australia v Ward*[100] the High Court limited the legal recognition of economic and resource rights by characterising native title as a 'bundle of rights', and not as a title to land.[101] In other Western Australian native title cases Aboriginal claimants have had varying success,[102] for example for the Jurruru[103] peoples in the Southwest Pilbara in a consent determination of non-exclusive rights and the Ngadju[104] peoples recognition of exclusive possession in the Goldfields region.

Native title decisions on water rights issues

It is important to note the comments of the Australian Law Reform Commission (ALRC) in its inquiry on the Australian Government's proposed amendments to native title, and in particular the 'concern around statutory rights vested in the states and territories' – including 'surface water rights'.[105] The ALRC recognised the need for a 'broader review of native title rights to water'.[106] I have also argued for a national review of Aboriginal water rights, sooner rather than later.

This section summarises a number of native title decisions on water to high-light the nature and extent of how Western value systems interpret a claim in Aboriginal water rights.

In recent times the High Court decision in *Akiba* opened up new dialogue on water rights to sea country. The Court in *Akiba v Commonwealth*[107] 'unanimously held that certain reciprocity-based rights between members of the Torres Strait Island communities did not constitute native title rights and interests within the meaning of s 223 of the *Native Title Act* 1993 (Cth)'. However, the Court recog-nised that Torres Strait Islander groups had a 'non-exclusive right to exercise their commercial fishing rights and that their right to fish was not extinguished by statutory licences'.[108]

In *Ngalpil v Western Australia*[109] the court held that the Tjurabalan peoples had exclusive possession 'in relation to flowing and subterranean waters'.[110] The court in *Nangkiriny v Western Australia*[111] held that the Karajarri peoples had exclusive possession of 'native title rights to use and enjoy the flowing and subterranean waters, including the right to hunt and gather'.[112]

In *Rubibi Community v Western Australia (No 7)*[113] the court held that an exception to exclusive possession for flowing and subterranean waters was limited to a right to take water 'for personal, domestic and non-commercial communal purposes'.[114] By contrast, in *Sampi v Western Australia (No 3)*[115] there was no recognition of 'exclusive rights to water, either in flowing or by natural collection or to underground water'.[116]

In *Lardil Peoples v Queensland*[117] the claimants, the Lardil, Yangkaal, Kaiadilt and Ganggalidda peoples, described their Aboriginal water rights:

[i]n respect of the lands and waters below the high water mark in an area adjacent to the Wellesley Islands [and] ... the right to exclusive and undisturbed occupa-tion, possession, use and enjoyment of the land and waters, including the natural resources within the sea.[118]

The *Lardil* decision recognised the existence of 'customary succession laws' possessed by the Aboriginal claimants,

[u]nder traditional law and customs at the time of sovereignty ... where the Ming-ginda peoples, no longer alive due to European colonisation, had land adjoined to the claimant group ... the Gangalidda succession had occurred under the tradi-tional law and customs.[119]

In this decision[120] Cooper J limited the Aboriginal claimants' rights, asserting that the *Lardil Peoples*

> [p]ossessed non-exclusive native title rights and interests over parts of the sea and Albert River ... which were manifest by a continuing connection to the claim area ... as one of sustenance and religious and spiritual belonging.[121]

Cooper J held that the Aboriginal claimants 'possessed non-exclusive native title water rights limited to personal, domestic or non-commercial communal consumption'.[122]

> [t]he right to utilise fresh water from springs in the intertidal zone and the right to access the land and waters seaward of the high water mark, and the Albert River, for religious or spiritual purposes, and to access sites of spiritual or religious significance.[123]

Cooper J went on to say that the Lardil, Yangkaal, Gangalidda and Kaiadilt Peoples' claim to the land and waters below the high water mark in sea country survived 'the tide of colonisation'.[124] Cooper J concluded that the Lardil peoples owned their sea country under their own laws and customs, as customary exclusive rights.[125]

The recent landmark native title claim for the *Rrumburriya Borroloola Claim Group*[126] in the Gulf country in the Northern Territory, recognised the exclusive right to trade, barter and exchange for commercial purposes and use of land and waters – based upon anthropological evidence of trade with the Macassan peoples.

Nicolas Peterson and Bruce Rigsby (1998) examined the customary marine tenure of Aboriginal peoples in Australia;[127] and research into Aboriginal marine tenure is yet to attract the attention it deserves. Since the *Mabo v Queensland [No 2]*[128] and the enactment of the *Native Title Act 1993* (Cth), the water rights and interests of Indigenous peoples have created a need for academic research on native title claims.[129] Peterson and Rigsby analysed how native title research into the customary marine tenure of Aboriginal communities addressed the issue of property rights in the sea.[130] They reported:

> It is evident that Aboriginal access to the sea has undergone a number of changes. The most recent of these, prior to European arrival, was the adoption of the dugout canoe in one of several forms. Its adoption clearly facilitated sea travel, made it possible to reach distant islands more regularly and influenced hunting and fishing patterns.[131]

Peterson and Rigsby noted that the archaeological literature on Aboriginal coastal economies is significant and provides indisputable evidence of Aboriginal peoples' relationship to and use of water – fish traps, middens and shell trading.[132] The authors' examination of Aboriginal customary tenure and values in the sea is relevant to any analysis of Aboriginal water values.

The water values held by Aboriginal communities are integral to the kinship relationships of all Indigenous peoples in Australia through either marriage or birth. Scott Cane (1998) undertook research in preparing the defended hearing for the Aboriginal fishing case in *Mason v Tritton*.[133] Cane acknowledges fishing as an inherent right and customary economy, as distinguished from Peterson and Rigsby's (1998) analysis of the 'social construction' of Aboriginal peoples' marine tenure.[134]

These examples on water rights highlight the extent to which the courts recognise such rights. The courts, in determining the use of customary waters, can either deliver extinguishment or partial extinguishment or deliver exclusive or non-exclusive rights and interests. The nature of defining Aboriginal property rights as either exclusive or non-exclusive is entrenched in Western concepts of property law. Aboriginal communities who cannot prove native title in water have limited opportunities to press for customary recognition.

In contrast, statutory laws pursuant to Part III of the *Rights in Water and Irrigation Act 1914* (WA) state that 'any native title rights to control the use and flow of waters were extinguished'.[135] The 'vesting of the beds of water courses, lakes and lagoons did not transfer legal estates to the Crown', only the control and management of water.[136] The High Court's 'unanimous' decision in *Karpany v Dietman* held that the applicant's (the Narrunga peoples') native title rights had not been extinguished and that native title rights were not inconsistent with statutory legislation to regulate fishing.[137] For many Aboriginal communities, the extinguishment of water rights becomes not only a legal impediment but a barrier for future generations to exercise customary laws and practices on country.

Indigenous Land Use Agreements (ILUA) under the *Native Title Act 1993* (Cth) have provided an alternative to litigated native title determinations. For instance, in the Wet Tropics World Heritage Area situated in the Daintree and Bloomfield River water catchments in Queensland,[138] the Eastern Kuku Yalanji peoples and the Queensland Government have entered into an ILUA which transfers 64,000 hectares into Aboriginal freehold land under the *Aboriginal Land Act 1991* (Qld) and the Eastern Kuku Yalanji peoples hold delegated powers to enforce the *Nature Conservation Act 1992* (Qld) regulations.[139]

The native title determination for the Butchulla peoples, traditional owners of K'Gari (Fraser Island), recognised their rights and interests in an ILUA – which affirms the Butchulla connection to the World Heritage-listed island.[140]

Under a native title consent determination, between the Djabugay peoples and the Queensland Government, 'native title was shown to exist in relation to water and land as a non-exclusive right, for personal, domestic, social, cultural, religious, spiritual, ceremonial and non-commercial communal need'.[141] The claim area included the Baron Gorge National Park where the 'Storywaters' and *Bulurru*[142] are ancestral creation areas.

The types of water rights and interests negotiated under ILUA under the *Native Title Act 1993* (Cth) do not provide compensation retrospectively for spent resources.

> Aboriginal people are denied any right to compensation where native title may have existed over timber, water or minerals … where native title may exist over these resources it will be extinguished …[143]

The High Court action brought by the Quandamooka Yoolooburrabee Aboriginal Corporation (QYAC), and recently discontinued, in relation to their ILUA[144] with the Queensland Government highlighted the wide-ranging impact for breach of the terms and conditions of such agreements – in amending legislation to extend mining operations without the consultation and agreement of the native title holders. This action also raised concerns for the validity of other ILUAs executed under the native title legislation.

An inferior water right — the limits of native title

The Native Title Report (2006) addresses the statistics on native title determinations, pointing out that 'Indigenous peoples have varying rights and interests to just over 8.5 per cent of the Australian land mass as a consequence of native title determinations'.[145] It also reports that 'just over 96 per cent of all Aboriginal land claims under native title are in very remote locations'.[146] The majority of Aboriginal peoples living in urban and rural locations will not be native title holders. Stephen Mueke (2006) argues that the doctrine of *terra nullius* in Australia's history resulted in a reluctance to legally recognise Aboriginal rights:

> The British invented the designation of *terra nullius*, empty land, 'nowhere', to justify their occupation, effacing in the process the specific modes of emplacement of Aboriginal cultures, which is tantamount to effacing the people themselves: if they are nowhere, where are they dwelling?[147]

Chief Justice French emphasised in a media interview that native title claims are onerous for Aboriginal peoples under the current burden of proof where Aboriginal peoples are required to prove claims to native title, where instead the Chief Justice asserts, Aboriginal claimants 'should be presumed to have continuous existence and vitality from the assertion of British sovereignty'.[148]

As discussed earlier, the native title amendments secured by the Federal Howard Government after the *Wik Peoples v Queensland*[149] decision, expunged the co-existence between Aboriginal and non-Aboriginal rights under certain pastoral leases – these amendments have narrowed Aboriginal rights and interests to land and waters.[150] For various reasons the native title system results in unsatisfactory outcomes for Aboriginal peoples, as the following illustrates. The New South Wales Aboriginal Land Council stated:

> [t]he *Wilson v Anderson* and *Yorta Yorta* decisions have further eroded the likelihood that native title will be recognised in NSW … Due to the likelihood that native title will have restricted benefits for Aboriginal people in NSW, cultural heritage rights should form the basis upon which Aboriginal people are afforded benefits through NSW Water Reforms and the state-based Implementation of the National Water Initiative.[151]

The Land Council submission made its position clear in relation to Aboriginal land and water interests under the New South Wales Government:

> It has been expected that Aboriginal rights and interests in water would be promoted through an approach similar to that contained in the *Aboriginal Land Rights Act 1983* (NSW). The *Act* recognises Aboriginal prior ownership of land, similar to the *Water Management Act 2000* (NSW) and the spiritual, social, cultural and economic values attached to land. The important distinction between the NSW Government approaches to the management of the Aboriginal claim on land as compared to the Aboriginal claim on natural resources is that the *Aboriginal Land Rights Act* provides mechanisms for compensation for loss whereas the *Water Management Act* and the Draft Implementation do not.[152]

Aboriginal communities' use of potable and cultural water rights, and their access to and use of water for other traditional or communal purposes, is considered by governments as an inferior water right among other interests. Stakeholders in sectors such as pastoral entities, agriculture and mining are highly valued within the Australian economy.

> The two major parties are confronted, on the one hand, by their desire to see social justice for Aboriginal Australians and, on the other hand, their concern about the effect that native title claims will have on the pastoral and mining industries which are of major importance to the Australian economy. Both parties have an ongoing interest in setting a firm regime specifying the limits of native title.[153]

Collins (2003) argues that the 'balancing of interests' in Australia is weighed against Aboriginal interests and that Aboriginal claimants in native title are required to conform to legal minutiae which entail a more complex, time consuming and cost exigent legal process than any other legal process of Australian law.[154] Holzberger (2003) notes that 'Aboriginal rights to water under native title do not prevail over mining rights' due to the High Court decision in *Western Australia v Ward*.[155]

> The issuance of a water licence for mining purposes may impair native title rights. According to Denholder and Gishubl, grants of licences under water legislation are generally not considered to be grants, which are likely to be construed as inconsistent with native title rights as to bar co-existence. The grants are not exclusive.[156]

In Australia there is an inequitable allocation of water resources by government to the majority of Aboriginal communities because they are divided into those who are native title holders and those who are not – and unable to meet the evidence required under native title law. Governments may choose to exercise their decision-making to accommodate or to enshrine Aboriginal cultural water rights and interests into Australian law. There is a range of Aboriginal water rights and interests that require legal certainty. If the water rights of the First Australians are ignored the increase in the level of social disadvantage among Aboriginal communities will continue.

> The Native Title Bill did not codify native title rights, but rather was arguably designed to give full play to the common law. It also sought to redress the effects of colonisation where native title could not be claimed ...[157]

Aboriginal water rights are not easily conceptualised or valued under the common law and statutory interpretation is often in conflict with an Aboriginal property rights paradigm. Aboriginal title is a 'creature' separate of the common law – and recognised as inferior to Australian law. The reluctance by governments to fully embrace the nature of Aboriginal ownership and Aboriginal property concepts is a barrier to ameliorate poverty. Although the introduction of native title rights was initially hailed as a significant victory, the subsequent amendments to the body of native title laws have sought to narrow the window of opportunity to reclaim the lands and waters.

PART B

TRADING WATER –
THE DISCONNECT IN WATER VALUES

Chapter 6

POLARISED PARADIGMS –
WESTERN AND ABORIGINAL CONCEPTIONS

Ownership of the land or the waters is highly valued because it enables the individual to increase personal wealth and status: 'private property is fundamental to a capitalist mode of production and, according to some, crucial to a nation's wealth and standard of living'.[1]

A conundrum arises when one tries to define Aboriginal property interests through Western legal concepts because the values, beliefs and laws inherent in Western and Aboriginal ontological concepts exist within polarised cultural paradigms. The distinct colonial histories of Australia experienced by Aboriginal peoples and settler societies have resulted in complex and historically difficult relationships, and such relationships continue to create conflict for resources. They also raise significant policy issues for developing inclusive Australian water policy and law and filling the gap that exists in understanding the themes around Aboriginal water values and Australian water management.

Professor Craig (Tony) Arnold (2002), an internationally recognised legal scholar, sought to define the concept of property rights as a 'web of interests'. He argued that 'property concepts applied to understand human beings' relationship with an object of property such as private property rights or the concept of the property right require a new metaphor'.[2] Arnold explained that this 'metaphor' is required to 'accommodate the human to human, human to object relationships' – and to 'define the legal interests within these relationships of property rights'.[3] Arnold said that there had been no attempt in legal scholarship to produce a broad metaphor of property based upon the interconnection of the property right to the person, to integrate the 'humanness and the thing, and to understand the interests of the property holders to each other'.[4]

This is relevant to understanding how Aboriginal peoples conceptualise water values within Western legal concepts and how Australian law seeks to merely accommodate Aboriginal water values into Western concepts of water management. The concept of using a metaphor such as 'a web of interests' in the area of Aboriginal water rights and interests is a new way to understand Aboriginal relationships to water and to demonstrate the depth and complexity of what water rights and interests represent to Aboriginal peoples.

This chapter analyses the ontological structure of Aboriginal water values – for example, the complexity of cultural meaning which pertains to Aboriginal water use and the treatment of Aboriginal values and meanings by Australia's legal system. It examines how the Western construction of Aboriginal meanings of Aboriginal water concepts and laws can misinterpret the context of Aboriginal ontology, and further argues that the nuances of Aboriginal language require a new approach to articulating these rights and interests to fully consider their ontological complexity.

The ontological context of water

The cultural ontology of Aboriginal peoples — 'the inherited ideas, beliefs and values and knowledge held by Aboriginal communities' is a unique cultural paradigm.[5]

The Western reconstruction of Aboriginal water values, such as the native title paradigm, often compromises an Aboriginal claim to rights and interests. Legal academic Bradley Bryan said,

> we are accustomed to see land and territory in terms of Cartesian space, and to see ownership as based in transactional value. The ontological structure of Aboriginal life necessarily means that 'ownership' per se never actually occurs or exists, because such things are simply not enframed as we would enframe them.[6]

Dr Bradley Bryan's essay, 'Property as Ontology' (2002), impressed upon me the importance of understanding Aboriginal ontology through conceptualising ownership rights and cultural rights in property.[7] Bryan's argument encouraged me to develop a new conceptual framework and to compare Aboriginal conceptions and values in water as property rights to Western legal concepts, which seek to define the culturally complex norms of Aboriginal society.[8]

Bryan argued that the values and concepts of property, such as ownership and cultural authority over land, water and resources, must be understood as Aboriginal norms, as Western concepts in property and their respective values and beliefs are very different. His essay ignited my thinking on how different concepts are held by Aboriginal peoples and non-Aboriginal peoples, particularly non-Indigenous water stakeholders such as farmers, irrigators and pastoralists.

Bryan explains that understanding Aboriginal ontological concepts in property does not translate into the same values contained in Western legal concepts of property:[9]

> As we approach Aboriginal society in our quest to find property, we inevitably name practices and customs … we set out on a dialogical excursion that is neither invited nor welcomed by Aboriginal peoples. This is because to re-describe native reality is to actually change native reality: changed descriptions create new webs of meaning, and hence practices, identity, and worldviews will all be affected.[10]

Bryan's analysis of English conceptions of property argues that the ontological status of English conceptions is rooted in the fundamental identity of the English, where language conveys a metaphysical understanding.[11] The ontological understanding of Aboriginal property, on the other hand, is blended through Western property concepts – by applying simplistic interpretations of the Aboriginal creation story as myths, blending the meaning of ownership into common law framing to construct a false Aboriginal identity.[12]

Neither the common law nor the provisions of the *Native Title Act 1993* (Cth) constitute a bulwark against the presence of Western influences.[13] Western conceptions of native title have resulted in the reconstruction of Aboriginal traditional laws and customs, and as a result they often bear little resemblance to Aboriginal ontological meanings.

The principal characteristic of Aboriginal property rights or interests to water, either in birth or in death, is in a familial connection to 'place'. Connection can be represented by a river, an inter-tidal waterway, a waterhole or in the resources that rest on or beneath water. According to a Western perspective,

> [t]he meaning of land (ontic commitments) and explanations of its origins (epistemic commitments) are reduced to a concern for quantification, in contrast to Indigenous relationships to land which are based on highly developed epistemic and ontic commitments.[14]

The most significant property value in Western land tenure is based upon 'individual property ownership and the commercialization of Indigenous resources'.[15] The intrinsic nature of Western property values is based upon individual rights whereas Aboriginal rights and interests are collective rights and attach to Aboriginal ontological water concepts and relationships.

> The cultural properties of indigenous peoples have been under ever increasing danger of theft, appropriation and exploitation … The right to collective ownership is for many indigenous nations an essential element of culture yet it is a right with little significance and standing in international and states' government laws.[16]

An Aboriginal worldview is often expressed through Western frameworks of ecology and biodiversity:

> The maintenance of biological diversity on lands and waters over which Aboriginal and Torres Strait Islander peoples have title or in which they have an interest is a cornerstone of the wellbeing, identity, cultural heritage and economy of Aboriginal and Torres Strait Islander communities.[17]

Australian legislation generally refers to the environment as consisting of 'water, land, trees, plants or wetlands'. A Western environment is constructed on a set of values that represent an aesthetic and scientific meaning. The inclusion of Aboriginal peoples' water values into water policy and legislation requires a cultural acknowledgement of its unique characteristics.

> In countries where customary water rights play a significant role, particularly in rural areas where they govern access and rights to water in basic human needs, for the watering of livestock and for subsistence agriculture, customary law and customary water rights are a factor to be reckoned with when preparing 'modern' legislation regulating the abstraction and use of water resources through government permits or licences. Failure to recognize the existence and resilience of customary practices, and to take them into account in 'modern' water resources legislation, is a recipe for social tension.[18]

Waubin Richard Aken, a Traditional Owner of Cape York in Queensland[19] has suggested that

> Cultural democracy is based on processes of Spiritual Sustainability Development Principles. It is a system based on the Cycle of Life. It clearly identifies who we are and where we are from. The mainstream society perspective is based on

Materialisms …[20]

Aristotle argued the position of numerous Greek philosophers on the relationship of human beings to the environment, as well as on property concepts in nature and resources.[21]

> Property, in the sense of bare livelihood, seems to be given by nature herself to all … Now if nature makes nothing incomplete, and nothing in vain, the inference must be that she has made all animals for the sake of men.[22]

Aristotle's view highlights an ontological perspective that nature has made all things for human beings, bringing to the fore specific sets of values and beliefs in the European concept of property.[23]

The Australian colonies were founded on common law doctrine and later by Imperial enactment that embedded characteristics of the common law doctrine and informed the rules of statutory construction and interpretation in Australia.[24] The oral narrative of Aboriginal peoples has a basic similarity to the early development of common law because both are communicated orally.[25] The oral common law tradition was handed down as *lex non scripta* or unwritten law prior to the development of *lex scripta* or statute law.[26] The unwritten law of early England was later viewed as insufficient for adequately documenting the amendments or declarations of the law when doubts arose.[27]

However, the context of oral Aboriginal meanings and values differs significantly from the *lex non-scripta* tradition because of the additional cultural meanings which are implied or expressed in Aboriginal value systems.

> The whole idea of governing by fixed words inscribed on tablets is fascinating and strange. The words, which because of inadequacy of language and the infinite variety of circumstance, from the beginning never are better than approximate, are frozen in their imperfect state unless and until amended … the inadequate words grow less and less apt. The temptation the court feels is to depart from the literal meaning in order to do justice or make sense. Yet this natural urge marks a failure in communication. Words are designed for no other purpose than to transmit a message. If what the words say is rejected in favour of a meaning reached by other means, the message has not got through.[28]

'Cultural ontology' refers to the 'metaphysics that deals with the nature of being'[29] and pertains to 'the inherited ideas, beliefs, values and knowledge held by a particular people'.[30] Cultural ontology as a paradigm can be used to explain the values and beliefs of Aboriginal creation and Aboriginal relationships to all things. Aboriginal ontology also interprets the rights and interests of Aboriginal peoples in their unique relationship with the tangible and intangible environment. However, the value of recognising the importance of Aboriginal ontology was considered of minimal interest to the emerging Australian state.

The introduction of the Anglo-Australian legal system did not endorse the legal co-existence of Indigenous laws, customs and practices of Indigenous peoples if co-existence interfered with commerce and trade. The notion of legal pluralism, that is, the colonial power allowing Aboriginal laws to operate, in whole or in part, was tolerated only where it would not impinge upon non-Aboriginal group or individual rights, nor restrict the colonial development of the Australian landscape. As Benton states:

> Conflicts over cultural difference in the law were intertwined with disputes focussing on the control of property and its legal definition. Culture and economy were not separate entities …[31]

The Boomanulla Report (2002) resulted from information provided by Aboriginal government employees who were tasked to brainstorm and record the cultural values and the natural resource goals of Aboriginal communities in New South Wales and make recommendations. The Report identified the distinct conceptual differences between Aboriginal communities and Australian society:

> The planning process springs from European thinking, which is linear and focussed on measuring data. This way of thinking does not rest easily with Aboriginal (holistic) ways of thinking about the environment and about the people who live in the environment.[32]

Russell Goldflam, a lawyer and legal academic, explained that Edward Said's critique of 'Orientalism' reflects the social position held by Aboriginal peoples in Western society:

> Aboriginalism as a European power and knowledge constructs Aboriginal peoples and their Aboriginality isolating Aboriginal peoples in a conspiracy of silence through the exclusive use of the English language in the legal system whereby Aboriginal people are effectively absent.[33]

In the view of this critique, Western concepts have the power to influence and construct Aboriginal water rights and interests, and the meanings and values associated with Aboriginal water use. The Western concepts of what represents Aboriginality have a flow-on effect in how Australian policy and law constructs the values, customs and practices of Aboriginal communities.

Aboriginal ontology provides a context for evaluating whether Australian policy and legal drafting is effective in portraying the values and meanings of Aboriginal water use because the emphasis should focus on Aboriginal peoples defining their own identity.

> The Western ideological construction of Aboriginal cultural values strips the inherent nature of its endemic culture, which in turn minimises Aboriginal consultation and engagement in the use of water. In the *Water Management Act*, the word 'environment' is defined as all living things to include human beings. From a customary Aboriginal perspective, the environment and culture are enmeshed.[34]

The objects of the *Water Management Act 2000* (NSW) is an example of ineffective legal drafting, in terms of Aboriginal ontology, because the Act represents the values of Aboriginal peoples as generic concepts such as 'spiritual' or 'social' values. The Western concept of 'benefits' which flow to Aboriginal peoples in s 3(c) (iv) of the Act implies

> [b]enefits to the Aboriginal people in relation to their spiritual, social, customary and economic use of land and water.[35]

The legislative objectives in the *Water Management Act 2000* (NSW) also fail to achieve an Aboriginal ontological expression of water values as it omits to include how the 'benefits' will flow to Aboriginal peoples by the 'spiritual, social, customary and economic use of the land and water'.[36] Western legal concepts for interpreting Aboriginal ontological values and beliefs are inadequate for properly expressing Aboriginal water concepts.

Fragmenting Aboriginal water knowledge into generic Western legal concepts is inadequate to properly represent Aboriginal concepts of water. To apply terms such as 'cultural water', 'traditional use', 'communal purposes' and 'spiritual activity' in order to interpret Aboriginal water values is equally problematic because it constructs prescriptive definitions.

The words of a Senior Lawman (deceased), demonstrate that an English interpretation of Aboriginal ontology fails to represent the depth of Aboriginal meaning:

White European want to know …
asking 'What this story ?
this not easy story.
No-one else can tell it …
Because this story for Aboriginal story.
I speak English for you,
so you can listen …
so you can know …
you will understand.
If I put my words (language) in same place,
You won't understand.[37]

Australia has inherited legal traditions and a system of laws derived from English law and religious foundations — beliefs and values that are now deeply rooted in the practices and customs of governments, institutions and various groups of Australians such as farmers, pastoralists, irrigators and pioneer families. These worldviews are distinct from Aboriginal worldviews. The use of the word 'Western' identifies and acknowledges that Australian and British ontology holds worldviews that are divergent from Aboriginal belief systems.

New metaphors in property relationships

The range of competing interests in property rights and how these relationships relate to the principles of environmentalism are examined in Craig Arnold's, 'The Reconstruction of Property' (2002), which accommodates human relationships within the environment to define these legal interests in property as a 'web of interests'.[38] This concept, as discussed earlier, introduces a new way to describe the complex relationships of Aboriginal peoples and the impact of other interest groups post-contact upon Aboriginal communities.

Professor Arnold's metaphor is useful when applied to the relationship of Aboriginal people to their lands and waters, where water rights and interests are recognised within a web of relationships and interests in property such as kinship obligations to maintain water-holes and to monitor traditional boundaries and regulate access to land and water. From an Aboriginal perspective, a complex system exists because an Aboriginal claim to water in the property rights paradigm requires a Western legal system to formally recognise and not merely accommodate Aboriginal water values in Australian law and policy frameworks. Arnold (2002) explains in his research that:

a metaphor cannot answer all questions, but it can help us to know what they are and provide some mental scheme around organising the inquiry and analysis in accommodating human relationships in property rights.[39]

An argument put by Mark Blumer (2000) analyses how to incorporate incompatible views on water interests, suggesting for example that an accommodation between environmental needs and an irrigator's allocation of water rights requires a distinction of the types of rights at issue,[40]

> [n]ot by treating them as competitors of the same type for the same resource within the same system because the environment and the irrigation industry have fundamentally different needs.[41]

Aboriginal norms are the basis for defining and interpreting Aboriginal water rights and interests. If we use the web of interests concept to explore Aboriginal values and beliefs it is easier to understand Aboriginal relationships in water. Because of community diversity it is not feasible to use a generic web of interests concept to represent the intimate knowledge and law system of every community group. Aboriginal peoples' rights and interests can exist anywhere within the web and not in chronological or linear formation.

The web concept is also the blueprint for visualising how other non-Aboriginal interests interact with Aboriginal interests. Aboriginal ontology is the dominant feature of this web of interests because the creation of Australia, from an Aboriginal perspective, has its origins in ancestral story. The nexus with all things within the Aboriginal environment, Australia, is innately joined together as a 'web of relationships'.

Similarly, David Lametti's 'The Concept of Property: Relations through Objects of Social Wealth' (2003) proposes a new metaphor in property relationships centred upon the intangible and tangible 'objects of social wealth'.[42] Lametti suggests that the use of 'definitions can influence the substantive discussion on rights-based property paradigms'.[43] I argue that the Australian definitions of water and the construct of Australian property rights have misrepresented the definitions of Aboriginal water rights and the way property rights are understood and determined under Aboriginal laws.

Lametti argues that Western society's notion of 'private property is a social institution that engenders objects of social wealth and a variety of individual and collective purposes'.[44] He suggests that the Western focus on individual ownership in property rights characterises the private entitlement or property title in such a way as 'to exude the ultimate control and power over lesser entitlements'.[45] For example, in the powers of the Crown prerogative in England that frames Australia's colonial powers:

> In the time of the Stuarts the doctrine was maintained, not only by the King, but by lawyers and statesman who, like Bacon, favoured the increase of royal authority, that the Crown possessed under the name of the 'prerogative' a reserve, so to speak, of wide indefinite rights and powers, and that this prerogative or residue of sovereign power was superior to the ordinary law of the land.[46]

An example of the Crown holding 'absolute control and ownership in property' is argued by J W Harris, who conceptualises a 'hierarchy of rights, whereby a "full-blooded" ownership qualifies the owner above the rights and entitlements of others'.[47] Such concepts of ownership under common law rights were created through the feudal origins of English real property, where land interests developed into fee simple estates by a grant of seisin from a superior lord.[48] Ownership rights held under the common law doctrine of estates are not as straightforward, for example, in land held in trust in the interests of the beneficiaries, and protected under equitable rules and case law.[49]

Lametti (2003) examines other theories in private property and the ambiguities that exist, in particular where legal discourse articulates that property relationships connect to 'things or people'.[50] He points out that the definition of property to refer to 'things' and 'values in resources' or 'property rights' incorporates inherent ambiguities in legal discourse.[51]

Property concepts – a 'bundle of rights'?

To understand the impact of Western property concepts on Aboriginal water rights and interests, an analysis of the impact of private and public property rights on Aboriginal communities is vital. Water law in Australia is a highly regulated system of domestic laws and policies structured to allow or limit the exercise of water property rights. The Western concept of property characterizes property as 'a bundle of rights or a right or collection of rights, not to a thing',[52] which is directly opposed to Aboriginal ontological concepts of property.

Craig Arnold (2002) examines the Western concepts of private and public property regimes in relation to their effect on environmental values and the impact of the modern property concept in identifying property as a 'bundle of rights'.[53] Arnold argues that the contemporary metaphor of property as a 'bundle of rights' fails to recognise the 'importance of the human relationship and the environment'.[54] He rejects the contention that property is about 'things' and 'relationships to things'.[55] His concept of 'property as a web of interests' shows how Aboriginal rights and interests to water could be articulated within various cultural and contemporary Aboriginal concepts of water values and Aboriginal water use. As I have discussed, the idea of developing a metaphor for Aboriginal property rights would, in my view, be a useful tool to aid conceptualisation of the Aboriginal relationship to water.

Arnold's article focussed my attention on how the settlers and convicts transported to Australia interpreted and applied Western concepts of property and their environmental values in an Aboriginal landscape. This played out in their interaction with Aboriginal peoples and in the conflict which often occurred on issues such as clearing Aboriginal land for development, water resource use, removal of Aboriginal sites and ceremonial areas and moving Aboriginal people off their traditional camp sites. It also explains the difficulty Aboriginal communities had in understanding the nature of Anglo-Australian property rights.

Arnold argues that 'environmental law scholars narrowly focus research on environmental protection and not on the interconnection of the uniqueness of the objects of property and 'things', which engages distinct values of human beings with the natural environment' within the paradigm of property concepts.[56] Aboriginal water values and Aboriginal environmental concepts are perceived and interpreted by foreign knowledge systems as 'cultural beliefs and practices', which in Australian property law are not representative of property rights. In Arnold's view a 'web of relationships' exists within 'all aspects of property'.[57]

According to Arnold, Thomas Grey in 'The Disintegration of Property' (1980) asserted the notion that 'property as a distinct and coherent concept was redundant'. Grey argued that property is a 'bundle of rights equally malleable, divisible, disaggregable and functional rights among people'.[58] Arnold explains Grey's position as 'inconsistent with the tenets of an environmental ethic' and that 'the value of the object within the property concept is more important'.[59]

The bundle of rights concept appears in judgements on determinations of native title, neatly compartmentalising cultural or legal rights as unconnected separate strands. Dr Lisa Strelein asserts that the debate on characterising 'rights and interests was distracting'[60] as applied in the judicial reasoning of the High Court's *Western Australia v Ward* [2002].[61] The Court held that 'native title was not a possessory title'[62] and 'raised issues on whether native title was an interest in land or characterised as a bundle of rights'.[63] Grey's position contrasts with the conceptualisation of Aboriginal culture and laws, because the bundle of rights concept, as outlined above, is not 'divisible or malleable' within an Aboriginal paradigm. Such values are exercised in accordance with Aboriginal laws and on the basis of these law relationships.

Glaskin (2003) argued that the legal recognition of Aboriginal land rights is steeped in contested property ideology of competing interests.[64] The notion of Australian property concepts is foreign to Aboriginal belief systems. Glaskin states:

> In Western societies, the concept of property is constrained by assumptions about economic value and governed by commodity logic that assumes the detachability of persons and things.[65]

Arnold (2002) argues that the bundle of rights theory fails to grasp the concepts of 'interconnection between things and human relationships in property'.[66] Glaskin (2003) also highlights the problems associated with attempting to 'detach persons and things' in conceptualising property. Problems arise in regulating Aboriginal water rights and interests when governments and other institutions detach or separate Aboriginal water values, laws and relationships from property concepts. In my view, the bundle of rights theory applied to Aboriginal water rights and interests fragments and weakens Aboriginal relationships and the meaning of water. Penner states that 'conceptualising property as a bundle of rights is not a useful concept and does not assist the judiciary in determining property rights'.[67]

The central aspect of private property is 'the right of an owner to the use, possession and enjoyment of the object to the exclusion of the rest of the world'.[68] The perspective of English jurist Sir William Blackstone in his theory of property law, asserts human beings hold an 'absolute dominion and control over all things'[69] based upon 'natural law and the will of God, and underpinned by rules and regulations to govern society'.[70] Blackstone declared that human beings have free will but the law of nature and the law of revelation require the observance of human laws.[71] Like the Western legal perspective of Blackstone's time, other 'legal systems emerge from cultural contexts, social relations, and concepts of law', that 'predetermines legal obligations and legal rights'.[72] Blackstone's *Commentaries* state that the 'way to acquire title to property that belongs to no one is by occupancy and the actual possession of such property'.[73] Western property interests also include equitable proprietary interests, statutory proprietary interests or movable chattels.[74]

Arnold's proposal of describing a new metaphor[75] would provide a significant contribution to reforming Aboriginal water rights and interests in Australia. Western academic dialogue simply applies its own conceptualisation of what property right norms are, and the determination of those norms 'is understood through Western values, legal theory and the characteristics of property rights'.[76]

The usefulness of conceptualising property and relationships in an inter-connected paradigm as Arnold (2002) proposes enriches the property concept. Understanding the rights to a 'thing', for instance in the case of land rights, leads to recognition of an Aboriginal relationship that interconnects with land and characterises cultural values to property.

Aboriginal property or private property

The meaning of property changes when values or relationships to property are conceived differently in political, social and legal paradigms, such as in the pronounced difference between Western and Aboriginal conceptions of property.[77] Such differences between these concepts of property rights and inter-ests are well recognised in the point of first contact of British settlement/invasion when the existence of Aboriginal laws and Aboriginal occupation were recognised but disregarded.

The social aspect of private property is introduced by Lametti with the words of Aristotle, who recognised that social benefits in ownership should flow to others, as captured in the phrase, 'private in ownership, common in use'.[78] Lametti argues that the 'degree of control and exclusivity continues to be the hallmark of private property, which includes usage rights and limitations in private rights'.[79] Aboriginal customary property concepts recognise property relationships that also identify a right to exclude, a right to control, and usage rights to property that are limited for customary purposes and regulated by laws.

The communal title of Aboriginal ownership is at odds with the Western concept of private ownership.[80] For example, the Aboriginal 'permission' system is underpinned by Aboriginal laws that establish a legal right for the Traditional Owners to exclude others, and this customary law informed the Aboriginal permit system in the *Northern Territory Land Rights Act 1976* (NT). A Senior Elder of an Aboriginal community expressed the importance of adherence to the permit in observance of Aboriginal laws:

> In early days the white man just put trouble all over blackfellas … he was under
> a pastoral property … they didn't want to talk. [If] they just wanted to put

something up there, they just went on ahead and put it up. But now we comin' in together. We should share something, then we happy to do that. But it gotta be court proper way proper processes which recognise our right of consent, whether we can give him go ahead to put the bore in there, or might be we say no, might be find another place away from that sacred site. Well, we have to negotiate the proper way, good relationship for share the water, together. Because [it's] their water and our water too, same way. Well, government say, 'no, everything under the ground belong to us', but we got our dreaming too, you know, all the way. That's what our ceremony and law is, underneath the ground.[81]

Lametti (2003) draws a nexus between property rights, social wealth and values held in private property. In making his point Lametti identifies that the notion of 'scarcity linked to social values produces economic worth', and in the 'value of the resource measured by its fulfilment to human needs'; value is the critical concept in the object's assessment.[82] The contextual analysis of Aboriginal concepts of property and the relationships which connect communities or individuals to land, water or other resources are normative law systems.

The view of Governor Gawler in the settlement of South Australia indicates a fuller appreciation of what the land represents to Aboriginal peoples and to the extent to which Australian law should recognise Aboriginal rights and interests:

Governor Gawler, in particular, tried, in accordance with his instructions, to adopt the principle that the aboriginal inhabitants of this province have an absolute right of selection … of reasonable portions of the choicest land, for their special use and benefit, out of the very extensive districts over which, from time immemorial, these Aborigines have exercised distinct, defined, and absolute rights of proprietary and hereditary possession.[83]

Lametti says the use of 'definitions can influence the substantive discussion on rights-based property paradigms', such as in the concept of private property ownership which is the most powerful of these.[84]

Attention to economics in property rights and property law is justified, Lametti (2003) states, because they are 'objects of social wealth in society'[85] and the focus of economic value of natural resources and land. Since the introduction of national water reforms, 'objects of social wealth' are accumulating through the economic value in water as a property right and asset. Lueck and Miceli argue that to 'measure and define water according to consumptive use is very costly', because water is a 'complex asset' where instead 'water rights should be defined above water diversion, consumption and water quality'; defining water rights as property rights does not allow for economic fundamentals when restrictions are required.[86]

The themes examined by Lueck and Miceli are relevant for Aboriginal peoples. One of the significant water issues is the inalienability of property rights such as native title, which is relevant to Aboriginal wealth creation. The principle of inalienability suspends or restricts the transfer of an asset or water resource, or prohibits a particular water use, and ensures the water resource is not transferred or traded out of the location where the water exists.[87]

Aboriginal perspectives on water are framed within a different ontology than that of Western water values. Craig Arnold argues that the Western concepts of private and public property regimes in identifying property as a bundle of rights, requires reframing a 'new metaphor'.[88] I support Arnold's metaphor of a web of interests because it is relevant in terms of reframing property concepts from an Aboriginal perspective, and it can reconstruct the inadequate Western interpretation of Aboriginal water rights in statutory regimes.

Arnold's (2002) metaphor could reframe Aboriginal water rights under the National Water Initiative and a framework for defining those rights and interests, which is discussed in the following chapter. Arnold's concept can help address the lack of inclusion of Aboriginal property rights and conceptualising water through Aboriginal ontology.[89]

Bradley Bryan suggests that 'Aboriginal concepts of property cannot be articulated into singular concepts of Aboriginal ontology'.[90] His view is that it is important to question conceptions of property law to assess whether property regimes are compatible with cultural interpretations of their relationship with property.[91]

The examination of Western property theories helps to understand how Aboriginal water rights and interests are framed within the Western property paradigm.[92] The Australian Government policy of separating the water from the land within an economic framework, such as in the National Water Initiative and regulating water resources as a commodity, has had significant and detrimental consequences for Aboriginal water use.

Chapter 7

'A FLUID ELEMENT' —
WATER IN AUSTRALIAN POLICY

In an ideal world, 'good governance principles in water management such as transparency, accountability, decentralisation and participation should be widely incorporated in government policies to advocate for the better management of natural resources'.[1] From an Aboriginal perspective, however, Australian governments have largely ignored the cultural and economic values inherent in Aboriginal knowledge systems, and Aboriginal ontological water concepts in policy development. Their incorporation into water policy requires the participation of Aboriginal communities in water management in order to guide good governance principles for Indigenous outcomes.

In Australian water policy the Western characterisation and use of water is compartmentalised into water policy categories such as 'environmental and cultural flows' and 'consumptive and non-consumptive use of water'. In the previous chapters I have argued that water values in Aboriginal customary laws have been simplified into wholly deficient cultural definitions of water values.

> The testimony of Aboriginal people is a difficult basis on which to develop policy, particularly in land management … Culturally specific issues of 'health', 'well-being', 'place' and 'identity' are culturally complex …[2]

The legal implications for water as a new type of property right has been problematic for Aboriginal peoples because it characterises water as having economic value, as distinct from social and cultural values. Because water is separated from the land there is an increasing tendency by policy makers to prioritise economic values in the context of water rights and interests above other value systems.

Accommodating or integrating Aboriginal water rights and interests into mainstream water management in state and federal legislation has been adopted and has failed because it undervalued Aboriginal values as a minor interest in

Australia's water framework. Policy development in relation to Aboriginal rights and interests slowly emerged into the national dialogue on water management through the advocacy of Indigenous peak bodies.

This chapter examines the participation and representation of Aboriginal peoples in the allocation of water rights and interests by governments administering Australian water policy. It also analyses whether the legislative regime provides adequately for the inclusion of Aboriginal water rights and interests and allows for the unique Aboriginal values attached to water. Further, it examines how Australian governments have responded to Aboriginal water rights and interests as regards sharing water allocations and whether policy development takes full account of the customary and cultural requirements of Aboriginal communities.

Contested values in water policy

David Pannell suggests that 'there is often a mismatch between the complexity of policy problems and the simplicity of responses'.[3] Pannell argues that the critical founding principles in politics and bureaucracies in Australian policy are underpinned by 'simplistic and bland agreements' which 'drive the lowest common denominator in policy proposals'.[4] The impact of unresponsive and ill-conceived policy planning, in light of Pannell's position, is that Australia's policy framework has the potential to negatively affect Aboriginal policy development and the capacity to provide effective responses to the customary water values of Aboriginal peoples.

Australian water policy fails to incorporate the breadth of Aboriginal water knowledge and the context of this knowledge, such as seasonal foods sourced from the knowledge of Aboriginal weather cycles, water connectivity across the landscape, customary fishing and eel trapping or fire farming practices. For example, Aboriginal communities' use of spring water in preparing numerous Aboriginal medicines requires that no other type of water may be used.[5] The central conflict in water policy for Aboriginal water use results from the fact that Aboriginal rights or interests are categorised into economic or non-economic interests.

Water policy reform in Australia has generally marginalised the rights and interests of Aboriginal peoples in the policy development of the states and territories. Jackson and Morrison (2007) comment that:

> Indigenous interests were not formally considered in water policy documents prepared during the 1990s ... and were not addressed in water resource law until 2000.[6]

The 1994 COAG report 'informed water users that the price of water would regulate future water use thus water efficiency would follow':

> [t]he concept of tradeable water rights or entitlements, given that it would operate within a market framework, is generally considered the maximum benefit from the use of the resource.[7]

The Howard Federal Government in 2007 funded other water rights across Australia and gave limited support for Aboriginal water interests.

> As part of the Howard Government's hastily conceived $10 billion national water plan ... nearly $6 billion of the plan was dedicated to assisting irrigators to improve the efficiency of existing irrigation infrastructure.[8]

Marcia Langton argues that the national policy change introduced by the Australian Government indicates that 'water is treated as a fluid element', and under these changes 'Indigenous water rights are poorly defined'.[9] Syme and Hatfield-Dodds (2007) argue that COAG 'ignored the social implications in water use during water reform development to favour the triple bottom line':[10]

> The social bottom line was given little emphasis in the early period of reform, the main emphasis being on the delivering within 'social constraints'. These constraints were not explicitly defined, although there was to be emphasis on consultation and public education ... culture as an input to water resource policy has been given little or no substantive attention.[11]

Syme and Hatfield-Dodds (2007) argue that 'the issue of resolving contested value systems is complex':[12]

> It is evident that growth in population, irrigation water demands, the expanding metropolitan footprint and climate change have placed strains on institutional structures ... Contested values present both well-known challenges and less recognised opportunities. Recognition of multiple currencies of value allows a more nuanced approach ... rather than framing the entire process in terms of trade-offs between opposing values ...[13]

The tension between Aboriginal communities and water stakeholders is growing because of strong lobbying by industry, farmers, pastoral entities and irrigators who seek to maintain or increase their water allocations. The emphasis on economic values in water has impacted significantly upon Aboriginal water rights and interests for customary and Aboriginal economic development. Aboriginal peoples' water rights are first rights – Aboriginal people are not just another stakeholder group.

Water management in Australia has moved to address serious concerns in water use and issues of sustainability because of the significant increases in water consumption for consumptive and non-consumptive use. The expansion of irrigated agriculture and advocacy from sectoral interest groups pressuring the Australian Government to expand the northern region of Australia for irrigated broad acre farming directly affects Aboriginal communities because northern Australia has significant areas of Aboriginal-owned land.

Jackson, Storrs and Morrison (2005) argue that industry and government planning have significantly altered the Aboriginal landscape and the water systems, undervaluing the millennia of Aboriginal laws and kinship.[14] The inclusion of Aboriginal water interests in Australian water policy is inconsistent among the states and territories because the language used in the Commonwealth Bilateral Agreements only requires governments to 'account for' Aboriginal water requirements.[15]

From the commencement of national water reform policy in the 1990s, Aboriginal water rights and interests were not included in the policy framework. Nearly a decade later, Aboriginal water rights and interests emerged as a footnote to the national water plan. The lack of formal and meaningful consultation by governments with Aboriginal communities has resulted in a significant policy gap for Aboriginal water values and community water needs.

In relation to allocating future water resources, it is unlikely that Aboriginal ownership or permanent water rights for Aboriginal communities will be included in the same way as legal certainty has been provided to other stakeholders. On this basis, it is clear that Aboriginal organisations and communities will be unable to participate in and enjoy the benefits of these water reforms because of non-tradeable Aboriginal water licences and the over-allocation of water resources to other interests. Gleeson CJ, in his argument that 'the next legal battleground for Australia will be water', said:[16]

> If someone asked me to predict – and said it was income tax 30 years ago, and it is immigration cases now – I would say in 30 years from now it will be water …
> When there is an important topic of public policy and the likelihood of government regulation, then lawyers are likely to get involved, too.[17]

The prediction of Gleeson CJ may well indicate the potential for litigation in the future where the development of public policy and legislation has not adequately addressed water issues.

The National Water Initiative

The National Water Initiative (NWI) which was initiated by COAG as the primary driver of national water policy requires the co-operation of the states and territories under a national agreement. The NWI led to the establishment of the National Water Commission (dismantled by the Abbott Federal Government).

The NWI, established in 1994 with Australian Intergovernmental Agreements between the Commonwealth and the States and Territories, was the policy driver for national water reforms. The NWI identifies methods for future water management, for example, in regulating water through price structure, statutory protection for environmental water allocations and national water sharing plans.[18]

Under the NWI, a framework and set of characteristics was implemented to provide a nationally compatible water entitlement system.[19] Water access entitlements, under this framework, were intended to create effective water management and certainty for business and industry, as well as commercial opportunities for investment in water trading.[20] In Clauses 28 to 31 of the NWI Agreement, the consumptive use of water enables water access entitlements as separate from land, consistent with water sharing plans.[21]

In a review of the national water reform policy, Tan (2001) argues that private rights such as 'domestic and stock use, water licences and the right to use surface flows' remain a high priority for governments.[22] Tan notes that the 'primary concern for governments in water policy was to protect the interests of irrigators'.[23]

> Water law reform was to define and simplify private rights to water, reduce potential for dispute between neighbours over drainage and water, and to make sure that disputes are resolved in ways to protect the wider interests of the community.[24]

The NWI reforms have provided governments with discretionary powers to accommodate Indigenous rights and interests, and any implementation of the reforms will rest with each jurisdiction.[25] The Indigenous Actions (Clauses) in the NWI Agreement recognise Indigenous water interests under the following clauses.

Clause 52(i) and (ii) state that 'the planning process ensures the inclusion of Indigenous representation in water planning wherever possible and will incorporate social, spiritual and customary objectives and strategies wherever they can be developed'.[26]

Clause 53 'will take into account in the water planning processes of the possible existence of native title rights to water in the catchment or aquifer area, following the recognition of native title rights, to allocate water to the native title holders'.[27]

Clause 54 refers to 'water allocated to native title holders for traditional cultural purposes and that it will be accounted for'.[28] The Indigenous objectives under these clauses are clearly inadequate because they do not seek a mandatory commitment from governments to include Indigenous water rights and interests, except for those rights and interests that are native title.

In Clause 53 the use of the words 'where possible' makes government action discretionary. There is no enforceable power to include Indigenous water use, or water resources plans. There is a lack of certainty about Indigenous water rights and interests implied in the phrase 'wherever they can be developed' and because words like 'cultural' and 'spiritual' fail to take into account the complex layers of customary laws.[29]

The Clauses in the NWI Agreement do not provide any meaningful recognition of the water requirements of Aboriginal communities or of Aboriginal values. In this way, 'customary objectives' receive a generic treatment and reflect little more than a baseline of Aboriginal values. As an analogy, the complex layering of Aboriginal laws are as central to Aboriginal water rights as the rule of law is central to underpinning the stability of the Australian legal system. For example, 'the upholding of the rule of law under English law was affirmed in representing the dominant values of its society, embodying the concept of English law, and acting as the ideological cornerstone of English society'.[30]

Similarly, Aboriginal laws underpin the social, cultural and familial order of relationships and the obligations expected by the individual and the collective group and because of this Aboriginal laws are held as the cornerstone of Aboriginal society. As the previous chapters have shown, Aboriginal values and concepts, and the use of water resources among Aboriginal communities, requires a nuanced approach to incorporating Aboriginal water requirements into a statutory framework.

The Aboriginal and Torres Strait Islander Commission raised dissatisfaction with the lack of engagement with Aboriginal rights and interests in water reform:

> The impending implementation of ... water management plans, as they stand, will have significant impact on Aboriginal rights and interests in the waters of those

catchments. Aboriginal communities throughout New South Wales are requesting more time to allow for effective discussion and feedback on the Catchment Blueprint Documents. I am advised by my constituents that this situation in New South Wales is a consequence of the failure of the Water Reform Agenda nationally, to take Indigenous interests into consideration from an early stage.[31]

National water reforms included water resource plans as a requirement of the Commonwealth Basin Plan 2012 and sustainable diversion limits on the quantities of surface and groundwater that can be taken for consumptive use. The Water Sharing Plans in New South Wales were not afforded any level of Aboriginal consultation because community consultation was considered 'time-consuming' in the view of the New South Wales Cabinet.[32] Instead, the New South Wales Government expedited the draft water legislation through the parliament.[33]

During the New South Wales Water Sharing Planning workshops by the Office of Water, Aboriginal participants agreed that the government was not prepared to listen to Aboriginal community views on the planning process for Aboriginal water allocation.[34] The community participants argued that the government prioritised legislative protection for other groups above that of Aboriginal peoples, in prioritising agricultural, industrial and town use.[35] The economic rights to water were not clarified at the Planning workshop. Windle and Rolfe (2002) contend that:

> The issue of whether Indigenous rights to inland waters includes commercial rights is still undetermined, but there are clear precedents overseas that it should include such rights.[36]

Jackson (2008) argues that 'in spite of national water reforms in Australia the process had not provided Aboriginal peoples with consultation or information on water sharing plans'.[37] According to Jackson, 'not one Aboriginal person knew about the water reforms in rural and remote communities'.[38]

Murray Radcliffe, a member of the National Water Commission, noted that 'the Indigenous actions in the National Water Initiative Agreement cannot be changed', however, 'they can be added to later'.[39] The National Water Commission did not indicate when any future amendment would occur.

Tan (2002) suggests that governments may incur future legal action from stakeholders because of inadequate policy and legislation:

> [w]ater agencies and their political masters were extremely vulnerable to litigation.
> They were prepared to make decisions that would affect availability of resources

in the long term, not to mention adverse environmental impacts, for short term political gain.[40]

Jackson and Morrison (2007) said that various issues need to be addressed in establishing Indigenous water interests under the NWI Agreement because there is a significant knowledge gap among governments on how to meet Indigenous water rights and interests. Issues identified are

[l]imited knowledge of the means of addressing Indigenous water requirements; the degree of technical difficulty; the lack of capacity in the Indigenous community; the impediments posed by uncertainty; and contestation and lags in native title claims processes.[41]

In November 2008, shortly after Garma, the National Water Commission convened an 'Australian Indigenous Water Focus Group' to progress the guiding principles for Indigenous water planning and Indigenous engagement in future policy development,[42] and I attended. Although a range of Indigenous water issues were discussed with the National Water Commission's representative, the Government's policy position did not prioritise Indigenous ownership in water, Indigenous peoples' management of their water resources or any direct input into national strategic water planning. The Australian Government did not meet the expectations articulated in our discussions.

The most significant failing of the NWI is that Indigenous Actions are discretionary for all jurisdictions.[43] The discretionary nature of these actions narrows the outcomes for Indigenous water policy and creates uncertainty regarding Aboriginal water rights and interests in Australia.

The NWI Agreement does not represent the profound nature of Aboriginal laws and the beliefs or values expressed because Aboriginal laws are founded on the conviction that water cannot be separated from land:

Land tenure is not a neutral ingredient: it is pervasive and the question is whether it encourages a positive or a negative expression of the human relationship with place.[44]

The NWI does not deal with Aboriginal ownership in water, apart from taking into account water for native title use. The national water policy and legislation remains a barrier for Aboriginal peoples if they seek to pursue Aboriginal economic or cultural rights in water use. Water has become a new property interest and the commercial benefits in water trading and water licences appear to exclude certainty for Aboriginal communities. Instead, profitable water assets such as water trading have developed additional property rights for industry, farmers, pastoralists and water companies.

The Indigenous Clauses under the NWI should be subject to the scrutiny of human rights standards to examine whether the complex needs of Aboriginal communities are met. Because water rights and interests of Aboriginal communities are not consistently implemented across the states and territories, a benchmark of human rights standards is required. The access to and use of water by Indigenous peoples is recognised as an international human right, as Chapter 11 examines.

Biennial Assessments of water resources

In 2008, at the Australian Indigenous Water Focus Group meeting in Adelaide, the progress on native title interests was presented by Murray Radcliffe, Manager of Programs for the National Water Commission, who stated:

> [t]he Biennial assessment under the National Water Initiative in relation to Indigenous Water Planning does not talk about cultural flows and economic interests ...
> the 2007 review of Indigenous engagement was 'patchy at best'.[45]

The National Water Commission under its legislation was required to advise COAG of the progress made by the states, territories and basin regions to meet the objectives and outcomes of the NWI in undertaking a biennial assessment.[46]

The National Water Commission's first assessment, the *Biennial Assessment 2009*, and the second, the *Biennial Assessment 2011*, reported on the NWI outcomes progressed by the States and Territories and to demonstrate how they had met the national water management objectives.[47] What is clear from both the 2009 and the 2011 Biennial Assessments is that the States and Territories have, in the majority of cases, failed to implement many of the Indigenous objectives under the NWI. According to the 'Biennial Assessment 2011' the summary of findings identified that 'most jurisdictions have failed to incorporate effective strategies for Indigenous social, spiritual and customary objectives in water plans'.[48]

The 'Biennial Assessment 2009' noted in the findings that 'it was rare for Indigenous water requirements to be explicitly addressed in the water plans of any jurisdiction'.[49] The National Water Commission's 'Biennial Assessment' findings on Indigenous water requirements are useful in tracking the progress of the jurisdictions across Australia under the benchmark of the NWI and the Intergovernmental Agreement between the Commonwealth and state governments.

The States and Territories are not penalised for failing to comply with meeting the water needs of Indigenous communities as set out in the Indigenous participation Clauses 25(ix) and 52 to 54 of the NWI.[50] There is no satisfactory method in place for compliance checking on the jurisdictions' commitment to implementing the National Water Initiatives; 'under the Intergovernmental Agreement at Clause 27 the jurisdictions agreed to modify their existing legislation and administrative regimes'.[51] The States and Territories were 'reluctant' to expressly identify over-allocated and overused water systems for progressing sustainable water extractions.[52]

It was noted in the *Biennial Assessment 2009* that 'a deeper assessment of Indigenous water values and needs in the water plan has not been undertaken'.[53] The *Biennial Assessment 2011* reports that the progress of initiatives to implement Indigenous water requirements in the jurisdictions is tardy and that 'where the Indigenous water values have been identified in the water plans it has not produced any additional water allocation'.[54] The outcomes for Indigenous water rights and interests have not improved under the NWI because, as the Biennial Assessments in 2009 and 2011 indicate, 'Aboriginal people face significant impediments in accessing water for economic, environmental and cultural needs'.[55]

The 'Biennial Assessment (2011)' reviewed the progress of national water reform strategies and raised the question of whether the benchmarks for the States and Territories had improved.[56] The Biennial Assessment identified the poor performance of the jurisdictions in meeting water-sharing planning and other water requirements for Indigenous peoples.[57] It also reported that Indigenous stakeholders' progress was deficient across all water management areas.[58] The National Water Commission's findings from the 2011 assessment indicate the performance by the States and Territories for incorporating Indigenous water interests under the Commission's benchmark for 'Water Access Entitlements and Planning Framework' under Clauses 25(ix) and 52 to 54 of the NWI,[59] and are summarised below.

New South Wales consulted with Indigenous communities across various networks to identify Indigenous water values in the water planning process and undertook consultation with Indigenous groups on water-dependent cultural assets.[60] The *Water Management Act 2000* (NSW) recognised native title rights as basic landholder rights and the New South Wales Government undertook discussions on defining water volume for determinations in native title.[61] In addition, Water Sharing Plans outside the Murray-Darling Basin would allow for an Aboriginal cultural water licence at no cost, where water was not fully allocated.[62]

The Australian Capital Territory under its statutory requirement to report responded that native title is extinguished in the Territory.[63] No outcomes were recorded for water planning to address Indigenous outcomes under the NWI.[64]

The Biennial findings for Queensland and the *Water Act 2000* (Qld) identified some public consultation and the formation of a community reference panel to identify Indigenous water issues in the water planning process.[65] The Queensland Government considered that Indigenous cultural values were already inherent in the regional water plans.[66]

South Australia had addressed Indigenous water issues in water planning through consultation and responded that the taking of, or use of, water for cultural purposes must not bring to a halt or interfere with the state's water flows.[67]

Victoria, under the *Water Act 1989* (Vic), has statutory requirements to address Indigenous water issues. However, no cultural flows were allocated under the Victorian Sustainable Water Strategies.[68] The government included Indigenous groups in the public consultation.[69]

The Barmah and Nyah-Vinifera National Parks in the Murray-Darling Basin, now co-managed by the 'Yorta Yorta and Wadi Wadi'[70] with the Victorian Government under the *Traditional Owner Settlement Act 2010* (Vic), made progress relating to Indigenous water management issues.[71] The Victorian Government amended s 8 of the *Water Act 1989* (Vic) to include native title rights to water and water for ceremonial and spiritual purposes.[72]

Finally, the 2011 Biennial Assessment reported that the interests of Indigenous peoples under Clauses 25(ix) and 52 to 54 of the NWI Agreement should 'more explicitly account for Indigenous water values and requirements in water planning and build the capacity of Indigenous peoples to increase Indigenous participation in water planning and management'.[73] Referring back to actions proposed by the 2009 Biennial Assessment of the NWI, it was acknowledged that 'Indigenous peoples were rarely included in water plans and rarely included in the objectives to meet Indigenous social, spiritual and customary water needs'.[74] The findings of the 2011 Biennial Assessment indicate that there has been inconsistent progress across all jurisdictions to meet the objectives of the Indigenous actions.

The Biennial Assessment reports by the National Water Commission are essential for identifying the level of commitment and progress in meeting Indigenous water requirements within the jurisdictions, even though the outcomes to date remain highly unsatisfactory. As the National Water Commission has been disbanded, its accumulated resources were transferred to the Australian

Government's Productivity Commission, with no reported outputs from the Commission.

First Peoples' Water Engagement Council

Prior to the formation of the First Peoples Council and the Water Summit, my involvement as a delegate to the National Water Commission's inaugural Indigenous Water Focus Group was to formulate the framework for Indigenous water rights. This dialogue provided the foundation for future discussions and convening the Indigenous Water Summit in 2012.

The First Peoples' Water Engagement Council (FPWEC) was established in 2011 by the National Water Commission to provide national policy advice on Indigenous water issues. The FPWEC acknowledged that 'Aboriginal peoples face significant impediments to access water for economic, environmental and cultural purposes and the impediments vary across jurisdictions and the regions'.[75] The FPWEC recommended, among other things, to establish an Aboriginal water fund or trust which would coordinate and facilitate the acquisition and management of Aboriginal economic water allocations.[76] The National Water Commission responded to the recommendation by acknowledging that a trust or water fund would make a legitimate contribution to the Australian Government's Indigenous policy, *'Closing the Gap'*.[77] However, the Council had limited potential to improve Indigenous water requirements.

> The national water policy position for the allocation of water to Aboriginal communities proposed by the Federal Government is represented by a handful of public servants and advocates that have imposed a national water rights agenda to freshwater Aboriginal interests.[78]

The FPWEC is not independent and not representative of the Indigenous community as a whole, as representatives are not elected by the community. In spite of the formation of the Council as a policy support group on Indigenous engagement on water issues, the jurisdictions were free to reject any of the Council's recommendations. The FPWEC was disbanded at the same time as the National Water Commission.

Aboriginal resource management

An analysis of the water resource allocation and entitlements is critical to understanding the impact on Aboriginal peoples of the competing interests for water in Australia and how Aboriginal peoples' relationship with water resources is undermined by water demands from other interest groups.

National legislation is often an expression of post-colonial positivist equality discourses. Equality refers to the right (and duty) to become equal to, among others, the image of the non-indigenous citizen or water user, to equalise the norms, rights and principles of 'modern' water management, to adopt occidental water use technology and to adapt exogenous forms of organisation.[79]

Jackson and Morrison (2007) noted the current gap in Aboriginal water allocation is the absence of a methodology:

We have no current overview of the various methods and means of identifying and incorporating Indigenous objectives within Australian water planning …[80]

Australian water management has become more complex because the competition over water use between irrigators, farmers, and the mining industry and water corporations is centred upon water trading. Aboriginal people are not considered a major stakeholder, let alone a *first rights* water holder, and this is unacceptable. There is no legal certainty with the allocation of Aboriginal water rights except where native title is determined. The cultural water rights of Aboriginal peoples are treated less favourably than the rights of other water users.

Journal articles by Poh-Ling Tan examine water management in New South Wales, Queensland and Victoria and consider the historical as well as the policy reform process among these states. In Tan's paper, 'An Historical Introduction to Water Reform in New South Wales: 1975 to 1994' (2002), the historical patterns of water use in the state are discussed, as well as the consumptive use of water for the development of the colony, the increased focus on irrigation and water extraction from major river systems, the progress of dam construction, and the conversion of water rights to property rights.[81] However, this article does not include an analysis of Indigenous water interests.

Tan (2002) argues that the patterns of 20th century water use and water management were primarily aimed at supporting irrigation schemes, and stock and domestic and riparian access rights, and not at conserving water and maintaining river and ecosystem health.[82]

As Tan points out, 'water licences were over-allocated because water agencies approved the over consumption of available water resources'.[83] The introduction of volumetric allocations, where limits were applied on licence-holders and catchment water extraction, did not impede the over-use of water, as diverted surplus river flows from high rainfall were stored on farms.[84] The definition of water flows in the landscape, under the *Water Act 1912* (NSW), within the common law meaning of a river and a creek, was determined by Lee J in *Latta v Klinberg*.[85] A river was defined under the meaning of a watercourse, where a river features 'continuity, permanence and unity'.[86] These Australian water concepts were in contrast to the Aboriginal values held in water:

> Under the National Water Initiative reforms, 'a common law right to take naturally occurring water, including water courses, wetlands, springs, groundwater and unconfined surface water, regulated under a statutory right' is abolished.[87]

The water reforms in New South Wales, as in the other states and territories of Australia, were introduced into water management systems that had not recognised or included Aboriginal water rights and interests. Other stakeholders maximised their water holdings and topped up already over-allocated water, exploiting the practice of 'licence stacking' – a method of requesting licences in bogus names – which was prevalent prior to national water reform.[88] Tan (2002) notes that the ad hoc approach to water management in New South Wales resulted in significant problems in auditing water use and addressing systemic issues such as 'integrated catchment management, floodplain management, water quality and pollution control'.[89] The National Land and Water Resource Audit stated:

> [t]he change in the condition of Australia's river basins is most strongly linked to intensity of land use; increased nutrient and sediment loads; and loss of riparian vegetation … only 3 per cent of rivers in NSW were classed as largely unmodified, with 18 per cent extensively modified.[90]

Tan's (2002) paper does not discuss the effect of these problematic issues on Aboriginal water resource management. What is important to glean from this discussion is to question how Aboriginal communities can claw back their rights to water in a historically over-allocated water system. After a century or more, the inability of government and water agencies to recognise the legitimate water rights of Aboriginal peoples has created significant hurdles to restoring water rights and interests to Aboriginal communities.

Tan (2000) also addresses the water resource conflict among stakeholders in the Lower Balonne region of Queensland and the historic and contemporary water issues that exist there, in particular the use of floodplain flows and water storage impact on downstream water users.[91] Tan argues that the history of water management in the Lower Balonne is symbolic of 'State water management under its legislative practices which were to disregard overuse and to allow unfettered access'.[92]

The Queensland Government for more than a hundred years has failed to recognise the importance of floodplain flows and environmental issues and in the late 1990s the government continued to allow farmers and other irrigation water users to flout the inadequate water legislation.[93]

The ineffective monitoring and management of the state's water resources inevitably led to environmental problems, which were experienced by all water users. These poor management practices impacted on Aboriginal peoples because they directly affected water quality, increased water scarcity and damaged the water landscape. The lack of Indigenous participation in the development and implementation of national water reforms and the lack of national discussion on appropriate levels of ownership and allocation of water to Aboriginal communities is a further indication that their water rights are a low priority. The Virginia Simpson Report (2007) highlighted that in Queensland Aboriginal participation in water planning processes remains 'unremarkable'.[94]

The issue of compensating irrigators and farmers for various water reforms under state water management is ironic given the lack of discussion of compensation for Aboriginal communities and the significant changes upon the Aboriginal environment. Sixty-five per cent of rivers existing in cleared areas have been reported to be in poor condition.[95]

> Current policy recognises that water should be allocated for the environment and where river systems have been over allocated ... some sort of compromise between competing interests must be reached.[96]

Tan (1999) argues that the basis for providing compensation to irrigators because of the reduced water entitlements under the national water reforms is small.[97] In contrast, a case for compensation was raised where a water licence was held in perpetuity and a perpetual water right was granted under the *Irrigation Act 1922* but was then amended under the *Water Resources Act 1989* (Qld).[98] Section 20B of the *Water Act 2000* (Qld) is the single specifically mentioned provision for Aboriginal and Torres Strait Islander peoples relating to 'the right to take or interfere with water for traditional activities or cultural purposes'.

The regulation of water resources in Victoria incorporated 'perpetual water rights' for irrigators and in the drawing of water from channels.[99] The expectation held by irrigators when bulk entitlements[100] were introduced was that they would confer perpetual tenure on their consumptive water right.[101]

> The purpose of water law reform was to clearly define and simplify private rights to use water, reduce potential for dispute between neighbours over drainage and

water, and to make sure that disputes are resolved in ways which protect the wider interests of the community.[102]

The Victorian Government White Paper, 'Securing Our Future Together' (2004), does not include any specific inclusion of Aboriginal water rights and interests in the government's 'principles for sustainable water allocation'.[103] The state's water allocation system consisted of tier one for rights held by the Crown; tier two for environmental water, caps and non-consumptive rights; and tier three for individual water rights.[104] A review of Victoria's White Paper does not indicate how Aboriginal water rights and interests were to be allocated, if at all. During the first part of 2016 the Victorian Government began a 'state wide forum with Victoria's Aboriginal community to discuss how to advance self-determination, a treaty, and an Aboriginal representative body'[105] – the issue of Aboriginal water rights rests in treaty discussions with the government.[106]

The primary concern of water bureaucrats in framing the objectives to the *Water Act 1989* (Vic)[107] was to protect the irrigators, which also appears to be a common theme in the history of water use in Australia. Aboriginal peoples' use of water was permitted to co-exist in the areas of land where Aboriginal peoples were tolerated, but not to challenge the water use of farmers, pastoralists and squatters. The Australian environment *is* the Aboriginal environment, and Aboriginal peoples had only competed for water because the expansion of farming and pastoral interests was driven by economic benefits.

Australian society has a long history in devaluing Aboriginal culture and Aboriginal peoples, which has permeated the development of government policy as evidenced by various social policies and legislative instruments such to assimilate Indigenous peoples and segregate communities on reserves and missions. Henry Reynolds (1987) has suggested that racial stereotypes held about Aboriginal peoples have been prevalent throughout Australia's history:

> Racism flourished in Australia in the nineteenth and in the early twentieth century. It shaped an orthodox view of Aborigines which survived intact until the 1940s and 1950s.[108]

It would be fair and reasonable to recognise that racial stereotypes of Indigenous peoples have influenced the conceptualisation of Aboriginal values in Australian society and in how governments identify Aboriginal water values and use.

Jackson's article, 'Compartmentalising Culture: The Articulation and Consideration of Indigenous Values in Water Resource Management' (2006) argues that there is more interest in the 'human dimensions of natural resource management and conservation to identify the values and relationships which exist to inform the policy paradigm'.[109] Jackson suggests the reasons for the emergence of 'human perspectives of culture' was due to the development of ecological economies and a pluralistic consideration for embracing knowledge, environmental use and values of social groups.[110]

I would argue that this policy shift has developed as a result of the activism and the increased agency of Aboriginal peoples and their peak bodies. The incorporation of Aboriginal values in water within the framework of national water reforms did not occur until Aboriginal organisations urged government to recognise Aboriginal rights and interests. An Aboriginal 'ecological' economy has always existed through barter, trade and environmental stewardship.

Jackson (2006) highlights the deficiency of the Northern Territory water resource legislation in broad definitions used in the legislation to identify cultural values: for example, the *Water Act 2004* (NT) defines these values as 'aesthetic, recreational and cultural needs'.[111] The conceptual framework of water values from an Aboriginal community perspective is not addressed. The generic reference to 'cultural values' has a pluralistic meaning and can apply to the water values of Aboriginal and non-Aboriginal groups. It does not assist in defining Aboriginal cultural values.

Jackson (2006) identifies the inadequate usage of Western concepts used to filter information on natural values from the Daly River Aboriginal Community Reference Group; the four values to be equally weighted were economic, environmental, cultural and social values.[112] She argues that the 'Daly River Community Reference Group did not articulate their values by a theory of value or some other methodology which Western science might use to analyse and evaluate the cultural value paradigm'.[113]

The construction of water values arises not as a utility resource, but through the cultural relationship that Aboriginal peoples have with water and cultural knowledge and according to the cultural seniority of the individual:

> In Aboriginal society, knowledge is a function of age and status. It is imparted by
> degrees, as and when appropriate, by those steeped in knowledge. Knowledge may
> be held in common by people of varying ages and rank … Cultural inhibitions
> may well cause such a person to give the impression that he or she does not know
> the information sought.[114]

'Indigenous Perspectives in Water Management, Reforms and Implementation' by Jackson and Morrison (2007) deals with the statutory acknowledgement of

Indigenous Cultural Values under the National Water Initiative; the authors indicate that the inclusion of these water values maintains a 'symbolic part' of being Indigenous.[115] I argue that Aboriginal water values exhibit more than symbolism and expressions of Aboriginal peoples' relationship to the land, the waters and resources, since they are the life-blood connection for Aboriginal identity.

According to Jackson and Morrison future challenges exist in allocating water to native title holders within water sharing plans; however, the National Water Initiative framework does not outline how this can be achieved.[116] As native title represents property rights, how will native title holders be compensated for the loss or frustration of their water use?[117] Important gaps identified by Jackson and Morrison include 'understanding the barriers and incentives for Indigenous participation in the water sector',[118] and quantifying Aboriginal water resource values within the Indigenous economy.[119] The authors also note a lack of empirical data on Aboriginal peoples who wish to pursue commercial interests and innovation in developing customary water economies.[120] The authors point out that the National Water Initiative does not foster Aboriginal economic aspirations,[121] whereas the recognition of Aboriginal water rights as property rights would provide such opportunities.

The former Federal Minister for Indigenous Affairs, Mal Brough, stated prior to the 2007 Federal election campaign that 'there are no votes in Aboriginal policy'.[122] Similarly, during the Goulburn electoral launch of Pru Goward in 2007, Barry O'Farrell, then Liberal Deputy Leader for New South Wales, responding to a question on the Liberal Party's Aboriginal policy, remarked that 'there are no election votes on Aboriginal issues and a formal policy is not required'.[123]

The recognition of Aboriginal interests in water resources is a jurisdictional conundrum. Sharon Beder (2006) explains that Indigenous minorities endure a lesser right in the management of environmental principles and policies[124] and this disenfranchises Indigenous communities and leaves them with less than the minimum living standard on their traditional lands.[125]

The Aboriginal and Torres Strait Islander Commission

Although relations between the Australian Government and the Aboriginal and Torres Strait Islander Commission were often challenging and at times openly combative on Indigenous policy development and human rights, the Commission held the view it was acting on a legislative charter to represent Indigenous Australians.

ATSIC maintained a presence in the media to remind the Government of its failures. The tension between the Federal Government and ATSIC was obvious, and it was clear that Indigenous Australians would be left to deal with the outcomes of this uneasy relationship.[126]

The level of advocacy maintained by the Aboriginal and Torres Strait Islander Commission (ATSIC) both in Australia and internationally has left a legacy of important research resources and academic literature. The Parliamentary Select Committee report (2005), 'After ATSIC: Life in the mainstream?', acknowledged that the abolition and transfer of the functions of ATSIC led to a rudimentary 'mainstreaming of Aboriginal programs within the Commonwealth government'.[127] The abolition of the Commission also diminished the available research material on Aboriginal water rights and interests in Australia.[128]

Our rights in relation to waters struggle to find recognition within the structure of common law, and the categories of rights and interests in water that are capable of recognition within the common law tradition. There is no genuine acknowledgement of their true character within our law and their *sui generis*, or unique, nature ...[129]

A report by ATSIC and the Lingiari Foundation on 'Indigenous Rights to Waters for Offshore and Onshore Waters' (2002), provides insight into domestic and international contexts for Indigenous peoples, including the development of a national 'Rights to Waters' database for Indigenous communities.[130] The Report identified that 'there was no reference to Indigenous peoples and their rights and interests to water in the Council of Australian Governments policies'.[131]

There is a profound disjuncture between Indigenous and non-Indigenous perspectives on water, in all its forms. This disjuncture existed at the time of first contact and persists today. It results in a lack of recognition of Indigenous rights and interests in waters by government policy, and by the Australian legal system.[132]

The recommendations of the Report identified outstanding issues in establishing the recognition of Indigenous peoples' rights and interests in water, both onshore and offshore. One of the recommendations was for 'the formation of a key water portfolio for Indigenous peoples to provide legal recognition for Indigenous rights and interests and identify best practice in the protection of Indigenous cultural rights in significant waterways sites'.[133] The Australian Government failed to adopt the formation of an Indigenous water portfolio and this proposal has not been revisited. A recommendation to establish an Indigenous water portfolio for onshore and offshore water would have advanced the status of Indigenous peoples water rights.

It has been widely reported by governments, organisations and the international community that the standard of living for Aboriginal peoples' is appalling, as reflected in life expectancy data published by the Australian Bureau of Statistics.[134] The marginalisation of Aboriginal communities on their traditional lands remains. The national water reforms and governments have failed to provide for the water requirements among Aboriginal communities.

This chapter has examined the participation and representation of Aboriginal peoples in the allocation of water rights and interests by governments administering Australian water policy. It has analysed whether or not the legislative regime provides adequately for the inclusion of Aboriginal water rights and interests and allows for the unique Aboriginal values attached to water. Finally, it demonstrates that since the 1990s research into Indigenous water rights and interests has not been a high priority of Australian governments. Nearly a decade later, the national water reforms concentrated on achieving water allocations to ensure the smooth transition of water trading and pricing, and a new property right in water for every water user but not for the First Australians.

Chapter 8

THE MURRAY-DARLING BASIN
AND THE COMMONWEALTH WATER ACT

The Murray-Darling Basin is the most iconic river system in Australia. It comprises more than one million square kilometres of south-eastern Australia and covers three-quarters of New South Wales, nearly half of Victoria, and a large portion of Queensland and South Australia.[1] Aboriginal peoples in the Basin have long-standing, inherent connection to the land and the waters – with laws, language groups and tribal boundaries.

The Murray-Darling Basin has 23 river valleys within 19 regions,[2] and represents around 40 per cent of Australian farms, where agriculture is the dominant water user, its share accounting for 83 per cent of the consumptive water use,[3] calculated on the use of surface and ground water.[4]

This chapter examines how water scarcity and competing interests in the Murray-Darling Basin impact upon Aboriginal water rights and interests and whether the customary, cultural, social, economic and spiritual water needs of Aboriginal communities are effectively represented in water allocation. It examines the broad experiences of Aboriginal communities within the Murray-Darling Basin, and the flow-on effect of the national water reforms to the Murray-Darling Basin Authority and the Basin regions. The chapter also examines the overall impact of the *Water Act 2007* (Cth) (*Water Act*) and the *Water Amendment Act 2008* (Cth) (*Water Amendment Act*), and further amending legislation, on Aboriginal communities' water rights and interests, with the provisions that directly affect Aboriginal communities and their water requirements.

Cultural rights in the Murray-Darling Basin

In a discussion paper on 'Indigenous Rights to Water in the Murray-Darling Basin' (2004), Morgan, Strelein and Weir examine Aboriginal peoples' relationship to the land and water. They comment:

Indigenous rights to onshore waters are part of a holistic system of land and water management. This holistic system has been fractionalised and encroached upon by European systems of land and water management, and by accompanying environmental impact.[5]

Aboriginal traditional groups in the Murray-Darling Basin assert that cultural rights to water are important to their survival.

> Water is central to the survival of Indigenous peoples in Australia. Indigenous peoples' survival depended upon knowledge of the both episodic and seasonal behaviour of the creeks and rivers, reliable water holes, and the availability of swamps, springs and soaks.[6]

The Boomanulla Report (2002) described water rights as a platform of social justice for Aboriginal communities:

> Access to water should be seen as a matter of social justice allowing Aboriginal communities priority access to the water market (that is through provision of allocation of water licences to Aboriginal people through an appropriate management structure such as a Trust).[7]

The New South Wales Aboriginal Land Council in 2011 addressed the United Nations Permanent Forum on Indigenous Issues, advocating for Indigenous peoples' water interests in the Murray-Darling Basin:

> [i]t must also be appreciated that the mere recognition of our rights and entitlements alone, is not enough. We also need to see Governments addressing the barriers our peoples face in accessing our rights and entitlements to water … Rights and entitlements that are given without practical support for accessing those entitlements amount to mere symbolic gestures.[8]

Raising its concerns, the Land Council indicated that the recognition of Indigenous water rights and interests is not an effective process where there is no guarantee to implement those rights and interests. Years later the 2016 Senate Select Committee Report on the Murray-Darling Basin Plan still failed to include any specific reference to the water rights and interests of Aboriginal peoples of the Murray-Darling Basin.[9]

An over-allocated resource

Water resources have featured as the central focus for facilitating economic wealth production for non-Aboriginal interests since the commencement of the

Murray-Darling project in the late 1800s. The Murray-Darling Project – an 'irrigation system designed in the late 19th century by the Chaffey brothers, who were lured from Canada to Australia by Alfred Deakin on the promise of 250,000 acres (101,000ha)'[10] – was critical in the late 1800s to advance agricultural research and enterprise potential in irrigation planning, as well as a significant experiment combining settlement and irrigation.

> During the 1890s the Mildura settlement in Victoria was an irrigation experiment where the Government, on the fulfilment of conditions, 'freely' gave away hundreds of thousands of [acres] and a large portion of the Murray River waters which 'cared for' the rights and interests of settlers.[1133]

However, the Murray-Darling Project accelerated the disenfranchisement of Aboriginal communities from Aboriginal economic opportunities and the continued use of water for customary purposes.

The national dialogue on water reform in Australia has regularly reported on the poor condition of the Murray-Darling Basin. The Murray-Darling Environmental Resources Study (1987) identified the significant changes to the Basin's river systems:

> Development of the river systems has involved extensive modification of the rivers through the construction of dams and weirs, river 'improvement' operations, levees, and water allocation and management practices designed essentially to supply water for domestic and industrial consumption, irrigation and livestock ... the changed flow from river regulation and the physical barriers of dams are two significant factors affecting the aquatic resources ...[12]

The significant impact of drought conditions and seasons of severe flooding across the Basin's region has greatly affected the water rights and interests of all water users.

> [T]he basin's rivers and groundwater is shared between all these interests ... the relentless expansion of irrigation, dam building and takes from groundwater. Along with the projected impact of climate change, all this [has] put the Murray-Darling on 'a knife edge'.[13]

The historic over-allocation of water resources in the Basin catchments has limited Aboriginal peoples' access to and use of water.

> [T]he mouth of the Murray River is silting-up as decreased water flows in the river are unable to carry sediments out into the sea. This environmental catastrophe is

attributed to the over-consumption of river waters by irrigators, and to massive land clearing in the Murray-Darling Basin over the past century ... Loss of bio-diversity threatens the identity and the way of life of the Ngarrindjeri people, their culture, stories and spirituality and their entire cosmology.[14]

The Murray-Darling Project was unable 'to withstand foolish allocations of rival state governments and their absurdly optimistic advisers'.[15] The results from the National Land and Water Resource Audit state that the historic impact of the over-allocation of water resources has been underestimated.[16]

[F]rom 1985 to 1996/97, total water-use in Australia increased by 65 per cent. Use for irrigation grew by 76 per cent, ... over commitment and over extraction of water resources has led to riverine ecosystem degradation.[17]

The overriding emphasis on economic wealth creation for the pastoral and agricultural industries in Australia is most apparent in the Murray-Darling Basin region. The expansion of agricultural operations and other industries has resulted in the over-allocation of water in the region.

Tan (2000) argues that the 'non-fettered discretion'[18] of government bureaucracy has over-allocated water licences to appease farmers and industry for political gain and that this approach has contributed to the water and environmental concerns affecting the Australian landscape.[19] The endemic problems in the Murray-Darling Basin catchments are attributable to current and former government water policy and the expansion of irrigation.

Awash with regulation — Acts, inquiries, plans and assessments

The management of Australia's rivers has become one of the most urgent public policy problems for each tier of government in Australia, due to the length of severe drought cycles and floods.[20] The Australian Constitution determines the framework for water resource management and the extent to which the state or the Commonwealth may exercise their respective powers.[21] Since federation, the primary heads of the Commonwealth's legislative powers in relation to water resources has expanded most notably, in particular the constitutional powers in relation to corporations, external affairs, trade and commerce and acquiring property on just terms.[22]

With the introduction of the Murray-Darling Project in the 1880s, Australia's most significant river system has been subject to increasing competition, regulation and policies to control the amount of water and decisons about which water use has priority. Governments have sought to balance interests, in various water *Acts* and policies which include: the Murray-Darling Basin Agreement, the 2010 Murray-Darling Basin Plan, the revised 2011 Draft Murray-Darling Basin Plan and the Windsor Inquiry.

The Murray-Darling Basin Agreement of 1992 was ratified by the parliaments of the Commonwealth, New South Wales, Victoria and South Australia, and then by Queensland in 1996 and the ACT in 1998 under a Memorandum of Understanding.[23] The Murray-Darling Basin Agreement replaced the River Murray Waters Agreements of 1915 and 1987.[24] In 1994 the Council of Australian Governments agreed to drive the national water industry to use water efficiently and to address environmental problems created by the historic over-allocation of water by governments and water stakeholders.[25]

The significant reform to water management sought by the Council of Australian Governments' decision – namely, institutional reform – was to deliver environmental flows, recognise a market value in water that relates to its cost, separate water entitlements from land title, and expand the right to trade water.[26]

In 2004 the Murray-Darling Basin Ministerial Council identified six factors that posed a risk to the competing water interests within the Basin, factors that included the impact of climate change, a rise in the number of farm dams and increased groundwater extraction.[27] The Murray-Darling Basin Commission, the executive arm of the Ministerial Council, was responsible for developing, supporting and evaluating natural resource management policies across the Basin's catchments.[28]

The Commonwealth Water Act and the Water Amendment Act

The *Water Act 2007* (Cth) implemented key reforms for water management in Australia and the key features of the Act vested the Murray-Darling Basin Authority with the functions and powers to ensure that Basin water resources are managed sustainably.[29] The *Water Act* requires that a Basin Plan is devised for strategically managing water resources and establishes a Commonwealth Environmental Water Holder to manage the Commonwealth's environmental water within the Basin as well as external to other areas where the Commonwealth owns water.[30]

In addition, the *Water Act* provides the Australian Competition and Consumer Commission with a key role in developing and enforcing water charges and water market rules under the National Water Initiative. The *Water Act* also provides the Bureau of Meteorology with water information functions, together with the *Meteorology Act 1955* (Cth) under which the Bureau operates.[31]

The introduction of the *Water Act* provided for the management of water resources in the Murray-Darling Basin and established the Murray-Darling Basin Authority as an independent statutory body to integrate a water management plan for the Basin.[32] The Murray-Darling Basin Authority absorbed the functions of the Murray-Darling Basin Commission, engaging with non-government stakeholders such as the Indigenous Water Subcommittee.[33] Under its mandate from the *Water Act* the Basin Authority compiles information on water resources, including issues that affect the Basin's environment and socio-economic framework.[34]

The Murray-Darling Basin Authority, under the *Water Act*, has been mandated to develop water planning and water management that promotes economic return and that does not compromise environmentally sustainable levels of extraction or the ecological values of the Basin.[35]

The *Water Amendment Act 2008* (Cth) amended the *Water Act 2007.* A key feature of the *Water Amendment Act* is that it was intended to transfer the Murray-Darling Basin Commission into the Murray-Darling Basin Authority to form a single body responsible for water resource planning in the Basin.[36] The *Water Amendment Act* allowed the Basin Plan to provide arrangements for meeting critical human water needs and increased the powers of the Australian Competition and Consumer Commission to ensure that water charge rules and water market rules apply to all water service providers and transactions, and to determine or accredit determination arrangements for all regulated non-urban water charges.[37]

The *Water Amendment Act* is based on a combination of Commonwealth constitutional powers and the referral of certain powers under s 51 (xxxvii) from the Basin States to the Commonwealth – in particular Queensland, New South Wales, Victoria and South Australia.[38] In Schedule 1 of the *Water Amendment Act* the purpose and functions of the Murray-Darling Basin Agreement and the powers of the Murray-Darling Basin Authority are set out, including state entitlements to water;[39] water accounting;[40] water sharing;[41] reporting; audit and review processes[42] and the interstate transfer of water entitlements.[43]

Amendments have been made to the *Water Act* and additional legislative functions in the *Water Amendment Act 2008* (Cth). Included in the 2008 *Act* is a referral of certain state powers to the Commonwealth;[44] under various subsections of s 18B of the *Water Act*, the Commonwealth coordinates arrangements between governments for the Basin.[45]

The purpose of the Murray-Darling Basin Plan, under the *Water Act*, is to provide for the integrated management of the Basin's water resources and to give effect to relevant international agreements, to the extent that agreements are relevant to the use and management of water resources.[46] The *Ramsar Convention on Wetlands (1971)* is recognised in the literature on the conservation of the declared wetlands in the Murray-Darling Basin as setting a benchmark for international standards. However, the significance of the *United Nations Declaration on the Rights of Indigenous Peoples 2007* is no less relevant to the purposes of the proposed Basin Plan for promoting the sustainable use of water resources.

In 2011 the Murray-Darling Basin Authority, pursuant to s 43(4) and (5) of the *Water Act 2007* (Cth), called for public submissions to revise the Murray-Darling Basin Plan.[47] The 2011 Draft Basin Plan sought to find a balance of competing water interests between the environment, the economy and Basin communities.[48]

The Windsor Inquiry

A Parliamentary 'Inquiry into the Impact of the Murray-Darling Basin Plan in Regional Australia' (Murray-Darling Basin Plan Inquiry 2011) and its report 'Of Drought and Flooding Rains' (2011) was tabled in June 2011. The inquiry was undertaken because of the 'hostile public reaction'[49] to the lack of consultation by the Murray-Darling Basin Authority with the community and stakeholders on the release of the 'Guide to the Proposed Basin Plan' in 2010 and given effect by the *Water Act*.[50] Concerned Basin communities held that the original Plan was too complex, and that it erred 'in stripping irrigators' water rights away and in lacking broad public consultation'.[51]

The inquiry (referred to as the 'Windsor Inquiry' after Tony Windsor MP, Chair of the inquiry in the House of Representatives) received over 700 submissions, held public hearings across the Basin region and heard evidence from 274 witnesses[52] in order to identify the basis for recommendations in an integrated response to Basin community needs.[53]

The Windsor Inquiry highlighted the communities' confusion regarding the proposed re-distribution of the region's water rights and interests. The Australian Government and the Murray-Darling Basin Authority attracted constant media attention because of this, which further highlighted the lack of community and stakeholder consultation. Adding to the communities' frustration was the fact that the highly technical reports by the Murray-Darling Basin Authority about the

2010 water reforms were too complex for communities to understand. This led to the launch of a Plain English Summary of the 2011 Draft Basin Plan.

In the Murray-Darling Basin catchments the focus on water scarcity and the length of the drought in Australia had intensified social and political debate on water issues. To improve government coordination in the management of water resources, state and territory governments responsible for the Basin catchments agreed to the referral of certain legal powers to the Commonwealth.

The key feature for achieving the proposed major water reforms in the Murray-Darling Basin was the proposed implementation of sustainable diversion limits, to regulate environmental water requirements within the Basin catchments.[54] The poor state of the Basin's environmental health had resulted from bad management and unsustainable water use, as the Basin rivers were over-extracted and facing serious risk of biodiversity decline.[55]

The Commonwealth Environmental Water Holder, established under the *Water Act 2007* (Cth), has the responsibility of managing the Commonwealth's water entitlements, in accordance with the Environmental Watering Plan.[56]

The Windsor Inquiry highlighted the need for a greater involvement of Aboriginal peoples in the Basin region with respect to the water planning process, the development and implementation of the Environmental Watering Plan and finding innovative ways to provide for self-managed cultural water use.[57] The Chair of the Northern Basin Aboriginal Nations, in a submission to the Windsor Inquiry, argued that 'cultural flows are distinct from environmental flows'; cultural flows provide water needs for Aboriginal people and environmental flows relate to biodiversity.[58] The final report from the Windsor Inquiry did not outline solutions to address the lack of Aboriginal water rights and interests or how to increase Aboriginal water holdings.

The Windsor Inquiry reported that Aboriginal people in the Basin argued 'they had not been consulted, lacked recognition of their cultural association with the Basin and drew attention to the significant level of disadvantage experienced by Aboriginal communities'.[59] Further, the inquiry report stated that although Aboriginal cultural values are considered under the *Water Act*, these values have not provided for cultural flows within the Basin Plan, irrespective of the overlap of environmental and cultural flows.[60] The Report also highlights the large Aboriginal population living in the Basin, and that the high level of unemployment among Aboriginal people is a negative impact, in addition to the underrepresentation of Aboriginal communities in water planning.[61]

The Windsor Inquiry made recommendations which specifically identify Aboriginal interests. In recommendation 4 it states that, in developing the Murray-Darling Basin Plan the Murray-Darling Basin Authority must 'recognise the social and cultural needs of Aboriginal people'.[62] Recommendation 5 states that 'the Commonwealth Government should develop separate community basin planning for the recognition of the specific needs and economic circumstances of Aboriginal communities'.[63]

The Windsor Inquiry did not recommend any substantive strategies to address Aboriginal peoples' loss of control of the river systems, nor did it address research and development opportunities, nor promote dialogue on the review of the legal and policy processes to enhance the equitable sharing of water rights and interests for the Basin's Aboriginal communities in cultural flows, nor how to restore economic opportunities in the water market and native title interests.

Perhaps the limited response to the Windsor Inquiry was predictable, given that powerful economic interest sectors such as irrigators have greater political clout and command greater attention than Aboriginal groups. The revised and the Proposed Murray-Darling Basin Plan 2011 did not advance the recognition of water interests and rights for Aboriginal people and did not engage in water reforms to equip Aboriginal communities in the Basin with any tangible benefits flowing from the Basin's water resources.[64]

The revised Draft Basin Plan and Aboriginal communities

The most recent policy development for the Murray-Darling Basin is the revised version of the proposed Draft Plan by the Murray-Darling Basin Authority, developed under the *Water Act*.[65] The Draft Plan includes a 'Plain English Summary of the Plan', a 'Catchment by Catchment' Plan for the proposed changes, and 'A Healthy Working Basin' discussion paper for sustainable integration of water use for public consultation.

The 'Draft Basin Plan: Catchment by Catchment' (2011), issued for public comment, provides an overview of the key elements of the Basin Plan in each catchment, and includes changes to water use which will result in social and economic benefits or costs to communities.[66] The 2011 Draft Plan sets out features that categorise water use into social, cultural, economic and environmental profiles in the Murray-Darling Basin – for example, the contribution to agricultural or industrial production, the environmental biodiversity of the catchments, and the cultural profile of Indigenous groups.[67]

In s 21(4)(c)(v) of the *Water Act*, a Basin Plan must give attention to 'social, cultural, Indigenous and other public benefits'.[68] The unpopular 2010 Basin Plan and the revised 2011 Draft Basin Plan are equally deficient in providing for Aboriginal water rights and interests. Neither plan identified tangible benefits that should flow to Aboriginal communities. There was also no proposition in the 2011 Draft Plan to establish perpetual and Reserved Indigenous Water Rights (RIWR) for Indigenous communities outside the consumptive pool, as I have sought in my recommendations.

Under the revised 2011 Draft Plan there is no significant inclusion of Aboriginal communities other than in identifying the names of the Aboriginal groups. The unique relationship of Aboriginal peoples to the Basin is not discussed and neither is Aboriginal use of the environment, such as the river providing for cultural, spiritual, social, customary and economic values.

The Plain English Summary of the Proposed Basin Plan (2011), aims to assess the environmentally sustainable level of take for water resources to ensure sufficient water to improve the rivers, Basin biodiversity and water availability.[69] Part 14 of the 2011 Draft Plan, titled 'Indigenous values and uses', is to identify cultural flows in the water resource plans.[70] The 2011 Draft Plan does not sufficiently examine native title rights and interests, Aboriginal consultation or strategies to meet social, cultural, spiritual and customary objectives.[71]

The introduction to the 2011 Draft Plan summarises the relevance of water to Aboriginal communities in the Basin:

> The Murray-Darling Basin Authority acknowledges and pays respects to the Traditional Owners and their Nations of the Murray-Darling Basin ... The Murray-Darling Basin Authority recognises and acknowledges that the Traditional Owners and their Nations in the Murray-Darling Basin have a deep cultural, social, environmental, spiritual and economic connection to their lands and waters.[72]

The 2011 Draft Plan fails to incorporate Aboriginal water management and Aboriginal water values. Nor does it include any provision for the economic use of water by Aboriginal communities in the Basin catchments and there is no discussion of guaranteed rights and interests for Aboriginal peoples.

The 2011 Draft Plan merely acknowledges the cultural or spiritual relationship of Aboriginal communities to water resources but stops short of identifying any strategies to progress any type of generational water rights for communities. In addition, there is no mention of linking the Australian Government's *Closing the Gap* policy to the proposed water reforms for the Murray-Darling Basin, to improve Aboriginal living standards.

Aboriginal communities gain little, if anything, from the 2011 Draft Plan. The opportunities to exercise water rights and interests are limited. The main participation of Aboriginal communities is to identify 'Indigenous values and uses in water management' in the development of a water resource plan.[73] The Plan should provide the same level of protection as a transitional or interim water resource plan,[74] and 'must have regard to cultural flows in view of Indigenous community objectives'.[75]

Although the documents to inform the 2011 Draft Plan focus on providing community information, without technical jargon, the Plan does not in any way address the water rights, interests and requirements of Aboriginal peoples living in the Murray-Darling region and there is no discussion in the Plan on ways to restore water rights and interests to Aboriginal communities.

As part of a panel discussion on Aboriginal sovereignty at the University of Wollongong I called for an inquiry into Aboriginal water rights and interests in Australia:

> The Australian Government should, as a priority, hold an inquiry to examine the status of Indigenous water rights and interests in Australia, for example, in the cultural, spiritual, social, and legal rights of all Indigenous peoples and if the Commonwealth, State and Territory water legislation meets the water requirements of Indigenous peoples. The inquiry should include in its terms of reference the issue of Aboriginal sovereignty, constitutional amendments and the incorporation of international law into Australia's legal system.[76]

The Indigenous Action Plan

In 2000 the Council of Australian Governments' Reconciliation Framework[77] led to an initiative in 2002 by the Murray-Darling Basin Commission to develop an 'Indigenous Action Plan' with Murray-Darling Basin Aboriginal communities.[78] The Australian Government commenced negotiation with 44 autonomous Aboriginal groups in the Murray-Darling Basin to inform the planning process for Indigenous water interests.[79]

The Aboriginal population in the Murray-Darling Basin comprises over three per cent of the general population, and is increasing.[80] In the Basin there is Aboriginal representation from the Northern Basin Aboriginal

142

Nations[81] and the Murray Lower Darling River Indigenous Nations.[82] Both groups advocate for Aboriginal water rights and interests in the Basin.[83]

The Indigenous Action Plan recommends principles to acknowledge the cultural diversity of Aboriginal communities within the Murray-Darling Basin, including the recognition of customary laws and Aboriginal cultural obligations to water and to establish an equitable share in the benefits from natural resources.[84] The Murray Lower Darling Rivers Indigenous Nation makes the point that:

> Water entitlements that are legally and beneficially owned by the Aboriginal nations and are of sufficient and adequate quality and quantity to improve the spiritual, cultural, environmental, social and economic conditions of those Aboriginal nations, is our inherent right.[85]

The Indigenous Action Plan has been signed by only 40 representative Aboriginal groups in the Basin. The Plan is designed to engage Aboriginal participation in the management of natural resources and environmental governance, and to reduce Aboriginal communities' socio-economic disadvantage under a revised protocol framework.[86]

The potential benefits of the Indigenous Action Plan have remained purely symbolic, and tangible outcomes for Aboriginal water rights and interests have not eventuated. The Plan for the Murray-Darling Basin was made as a non-binding agreement that has failed to deliver economic and cultural outcomes for water.[87]

The Murray-Darling Basin Authority has to date had no meaningful involvement with Aboriginal peoples in the management of the Basin's water resources.[88] Its failure to legally recognise the needs of Aboriginal communities marginalises the spiritual, cultural, environmental, social and economic water requirements of Aboriginal communities.[89] The Murray-Darling Basin Authority implemented the Aboriginal Partnerships Action Plan (2015) in an attempt to involve Aboriginal traditional owner groups of the Basin region.[90]

The impact of water legislation on Aboriginal peoples

The inadequate provision of legally recognised cultural water rights in the national water reforms equates to a loss of Aboriginal identity because water is inherent to kinship. Jackson and Morrison (2006) argue that in the National Water Initiative 'there is negligible empirical evidence of the impact of various water reforms and a range of knowledge gaps in Aboriginal water management'.[91] (see Chapter 7) Jackson and Morrison explain that unless further research is undertaken there is considerable doubt about the benefits that can flow from the water reforms to Aboriginal interests.[92] Because the Indigenous actions under the National Water Initiative are unenforceable, there is an increased possibility of inconsistent outcomes.[93]

The *Water Act 2007* (Cth) states in s 21(4)(c)(v) that 'the National Water Initiative has regard to social, cultural, Indigenous and other public benefit issues' in the Basin Plan. For Aboriginal water rights to be accorded a value balanced with other water rights it is necessary for Aboriginal water rights and interests to be incorporated into legislative instruments.

The drafting of the *Water Act* to provide 'social, cultural or other public benefit issues' is too narrow. This does not properly represent the range of Aboriginal water rights and interests within the Basin. Spigelman CJ has expressed the view that the interpretation of legislation has moved to a 'contextual interpretation':[94]

> Over the last two or three decades the fashion in interpretation has changed from textualism to contextualism. Literal interpretation – a focus on the ordinary meaning of particular words – is no longer in vogue. Purposive interpretation is what we do now ...[95]

This contextual approach to legal interpretation would help to redress the gaps in Aboriginal water knowledge and rights and interests in Australia's water legislation. The national water reforms must incorporate human rights benchmarks in order for Aboriginal water rights and interests to be recognised according to the basic standards for human rights.

Jackson (2006) argues that the 'creation of a distinct category associated with Aboriginal values is glossed over as cultural values':[96]

> [t]he implicit dichotomy between the material (e.g. environmental, economic) and a separate symbolic sphere of meaning (belief and value), otherwise understood as cultural, relegated Aboriginal interests to a realm of negligible significance to the political economy of regional agricultural development and marginalised them within environmental research and action.[97]

In s 20(b) of the *Water Act*, the purpose of the Basin Plan is 'the establishment and enforcement of environmental sustainable limits to the taking of surface and groundwater and to also protect the land and the waters valued by Aboriginal people'. The 'environmental limits' impact the available water resources for cultural water activities and cultural water licences.[98]

As the chapters explain, the nurturing of Aboriginal water and landscapes for Aboriginal peoples is bound to the inseparability of land and water. Section 20(b) of the *Act* refers to 'cultural water activities' that are conditional upon an Aboriginal right to take and use water. Aboriginal laws of themselves limit the taking of water so that they maintain a holistic relationship with the environment, because surface and groundwater are not severable components of the water and the land.

Although s 86A of the *Water Act* states that the Basin Plan 'must have regard to critical human water needs', the provision does not specifically include Aboriginal water requirements as critical needs, or basic human rights.

Part 14 of the *Water Act* sets out requirements to address 'Indigenous Values and Uses' and includes requirements for a Water Resource Plan.[99] A Water Resource Plan, in light of this provision, must identify a range of issues which meet 'the objectives and outcomes for Indigenous people'.[100] It includes 'consultation with relevant Indigenous organisations in the management of water resources' and 'to have regard to the social, spiritual and cultural values of Indigenous people' of the Plan area.[101] The preparation of a Plan is 'to have regard to the desirability in minimising any risks to the Indigenous values and Indigenous use of water', and discretionary scope to 'identify opportunities to strengthen the protection of Indigenous values and uses'.[102]

Western concepts of water use are represented in government water policy, planning and the development of water allocations. The Commonwealth water legislation has decoupled Aboriginal ontological water concepts from the provisions that could well identify Aboriginal water interests. The definition of environmental water under the *Water Act 2007* (Cth) does not represent an Aboriginal understanding of the environment. Both access and use of surface and ground water are governed through Aboriginal laws.

In section 3 of the objects of the *Water Act*, the management of Australia's water resources and how these resources should be dealt with and monitored is set out. The objects in the *Act* under s 3(a) enable the Commonwealth, in conjunction with the Basin States, to manage the Basin water resources in the national interest. Section 3(b) gives effect to relevant international agreements 'for special measures' and s 3(c) gives effect to 'relevant international agreements', in order to 'promote the use and management of the Basin water resources to optimise economic, social and environmental outcomes'.[103]

Section 3d(i) of the *Water Act* seeks to ensure a return to environmentally sustainable levels of extraction for water resources that are over-allocated or overused. Section 3d(ii) is intended 'to protect, restore and provide for the ecological values and ecosystem services of the Murray-Darling Basin taking into account, in particular, the impact that the taking of water has on the watercourses, lakes, wetlands, ground water and water-dependent ecosystems and biodiversity'.

Definitions which refer to 'social, economic and environmental outcomes' in s 3(c) of the *Water Act* currently fail to include recognition of Indigenous water rights and interests as a significant group in its own right and also fail to identify that the rights of Indigenous communities are not fully represented in consumptive or non-consumptive use. Indigenous water rights and interests should be defined as collective rights because in the timeline of Australia's water use these are First Nation rights. An economic perspective has a limited capacity to respond to many moral and ethical issues even though substantial political threats can come from groups driven by such considerations.[104]

A significant role in co-managing the Murray-Darling Basin's water resources requires the recognition of Aboriginal peoples as possessing a prioritised 'first right' in the hierarchy of water users. The Commonwealth water legislation has failed to meet the water needs of Aboriginal communities in the Basin.

> In Australia, Aboriginal cultural values are generally regarded as subservient to the economic progress of the nation. Where any public purpose or planning requirement is proposed, the value of Aboriginal sites is doomed … Natural waterways continue to succumb to the urgency of improving and expanding the 'frontier'.[105]

In 1995 the Council of Australian Governments' Task Force on Water Reform, 'Water Allocations and Entitlements: A National Framework for the Implementation of Property Rights in Water', omitted Indigenous water rights:

> [t]his national policy position paper made no reference to native title, or any other form of Indigenous entitlement that might require recognition and accommodation when developing national principles designed … to turn water entitlements … into full property rights which will form the basis for inter-jurisdictional trade …[106]

Tim Fisher of the Australian Conservation Foundation stated:

> The Council of Australian Governments' Water Resources Policy also included water property rights. Classification of rights is required to free-up markets,

enabling irrigators to cash-in on unwanted entitlements and speeding up transition to the use of water for higher-value products …[107]

Australia's blueprint for the National Water Initiative Agreement did not include Aboriginal water rights and interests. However, the Federal Government did include discretionary provisions in the National Water Initiative, without community consultation to identify whether these national Indigenous Actions met the water needs of communities.

The *Water Act* fails to include any substantial water rights and interests for the Aboriginal communities of the Murray-Darling Basin. There has been a lack of recognition and inclusion of Indigenous peoples in water management reform since the 1990s, and the policy malaise displays no genuine shift towards establishing Indigenous water rights and interests in the national water blueprint. The development of case law in relation to the operation of the *Water Act* is still emerging.

Establishing environmental flows is necessary for improving the Murray-Darling Basin's ecosystem. However, the provisions fail to recognise that Aboriginal people's knowledge and relationship with these ecosystems has existed for hundreds of generations. Although Aboriginal cultural flows are congruous with Aboriginal water values for nurturing the river systems, Aboriginal water management is inadequately acknowledged in the Murray-Darling Basin's policy and legislation.

In spite of the environmental objectives of the 'Living Murray Initiative'[108] and the objectives of the proposed Murray-Darling Basin Plan, these policies do not adequately recognise a major role for Aboriginal communities in managing water resources. The *Water Amendment Act* only includes Indigenous water rights and interests as merely part of other stakeholder interest. For example, s 21(4)(c)(v)[109] of the *Act* reads: 'to have regard to social, cultural, Indigenous or other public benefits in water'. The words 'to have regard to' are a passive proposal which does not require governments to commit to providing water resources for Aboriginal communities.

As I have discussed, the land, waters and resources have interconnectivity to the spiritual and cultural meaning of country and connect to Aboriginal kinship. Water management legislation must recognise Aboriginal water rights and interests in such a way as to reflect the contextual meaning of Aboriginal relationships *with* the environmental landscape. The right to water is integral to Aboriginal peoples as a human right and their relationship to water lies at the centre of community identity.

The significance of water being everywhere culturalized as sacred in Aboriginal societies, the settler society was and remains in conflict with Aboriginal constructions of the landscape in ever more complicated ways.[110]

In Schedule 1 of the 2011 Draft Basin Plan, an Indigenous use of the Murray-Darling is expressed in terms of Indigenous values in water as 'inextricably connected to the land and the rivers and integral to the river system'.[111] Schedule 1 also states that 'the concept of cultural flows helps to translate the complex relationship of Indigenous peoples to the language of water planning and management'.[112] An acknowledgement of commercial water interests for Indigenous Basin communities and organisations is mentioned, including native title interests.[113]

The 2011 Draft Basin Plan fails on many levels to deliver significant water rights for Aboriginal communities because their water rights and interests have to compete with other high-value stakeholders. Aboriginal cultural flows and native title water rights compete with the allocation of environmental flows, and Aboriginal Commercial Water Licences and Aboriginal cultural water licences are made to compete with stakeholders in the consumptive pool.

The Commonwealth Scientific and Industrial Research Organisation (CSIRO) report, on the 'Effect of Water Availability on Indigenous People in the Murray-Darling Basin' (2010) said that the current legislative framework for water management in the Murray-Darling Basin makes minimal provision for the water rights and interests of Indigenous communities.[114]

> The Basin's water resources are now so tightly constrained that Indigenous people find it extremely difficult to compete with those accessing water for either consumptive or non consumptive uses. Indigenous water requirements have not been ascertained in any systematic or comprehensive manner at a catchment scale …[115]

This Report considers that Indigenous communities within the Basin region should have shared control of water management if tangible benefits to Indigenous peoples are to be delivered.[116] The Report also recommends government financial investment in the capacity building of Indigenous Basin communities, to provide opportunities for the contribution of Indigenous water knowledge[117] in managing environmental water allocations.[118]

Jackson, Moggridge and Robinson (2010) agree that the Murray-Darling Basin Plan presents a significant opportunity to address the longstanding neglect of Indigenous water interests and call for further research, as well as monitoring of any benefits from the national water reforms for Indigenous communities.[119]

Research on the Murray-Darling Basin

Most of the earlier written resources on the Murray-Darling Basin region have focused upon the economic values and opportunities that can be produced from farming and agriculture. Contemporary documents on the Basin region also identify the range of opportunities for maximising wealth production in the commercial use of water resources. The national water reforms promote the provision of water resources for the environmental requirements of the Basin and also acknowledge limited inclusion of Aboriginal water rights and interests.

The various government and agency reports offer insight into how government agencies respond to Aboriginal water interests and relationship with the land and the waters. Aboriginal narratives orated by Aboriginal peoples about their relationships in the Murray-Darling Basin are instructive as to why Aboriginal communities are forever connected.

The 'Murray-Darling Basin Environmental Resources Study' (1987) ('Environmental Resources Study') prepared for the Murray-Darling Basin Ministerial Council, presents a Ngurunderi creation story of the Lower River Murray, describing it as a 'myth' and reconstructing it through an anthropological gaze.[120] The section of the study deals with the cultural heritage of Aboriginal peoples in the Basin, identifying 10,000 significant Aboriginal sites that have been recorded and generally found along the rivers and using the word 'mythological' to describe the significance of sites such as middens, burials and quarries.[121] Approximately 20 rivers drain into the Basin system; along with the Great Artesian, which is significant for the environment.[122] Two of the oldest Aboriginal areas in the Murray-Darling Basin have been identified as Lake Mungo and Kow Swamp, where features in the landscape have been created by ancestral beings.[123]

Across the Basin landscape the development of this region caused considerable negative impact at the hands of explorers (since 1813), squatters (pastoralists), timber-getters, farmers and gold miners, as well as the introduction of irrigation in Renmark and Mildura around the 1880s.[124] In looking ahead to the contemporary use of the Basin, the Environmental Resources Study clearly indicates that the present problems in the Basin have resulted from over-development and unsustainable water use, and that significant environmental problems such as rising salinity in the groundwater systems should address the cause – recognised by submissions to government in 1985.[125]

Chapter 3 of the Environmental Resources Study examines water resources in the Basin, including the result of degradation to the water landscape from irrigated landholdings, agriculture run-off from fertilizers into the water system, erosion of the landscape from the increased demands of industries such as forestry, land clearing for agricultural production and salinisation from extensive irrigation.[126] There is no inclusion of Aboriginal interests in water resources within the Basin study and no discussion of the effect of these significant environmental problems upon Aboriginal communities.

In Chapter 8 of the Environmental Resources Study, the only focus on Aboriginal peoples in the Basin is concentrated on cultural heritage through an anthropological framework; this includes information on Aboriginal sites, the Aboriginal Site Register, the distribution and type of Aboriginal sites, and attributes the negative impact on Aboriginal sites to such activities as recreation, tourism, rural development and rising non-flood river levels.[127]

Tan (2001) concludes that 'flood plain water resources, the recognition of environmental values in water and flood plain capture have historically been disregarded in Australia by the common law, State water managers and politicians'.[128]

Here, once again, there is no information on the relationships of Aboriginal peoples, or reference to the complex connection of water resources within Aboriginal culture, and no attempt to make recommendations to the Murray-Darling Basin Ministerial Council to protect the rights and interests of Aboriginal communities to their traditional lands and waters.

The Environmental Resources Study identifies several main issues. It points out that the contemporary problems that plague the Basin have resulted from the impact of inappropriate development. The failure to include Aboriginal relationships inherent to the lands and the waters of the Murray-Darling Basin also undermines an Aboriginal claim to water rights and interests. Applying a largely anthropological framework, and concentrating only on cultural heritage, fractures the inherent relationships of Aboriginal communities in the Basin and disregards their historic and contemporary connections.

A paper by Monica Morgan, Lisa Strelein and Jessica Weir, 'Indigenous Rights to Water in the Murray-Darling Basin' (2004), examines the rights and interests of Indigenous peoples to water, not as a mere stakeholder in water, but as the Indigenous Nations of 'First Peoples' and underpinned by the inherent Indigenous sovereignty to water resources.[129] The right to water for Indigenous peoples is facilitated through the *Racial Discrimination Act 1975* (Cth) whereby governments have an obligation to exercise non-discrimination principles in relation to Indigenous rights.[130]

The recommendations put forward by Morgan, Strelein and Weir for conceptualising Indigenous water rights in the Murray-Darling Basin are: an application of the precautionary principle to ensure that water flows returned to the environment are linked to Indigenous interests, an Indigenous priority in water allocation accorded to Indigenous cultural flows before economic allocations, economic water rights allocated for Indigenous peoples such as water trading, and the implementation of a co-management model between Indigenous Nations within the Basin to protect water systems.[131] In addition to the recognition of Indigenous water rights and interests identified in their paper, there is a call to acknowledge Indigenous diversity, procedural rights in decision-making, principles of self-determination and Indigenous governance to regulate property rights in water.[132]

Morgan, Strelein and Weir do not include all Indigenous Nation Groups within the Murray-Darling Basin, effectively excluding consultation with other Indigenous groups regarding water rights and interests. The authors fail to identify the nexus in the diverse cultural, economic and environmental water requirements of Indigenous peoples. The legal recognition of water rights and interests requires meaningful engagement with all Indigenous peoples within the Murray-Darling Basin region.

In hindsight, the vesting of water management in the States and the administration of water resources by the Commonwealth has undermined the inherent rights of Indigenous peoples to self-manage the Basin's water resources. Further academic research on the Murray-Darling Basin should address Indigenous peoples' inherent customary rights in water in future policy reform. In addition, the National Water Commission should have supported the introduction of Indigenous water rights to be legally recognised and protected under water management legislation as a separate category for Indigenous peoples under the Murray-Darling Basin Plan.

The gross under-allocation of water resources to Indigenous communities in the Murray-Darling Basin Plan has serious consequences for future generations of Aboriginal peoples. The historic over-allocation of water resources to other stakeholders has left Indigenous communities with limited opportunities to participate in water management and economic development such as water trading.

The Murray-Darling Basin Authority should consider Aboriginal water rights and interests as a critical issue in restoring water and to deliver water policy strategies which improve the living standards and health of Aboriginal peoples in accord with Australia's Closing the Gap initiatives.

As this chapter demonstrates, the Murray-Darling Basin Plan has experienced reform but yet failed to address Aboriginal water requirements and it appears that governments prefer discretionary rights over legal certainty for Aboriginal peoples.

Chapter 9

WATER RIGHTS –
FOR ECONOMIC INDEPENDENCE

In relation to Aboriginal water rights and interests in Australia, an economic analysis of the qualitative and quantitative impact on the Aboriginal water economy has generally been ignored in research.

The historical marginalisation of Aboriginal communities has occurred as a result of the development of the Australian economy. The creation of a water market provides considerable gains for government, industry and agricultural development and leaves Aboriginal peoples with little other than symbolism. Australian Government policy and the lack of the planning for generational wealth of Indigenous peoples has been a strong contributing vehicle in the contin- uation of Aboriginal poverty.

> [T]he worth of rural land lies not only in its market value. It also offers some assurance of an economic future and grants the autonomy of self-employment which is part of the bourgeois occupational ideal … In the country land is the basis for the most privileged class relationships, which can only improve in char- acter and potential with improved quality and quantity of the property. Moreover, land ownership has symbolic value: it attests a person's worth and standing in the community.[1]

Collings and Falk (2008) argue that Aboriginal peoples' ability to exercise any future demand for Aboriginal water rights and interests is measured against the national economy:[2]

> The far-reaching implications of the Commonwealth's National Water Initiative reforms through the Intergovernmental Agreement between the Commonwealth, States and the Territories mean for Aboriginal and non-Aboriginal Australians things remain clear in terms of the commodification of water: Australia will buy and sell water as the market price determines its private and public value.[3]

The participation of Aboriginal peoples in the water economy is essential to stimulate the intergenerational growth of wealth in Aboriginal communities. The national water reforms have been weak in delivering substantive water rights for Aboriginal communities.

> There is an apparent disjuncture between the significant attention given to Indigenous economic rights in the academic literature and the content of resource management discourse which rarely addressed property rights issues, or economic opportunities arising from Indigenous access to water rights.[4]

This chapter examines the potential for wealth creation through ownership in water, for example, in the allocation of what I refer to as Reserved Indigenous Water Rights (RIWR). This would ensure water resource availability for Aboriginal communities to self-determine rights and interests before other water users in the consumptive pool. National policy reforms are needed to stimulate wealth development, including statutory Aboriginal ownership of water.

The chapter demonstrates that the status quo of Australia's water laws does not provide opportunities to develop economic benefits in native title or cultural water licences and barriers exist because of historical over-allocation in water and the economic value of water. While the advancement of national water reforms has secured economic benefits for stakeholders, assisted by the separation of water from the land to convert water into a type of property right, governments should turn their minds to securing economic certainty for Aboriginal communities.

'The river of gold' — the economic value of water

As Chapter 4 has shown, the poor outcomes in health, wealth and wellbeing of Aboriginal peoples in Australia result from the significant failure in Indigenous policy implemented by successive Commonwealth, State and Territory governments. Since Australia's settlement by the British, the historical inequities experienced by Aboriginal communities have produced a challenging environment for policy planning. Ineffective government policy has led to the entrenched social, economic and cultural dysfunction experienced by the majority of Aboriginal peoples in Australia. The Western economic concept can be explained in this way:

> The discipline of economics is concerned with scarcity. In the face of scarcity of resources, there is the need to allocate resources within society among competing ends.[5]

The Commonwealth Senate Committee heard evidence on 'Rural Water Usage in Australia' (2003) for Australian farmers and the highlighted economic values in water. The Deputy Chair stated:

> Twelve months ago a lot of key politicians from both sides of the political spectrum thought Australia was going to have some sort of nationally traded water right, which was dreaming, and there is no question that the banks and investment vehicles in Australia are lobbying heavily to be able to capture the river of gold, which was the capital base of the value of water, where they should not allow the transfer of the wealth of water, where they will have a regime, as they see it, to have a farmer as the tenant to the water. I say that we should not allow the transfer of wealth of water from the farm to the bank vault … when you go to borrow the money at the bank you have to have equity.[6]

In New South Wales no commercial water licences for Aboriginal peoples were granted by the NSW Department of Natural Resources; the Aboriginal licences were deemed non-tradeable and Aboriginal communities have strongly criticised the government's approach.[7] Both water access and water infrastructure are integral to a successful economic enterprise in Aboriginal communities.

The Commonwealth land acquisitions by the Indigenous Land Corporation, on behalf of Aboriginal communities, did not include investment in capital infrastructure or the purchase of water rights for Aboriginal leaseholders. Because of this policy omission, Aboriginal farm enterprises invariably failed.[8]

The 'father' of the New South Wales Constitution, William Charles Wentworth, wrote in 1819 of the potential worth of rivers for exploitation in Australia's economy:

> [i]n promoting the progress in this fifth continent, will be prodigious, and in all probability before the expiration of many years, give an entirely new impulse to the tide of population: and here it may not be altogether irrelevant, to enter into a short disquisition on the natural superiority possessed by those countries which are most abundantly intersected with navigable rivers. That such are most favourable for all the purposes of civilized man, the history of the world affords the most satisfactory proof. There is not, in fact, a single instance on record of any remarkable degree of wealth and power having been attained by any nation which has not possessed facilities for commerce, either in the number and size of its rivers, or in the spaciousness of its harbours, and the general contiguity of its provinces to the sea.[9]

Wentworth's vision for creating wealth was to advance the economic development of Australia, not for Indigenous peoples. The acquisition of land by the Crown dispossessed Aboriginal peoples but 'allowed the Crown to make free land grants to individuals on the basis of a nominal rent'.[10] Most of Australia's land holdings were privately owned, either by the purchase of freehold land or in leases by the Crown; leasehold estates were for a term of years or in perpetuity, where in the case of the latter a reversion to the Crown occurred for non-payment of fees or other breaches.[11] Crown grants of land were able to be passed on to the heirs and successors of the land owner.[12]

The Crown's legal powers to withhold or confer the ownership of land directly impacted upon Aboriginal water use because water ran with the land. With few exceptions, Aboriginal peoples were disenfranchised from their customary connection to the Aboriginal environment by the Crown's powers to grant land and to set aside land for Crown purposes, individuals and others. These past practices have directly resulted in the paucity of Aboriginal owned land and water resources.

The 'Two Ways Together Report' (NSW) produced by the Department of Aboriginal Affairs (NSW) identified the total amount of Aboriginal owned or controlled land in New South Wales as 0.45 per cent.[13] The report 'An Effective System of Defining Water Property Titles' (2004) also argues the power in ownership:

> One can have property rights over a resource without being the owner of the resource, such as in a leasehold arrangement to real estate … property rights in an asset or resource can be viewed as a spectrum from a minimal interest through to private ownership … The distinction between ownership and rights is relevant to water because the bundle of rights that have been allocated do not collectively amount to a legal ownership of the underlying resource, in the pure property sense of the word.[14]

Commonwealth and State pastoral leases in Australia exist under a combination of freehold, Crown leasehold and Crown reserves, which it is estimated amounts to 42 per cent for the Commonwealth and between 70 and 80 per cent for the States.[15] Queensland has the largest area held by Crown tenants under non-perpetual Crown leasehold tenure.[16] The water interests held by Aboriginal communities under these pastoral leases have generally been extinguished as a result of the 1998 amendments to the *Native Title Act 1993* (Cth).[17] The NSW

Legislative Council Inquiry into Crown Lands[18] undertook a review of managing existing Crown land assets including the NSW Government's aim to transfer Crown title to local government, which the NSW Parliament passed as the Crown Lands Management Bill 2016.

As Crown lands may be subject to the *Native Title Act 1993* (Cth), the *Aboriginal Land Rights Act 1983* (NSW) and the *Environmental Planning and Assessment Act 1979* (NSW) there are serious concerns about the future of Aboriginal land claims, travelling stock routes, the conversion of Western Land Leases to freehold and the future involvement of Aboriginal peoples in managing Crown Lands.

A legacy of government failure

In 1964 Donald Horne, a social critic and academic, analysed the government's Indigenous policy and its effect upon Indigenous communities.[19]

> Economically they are still exploited, often being paid lower minimum wages than people of European descent … most of them are second-class citizens (although they now have the Federal vote), and the necessary accompaniment of paternalism, lavish expenditure on welfare and imaginative planning was not present … a lack of a policy is itself a policy.[20]

Peter Shergold, former Secretary of the Department of Prime Minister and Cabinet, acknowledged the failure in government policy across all areas of Aboriginal life.[21] Shergold outlined a bleak assessment of the 'lost years' and the plethora of Aboriginal programs and schemes that had failed.[22] The 2007 Oxfam Australia study found that the 'lack of progress in Aboriginal living standards is undeniable'.[23]

Mick Gooda, the former Aboriginal and Torres Strait Islander Social Justice Commissioner, addressed the role of governments upon Aboriginal communities:

> Governments need to be aware of the legacy of previous government policies and make sure that their actions empower rather than disempower. Governments must work with our communities as enablers and facilitators. They can also work to remove existing structural and systemic impediments to healthy relationships within our communities.[24]

The removal of Aboriginal peoples' control over customary ownership of the land, waters and resources, and the impact of British sovereignty, along with the staggered establishment of the colonies have resulted in the disenfranchisement of customary Aboriginal economies. For generations, customary practices on country sustained the health of Aboriginal communities. These included customary trade practices, cultural sharing practices and access to water sources during seasonal cycles. In contemporary water practice, Aboriginal water rights still remain central to the cultural and economic development of Aboriginal peoples.

A scoping study by Jon Altman and William Arthur (2009)[25] offers an estimate of commercial water licences and allocations for Indigenous people across all States and Territories in Australia.[26] The number of water licences held by Indigenous individuals or organisations are given as follows: 122 in New South Wales, 23 in Queensland, 4 in South Australia, 5 in Victoria, 3 in Western Australia, 1 in Tasmania and 4 in the Northern Territory.[27]

Altman and Arthur argue the need for comprehensive research to calculate the exact number of Aboriginal commercial licence holders in Australia and for the establishment of a national Indigenous water register in Indigenous customary water allocations and water licences.[28] They conclude that the policy objectives for Indigenous peoples may improve when these issues are addressed.[29] Further extensive research would identify the specific commercial and customary water requirements of communities.

The NSW Government in 2009 held government-led workshops across the state to identify the unique water issues for Aboriginal communities and to consult on the impact of water reform. During the workshops Aboriginal community participants responded that 'they were unaware of their status in the water sharing process or the allocation of the Aboriginal cultural water access licence'.[30] Aboriginal participants raised the 'need to develop cultural and economic opportunities in water and to recognise the NSW Aboriginal Water Trust as an important body that represents the interests and community objectives of Aboriginal communities'.[31]

Edith Weiss remarked that 'intergenerational equity is to prevent the squander of natural and cultural resources and to underpin the wellbeing of earth's future generations'.[32]

> We, as a species, hold the natural and cultural environment of our planet in common, both with other members of the present generation and with other generations, past and future. At any given time, each generation is both a custodian and trustee of the planet for future generations and a beneficiary of its fruits.[33]

Sharon Beder (2006) considers the concept of intergenerational equity in global terms under the definition provided by the World Commission on Environment and Development:

The Brundtland Commission's definition of sustainable development is based on intergenerational equity, development that meets the needs of the present without compromising the ability of future generations to meet their own needs.[34]

The concept of intergenerational equity is articulated through environmental philosophy. To establish an economically sustainable future for Aboriginal water rights and interests, the Australian legal system should recognise Aboriginal ownership rights. The practical benefits derived from intergenerational equity through Aboriginal water rights would enable Aboriginal communities to plan for future water needs and establish economic growth.

The 'acquisition of native sovereign territory in the United States of America is held under the legal doctrine of domestic dependant nations'.[35] Nation is understood to mean 'a people distinct from others'.[36] Native peoples in the United States are recognised as 'domestic dependant nations because some native tribes retained their powers as autonomous sovereign states and thus manage their internal affairs'.[37] The sovereign powers of native peoples are 'lost only if surrendered by specific treaty provisions or expressed in legislation as terminated by the Federal Government'.[38]

Professor Kent McNeil (2004) suggests that Aboriginal self-governance under the doctrine of domestic dependant nations relates to

[t]he form of government it chooses, citizenship rules, laws relating to natural resources and land use within territory, family law matters, education, social services, and so on.[39]

In the High Court decision of *Coe ('Wiradjuri Tribe') v Commonwealth*,[40] the Court considered whether the Wiradjuri peoples were a 'domestic dependant nation, and if so, entitled to self-government and full rights over their traditional lands'.[41] The Court dismissed the claim by the Wiradjuri because a reasonable cause of action was not disclosed.[42] Aboriginal peoples in Australia are not recognized under Australian law as domestic dependant nations.

The inherent customary rights and obligations which underpin Aboriginal laws have become constrained under the common law as *sui generis* or usufructuary rights to take and use water for domestic purposes. Within the common law framework the concept of *sui generis* presents limited opportunities for economic outcomes and reduces Aboriginal rights only to a right to take. The national water reforms implemented by Australian governments also work against the concept of intergenerational equity because the focus of national policies is upon exploiting resources for national wealth creation.

Self-determination and economic development

The guarantee of economic benefits from water, under statutory water legislation, has provided a higher level of commercial certainty for non-Aboriginal stakeholders to water, as well as perpetual water entitlements and water trading. In Australia the capitalist nature of the economy has cultivated self-interest among water users.[43] The nexus linking water to the land has underpinned Australia's agricultural development for over a hundred years.[44]

The marginalisation of the Aboriginal economy seems inevitable, given the introduction of capitalist market forces and economic utilitarianism. Australian legal frameworks have subsequently undermined Aboriginal customary trade and community values in water. This market approach does not provide a framework of economic and cultural certainty for Aboriginal communities or increase Aboriginal participation in the water market under the existing regimes *if* Aboriginal communities are not participating in the water market.

The Federal Government's Indigenous Business Australia has replaced a number of business operations previously implemented by the Aboriginal and Torres Strait Islander Commission.[45] The Indigenous Business Australia Annual Report (2005) states that

> Indigenous Business Australia sees a direct correlation between Indigenous communities owning businesses and the future improvement in employment opportunities.[46]

The Victorian Government's Indigenous Business Development Strategy (2005-2007) under its main objectives for Aboriginal economic development identified self-determination as incorporating 'symbolic and practical measures to address the dispossession of land and culture'.[47] Restoring Aboriginal ownership rights to water is a practical measure to build capacity in an Aboriginal market economy.

There is no mention of Aboriginal water rights in the Victorian Government's business strategies; increased Aboriginal participation in the Australian water market and the ownership of water property assets could create a 'practical measure'.[48] As a general rule, Aboriginal economic policies should be based on the principles of self-determination because Indigenous economic strategies and policy planning should be driven by Aboriginal communities. Water market policies do not incorporate Aboriginal water values and concepts. The participation of Aboriginal communities in the water market and the Aboriginal customary economy is vital for community development and creating genuine pathways to intergenerational equity.

> Australia has one of the highest home ownership rates among Organisation for Economic Co-operation and Development (OECD) countries. At the 2001 Census, 70 per cent of all households in New South Wales lived in a dwelling that was either fully owned or mortgaged … only 16 per cent of Indigenous households in New South Wales lived in a fully owned dwelling … [the difference between] Indigenous and non-Indigenous rented accommodation [reported that] Indigenous households [were] far more reliant on State and community housing.[49]

Aboriginal communities should be free to exercise their native title water rights and cultural interests through unfettered ownership to facilitate Aboriginal water enterprise. The narrow interpretation of native title imposes limitations on realising community autonomy and wealth creation to achieve Aboriginal water strategies, as the chapters demonstrate.

> Achieving self-determination is difficult because of the dichotomy of a government that has a focus on the pursuit of individual wealth creation and Aboriginal and Torres Strait Islander peoples who may pursue self-determination as individuals or groups within a cultural context that focuses more broadly on social, cultural and environmental as well as economic benefits.[50]

The lack of economic leverage in Aboriginal communities cannot facilitate the concept of intergenerational equity and hinders the economic participation of Aboriginal communities. Aboriginal water rights require legal recognition as property rights to allow Aboriginal communities to utilise communal and private water rights. Without the incorporation of Aboriginal water ownership strategies, the National Water Initiative will never deliver economic outcomes to Aboriginal communities.

Western property rights in water are highly valued because ownership can provide exclusivity. Exclusive ownership rights in water enable the individual or entity to exercise a temporary or permanent right to transfer, trade or sell their water rights.[51] The non-tradeable status of Aboriginal water licences fails to provide economic benefits. In New South Wales Aboriginal peoples may apply for a 'Specific Purpose Water Access' licence that is non-tradeable or an 'Aboriginal cultural water access licence' that is for a specific activity over a period of time, subject to the available water determination.[52] This narrow policy approach is a static approach to Aboriginal water requirements and fails to provide allocation certainty for Aboriginal licence holders because it is subject to the available water. A non-tradeable water licence has no commercial value.

To improve the living standards of Aboriginal peoples, the focus should therefore be on providing Aboriginal communities with legal certainty in all aspects of water use and the autonomy to manage water resources. The Aboriginal concepts of water are not diminished by exercising private property rights if they ensure that Aboriginal communities are able to determine and self-manage their needs.

The Productivity Commission Report 'Overcoming Indigenous Disadvantage: Key Indicators' (2011) recognised that the economic participation of Indigenous peoples directly influences the living standards of Aboriginal peoples, including health and wealth development.[53] The Report points out that Aboriginal health improves significantly when Indigenous peoples hold Indigenous-owned or -controlled land and business.[54] In view of the Commission's findings, it should be incumbent on the Australian Government to incorporate Indigenous economic rights to water within the framework of national water management policy and legislation.

The Productivity Commission Report also states that 'land ownership and the control of land provides a range of benefits to Indigenous peoples and enables autonomy and economic independence within Indigenous communities'.[55] The primary measures identified in the Report recognise other economic participation indicators such as the recognition of native title, the size and number of Indigenous Land Use Agreements, the economic benefits of Indigenous rights to land and the opportunities for self-employment and Indigenous business.[56]

The Commission's Report notes that although an Indigenous customary economy such as fishing and 'hunting and gathering' is highly valued and important to communities the potential for commercial exploitation in these economies is negligible.[57]

> Native title is not a form of tenure and so has no market value … although Indigenous groups have an extensive land base; there are limited opportunities to use them as security for economic developments.[58]

The economic utilisation of natural resources by Indigenous peoples provides opportunities for the development of a vital economy and enables Indigenous peoples to maintain Aboriginal laws, customs and practices on Indigenous-owned and -controlled land and waters.[59] The national water management regime could incorporate the economic participation of Aboriginal peoples in the water market by creating a reserved Aboriginal water right external to the consumptive pool. The improvement of Aboriginal health and living standards requires future reforms to benefit future generations and to provide the necessary framework for self-determination for Aboriginal communities.

Competing water rights – environmental and cultural values

The Annual Report on Indigenous Reconciliation in Primary Industries and Natural Resource Management (2006-2007) identified the Australian Government's inaction in providing an equitable or cultural water use for Aboriginal peoples:

> Water is a critical issue for Natural Resource Management and Primary Industries in Indigenous communities, as many communities have unreliable water source or lack of potable water. A reliable water supply is required for sustaining business ventures e.g. irrigated agriculture and aquaculture in remote and regional areas and may promote the economic independence of Indigenous communities.[60]

In his doctoral research on the Murray-Darling Basin, Daniel Connell (2007) comments on the 'ambiguous nexus between water commodification and water management':

> It is hard to avoid concluding that if the National Water Initiative system as described is needed for water trading to be environmentally beneficial then this is, in effect, a statement that water trading under achievable standards will be bad for the environment in many instances. These uneasy compromises suggest unresolved tensions between the desire to promote economic activity by strengthening or creating property rights, and the legal responsibility of Australian governments to manage water resources for the benefit of society as a whole.[61]

Jakeman, Letcher and Chen (2007) argue that the use of an 'integrated assessment of the interconnected issues surrounding water allocation with the integration of stakeholder water demands may resolve allocation issues'.[62] The authors considered the

> [i]ntegration of knowledge from different disciplines with the goal to contribute to understanding and solving complex societal problems, that arise from the interaction between humans and the environment, and to contribute in this way to establishing the foundation for sustainable development.[63]

In Australia over the past decade, new concepts in environmental policy and law have evolved through environmentally sustainable development principles which 'apply to water resources to maintain ecological values of ecosystems'.[64] Sustainability principles seek to achieve economic development without increasing the over-exploitation of natural resources.[65] The application of environmental concepts in relation to traditional ecological management requires the inclusion of Aboriginal people's water use as an environmentally sustainable measure.

Aboriginal water rights in Australia do not have the legal protection recognised in other common law countries such as Canada, the USA and New Zealand. Apart from native title determinations and areas of Aboriginal freehold land, the allocation of water rights and interests for Aboriginal peoples in the National Water Initiative is framed with discretionary jurisdictional actions under Indigenous Clauses, 52, 53 and 54.[66] The National Water Initiative policy underpins a broad agenda of 'water reform in water allocation, water trading, environmental considerations, public participation in water management principles and a market-based and regulatory regime that requires state and territories to compete for water use'.[67]

The recognition of native title rights is available to Aboriginal communities who are able to meet the complex standard of proof required under statutory native title legislation and the common law. For this reason alone there is a compelling case to incorporate a reserved water right for Aboriginal peoples in the Australian Government's National Water Initiative.

In South Australia the government has failed to provide economic development of Aboriginal water rights and interests.[68] Equally, other states or territories have also failed to implement a policy pathway to incorporate Aboriginal economic benefits.[69] Virginia Simpson's report (2007) strongly argued that 'governments should allow Aboriginal people to extract water for economic development through water licences and by other means'.[70]

The 'Review of the 1994 Water Report' (2001) highlights that the Australian Government water reforms have also failed to recognise the intrinsic economic and cultural values which exist in Aboriginal water use.[71] I submitted in my report to the Western Australian Government that the concept of water royalties be included in the policy framework on Aboriginal water rights. My position is drawn from mining royalties on Aboriginal-owned land because water royalties could provide economic benefits. A water royalty would ensure certainty in economic planning in Aboriginal communities where third parties seek to access and use water on Aboriginal owned lands.

The Federal Government's '*Closing the Gap*' policy was implemented to improve opportunities and living standards for Aboriginal communities. However, the Productivity Commission Report (2011) states: 'any improvement from this federal policy is minimal'.[72] The '*Closing the Gap*' policy is summarised as follows:

> Our challenge for the future is to embrace a new partnership between Indigenous and non-Indigenous Australians. The core of this partnership for the future is closing the gap between Indigenous and non-Indigenous Australians on life expectancy, educational achievement and employment opportunities. This new partnership on closing the gap will set concrete targets for the future.[73]

For a decade from the 1990s, the mining boom in Western Australia secured the main source of national economic wealth, and in certain extractive industries 'mineral exploration across Australia continues to expand at a rapid rate but living standards among Aboriginal communities remained poor'.[74] Traditional Owners are impacted in the Northern Territory where 80 per cent of the land is covered by exploration licence applications.[75] Mining exploration and development in coal, uranium ore and other base and precious metals require high levels of fresh water.[76] If Aboriginal communities owned the water resources, under native title or other water rights, communities could commercially exploit these resources and develop economic viability.

> Australia is a major world producer of iron, aluminium, lead, zinc and uranium. It is the world's largest exporter of bauxite (aluminium ore) and alumina. It is the world's largest exporter of lead and the second largest exporter of zinc. It is the world's largest producer of both nickel and gold.[77]

The ongoing national competition for water resources between governments, industry and native title holders has not placed Aboriginal communities in a favourable position. The wealth creation from spring water extraction and bottled water is estimated at over $800 million dollars annually, primarily developed by global companies such as Coca-Cola Amatil and Nestle.[78] The current commercial requirements for spring water supplies can impose a direct threat to many Aboriginal cultural water sites and in sustaining levels of available spring water in aquifers: 'Maintaining water flows is fundamental to ensuring the vitality and existence of Indigenous heritage and spirituality.'[79]

In the village of Bundanoon in New South Wales where I lived, the community residents held a meeting to ban bottled water, and instead provide several drinking fountains to reduce the use of wasteful plastics.[80] The bottled water ban, believed to be a world-first, was aimed at highlighting the excessive production of plastic bottles and the impact upon the environment.[81]

As the only Aboriginal presenter during the community meeting, my focus was on the implications of the proposed spring water extraction from Bundanoon. However, the event organisers were not interested in Indigenous water issues or in the impact upon Bundanoon's aquifer. My observations of the meeting were:

> Through the evening the presentation emphasised the pollution factor to plastic bottles, not the entire still and sparkling water business practice that should expose Australia's well-documented over-extraction of groundwater and the significance of water holes, springs and the existence of Indigenous heritage sites to these water systems.[82]

Spring water has been exploited around the globe irrespective of Aboriginal water values. The extraction and commodification of spring water is dominated by Coca-Cola Amatil, a world leader in the bottled water market.

> Mount Franklin dominates the $544 million bottled water market and is an expert in marketing campaigns that tap into community issues …[83]

The human consumption and demand for bottled water throughout Australia has increased the establishment of other spring water companies entering the market and the ramifications for Aboriginal communities are many. Aboriginal cultural values in spring water have not been fully considered by government in allocating water extraction permits. The incorporation of Aboriginal business opportunities have not been developed in this market and the policy paradigm for culturally appropriate and sustainable Aboriginal water enterprise has been virtually ignored.

Hawken, Lovins and Lovins (1999) argue that exploitation for wealth production requires compromise for the benefit of the environment and people.[84]

> Industry ingests energy, metals and minerals, water, and forest, fisheries, and farm products. It excretes liquids and solid waste – variously degradable or persistent toxic pollutants – and exhales gases, which are a form of molecular garbage … The molecular waste goes into the atmosphere, oceans, rivers, streams, groundwater, soil, plants, and the flesh of wildlife and people.[85]

The exploitation of land and resources has always been part of the settlement history of Australia. In the establishment of New South Wales no land would be sold for fewer than five shillings an acre, where sales were generally for lots of 640 acres.[86] The Crown reserved the right to build on the land for public purposes and 'reserved for itself indigenous timber, stone and all minerals of precious metals and coals'.[87]

The NSW Government's 2006 'Water Sharing Plan' for the Greater Metropolitan Region identifies that Sydney's population is expected to increase by one million people over the next 25 years, which represents an average increase of 110 people and 40 dwellings every day.[88] If water consumption remains at its current levels the government will need to find an extra 200 billion litres of water each year.[89] This increased demand in water use will directly impact upon meeting the water requirements for Aboriginal communities in the future.

The contemporary sustainability of the Aboriginal environment and the protection of Aboriginal water resources have not been meaningfully considered under national water planning reforms. The amount of water used by the mining sector and other industries is prioritised above the needs of Aboriginal peoples and their water use. Water requirements for both consumptive and non-consumptive purposes under the National Water Initiative framework do not take into account Aboriginal ontological concepts of water.

> The minerals sector invests its risk capital in investigating and developing water sources and infrastructure and provides significant data to Government on these water resources ... the bulk of water used by mining is from underground aquifers, in the more remote regions and [is] non-potable.[90]

In the Pilbara region of Western Australia, water contamination from mining operations has posed significant threats to Aboriginal water use.

> The Weeli Wolli Spring in Western Australia ... has been central to local language groups' lifestyle and spiritual beliefs for about 18,000 years, [and] will take at least 20 years to restore after mining ... the drinking water has been polluted by the mining process ... we want to make them the mining companies and the Government accountable ...[91]

A Senior traditional Witjira Elder and Ranger observes that 'Aboriginal health is interconnected to a holistic purpose for water and its Aboriginal values'.[92]

> [W]e have a holistic approach to water. For this is a source of healing when we are sick ... it is our life blood which we need to survive. It allows us to continue our ceremonies which incorporate our rich and unique culture ... it is these sources

of water that provide an adequate and valuable food source rich in fish and other foods for my people.[93]

In 2006 the Leichhardt River near Mt Isa was reported to have excessive lead toxicity from smelting and mining operations, which dispersed dust contamination from the mine's heavy metal production.[94] At the Pacific Basin Consortium for Environmental and Health Conference, research was presented on 'the health effects of lead in Mt Isa and identified that children were at risk from intellectual deficits and fatal health outcomes as a result of lead poisoning from mining residue'.[95]

> Children are exposed to dust laden with lead … Youngsters ingest dust when crawling on contaminated floors, playing in contaminated yards, swimming in contaminated water or engaging in hand-to-mouth behaviour.[96]

The contamination of water resources is an additional threat to Aboriginal water use. Equally, the over-allocation of freshwater for industry and mining directly impacts on Aboriginal communities. The competing interests within the water market are not accounted for by the Federal Government and other peak bodies, according to the 'Statement of Intent to Close the Gap on Indigenous Health Equality' (2008). The Statement of Intent expresses

> [a] commitment to work collectively to systematically address the social determinants that impact on achieving health equality for Aboriginal and Torres Strait Islander peoples.[97]

The Department of Water (WA) has stated in its proposed Water Resources Bill that 'native title rights for Aboriginal peoples are to be recognised on the same basis as stock and domestic or riparian water interests'.[98] The department did not propose any economic use of water for Aboriginal peoples under the government's water policy.[99]

A further example of excluding Aboriginal economic development is in the Ord River Irrigation Area in Western Australia, which was originally designed to develop wealth for northern Australia and increase the settlement of Anglo-Australians.[100] The Ord consists of tens of thousands of hectares in irrigated horticultural crops,[101] and the gross value in production is around $60 million annually.[102]

The Miriuwong-Gajerrong peoples, Traditional Owners of this area, were not consulted in the preliminary discussions on the redevelopment of their lands[103] and did not directly benefit from the early development of the irrigation area.

There is no indication in available records that Aboriginal people were consulted about the Ord River Irrigation Area development, nor were they given advance notice of the flooding of their traditional lands ... As the waters rose the traditional landowners were moved to short term leasehold areas and communities with no means of employment except day labouring ... The land and the wealth created through their long involvement in the pastoral industry were in the hands of the pastoralists, and so Aboriginal peoples had no capital or assets to invest in the project.[104]

In Western Australia a 'Study of Groundwater-related Aboriginal cultural values of the Gnangara Mound' (2005) identified major groundwater sources of freshwater in the Mound (which extends from north Fremantle, to Moore River and Gingin Brook and east to Ellen Brook and the Swan River in the South) to determine the 'Social Water Requirements' of the Nyoongar communities.[105]

The 'Gnangara Mound Report' articulated the traditional creation story of the 'Emu cave of Nyungar peoples, in which the modern Emu[106] and the serpent Waugal[107] are associated with certain freshwater springs'.[108] Nyoongar peoples, as with other Aboriginal communities, have traditionally used swamps or wetlands as a source of water.[109] Due to increasing industry and housing developments, the Nyungar peoples have lost staple foods such as typha reed (*yandiji*)[110] and their customary access to water.

The increased development of coastal and inland areas of Western Australia has implications for the 'public and private alteration of the natural flow of surface and ground water'.[111] The Gnangara Mound, a significant Aboriginal water site for Nyoongar peoples, has been significantly affected by the 'use of private water bores, the increase of housing estates, the operation of market gardens and turf farms'.[112]

The correlation between poor Aboriginal health, the lack of Aboriginal wealth creation and the over-allocation and contamination of water resources has not been taken into account within the national dialogue on water and water reform policy.[113]

This chapter demonstrates that Aboriginal values in water and the customary purposes inherent in water under Aboriginal laws and practices should not preclude Aboriginal peoples from adapting these customary practices and beliefs for economic development. It is not viable for Aboriginal communities to compete with stakeholders in the water market with an inferior legal right because there is an obvious power imbalance.

In summary, the strategies directed at generating wealth in Australia, since the Crown asserted possession of the land, have resulted in creating the conditions for extreme Aboriginal disadvantage and unacceptable levels of poverty. At the point of British settlement in Australia and over the various stages of colonising the land and the water, Aboriginal peoples were disenfranchised from their traditional rights and interests and from the ability to create an economic base to sustain their communities. The national water reforms have again focused upon industry, pastoralists, farmers and irrigators, and continue to disenfranchise Aboriginal communities from property rights in water and embed disadvantage. If governments choose to ignore Aboriginal water rights and interests within their respective legislative instruments and water policy strategies, the dire conditions of Aboriginal communities will remain.

Chapter 10

ABORIGINAL WATER VALUES IN AUSTRALIAN POLICY AND LAW

In Australia the allocation of water resources has become one of the most politicised and contentious issues among national and state water departments and their agencies. Water scarcity is a global concern. In the words of early explorer and barrister William Charles Wentworth, the 'competing interests of commerce in the access and use of water to attain power and wealth' was paramount.[1]

The *Australian Constitution* has determined the extent of state and Commonwealth powers in water management.[2] Because of the 'artificial political borders which lie over Australia's river system this fragments the governance of water'.[3] In recent times there have been few cases in the High Court examining Australia's water issues.[4] Section 100 of the *Australian Constitution* places limits upon Commonwealth intervention in the States' control of water resources:

> The Commonwealth shall not, by any law or regulation of trade or commerce, abridge the right of a State or of the residents therein to the reasonable use of the waters of rivers for conservation or irrigation.[5]

Water is vested in the Crown for the purposes of management and conservation, although access rights to use water are granted by the respective States.[6] Indigenous peoples' water rights and interests do not appear in the Australian Constitution or in the constitutions of any state.

The management of water sources in the early days of British settlement was treated in an ad hoc fashion where common law riparian water rights were used at the discretion of the land owner; water ran with the land and had no separate property rights attached to it. The Australian colonies did not implement a management regime to regulate the use of water until the late 1800s. From Federation the Australian states sought to 'softly' regulate water used by irrigators, as well as water users such as pastoralists, farmers and squatters.

The Howard Federal Government's national review of water management unequivocally altered Australian water policy and the legislative framework for water management by separating water from the land; water rights could be temporarily or permanently transferred or traded to other parties or entities, and could be mortgaged to secure economic benefits.

This chapter examines the treatment of Aboriginal water rights and interests in policy development and the extent to which Aboriginal cultural customs and practices are considered in the management of water resources under Australian law. The chapter analyses the position of Aboriginal water rights and interests within the hierarchy of other water interests, and considers whether Aboriginal cultural, customary practices and economic needs in water are sufficiently considered in water policy development and effectively incorporated into Australian law. This chapter demonstrates that the primary focus of water use and water management in Australia is the economic prosperity of a small group of stakeholders and governments.

The poor recognition of Aboriginal water rights

Aboriginal water rights and interests were not included in national water reforms until 2004, resulting from the persistent advocacy of Aboriginal peak bodies raising their concerns with the governments on the disregard of Indigenous water rights and interests. The National Water Initiative has barely progressed these rights and interests to anything more than inadequate provisions coined in passive language such as 'accounting for native title water' and 'where possible, to acknowledge these water interests exist'.[7]

Tan (2002) argues that early government water policy did not take into account the impact from the inadequate regulation of Australian water resources.[8]

> Public debate over policy and law reform has challenged expectations about water use. It must be acknowledged that the economic prosperity of inland irrigation has been bought at considerable environmental cost. River systems have suffered much degradation in the two centuries since colonial occupation … Water resources have become fully committed, wetlands have been drained, natural habitats destroyed, and native species have dwindled under the burden of highly modified flow regimes and spreading exotic species.[9]

In Australia, water management legislation was first introduced in the 1880s to regulate a consumptive use of water, generally for irrigated agriculture, where water was regulated through an administrative system rather than a riparian doctrine of the common law.[10] The doctrine was shaped upon the legal concept that 'flowing water is in a constant state of change and cannot be possessed or appropriated' by water users.[11]

This approach became less than ideal for Australian conditions because Australian watercourses differed vastly from English watercourses, as did the climatic conditions.[12] Water resources in Australia were administered in a manner that was inconsistent with how Aboriginal water use was understood. Aboriginal water use knowledge was not highly valued. The priority in allocating water resources was instead focused upon ensuring the social and economic benefits flowing to the nation and the states.

Jackson, Storrs and Morrison's research paper (2005) analyses the recognition of Aboriginal rights and values in the Western legal system:

> [w]estern and customary legal systems allocate rights and responsibilities to land and resources … the greater significance of land over water in the western environmental consciousness explains why Indigenous relationships to land, rather than water, have tended to be more readily recognised and documented. Western law has treated water as a fluid element and, as a consequence, rights to water have been poorly defined … land is more or less fixed, is more readily traded and valued.[13]

Jason Behrendt and Peter Thompson (2004) argue that there has always been a lack of recognition of and protection for Aboriginal rights and interests in the state management of New South Wales river systems.[14] Behrendt and Thompson recognised the plight of Aboriginal peoples regarding access to and use of water resources and the impact from the commodification of water and the allocation of water extraction licences to other water users.[15] The authors conclude that water reforms implemented without Aboriginal consultation have had negative consequences for Aboriginal communities, including inadequate provision for cultural, spiritual, social and economic water use.[16]

Murray Radcliffe, the Manager of Water Planning for the Australian Government's National Water Commission, confirmed the poor recognition of Indigenous water rights in addressing the Indigenous Water Focus Group (2008) in Adelaide:

> [t]he National Water Commission and the Commonwealth government may amend the National Water Initiative in relation to Indigenous Water Planning … Indigenous spiritual and social water requirements are currently neither included

by Indigenous cultural flows or economic interests. The Biennial Assessment of the National Water Initiative in 2007 showed Indigenous engagement was patchy at best.[17]

Radcliffe also stated to the Indigenous Focus Group meeting that

[f]rom the Indigenous actions under the National Water Initiative only 10 Indigenous groups were represented nationally … with nil incorporation of Indigenous cultural inclusion, or Indigenous consultation, native title rights allocation, or where water was to be taken into account among water sharing plans.[18]

The national focus of water policy reform is not concerned with improving the water rights and interests of Aboriginal communities. The Howard Federal Government instead prioritised national issues such as the development of Northern Australia for new and expanded agricultural lands and increased financial investment[19] – which has now resurfaced as a key policy for the Turnbull Federal Government. However, to achieve this sizeable development, the Federal Government would have to acquire Aboriginal land and water rights.[20] The government's policy position to acquire Aboriginal land would compromise land and water rights of Aboriginal communities for the sake of achieving national wealth.

Towards inclusion: the case for tradeable Aboriginal water licences

The ability to trade water allocations under Australia's water legislation provides a secure asset which can be leased or used as equity, and also allows water to be temporarily leased without selling land. In NSW water legislation there are various categories of water access licences for water users. Trading water is voluntary and based on the market price – it may be sold for the price of a peppercorn.[21] Interstate water can be traded permanently, temporarily or leased. A water register records water allocation ownership and water allocations. For example, a water access licence can be subdivided and new water access licences made available to bequeath on death or as settlement of property interests in family law matters.

The assessment of groundwater systems in New South Wales is flawed, as the Department of Natural Resources (NSW) identified:

The primary tool currently available for managing groundwater in highly connected alluvial systems is the 40m rule — where groundwater extractions within 40m of a river are managed to the daily access rules of the adjoining river — which falls short of the National Water Initiative requirement, as there are literally thousands of alluvial aquifers which are highly connected to their parent streams and extend well beyond the 40m zone.[22]

The Department of Natural Resources (NSW), under the department's 'Macro Water Plans Project', advised 'that the introduction of Aboriginal Commercial Water Licences in the state's water plans would address Aboriginal disadvantage'.[23] The granting of Aboriginal commercial water licences is subject to lenient access provisions because of their availability in low-risk ground-water.[24]

In New South Wales, the Macro Water Sharing Project Control Group recommended that the New South Wales Minister for Water should restrict the economic interests of Aboriginal peoples in the proposed policy of a commercial water licence:[25]

> [t]hese licences are not fully commercial. While they may be temporarily traded, they cannot be subject to permanent trade [and] as such [they] will remain in the community for the life of the licence. Aboriginal communities, enterprises and individuals are encouraged to seek financial assistance from funding bodies to purchase fully commercial licences.[26]

However, the Project Control Group agreed to allow Aboriginal Commercial Water Licences to be tradeable and to allow licence holders to convert the licence to an unregulated river licence and trade or sell their share to other Aboriginal organisations or individuals and sell their allocations to other licence holders.[27] A recommendation by the Project Control Group was to create an additional category of 'Aboriginal Community Development' under the Water Management Regulations, to progress Aboriginal commercial licences, including unregulated river and aquifer licences.[28]

The Aboriginal Community Development Water Access Licence was included within the water sharing plans. However, these licences have highly restrictive conditions. They are not made available to Aboriginal individuals, are only for coastal water and some aquifer systems, and are not available where cap limits apply such as in the Murray-Darling Basin region.[29]

The State water policy was incorporated into the Macro Water Sharing Plans under the *Water Management Act 2000* (NSW).[30] The government had not engaged in consultation with Aboriginal communities in New South Wales, and the State's water policy reforms were instead driven by internal policy advice.[31]

Aboriginal non-tradeable commercial water licences were aimed at unregulated coastal water systems where low impact and high flows are a condition for granting an Aboriginal licence.[32] Government policy stipulated that no licences would be issued for inland regulated rivers and that potential licences in unassigned groundwater systems are all subject to environmental assessment.[33]

The water entitlement licences in New South Wales are generally for 'domestic and stock access licences and local water utility access licences'; aquifer licences in not fully allocated groundwater sources and the introduction of Aboriginal cultural purpose access licences are restrictive.[34] In contrast to the cultural licence, a commercial licence for Aboriginal applicants was designed as non-tradeable, non-perpetual water licences that cease when the commercial activity has finished.[35]

Craig (2005) highlights the cultural needs for Aboriginal peoples for cultural purposes:

> Cultural flows should be an essential component of river management. A cultural flow can be set and monitored as sufficient flow in a suitable pattern to ensure the maintenance of Aboriginal cultural practices and connections with the rivers. In circumstances where rights to water are being turned into a commodity and schemes for tradeable water rights being expanded, it becomes increasingly important to ensure that Aboriginal cultural flows are secured in legislation as a non-tradeable interest. Aboriginal people do not have the means to purchase those water flows on the open market.[36]

The New South Wales 'Two Ways Together 2003-2012' policy, developed by the Department of Aboriginal Affairs (NSW), committed to developing and delivering government partnerships with Aboriginal communities. Culture and heritage were key priorities identified to improve Aboriginal policy outcomes through 'social, economic and cultural' policy objectives.[37] However, this policy was mute on outcomes in water rights and interests for Aboriginal peoples.

State approaches to Aboriginal water enterprise

Australian governments do not appear to have addressed any level of certainty for Aboriginal communities' cultural and economic use of water. In recent times governments have had the opportunity to formally recognise and incorporate Aboriginal water requirements into water management legislation. However, governments instead have marginalised Aboriginal water rights and interests as an inferior right.

The Draft Annual Report by the Working Group for Advancing Reconciliation (2006) to the Primary Industries Ministerial Council and the Natural Resource

Management Ministerial Council addressed where the states and territories met the priority areas identified by the Council of Australian Governments.[38] The Draft Report indicates a desire for reconciliation within the National Action Plan in natural resource management and primary industries, and includes a key theme of water and land.[39]

In the submissions made to the Australian Government on the Draft National Water Initiative Implementation Plan in 2005, the complaints raised in the submissions included 'a lack of federal funding to State and Territory jurisdictions to implement the national plan and funding water reform implementation from their resources'.[40] There was no funding set aside for the National Water Initiative by the Australian Government to assist the States and Territories implement water reforms under the plan.[41]

> The only funding available for specific National Water Initiative related projects is the $1.6 billion Water Smart Australia program under the Australian Water Fund. The Water Smart Australia program is designed to support the National Water Initiative by funding projects that improve river flows, desalinate water, recycle storm water, re-use grey water, better manage sewerage, store water more efficiently, and design more efficient houses.[42]

Daniel Connell in 'Water Politics in the Murray-Darling Basin' (2007) suggests that 'solutions must be culturally acceptable'.[43]

> An economic perspective also has limited capacity to respond to many moral and ethical issues even though substantial political threats can come from groups driven by such considerations. Those involved often lack market power but that does not mean that they lack political power. Examples in Australia include the Green and Indigenous land and water rights movement. Consequently, medium term security and predictability for management programs and water-based economic activities cannot be provided without a policy and management frame-work that is able to integrate many different interests, not just those that can exert market pressure, in ways that are acceptable to the wider community.[44]

The Productivity Commission Report (2011) states that, 'in order for Indigenous peoples to participate in the economy government policy must address strategic areas for any significant and lasting effect in Aboriginal health reform'.[45] The Productivity Commission identified the 'correlation between improved incomes, economic participation and socio-economic development'.[46]

According to the Virginia Simpson Report,[47] the implementation of water management in 'partnership' with Aboriginal peoples remains unsatisfactory.[48] Aboriginal engagement in national water reform is under-resourced in funding for capacity building of Aboriginal water enterprise, and the level of genuine engagement by governments with Aboriginal communities has been described as dysfunctional.[49]

In Queensland the *Water Resources Act 1989* avoids any substantive recognition of Aboriginal water requirements; the rights of the Crown prevail.

> The perpetual water rights provision was superseded by the *Water Resources Act 1989* (Qld) which concentrated upon the powers of the Crown to water resources, the development and consumptive use of water ... avoiding the relevance of ecosystems and the environmental aspects of water management.[50]

The *Irrigation Act 1922* (Qld) held that perpetual water rights for irrigators were 'attached to the land' and water availability was defined.

> A water right was circuitously defined as a right in respect of irrigable land to a quantity of water annually out of the water available for irrigation in an irrigation area.[51]

In contrast, water availability is defined by restricting water trading and economic development for Indigenous peoples. The Cape York Peninsula Heritage Bill 2007 was the singular provision for water in Aboriginal communities, where river extraction is capped at 1 per cent of the mean annual flow.[52] Fifty per cent is to be allocated as non-tradeable Aboriginal water licences.[53] The Queensland Government, for example, 'bundles Aboriginal peoples' cultural water into environmental water flows'.[54]

In Victoria the *Water Act 1989* promotes a 'water reserve' for environmental values,[55] but does not address a 'water reserve' for Aboriginal cultural values. In Victoria there is no provision for allocating water for traditional purposes under native title.[56] A consent determination in the Federal Court recognised that the Gunditjmara peoples in Victoria held non-exclusive native title rights and interests over 133,000 hectares of vacant Crown land, national parks, reserves, rivers, creeks and sea north-west of Warrnambool.[57] The Gunditjmara peoples have traditionally farmed eels and fish in a highly organised construction of channels and stone holding areas for thousands of years.[58] The *Water Act 1989* (Vic) does not include permanent access and use of water for native title holders.

New South Wales in terms of national achievement was the only jurisdiction to meet the key priorities identified by the Council of Australian Governments to improve the lives of Indigenous peoples, which included the creation of the NSW Aboriginal Water Trust and the appointment of an Aboriginal Executive Officer to establish and administer the state program.[59]

The Northern Territory legislation does not recognise Aboriginal water rights and interests at all. In s 9 of the *Water Act 1992* (NT), the Crown owns all water.[60]

> The Northern Territory Water Act refers to recreational, social and cultural uses of water, but no reference is made to Aboriginal rights and interests in water.[61]

The *Aboriginal Land Rights Act 1976* (NT) does not allow for the transfer of Crown-owned water to Aboriginal ownership.[62] Research on the water rights of Aboriginal peoples in the Maningrida region highlights the impact of the Northern Territory National Emergency Response legislation in 2007.[63] The legislation initiated a compulsory lease of the Maningrida Township and took compulsory acquisition of Aboriginal assets, including water, bore fields and sacred water sites.[64] The government's compulsory acquisition of Aboriginal property disenfranchised the Maningrida community from exercising their customary water rights and interests and management of their country.

New South Wales

The New South Wales Aboriginal Land Council submission on the Draft National Water Initiative Implementation Plan outlined to the Department of Natural Resources (NSW) that the Draft Plan had failed to adequately promote Aboriginal water rights and interests in the state.[65] The Aboriginal Land Council letter to the Deputy Director General of the department highlighted various issues that did not promote water rights for Aboriginal communities such as: the omission of a mandate for Indigenous representation in water planning and implementation of the Indigenous objectives under the Plan; the need to guarantee Aboriginal peoples access to, and use of water; to allow Aboriginal peoples to participate in the decision-making processes; and to recognise the need for compensation for the loss of Aboriginal water rights and interests.[66]

The New South Wales Aboriginal Land Council emphasised that, irrespective of a determination in native title, Aboriginal peoples are the rightful custodians of their cultural heritage and the prior owners of the lands, the waters and natural resources in their 'country'.[67]

Prior to the establishment of the Aboriginal Water Trust, during negotiations between the New South Wales Government and the New South Wales Native Title Services, the latter requested $250 million to compensate native title holders for their share of the estimated $5 billion value in water trading rights resulting from the introduction of national water reforms impacting on the New South Wales water legislation.[68] The compensation was sought to establish the Aboriginal Water Trust with the financial capacity to purchase water.[69] Instead, the New South Wales Aboriginal Water Trust received five million dollars for the establishment, administration and funding of community activities.[70]

The Aboriginal Water Trust (NSW) was established to facilitate the delivery of potential benefits to Aboriginal communities in New South Wales through funding Aboriginal water enterprise under objectives of the *Water Management Act 2000* (NSW).[71] The New South Wales Cabinet directed that the Aboriginal Water Trust would be incorporated into the State corporate water management plan with a key performance indicator to estimate the volume of water purchased for Aboriginal peoples within the State.[72] Water licences on the 'open market' are highly inflated in price and are held primarily by non-Aboriginal persons or legal entities.[73] To address the limited opportunities for Aboriginal peoples to access the water market and to participate in 'benefit-sharing', the Aboriginal Water Trust was established as a 'protected state project'.[74]

The Department of Natural Resources (NSW) stated that 'a reliance on native title rights to provide benefits to Aboriginal peoples in the state was unlikely to occur'.[75] Furthermore, the Department recognised that 'all water sharing plans should provide for Aboriginal cultural access licences and Aboriginal commercial access licences, in conjunction with the NSW Aboriginal Water Trust'.[76]

In my capacity as the Executive Officer of the NSW Aboriginal Water Trust, and leader of a state water project, I was responsible for generating, assembling and disseminating a range of working papers, discussion papers, briefing papers, reports and correspondence that relate to Indigenous rights and interests in water resources. The significance of these documents lies in their relevance to the emerging Aboriginal water rights dialogue and in the response elicited from state and federal government agencies and other water users. These documents provide an important insight into the development of Aboriginal water policy and a rich source of reference material.[77]

Following a meeting between the NSW Aboriginal Water Trust, and the Indigenous Land Corporation (ILC), the ILC supported a partnership with the Water

Trust to 'enhance the benefits for Aboriginal peoples through combining water and land ownership'.[78]

The successful Aboriginal Water Trust was shelved several years later. The New South Wales Government suspended further grant funding and withheld the accumulated interest owed to the Aboriginal Water Trust on the remaining funds.[79] Following a review of the Aboriginal Water Trust by Andrew Refshauge, a former New South Wales Minister and consultant to the review, the government then dissolved the Aboriginal Water Trust and returned remaining funds to consolidated revenue.[80] The Water Trust has not been replicated anywhere in Australia.

The Aboriginal Water Trust's administrative and grant funding budget of $5 million for the life of the project was insufficient funding to realise significant economic benefits for Aboriginal peoples.[81] The increase in water pricing through water trading and the increased value in commercial water licences significantly impeded the capacity of the Aboriginal Water Trust to purchase Aboriginal water licences because of the modest funding.[82] The allocation of funds by the State Government for purchasing water licences had not included the calculation of the higher cost to purchase water licences as a result of the national water reforms for water trading.[83] The maximum grant of funds to an Aboriginal-owned organisation was approximately three hundred thousand dollars to assist with the modernisation of commercial water infrastructure.[84]

The Draft New South Wales Water Management Business Plan (2006-2007) involves Aboriginal communities only through its heading, 'Indigenous Engagement', which covers the development, construction and implementation of State water projects that are overseen within the corporate structure.[85] There is no inclusion of Aboriginal self-determination or how Aboriginal communities are to be involved in the state water management plan.

> [From] the State 'Water Sharing Workshops' for Aboriginal community groups in New South Wales, the range of Aboriginal participant comments highlighted the lack of government communication and consultation with Aboriginal communities, in conjunction with the State Water Sharing Plans and the post-policy process that was rushed through to suit government timeframes.[86]

The Water Management Division Business Plan (2006-2007) for the Department of Natural Resources (NSW) requires that Indigenous engagement must be undertaken in the development, construction and implementation of State water programs, and water management plans for iconic sites.[87]

The Water Management Principles in the *Water Management Act 2000* (NSW) address Aboriginal cultural values; the legislation refers to the protection of 'geographical and other features of major cultural, heritage or spiritual signif-icance'.[88] However, the legislation is silent on how these benefits of equitable sharing are to be delivered to Aboriginal peoples.

The Objects of the *Water Management Act 2000* (NSW)[89] provide for 'equi-table sharing of water resources'.[90] Further, the objects of the Act are to 'ensure' the flow-on in 'benefits to Aboriginal people in relation to their spiritual, social, customary and economic use of land and water' through the State's provision of 'sustainable and integrated management of water resources'.[91]

In New South Wales the Indigenous principles in the *Water Management Act 2000* (NSW) provide protection to Indigenous areas of significance in s 5(2)(e) in the 'geographical and other features of indigenous significance' and s 5(2)(f) in the 'geographical and other features of major cultural, heritage or spiritual signifi-cance'. There is no indication in the legislation whether these water sites in 'areas of Indigenous significance' are protected water resources under this legislation.

The purpose of the *Water Act 1912* (NSW) was to consolidate legislation relating to water rights, water drainage, drainage promotion and artesian wells. In contrast, the *Water Management Act 2000* (NSW) provides for the protection, conservation and ecologically sustainable development of State water. For example s 55 of the *Water Management Act 2000* (NSW) includes native title rights and Aboriginal ownership not contemplated by the *Water Act 1912*.

Behrendt and Thompson explained that a 'just and equitable sharing of water resources epitomises an act in reconciliation'[92] and the 'implementation of inter-national human rights standards to secure the water rights of Aboriginal people'.[93] They identified the lack of protection and recognition of Aboriginal rights and interests to river systems in New South Wales, and included a number of recom-mendations.[94] The issues remain relevant because the recognition of Aboriginal water rights and interests is still emerging as jurisprudence in Australia. It would appear that mandating Aboriginal water rights and interests needs serious consideration.

Western Australia

This section highlights Aboriginal issues that arise under the National Water Initiative and how the Australian Government's water policy framework has been dealt with by the West Australian Government.

The Draft Water Resources Management Bill (WA) (Draft Water Bill) is modelled on the *Water Management Act 2000* (NSW).[95] Section 55 of the *Water Management Act 2000* (NSW) was adapted for the Western Australian Draft Water Bill, under instructions by the Department of Water 'to limit water use'.[96] The Draft Water Bill provides a broad definition of water resources:

> [a]ll waterways, wetlands, aquifers and groundwater, and all surface or overland flow; adding spring water flowing to the surface on private land, water in privately owned wetlands, and all floodplain and overland flow.[97]

The Draft Water Bill does not account for Aboriginal cultural and spiritual rights and interests in the proposed legislation and there is no inclusion of any economic water value for Aboriginal peoples under the proposed statutory provisions. The Bill recognises that native title holders are defined for the purposes of the *Native Title Act 1993* (Cth) as follows:[98]

> [n]ative title means a non-exclusive right to take and use water for personal, domestic and non-commercial communal purposes (including the purposes of drinking, food preparation, washing, manufacturing traditional artefacts, watering domestic gardens, hunting, fishing and gathering and recreation, cultural and ceremonial purposes).[99]

In drafting the new legislation, the Western Australian Government was reluctant to include native title rights at all:

> A question has arisen should the rights under the proposed Water Resources Management Bill be extended to the registration of Native title interests? If rights are to be extended, the Legislation Reform Branch will require a written policy position on this issue that outlines the justification for this position.[100]

The legal instruction for the Draft Water Bill was centred upon non-Aboriginal rights and interests, with 'a default policy position to maintain the status quo for the consumptive pool regime'.[101] The consumptive pool incorporates all water users in a competitive market-place where pricing is driven by the economic utility values of 'supply and demand'.[102]

The primary policy position of the North Australian Indigenous Land and Sea Management Alliance (NAILSMA) and the Indigenous Water Policy Group, which represents Aboriginal water interests in northern Australia, states 'it is imperative that Indigenous people are allocated rights to the consumptive pool, to ensure that we are not further marginalised.'[103]

The proposal for Aboriginal peoples' water rights to exist within the consumptive pool is short-sighted because the pool includes all water stakeholders with an interest in water. The legal advice for the Draft Water Bill sought to minimise the legal rights of Aboriginal communities stating 'The Minister may restrict native title rights to take water or to protect a water resource and its dependent ecosystems'.[104]

Further, advice on the Draft Water Bill identified a process to quantify water use under native title rights:

> [i]t would be unusual for a determination of native title to specify the maximum amount of water that could be taken or used by native title holders, for instance under section 211(2)(a) of the *Native Title Act*.[105]

In the Draft Water Bill, where native title holders seek to exercise a water right under the *Native Title Act 1993* (Cth), the draft proposes that, if the taking of water exceeds the volume specified, a penalty is likely to be incurred by the native title holder.[106]

Under the *Rights in Water and Irrigation Act 1914* (WA), vesting rights in the State were recognised as follows:[107]

> [t]he right to the use and flow, and to the control, of the water [in various natural water resources] vests in the Crown except where specified in other legislation.[108]

The Western Australian State Solicitor considered that 'the recognition of common law rights and interests in inland waters[109] was settled after the High Court decision in *Western Australia v Ward*' where 'the Court determined that the state held exclusive possession'.[110]

> [T]he vesting of the right to the use, control and management of inland waters in the Crown under the *Rights in Water and Irrigation Act 1914* (WA) have put to rest any possibility of exclusive rights …[111]

The Department of Water proposed that the Draft Water Bill identify the provision for native title holders:

> Subject to there being sufficient unallocated capacity in the system, a maximum of 5% of the water resources identified in the water resource allocation plan as being available for consumption on land subject to native title is to be reserved for use.[112]

Legal definitions in the Draft Water Bill are ambiguous, notably where it is stated that 'allocation' means the 'bucket of water' attached to a water licence or a water access entitlement.[113] The proposed draft would define a 'water access entitlement' under the Water Sharing Plans to mean, 'where a consumptive pool may exist or a consumptive pool that cannot be defined'.[114] The proposed advice raises the potential issue that 'if the amount of water in the native title determination was quantified and statutory legislation or regulations prescribed a cap on taking, then *prima facie* the native title holder may require a licence to exercise a right beyond the prescribed amount'.[115]

Aboriginal communities in Western Australia were not consulted on the Draft Water Bill and this omission brings into question how the state will recognise and implement Aboriginal water use.[116] The government has sought to marginalise native title water requirements, and failed to include a methodology for Aboriginal consumptive water use and address sharing water allocations within a geographically diverse state.[117]

Western Australia's Department of Water developed proposals for statutory water plans without specific consultation with Aboriginal communities, and without ascertaining the nature of Aboriginal water use and cultural ontological values.[118] Aboriginal interests in water were not a government priority in Western Australia's water policy reform.

The Department of Water (WA) considered that allocating water rights to Aboriginal peoples was discriminatory to other water stakeholders,[119] claiming that

[a] reserve of water rights for Aboriginal peoples would be discriminatory for other stakeholders and would create a precedent. The National Water Initiative is to drive water entitlements not a reserved allocation. The Water Trust model initiated in New South Wales is considered a welfare model. The allocation of water via water licences to Aboriginal peoples would be seen as discriminatory to other stakeholders. Allowing Aboriginal cultural values in water *in situ* means where water allocation is currently held by other stakeholders and not a transfer for Aboriginal peoples.[120]

David Collard, the then Indigenous Affairs Coordinator with the Department of Water of Western Australia, highlighted the lack of government engagement in allocating water for Aboriginal peoples:

The Western Australian government have watered down Aboriginal rights and interests … COAG Reconciliation Committee didn't address water or resources for Aboriginal peoples ... Government will look at how much it will cost them and not Aboriginal peoples ... There is no budget for Aboriginal consultation for Aboriginal engagement.[121]

My recommendations to the Department of Water (WA) were for a reserved water allocation for Aboriginal water use outside the consumptive pool.[122] The terms of reference of the report were to take into account the range of water rights and interests of Aboriginal communities and to identify how to incorporate Aboriginal water rights and interests into the State water policy for the proposed Draft Water Bill.[123] However, the Western Australian Government has deferred further action on Indigenous water allocations or entitlements and the Water Bill remains in limbo.[124]

It is surprising and odd that the Draft Water Bill recognises the legal definition of *first rights* water use for non-Aboriginal water licence holders, where a person explores for water, and that their licence 'takes priority over a person applying for a licence to take water'.[125] A water exploration licence holder is afforded greater certainty than Aboriginal water users.

The proposed first rights provision under the Bill was drafted

[t]o protect people who conduct their own investigations for water resources to allow them the first rights to water they have spent time and money in exploring for, over another person who has not done the work for determining the nature of a water resource.[126]

This thought bubble in the Draft Water Bill gives legal certainty for the exploration of water as first rights, which is a non-exclusive right based upon the financial investment expended by the licence holder. Under the same Draft Water Bill a native title holder may hold an exclusive or non-exclusive right to water under the *Native Title Act 1993* (Cth), and it seeks to narrow the exercise of those rights.

The Virginia Simpson Report (2007) argues that Aboriginal participation, in view of the national water reforms, is minimal under the Draft Water Bill, and points out that the economic water use for Aboriginal communities was not included in the draft legislation.[127] Further, the report identifies a lack of progress in the delivery of water services to discrete Aboriginal communities, and points out that the dormancy of Aboriginal participation in Water Sharing Plans was exacerbated by the legislative delay of the Draft Water Bill.[128]

The Simpson Report highlights that 'the consideration of water use for economic purposes in Aboriginal communities is considered a competing threat by governments and non-Aboriginal stakeholders'.[129] The Western Australian Government was provided with policy advice to set aside a reserved water right for Aboriginal peoples, in order that Aboriginal communities are not exposed to unfair competition in the consumptive pool.[130] The state government has not considered incorporating a reserved water allocation.

The approach taken by the Western Australian Government to account for Aboriginal water rights and interests illustrates the weakness of provisions of the National Water Initiative Agreement. The discretionary nature of the National Water Initiatives does not provide certainty for Indigenous access to and use of water resources. The legal advice provided to the government on Aboriginal rights and interests regarding water seek to minimise the legal rights of native title holders and to narrow the cultural interests of Aboriginal communities. As at May 2016 the Draft Water Resources Management Bill has still not progressed in Parliament and the absence of state legislation directly impacts on the ability of Aboriginal communities to access and use consumptive and non-consumptive water.

In drafting the early stages of the Water Bill, the Western Australian Government did not widely consult with Aboriginal communities within the state and does not take into account the range of Aboriginal water use exercised by Aboriginal communities, so as to include, for instance, the cultural context of water, the complex nature of the water landscape within Western Australia and the range of water requirements required by native title holders. The Western Australian case demonstrates the inconsistent implementation of the national water reforms and the gaps in the national legislation that allow the marginalisation of Aboriginal water rights and interests.

Northern Territory

The Northern Territory Government has also been slow to address domestic water access and use, as well as business or economic development in water and the development of Water Allocation Plans.[131] The National Water Initiative has significant policy gaps regarding Aboriginal water rights and interests because of the discretionary nature of the Indigenous clauses.[132]

In the *Water Act 2004* (NT) there is a definition of a generic cultural value, expressed as 'water to meet aesthetic, recreational and cultural needs'. The water legislation does not include Aboriginal cultural values in any of the seven definitions under the environmental and cultural values of water.

The broad reference to 'cultural needs' under the *Water Act 2004* (NT) is an example of the lack of recognition of Aboriginal water values and use. The concept of Aboriginal water use is included as a generic cultural value in the legislation.

Jackson (2006) identifies in her research on 'Indigenous values for water resource management' in the Northern Territory, that the Territory's water legislation defines environmental values as comprising seven categories, including generic social and 'cultural values'.[133]

Aboriginal water issues in Western Australia

My report 'Indigenous Access to Water Entitlements in Western Australia' (2008) provided advice to the Department of Water (WA) on the development of an Aboriginal water policy for Western Australia, and to identify particular water issues and water requirements for Aboriginal peoples.[134] The department was to utilise this report to further develop a state water policy in relation to Indigenous access to water.[135] The recommendations in the report were to inform the government on how to address the broad water rights and interests of Aboriginal communities and the inequitable water allocation and planning strategies for Aboriginal water users.[136] My report was endorsed by the Western Australian Department of Water and the Department's Indigenous Coordinator.

The Report recommended a legislative framework for the Draft Water Resources Management Bill[137] and identified that the legislation should 'recognise and protect the benefits of water resources for Indigenous people and recognise their role in managing water resources'.[138] This legislation should 'include principles of intergenerational equity',[139] 'avoid any contestation with native title holders where aquifer recharge reverts to Crown ownership'[140] and include 'the recognition of native title rights as a class of basic rights'.[141] My recommendations are yet to be acted upon by the Western Australian Government.

The Department of Water delayed the implementation of my report, which set back community consultation and further stalled opportunities to develop Indigenous water policy in Western Australia.[142]

The National Water Initiative and Western Australia

The Implementation Plan for the National Water Initiative (NWI) by the Western Australian Government (2007)[143] (the Plan) provided strategies for adopting the national water reform objectives under the Australian Government's Intergovernmental Agreement with the States and Territories. Western Australia became a signatory to the NWI in 2006.[144]

The Plan sets out comprehensive policy on how the state will meet the national water reform actions under the national agenda, setting aside two pages to deal with Aboriginal engagement in water resource planning.[145] Indigenous water planning is considered for non-consumptive cultural use but the Plan does not consider how native title rights to water will be accounted for.[146]

Under the National Water Initiative reforms, 'a common law right to take naturally occurring water, including from water courses, wetlands, springs, groundwater and unconfined surface water, regulated under a statutory right' was abolished.[147]

The foreword of the Plan 'draws and expands upon extensive consultation undertaken in developing the State Water Strategy, the State Water Plan and a Blueprint for Water Reform in Western Australia'.[148] However, it overlooks the water requirements, as well as the legal rights and interests, of Aboriginal communities.

The Plan indicates that the government 'seeks Indigenous ecological knowledge to make allocations for the environment'.[149] The Plan does not indicate whether Aboriginal community consultations will be forthcoming and how the provision for an environmental water allocation will harmonise with non-consumptive cultural water use. There is also no discussion on how the government will provide intellectual property protection for any Indigenous ecological knowledge that is collected during these community consultations.

The Western Australian Government as a signatory to the Intergovernmental Agreement has agreed to 'allocate water to native title holders and agreed that the allocation will be accounted for under clause 54'.[150] The Western Australian Government suggested capping the volume of water for native title holders. This policy decision is not supported by the Indigenous provisions of the National Water Initiative. The Western Australian Government stated:

> The quantification of water use on Aboriginal lands held under a native title determination should not be restricted under statutory legislation. The draft State Aboriginal Water Policy intends to 'quantify water use for native title holders in Western Australia at 5 per cent'.[151]

The lack of discussion on the geographically and culturally diverse Aboriginal water requirements exhibits a disregard for Aboriginal water rights and interests. Western Australia has significant water resources:

> [t]here are 44 surface water management areas in Western Australia, primarily determined with reference to major river systems and natural catchments ...

into four drainage divisions: Timor Sea, Indian Ocean, South West and Western Plateau.[152]

The *Country Areas Water Supply Act 1947* (WA) outlines the protection of water quality in water catchments and Aboriginal communities have had 'few water catchments proclaimed' where Aboriginal water use exists.[153]

> Aboriginal communities located in remote areas … have a long history of sub-standard services and circumvention of state or local government approval processes, and are affected by legacies of discriminatory practices, of insufficient and *ad hoc* funding and poor quality infrastructure.[154]

A review of natural resource management reports can provide insights for understanding the meaning of water and its use by Aboriginal communities. The 'Indigenous Reconciliation in Primary Industries and Natural Resource Management Annual Report' (2006-2007) reported on themes such as land management, and water management and water supply were introduced as new themes.[155]

As that report identifies, 'water is a critical issue for Natural Resource Management and Primary Industries in Indigenous communities as many communities have [an] unreliable water source or lack of potable water'.[156] The Annual Report highlights several critical factors in achieving success in Indigenous communities such as 'recognising the diversity in the process of applying Indigenous knowledge and traditions', 'ensuring outcomes beyond individual projects', providing 'a long-term commitment and ongoing support by governments in a multi-agency approach' and the need to 'build capacity for Indigenous communities to manage and implement programs'.[157]

Glen Kelly, Chief Executive Officer of the South West Aboriginal Land and Sea Council[158] in Western Australia, expressed concerns that the Western Australian Government has failed to address Aboriginal water issues:[159]

> [i]n relation to Nyoongar customary value in water resources there is an absence in statutory water provisions by government in accepting the Nyoongar identification in the cultural and spiritual environmental values of Nyoongar connection to aquifers, ground water replenishment, water quality and other water knowledge.[160]

Aboriginal peoples' relationship with groundwater and the cultural water values as documented in the 'Gnangara Mound Study' (2005) of the Swan Coastal Plain in Western Australia, traditional lands and waters of the Nyoongar peoples,[161] contrast with historic observations and records by non-Indigenous researchers which interpret Aboriginal values through the lens of Western social values.

Daisy Bates, who is regularly quoted in the 'Study of the Gnangara Mound', described Aboriginal peoples in Australia through the social values of her time:

> So far as their origin is concerned, that, too, belongs to the dreamtime. I am doubtful that it will ever be established, except in theory. I do not regard them as a race apart, but as a mixture, a nomad people picking up scraps of racial character in their different environments, and at last, in primitive Australia, gravitating to the primitive life that they have led here for centuries.[162]

Bates' observations by modern standards are offensive and disturbing. When research and interpretation is collated about Aboriginal peoples, and filtered through Western concepts and the framework of ethnographic literature, Aboriginal values in water are misrepresented. It is necessary to develop water policy and legislative frameworks through the active participation of Aboriginal peoples.

The Aboriginal community consultation and workshop facilitated by the Department of Water (WA) for Nyoongar communities to participate in the South West Water Plan review provided substantial advice to the department and an opportunity for Nyoongar participants to question technical water experts and government representatives.[163] I was invited as a guest speaker to address the Nyoongar community about the opportunities in the commercial water market which were provided by the NSW Aboriginal Water Trust.[164] The final workshop report from the department provided considerable evidence of the ongoing relationship of Nyoongar communities to water, and of the definitive Nyoongar knowledge on the cultural and spiritual water values that inform and frame Nyoongar identity to 'country'.[165]

The nexus in the health status of remote and discrete Aboriginal communities in Western Australia is significant because the 'Report for the Minister for Water Resources on Water Services in Discrete Indigenous Communities' (2006)[166] identifies that essential water services are not delivered for '300 discrete Indigenous communities'.[167]

The Report highlights the need for a 'specific policy advisor on water services for Indigenous communities'[168] to address the 'poor water infrastructure and operational maintenance',[169] and the 'elevated levels of uranium, arsenic and heavy metals which contravene the revised Australian Drinking Water Quality Guidelines';[170] and the need for 'whole-of-government responsibility and investment in providing legislated standards of water services to discrete Aboriginal communities'.[171] A journalist noted that 'Western Australia mining provides $334 billion of budget windfall for the Federal Government and [is] a substantial contributor to Australia's gross domestic product'.[172]

There is, however, a significant disparity in the state's investment and commitment to Indigenous water requirements and health conditions in discrete and remote Western Australia.

> In Western Australia Aboriginal communities did not receive $700 million in government funding for water services and infrastructure because Aboriginal communities refused to sign Shared Responsibility Agreements because it suspends their human rights.[173]

This chapter has demonstrated that Aboriginal communities have not been accorded a fair entitlement to water rights and interests where competing rights exist. Although the New South Wales water management legislation has provisions to protect and recognise Aboriginal water requirements, government policy and legislation has not delivered actual long-term benefits, apart from a short period of success during the operation of the Aboriginal Water Trust.

It is argued that the two-tier system of tradeable water licences for non-Aboriginal licence holders and non-tradeable water licences for Aboriginal communities reflects the inadequate level of government support for the economic development of Aboriginal communities. The lack of national and state commitment for a guaranteed reserved Aboriginal water right limits the opportunities for Aboriginal communities to exercise their customary and economic rights and impacts on receiving basic human rights.

Geoffrey Robertson QC, a human rights barrister, argues that 'the common law has been found to be defective', and, as the next chapter demonstrates, 'the application of human rights principles to balance judicial reasoning' is justified.[174]

Chapter 11

HUMAN RIGHTS –
INCORPORATING ABORIGINAL WATER RIGHTS

In 2009 the *Sydney Morning Herald* reported that, in the New South Wales town of Toomelah, Aboriginal peoples shared one water tap with hundreds of other community members and Aboriginal children played in raw sewage.[1] Recognised minimum standards of international human rights have little effect on the status quo among rural and remote Aboriginal regions and are hardly improving the living standards of Aboriginal communities.

Earlier chapters demonstrate that water requirements require responsive management processes to allocate the available water resources during drought cycles and to ensure water quality for human consumption. However, the chapters identify that Aboriginal communities in Australia have an inferior standard of water rights, water service delivery, water entitlements or allocations, and water management, with limited representation within the National Water Initiative framework. Aboriginal concepts of water within an Aboriginal ontological framework have not featured in any prominence in this nation's water paradigm.

This chapter examines the relevance of human rights instruments for securing water rights for Aboriginal peoples in Australia and whether Aboriginal water rights and interests are adequately protected under these instruments under Australian water law and policy. In an integrated analysis of domestic and international human rights, the chapter reflects on how these standards and principles strengthen the argument for Aboriginal water rights and interests to be recognised in Australian policy framework and water legislation – which is essential to reforming water management.

The chapter discusses whether human rights regimes can effectively influence the domestic recognition and protection of basic guarantees of international human rights instruments, which assert the inherent right of Indigenous peoples to water resources.

The book has examined the limited recognition of Aboriginal peoples' rights and interests in water within various jurisdictions across Australia. The framework of water rights and interests for Aboriginal communities under the 'Indigenous Access' Clauses of the National Water Initiative does not include the provision of human rights protection in the national reforms.

Australian water legislation does not formally recognise the inherent nature of Indigenous water rights as a platform for cultural and economic development. In the absence of human rights principles for Indigenous peoples in the national water reform process, there is a legal impediment to Aboriginal peoples claiming water rights and asserting ownership of water resources on Aboriginal-owned lands and where Aboriginal interests in water exist.

Michael O'Donnell, in his report 'Indigenous Water Rights in Northern Australia' (2011), notes that 'Indigenous rights to water are seen as an incident of the principle of self-determination and not part of domestic Australian policy'.[2] O'Donnell states that 'in terms of government water policy under the National Water Initiative and State and Territory water management legislation that there is a long way to go in meeting international standards for Indigenous participation'.[3]

Matthew Rigney, Ngarrindjeri and Chair of the Ngarrindjeri Native Title Management Committee, expressed to the National Water Commission that the 'separation of land and water should be considered a genocidal activity because Aboriginal peoples belong to the water'.[4]

International law – Standards and Principles

International law before 1945 was not generally concerned with how nation states treated individuals within their domestic sovereign borders; there were some exceptions but they were limited in scope.[5] The process in reaching the ratification of international instruments is said to consist of 'slow processes and lengthy, complex drafting that is debated within ideological and political battlefields'.[6] Although traditional international law existed before the adoption of the *Charter of the United Nations (1945)*, the Charter's extensive body of international and regional human rights law expanded human rights doctrine.[7]

John Rawls' 'A Theory of Justice' (1971) was significant in forming the modern development of human rights, as Rawls's theory is said to have introduced 'principles of justice to define the rights and duties of universal citizenship'.[8] In understanding the broader role of justice in defining water rights and interests of Indigenous peoples in Australia, the national framework of water policy and law would provide a more contextual analysis of Indigenous human rights. In relation to international human rights principles the enjoyment of substantive human rights for Indigenous peoples in Australia is put by Erica-Irene A Daes: 'society and governments have to align in the right political and social climate to support a shared autonomy'.[9]

Not all human rights instruments articulate every facet of a right or interest, for example, in the *International Covenant on Civil and Political Rights 1976* (ICCPR) 'the economic, social and cultural rights do not include the rights to property'.[10] Aboriginal water rights and interests should be based upon on the principle of justice and a shared autonomy, where the creation of substantive rights to access and use water is based upon Aboriginal ontological water concepts.

The *United Nations Declaration on the Rights of Indigenous Peoples 2007* (UNDRIP) in Article 26 expresses an Indigenous right to resources:

> Indigenous peoples have the right to own, develop, control and use the lands and territories, including the total environment of the lands, air, waters, coastal seas, sea-ice flora, fauna and other resources which they have traditionally owned and otherwise occupied or used. This includes the right to the full recognition of their laws, traditions, and customs, land-tenure systems and institutions for the development and management of resources, and the right to effective measures by States to prevent any interference with, alienation of or encroachment upon these rights.[11]

Further, Article 29 of UNDRIP states:

> Indigenous peoples are entitled to the recognition of the full ownership, control and protection of their cultural and intellectual property and have the right to special measures to control, develop and protect their science, technologies and cultural manifestations, including … seeds, medicines, knowledge of the properties of fauna and flora, oral traditions …[12]

The Rudd Federal Government endorsed UNDRIP and recognised the declarations influence on '*Closing the Gap*', to respond to the endemic disadvantage burdening many Aboriginal communities in Australia.[13] Incorporation of these articles in developing water policy and legislation would duly recognise a legal right to water and extend beyond mere dialogue on Aboriginal values in water.

In the *United Nations Declaration on the Rights of Indigenous Peoples* (2007), Articles 25, 26 and 27 deal with the recognition and protection of water rights. Article 25 states:

Indigenous peoples have the right to maintain and strengthen their distinctive spiritual relationship with their traditionally owned or otherwise occupied and used lands, territories, waters and coastal seas and other resources and to uphold their responsibilities to future generations in this regard.[14]

Article 25 articulates the principles of intergenerational equity and that Indigenous rights require protection so as to enable Indigenous peoples to develop and control their water resources. This includes Aboriginal-owned land and other tenure or Aboriginal occupation that is recognised under land rights legislation such as native title and township leases. Article 26 states:

1. Indigenous peoples have the right to the lands, territories and resources which they have traditionally owned, occupied or otherwise used or acquired.

2. Indigenous peoples have the right to own, use, develop and control the lands, territories and resources that they possess by reason of traditional ownership or other traditional occupation or use, as well as those which they have otherwise acquired.

3. States shall give legal recognition and protection to these lands, territories and resources. Such recognition shall be conducted with due respect to the customs, traditions and land tenure systems of the indigenous peoples concerned.[15]

Article 26(2) acknowledges that Aboriginal peoples have the right to control their resources, including water. In view of Article 26(3) these resources are to be afforded legal recognition and protection by the nation-state, and Aboriginal peoples are to 'exercise these rights as they see fit'.[16] Further, Article 27 states:

The States shall establish and implement, in conjunction with indigenous peoples concerned, a fair, independent, impartial, open and transparent process, giving due recognition to indigenous peoples' laws, traditions, customs and land tenure systems, to recognize and adjudicate the rights of indigenous peoples pertaining to their lands, territories and resources.[17]

James Anaya, former UN Special Rapporteur on the Rights of Indigenous Peoples, has reported upon 'the status of human rights and fundamental freedoms of Indigenous peoples in Australia', and observes that the recognition and application of these international law standards in the *United Nations Declaration on the Rights of Indigenous Peoples*[18] should be incorporated by the Australian Government in water, land and natural resource reforms:

The strengthening of legislative and administrative protections for indigenous peoples' rights over lands and natural resources should involve aligning those protections with applicable international standards, in particular those articulated in the Declaration on the Rights of Indigenous Peoples ... the Declaration effectively rejects a strict requirement of continuous occupation or cultural connection from the time of European contact in order for indigenous peoples to maintain interests in lands, affirming simply that rights exist by virtue of traditional ownership or other traditional occupation or use.[19]

Anaya observes that the high threshold of evidential proof required in the Australian native title system is not a requirement for recognition under international legal standards. Within the context of this observation, Anaya instructs that Australia's water legislation should recognise and protect Aboriginal rights to natural resources and that domestic legislation should incorporate international human rights standards.

Victoria Tauli Corpuz, Special Rapporteur on the Rights of Indigenous Peoples, reported to the UN General Assembly,[20] noting that Indigenous peoples account for 5 per cent of the world's population, while representing 15 per cent of those living in poverty. As many as 33 per cent of all people living in extreme rural poverty globally are from indigenous communities. Those figures are particularly alarming given the wealth in natural resources that are located within Indigenous territories.

The North Australian Indigenous Land and Sea Management Alliance emphasised that in order 'to maintain and strengthen Aboriginal peoples' spiritual relationship with their traditional owned territories and water it requires incorporating the *United Nations Declaration on the Rights of Indigenous Peoples* into Australia's water management regime'.[21]

Article 32.2 of the Declaration[22] recognises the rights of Indigenous peoples to the commercial use and development of water on traditional territories, through the principles of self-determination.[23] Article 32.2 of the *UN Declaration on the Rights of Indigenous Peoples* requires 'free, prior and informed consent of Indigenous peoples such as for lands, water and resources'. Indigenous individual and collective rights for Aboriginal water knowledge will gain status when it is incorporated into Australian law.

The National Water Initiative and State and Territory legislation do not currently comply with the international legal standards expressed in the *United Declaration on the Rights of Indigenous Peoples*. The Declaration points out that Aboriginal water rights are inherent primary rights in the stakeholder hierarchy.

According to international human rights standards Aboriginal water rights are unique. If the Australian Government incorporated Aboriginal water rights as human rights, then Aboriginal communities would be free to exercise their water rights through a more effective and fairer system.

It is not appropriate for Aboriginal water rights to be recognised by the Australian Government as merely rights of just another stakeholder group or special interest group. This policy approach has been adopted towards Aboriginal groups in the Murray-Darling Basin, by allocating water rights and interests of industry, irrigators, agricultural production and the environment above that of the First Peoples.

Tim Fisher presented a briefing in 1996 which highlights the lobbying power of industry in shaping policy:

> Irrigator groups, such as the NSW Irrigators Council, have raised the issue formally with state departments. They want freehold title to water with guaranteed security. ARMCANZ ... recommends that water entitlements should wherever possible be perpetual.[24]

The Australian Federal Government proposed to formally support the *United Nations Declaration on the Rights of Indigenous Peoples*,[25] as confirmed by Murray Radcliffe of the National Water Commission at the Indigenous Water Focus Group in Adelaide in 2008, prior to the government's formal announcement. However, the Australian Government failed to consult with Aboriginal communities on how to give effect to the Declaration, and other human rights standards, and this does not augur well for future reform in Australian water policy and recognition and protection of Aboriginal rights and interests in water resources.

The Australian Government has endorsed the *United Nations Declaration on the Rights of Indigenous Peoples* (2007), where Indigenous water rights are expressed in Articles 8, 20, and 24 through to 32. Indigenous water rights and interests in the Declaration are yet to be implemented in Australian water laws to protect the rights to water of Indigenous peoples. Because successive governments have failed to view the National Water Initiative within a human rights paradigm there is a significant negative impact on Aboriginal communities.

The United Nations declares access to water to be a human right.[26] The *International Labour Indigenous and Tribal Peoples Convention* (1989), ratified by seventeen countries, expressed provisions for Indigenous control over natural resources in Article 15 of the Convention:[37]

The rights of the peoples concerned to the natural resources pertaining to their lands shall be specifically safeguarded. These rights include the right of these peoples to participate in the use, management and conservation of these resources.[28]

Prominent principles of water resource management also appear in other international instruments – for instance, in the Dublin Principles (United Nations 1992), the water policies of the World Bank (1993, 2003), and those of the Asian Development Bank (2001).[29] The *Indigenous Peoples Kyoto Water Declaration* (2003) recognises the international law paradigm in Indigenous rights to water to include the ownership, control and management of lands, natural resources and traditional territory; the exercise of customary law; Indigenous representation in Indigenous institutions; the free, prior and informed consent to land development and to control and share the benefits of traditional knowledge.[30] The *Indigenous Peoples Kyoto Water Declaration* also includes the 'right to self-determination to exercise in full authority, control and as permanent sovereignty over water and other natural resources'.[31]

The right of Indigenous peoples to self-determination is affirmed under the United Nations Charter and other treaties, where many jurists consider it to be a customary norm, if not *jus cogens*.[32] While many disagree about what the terms 'peoples' and 'self-determination' mean, there is an international consensus that Indigenous claims should be recognised according to the principles of self-determination.[33]

Australia's Constitutions – more than words?

Kirby J in *Western Australia v Ward*[34] critiqued the reasoning by von Doussa J where the latter states that 'the legal recognition of Aboriginal property rights would fracture the skeletal principles of the common law'.[35] Kirby J responds that:

Skeletal principles are not immutable. When they offend values of justice and human rights, they can no longer command unquestioning adherence. A balancing exercise must be undertaken to determine whether, if the rule were overturned, the disturbance would be disproportionate to the benefit flowing from the overturning.[36]

The historic over-allocation of water resources by successive Australian governments was implemented without any regard to Aboriginal water rights and human rights. The rights and interests of Indigenous peoples have also been overridden in other areas of Australian policy.

Under section 109 of the Australian Constitution, the *Racial Discrimination Act* can operate to override any State or Territory legislation which contravenes its provisions … it can be overridden by the express legislative intent of the Commonwealth Parliament, as happened with the 1998 *Native Title Act Amendments*. The Federal government does have the legislative power to fully incorporate its obligations under International Convention on the Elimination of Racial Discrimination.[37]

George Williams has emphasised that the *Racial Discrimination Act 1975* (Cth) has proven vulnerable to political policy change, where 'the Act has been over-ridden twice in ten years'.[38]

[I]n 1998 for native title and in 2007 for the Northern Territory Intervention, a federal law provided that if it was racially discriminatory it was to operate despite the Racial Discrimination Act.[39]

The constitutional entrenchment of Aboriginal peoples' legal rights and interests has not been attempted in the *Australian Constitution*. There is no Aboriginal right inherent in the *Australian Constitution* to recognise, for example, a 'right to own, conserve and manage natural resources', as exists in s 35(1) of the Canadian Charter of Rights,[40] where, Canadian Aboriginal title is a 'constitutionally protected property right'.[41] Australia's states have symbolically recognised Aboriginal and Torres Strait Islander peoples in their constitutions in a statement, either inserted in the preamble or in a provision within the State and Territory Constitutiona that does not create legal rights and interests or give rise to legal action.[42]

There is a national dialogue on recommendations to amend the *Australian Constitution* to provide substantial improvement for Indigenous recognition and laws to protect Indigenous Australians from discrimination and to ensure that any laws made on behalf of Indigenous communities are beneficial. A national referendum on such changes will require significant support from all Australians. The Expert Panel on Constitutional Recognition of Aboriginal and Torres Strait Islander Peoples, appointed by the Australian Government, proposed a range of recommendations for consideration.[43] There is no firm commitment by the Australian Government when, or if, a referendum will take place.

Hill J proposed a Bill of Rights for Australia and highlighted that 'Chapter III of the *Australian Constitution* could be modelled on the provisions of Article III of the United States Constitution (1791); the *Australian Constitution* did not include the American model of entrenched rights'[44] because of 'the rigidity of its constitutional framework and laws'.[45]

> The fact [that] there is no real push for an enacted bill of rights in Australia may be the result either of apathy or satisfaction with the present system (or, which may be the same thing, at least no real dissatisfaction with it).[46]

Government opinion has generally dismissed the consideration of human rights in a constitutional instrument. The *Australian Constitution* is administrative in character whereas the United States Constitution expresses the role of government in a relationship with its citizens. Amar has summed up the American Constitution, saying:

> [the] brevity and bluntness of the document and its intimate relation to the central narrative of the American people make it a brilliant focal point drawing together ordinary citizens ...[47]

The Federal Government initiated the National Human Rights Consultation in 2008 to call for public submissions on how human rights and responsibilities should be protected in Australian society.[48] Submissions were to indicate society's preference for a statutory Bill of Rights or Charter of Rights to frame and protect society.[49] The Federal Government has confirmed that the United States Bill of Rights model, which is constitutionally entrenched, will not be considered.[50]

> The most important feature of a charter is a provision requiring the courts to interpret legislation, wherever possible, in a way consistent with the charter's recognition of rights.[51]

The National Human Rights Consultation Committee's, 'National Human Rights Consultation Report' (2009) indicates that from the 29,153 submissions there was support for a human rights act, and a random telephone survey had shown 87.4 per cent support for the introduction of a human rights act.[52] The 31 recommendations in the Human Rights Report also include the protection of civil and political rights and the possible inclusion of social and economic rights.[53]

The vulnerability of Aboriginal peoples has been amplified under the suspension or amendment of statutory legislation – for example, the Australian Government's suspension of the *Racial Discrimination Act 1975* (Cth), diminished the rights of Aboriginal peoples in Australia.[54] This clearly demonstrates the limitations of international law principles even when these principles have been incorporated into domestic law.

> Disparities between riparian nations – whether in economic development, infra-structural capacity, or political orientation – add further complications to water

resources development, institutions, and management. As a consequence, development, treaties, and institutions are regularly seen as, at best, inefficient: often ineffective; and occasionally, as a new source of tensions themselves.[55]

Tom Calma, of Kungarakan and Iwaidja peoples, and former Aboriginal and Torres Strait Islander Social Justice Commissioner, commented that the question of Aboriginal rights 'is left to the whim of government, where each jurisdiction in Australia has different procedural requirements'.[56] Since *Mabo* Australian governments have watered down the *Native Title Act 1993* (Cth) through statutory amendment. Without a modern treaty agreement with governments, the legal recognition of Aboriginal rights and interests in water, natural resources and land, remains tenuous.

There is a plethora of international instruments in law intended to urge nation states to provide international human rights standards for Indigenous peoples and to ensure active Indigenous participation within all levels of water governance, management and its use.

> The Aboriginal cultural concept of waters, as with the land and resources, would however be misinterpreted by a range of Western trained professionals such as lawyers, anthropologists and the judiciary. The representatives of non-Aboriginal interest groups to water, governments and the legal system itself have struggled under the 'fragility of the legal concept of native title' and Aboriginal water rights.[57]

Aboriginal peoples in Australia do not hold entrenched constitutional rights to water resources or the legal recognition of Aboriginal water rights as a human right under Australian law. The implication for Aboriginal water rights in Australia under the proposed statutory federal model has been discussed by Wilcox J, who compares it with the entrenched rights in the Canadian *Constitution 1982, Charter of Rights and Freedoms*:[58]

> [p]ublic servants and parliamentary counsel [believed] that one of the great consequences of the Canadian Charter was that it effectively required Ministers, and their Departments, to build human rights values into the scheme of their draft bills.[59]

Australian barrister Julian Burnside suggests that 'Australian society is unaware of the standard of rights because our society assumes they exist'.[60]

> Australians have a strong instinct for human rights. Although Australia does not have a written bill of rights, we havwe a shared sense that some ideals are basic to our society. Most of the basic elements of a constitutional democracy are found in

our constitution, but others are taken for granted: we tacitly accept them as basic and inalienable.[61]

Burnside (2007) argues that the value judgements which found currency in Australian society during the Howard Government, and were reflected in decreasing Australian support for the broad spectrum of human rights, has reinforced the notion of 'otherness'.[62]

> Australia's human rights record has been seriously damaged by our treatment of refugees. It will not be repaired by the cinematic simplicities of Russell Crowe. Utilitarianism [was] used in the eighteenth century to justify slavery, in the nineteenth century to justify child labour, and in the twentieth century to justify the Nazi's treatment of the Jews …[63]

Aboriginal peoples in Australia lack the historic and contemporary legal recognition of their inherent sovereignty. By the continued amendments to statutory and Commonwealth laws such as native title, water resources and the suspension of the *Racial Discrimination Act 1975* (Cth) to allow for the Northern Territory Emergency Response (the Intervention) into Aboriginal communities it is clear that Aboriginal peoples have little control over their future. In the absence of a federal treaty, which is being discussed more widely in Australia, there is no foundational legal document or agreement to restore Aboriginal peoples individual and collective rights and interests to land, waters and resources.

> The commodification of culture is a critical aspect of globalisation and has direct impact on Indigenous societies and ongoing survival of the local markets operating within them. Recent experience in Australia should highlight the fact that rights that have been recognised in the past – native title and heritage protection – can be extinguished …[64]

Richard Bartlett (2001), in summarising treaties and agreements negotiated in other common law countries, states:

> The policy and practice in Canada is dramatically different from that in Australia. The Canadian policy of reaching settlements by agreement has worked … The objectives of securing a bridge between traditional and contemporary approaches to development, and providing certainty and clarity for land and resource use and management, are being achieved … such objectives are being achieved without the gross denial of equality, or the ludicrously wasteful expenditure of the processes of the Native Title Act.[66]

Dialogue on a Federal Charter of Rights or a Bill of Rights for Australia has provided the opportunity to openly debate and examine whether Australia's legal system incorporates the values of our times. In relation to Aboriginal water rights, the failure to have entrenched legal protection for Aboriginal peoples is also a primary reason for the continued uncertainty in law and policy planning. In this context the exercise of cultural and economic rights will continue to be problematic for Aboriginal communities.

Former President of the Australian Human Rights Commission, Catherine Branson, argues that Australia's system of democracy has failed to protect human rights:

> We have not been confident that our democratically elected representatives had the possible implications of the laws made clear to them … for example, sedition laws, mandatory detention laws and the Northern Territory Response.[66]

Although both federal and state laws may recognise the existence of certain rights and protections in human rights, the mechanisms to implement human rights standards such as the right to water or the principles of self-determination for Aboriginal peoples cannot be presently enforced.

> The *Human Rights Act 2004* (ACT), the first Bill of Rights in Australia, has no provision for Aboriginal peoples to claim land or waters such as native title; land title is held under Commonwealth leases in the territory.[67]

In the Preamble of the *Human Rights Act 2004* (ACT) (ACT Act) there is recognition of Indigenous peoples which states, 'although human rights belong to all individuals, they have special significance for Indigenous people, the first owners of this land, members of its most enduring cultures, and individuals for whom the issue of rights protection has great and continuing importance'.[68] 'The *Human Rights Act* should be viewed as supporting the special agreements already existing between Indigenous people … for service delivery, land agreements and protection of other rights and development of protocols'.[69]

In s 27 of the *ACT Act* (Rights of Minorities) it states that 'anyone who belongs to an ethnic, religious or linguistic minority must not be denied the right, with other members of the minority, to enjoy his or her culture, to declare and practice his or her religion, or to use his or her language'.[70] There is no specific mention of Indigenous peoples and their rights under the legislation.

The *Charter of Human Rights and Responsibilities Act 2006* (Vic) includes recognition of Aboriginal peoples and their status as 'First Peoples' and recognition of cultural rights. However, the jurisdiction of the *Charter* to hear a legal cause of action in relation to denying a right to water is untested.[71] Section 19(2) (Cultural rights) of the *Charter* states:

> Aboriginal persons hold distinct cultural rights and must not be denied the right, with other members of their community:
> (a) to enjoy their identity and culture; and
> (b) to maintain and use their language; and
> (c) to maintain their kinship ties; and
> (d) to maintain their distinctive spiritual, material and economic relationship with the land and waters and other resources with which they have a connection under traditional laws and customs.

The Preamble of the *Charter* states that 'human rights have a special importance for the Aboriginal people of Victoria, as descendants of Australia's first people, with their diverse spiritual, social, cultural and economic relationship with their traditional lands and waters'. The *Charter* covers a class of rights that are predominantly civil and political rights, based on rights in the *International Covenant on Civil and Political Rights*, to which Australia is a party.[72]

In Colmar Brunton's research on the impact of the *Charter* the findings are relevant to advance the inclusion of water rights: 24 per cent of applicants accessed the *Act* under the Cultural Rights provision and 3 per cent of the applicant cases were based upon human rights law and native title.[73] The inclusion of water rights in the *Act* would provide for Aboriginal peoples to apply to an administrative body to hear their complaint.

There is no evidence that either the *Charter* or the *Human Rights Act 2004* (ACT) protects the rights of Aboriginal peoples or meets the expectations of protecting those rights. Article 17 of the *Universal Declaration of Human Rights and the International Convention on the Elimination of All Forms of Racial Discrimination* has implemented limited protection for Aboriginal peoples in Australia.[74]

In 2006 Amnesty International Australia commissioned a poll of 1001 voters by Morgan Research and reported that 61 per cent of people believed that a national Charter of Rights already operates in Australia.[75] The existing legislation fails to protect Aboriginal rights and interests to self-determine and manage water resources in Australia. Empowerment for Aboriginal peoples would be advanced by the incorporation of water rights, as a human rights principle into Australian domestic law.

In recent comments by Australia's Deputy Prime Minister, Barnaby Joyce, on whether Australia was "settled" or "invaded" by the British, Mr Joyce rejected the use of the word "invasion" saying, "my view is that if you are going to have an invasion, you need an army".[76] In fact the British Government in 1788 did invade this Aboriginal continent, by sending convicts, officials and the British Marine Corps.

Indigenous Water Declaration

Following the Garma Water Conference in 2008 a small Indigenous group of Garma participants, including the author, drafted the 'International Indigenous Water Declaration'. The Preamble of the Garma International Indigenous Water Declaration (2008) states:

> Recognising and Reaffirming that the Indigenous peoples of the World are and have been since time immemorial sovereign over their own lands and waters and that Indigenous peoples obtain their spiritual and cultural identity, life and livelihood from their lands and waters.[77]

The body of this Declaration calls on the States to 'fully adopt, implement and adhere to the international instruments recognising the rights of Indigenous peoples to land and water'.[78] Collings and Falk (2008) highlight that national water reforms in Australia are 'modest' – particularly the Indigenous clauses 52 to 54 of the National Water Initiative.[79] The National Water Initiative does not incorporate recognition of Indigenous water rights and interests as they are expressed under international instruments; nor has the Australian Government adopted the 'Garma International Indigenous Water Declaration' as a framework for articulating Indigenous rights to water. Without a national Indigenous framework that clearly expresses international standards, Australian governments will, in all likelihood, continue to give a low priority to Indigenous water rights and interests.

In collaboration with the United Nations University of Traditional Knowledge, the North Australia Indigenous Land and Sea Management Alliance and the Indigenous Water Policy Group, the Indigenous delegates at the Garma Water Conference produced a framework for a declaration of Indigenous Water rights to be presented at the 2009 World Water Forum in Turkey.[80] Following several drafts, it became clear that Indigenous perspectives on water were not dealing with the potential impact of the commercial exploitation of water and any advance to the debate on rights was set aside.

The Preamble of the Draft Indigenous Water Declaration (2009) states that 'we do not believe that water should solely be treated as a resource or a commodity' and that 'water is a being with a spirit'.[81] The Draft Water Declaration also stated that Indigenous peoples have 'inherent rights in water, including customary, cultural, economic, potable use, sanitation requirements and the control of water planning and allocation'.[82] The method for exercising these rights was not clearly articulated in the draft document and there was a compromise in the language and definitions used mainly to emphasize solidarity in Indigenous water rights.

The Draft Water Declaration did not attempt to reflect the history of water rights under the government system that relates to Australian law, nor the absence of domestic treaties and entrenched rights that are to be found in other countries. The Draft Water Declaration took the form of a generic international declaration, and the substance of the declaration was framed in language more reminiscent of international law instruments.

Nor did the Draft Water Declaration address the particular objectives and policy strategies regarding water rights for Indigenous peoples in Australia. I was deciding whether to endorse the Draft Water Declaration at that time, and decided against the endorsement because I believed the cultural, political and economic position of Indigenous peoples in Australia was poorly represented in the jointly drafted document. In essence, substance was being sacrificed in order to incorporate the particular views of a number of visiting Indigenous delegates, however well meaning.

This experience of drafting a declaration with international Indigenous peoples highlights the degrees of difference in perspective on water rights among Indigenous peoples. Notwithstanding our shared values and beliefs regarding water, the drafting process and the generic language used in this instrument watered down the water policy position and the recognition sought by Indigenous peoples in Australia.

Ethical principles: A water management benchmark

The lack of a water ethics discourse in Australian water management policy results in a serious deficiency of moral and legal commentary and critique on the competing water rights and interests and ethical benchmarks regarding the state of consumptive and non-consumptive water allocation. The national water reform policy and legislative framework have failed to recognise the ethical parameters of Australia's water governance arrangements.

Ethical standards and measurable indicators which relate to the impact of water property rights and allocations on Aboriginal-owned land and native title have yet to be framed. In relation to the national water market, there is a policy gap in Australia, where private and public financial investment is not assessed or measured for 'best practice', nor assessed on whether the proposed financial investment in the water market, and projects dependent on freshwater supplies, have negative impacts on Indigenous communities and other water users.

In recent times the introduction of ethical investment standards for environmental projects has raised the bar for establishing ethical principles for industry projects. One example of applying ethical considerations to financial investment and project development has been established by 'the international banking community under the Equator Principles, which provides a voluntary code of conduct for responsible project financing'.[83] The Equator Principles is a landmark agreement signed by some of the world's banks, agreeing 'not to finance projects that endanger communities or the environment'.[84]

The Equator Principles model could be used as a framework with water resources, to assess where there will be impact on Indigenous communities, governments and corporate entities in Australia, and those who seek to develop water intensive projects would be required to codify a framework of ethical water principles and implement a rigorous assessment of proposed projects to identify whether they are a socially responsible investment. Where such projects have high water extraction and the possible contamination of watercourses, projects could be refused investment capital by those banking institutions that are signatory to the framework principles.

The adoption of an Equator Principles model would also support the principles of environmental integrity in national water policy and water legislation. Currently, commercial investments in water projects do not have to adhere to any principles of ethics in water or corporate responsibility in water enterprise.

The Westpac Bank of Australia and the Australia New Zealand (ANZ) Bank are corporate signatories to the Equator Principles[85] and, as signatories, should fund financial investments in commercial projects only where the project is environmentally responsible. The contentious Gunns' pulp mill in northern Tasmania was partially funded by the ANZ Bank. The Tasmanian mill project received consistent criticism in the media in relation to the mill's potential toxic chemical residue that could contaminate the ocean and endanger important sea-life colonies.[86]

Due to the intense media coverage, the ANZ withdrew capital funding from the A\$2 billion Tasmanian mill project – an action underpinned by the bank's commitment to environmental corporate responsibility.[87] A potential investor, the Richard Chandler Corporation, pulled out of a bid for a large stake in Gunns' Tamar Valley pulp mill.[88] The Tasmanian Premier backed the Gunns project, and commented that 'it was quite alarming that big business could be undermined by small minority groups'.[89]

The inclusion of ethical principles framed with cultural integrity could provide the necessary checks and balances to the national water reforms and the National Water Initiative. The flow-on effect of establishing a benchmark of ethical principles in the use of water resources has the capacity to address the cultural and environmental concerns of Aboriginal peoples in relation to the high level of water extraction by industry under government-supported projects. In addition, proposed water projects which have unsustainable water requirements, such as high extraction levels of water and mining processes with significant potential for contamination of water resources, could have their funding withheld. What is required is

[a] foundation of identifying water ethics in drafting water interests … [and] ethical practices [that] underpin all policy, legislation and the private and public sector management of water.[90]

The Australian water policy position on the allocation and use of water resources would benefit from ethically informed government decision making and accountability. An ethical code of conduct is also required for water intensive projects or those that impact significantly upon water resources – fresh-water and marine. Australian governments have failed to adequately protect water resources required by Aboriginal peoples and to limit commercial projects which entail high environmental risk to contaminate or over-exploit water resources.

To ameliorate the poor living standards of Aboriginal peoples and advance the protection of their water rights requires more than merely acknowledging international law principles and standards or incorporating them into Australian law. It also requires a framework of ethical principles in national water policy and state and territory water legislation, to independently assess commercial projects as socially responsible investments.

The international standards and principles discussed in this chapter articulate a guarantee of rights. However, if they are not incorporated into Australia's legal system, they are merely construed as non-binding guiding principles. Australian governments in recent times have suspended the human rights of Aboriginal communities under the *Racial Discrimination Act 1975* (Cth) to implement government policy and this clearly identifies that the objectives of the *Act* are vulnerable to the whim of government policies. The treatment of Aboriginal water rights and interests will be determined by a government's commitment to utilise and incorporate human rights and ethical principles within Australia's legal system.

PART C

A PARADIGM SHIFT FOR ABORIGINAL WATER RIGHTS

CONCLUSION –
SECURING ABORIGINAL WATER RIGHTS

Tom Calma expressed his concerns for the future of Indigenous water rights in the 'Native Title Report' (2008)[1]:

> I am concerned that as Australia becomes increasingly scarce of water due to climate change, long periods of drought, over-allocation to industry and agricultural stakeholders, and population growth and migration, the capacity of recognition and security of Indigenous rights to water will become increasingly important and highly competitive.[2]

This book has examined and analysed, from an Aboriginal perspective, what Australia has generally ignored – namely, the rights and interests of Aboriginal peoples since European invasion/occupation and throughout the staggered colonisation of Aboriginal lands, waters and resources. But despite the application of common law and the sovereign right of the Crown to water resources, Aboriginal peoples continue to assert and exercise their rights and interests under Aboriginal laws – and revitalised customs and practices. Senior Law-men and women, and Aboriginal communities across Australia, conceptualise 'belonging to country' and their rights to access and use water through the lens of Aboriginal sovereignty.

From an Aboriginal perspective, the relationship with water is sacred and underpins a kinship connection through birth, life and death. Aboriginal laws exist in parallel to Western law, but there is limited common ground between Aboriginal and Australian law because the values in water are very different. Aboriginal laws regulate the access and use of water which are steeped in ancestral oral story and familial relationships, which inherently connect an Aboriginal person and community to country.

The significance of the Aboriginal 'social processes to protect, maintain and enhance relationships with the river system' has been ignored[3] in pursuing the development of land and controlling the use of water resources. Understanding Aboriginal peoples' relationships with water should be analysed from an Aboriginal ontological position, so as to inform the framework of Australian water policy. Aboriginal water values are more than a cultural value or an environmental value:

> [t]he implicit dichotomy between the material (e.g. environmental, economic) and a separate symbolic sphere of meaning (belief and value), otherwise understood as cultural, relegated Aboriginal interests to a realm of negligible significance to the political economy of regional agricultural development and marginalised them with environmental research and action … it should be analysed as a socio-cultural process ….[4]

Aboriginal perspectives on water are framed within a very different ontology than that of Western water values. As discussed in Chapter 6, the use of 'definitions can influence the substantive discussion on rights-based property paradigms'.[5] The Australian definitions of water and the construct of Australian property rights misrepresent the definitions of Aboriginal water rights and the way property rights are understood and determined under Aboriginal laws.

Aboriginal language is a conduit to comprehending one's rights and obligations to a water landscape, and marks the spiritual and physical boundary of Aboriginal water rights and interests on country. Aboriginal language carries the purpose of water, and the communal obligations to care for country.

In relation to Aboriginal water rights and interests, property concepts need to be reframed with an Aboriginal perspective. A Western interpretation of Aboriginal water rights is grossly inadequate and Aboriginal water values are simply distorted in statutory regimes.

What is required is a paradigm shift to assert the full recognition of Aboriginal property systems with the incorporation of human rights principles such as expressed in the UNDRIP. It is imperative to reconstruct and shift Western legal theories towards an inclusive Australian water policy framework that incorporates both cultural and economic Aboriginal water rights and interests. The accommodation of Aboriginal values and water rights is a mere act of tolerance, and undermines the status of the First Peoples of Australia. Australian law should be viewed through the lens of Aboriginal property relationships, and human rights, reflecting the water values Aboriginal communities hold in their relationship with country.

I argue that the exposition of Aboriginal water values and water concepts should be informed by Aboriginal communities to correctly interpret Aboriginal meaning. The Aboriginal concept of ownership is embedded in a unique and complex conceptual framework. These concepts possess inherent cultural characteristics that strictly determine how Aboriginal water rights and interests are managed.

The United Nations Permanent Forum on Indigenous Issues has put forward several concerns to other nation states in addressing contentious water rights issues in Australia. The UN Permanent Forum has urged that:

- water should not be privatised
- traditional values in Indigenous economic traditions to water are engaged
- Indigenous peoples be engaged with full participation and consultation for waterways
- water policy decision-making and development should include Indigenous men and women from all levels of government and
- a Charter of Corporate Accountability with Indigenous Peoples should be drawn up.[6]

To increase the substantive rights of Aboriginal peoples, and to move away from political symbolism in water policy development, an independent process to governments is required, led by Indigenous peoples, to review and amend the Indigenous Access Clauses of the National Water Initiative Agreement to fully incorporate the international standards expressed in the *United Nations Declaration on the Rights of Indigenous Peoples*[7] into Australian water law.

A national review must also include the recent developments in native title case law, with both consent and litigated determinations – for instance the legal recognition for the right to trade and right to economic water rights. The national reform process should focus on harmonising the water policy and laws of the Commonwealth, States and Territories to ensure a consistent approach in recognising and developing Aboriginal water rights as a cultural and commercial right. The review process should include mechanisms to ensure the consistent implementation of the amendments of the national water policy so that Indigenous communities are able to progress new opportunities in exercising their water rights and interests.

Governments across Australia are recognising that there is a lack of co-ordination among government agencies in designing policies and programs and delivering services to Aboriginal communities. Governments are also recognising that categorising Aboriginal issues and addressing them individually, does not work.[8]

RECOMMENDATIONS

On the basis of the arguments outlined in this book I advance the following recommendations for law reform. If the current situation is to change, Commonwealth, State and Territory governments need to work with Aboriginal communities, Traditional Owners and representative Aboriginal organisations to formalise Aboriginal peoples' ownership and cultural use of water as an Aboriginal property right.

Each recommendation for action presented below requires this commitment. The proposed review into reforming the current status of water rights and interests requires that Aboriginal communities lead the process. This includes drafting the terms of reference, the protocols for Aboriginal community consultation, the timeframes for the review process, assessment and analysis of the proposed reforms and the implementation of these reforms.

In order to evaluate Aboriginal water rights and interests in Australia there is an urgent requirement to consult widely among Aboriginal communities, not only communities who hold legal rights to land and waters. The key recommendations for action presented below outline the recognition and the actions needed to ensure change.

Recommendation 1: An Aboriginal ontological framework

The Commonwealth, State and Territory Governments should, with leadership from Aboriginal communities and representative Aboriginal organisations, review, redefine and implement an Aboriginal ontological framework to inform common law and statutory regimes regulating water rights and interests.

The book demonstrates the problems generated by the Western reconstruction of Aboriginal customs, laws and practices in water exhibited in the *Native Title Act 1993* (Cth), and the treatment of these customs, laws and practices by the courts.

For Aboriginal claimants seeking a determination of Aboriginal ownership under native title in Australia, the judicial interpretation of Aboriginal laws may recognise a continuing relationship of Aboriginal peoples to the land and the waters but will generally stop short of fully recognising Aboriginal rights and interests. Although the legal recognition of Aboriginal laws had been overdue, the introduction of native title laws has required Aboriginal claimants to reconfigure their laws, customs, and practices to convey Aboriginal concepts and values in terms of incongruent Western legal language.

In *Mabo v Queensland [No 2]* the High Court considered the common law reasoning on Aboriginal title in *Milirrpum v Nabalco*. According to that court's reasoning, Aboriginal peoples living in their community who enjoy only usufructuary rights, but not proprietary rights, do not impede the recognition of communal title. The notion of usufructuary or *sui generis* rights is not an Aboriginal concept under Aboriginal laws, and in many ways the legal construct of *sui generis* diminishes the capacity of Aboriginal peoples, because it fails to include the exercise of anything other than non-economic rights.

The book demonstrates the inappropriate use of certain descriptors under native title law. The Australian concept of Aboriginal title unduly constrains the exercise of water rights and interests of Aboriginal peoples. The narrow interpretation of water rights under native title provides limited opportunities for Aboriginal peoples to exercise customary rights and interests, under the principles of self-determination, within Australia's legal system. For Aboriginal communities to engage in opportunities of economic development in water resources held under their native title ownership, the concept of Aboriginal proprietary title must be redefined by native title holders.

I have argued that Aboriginal water rights and interests under the native title regime should encompass the full spectrum of water property rights and interests. For example, Toohey J held in *Mabo v Queensland [No 2]* that Aboriginal ownership was 'an abstract bundle of rights enjoyed by reason of the connection of ownership'. I have explained that the notion of a 'bundle of rights' as a legal concept thus applied to explain Aboriginal ownership is an inadequate rhetorical analogy because it is not an Aboriginal law concept. My research shows that it is not possible to neatly compartmentalise Aboriginal ownership rights into separate bundles of rights in property. These conclusions lead to the following law reforms.

Recommendation 2: Culturally appropriate definitions

The Australian Government should, with leadership from Aboriginal communities and representative Aboriginal organisations, review native title legislation and case law to provide for culturally appropriate definitions of Aboriginal land and water rights.

Aboriginal health is integral in any national dialogue on Aboriginal water rights and interests because there is an interrelationship between access to natural resources, such as clean drinking water, and the enjoyment of good health among Aboriginal communities. Jon Altman, the Australian National Director of the

Centre for Aboriginal Economic Policy Research,[9] has suggested that 'to close the gap of indigenous life expectancy in Australia [requires] amending the law to provide Aboriginal land owners with legal property rights over resources'.[10]

The omission of self-determination principles in Indigenous water management policy and legislative instruments directly impacts upon Aboriginal communities' water rights. As a consequence, Aboriginal communities lack the economic influence which other water stakeholders in industry and agriculture enjoy.

Recognition of a national Aboriginal reserved water right in Australia would provide economic certainty for Aboriginal peoples and a substantive legal recognition of Aboriginal water rights and interests. I have demonstrated the need to include permanent water allocations for Aboriginal communities outside the consumptive pool under the national water management regimes.

Recommendation 3: National Indigenous water reforms

The Commonwealth, States and Territories should, with leadership from Aboriginal communities and representative Aboriginal organisations, implement national water reforms to provide for:

a) *perpetual water allocations for Aboriginal communities outside the consumptive pool which meet the water requirements deemed by Aboriginal communities to be consistent with the principles of self-determination; and*

b) *a Reserved Water Right regime allocated for Aboriginal communities to develop economic capacity and intergenerational prosperity; and*

c) *biennial and independent reporting to Parliament on the progress of implementing these water reforms within the respective jurisdictions.*

This book highlights the failure of Indigenous policy and planning processes formulated and implemented by Australian governments – policies which have not addressed the poor outcomes in health, wealth and wellbeing of Aboriginal peoples in Australia, and Aboriginal peoples' right to water. The correlation between Aboriginal health, the lack of Aboriginal wealth creation, the over-allocation of water, and the contamination of water resources in Aboriginal communities has been neglected as a national policy issue. The Australian Government's '*Closing the Gap*' Indigenous policy has likewise failed to include Aboriginal water rights and interests as a pivotal policy response.

Although native title recognition of country is an important milestone in Australian legal jurisprudence, native title lacks the capacity to provide for economic development and to generate equity in commercial enterprise. This book has demonstrated that achieving intergenerational equity requires the inclusion within water policy planning of mandatory commitments to advance Aboriginal wealth development through perpetual water rights.

Recommendation 4: Enshrine Aboriginal water rights

The Commonwealth, States and Territories should, with leadership from Aboriginal communities and representative Aboriginal organisations, provide for:

a) *Aboriginal peoples' 'special association to water' to recognise this as a First Right before other water rights; and*

b) *government strategies to increase Aboriginal participation in the Australian water market and increase the ownership of water property assets in Aboriginal communities; and*

c) *economic benefits under statutory water legislation to promote wealth creation within Aboriginal communities; and*

d) *meaningful consultation with Aboriginal peoples to identify and allocate permanent water rights in under-allocated and over-allocated water resources; and*

e) *adoption of Aboriginal wealth creation policies and strategies, consistent with the principles of self-determination within national Indigenous policy frameworks, to include water ownership; and*

f) *Aboriginal water rights to ensure communities can utilise communal and private water rights and interests; and*

g) *tradeable Aboriginal water access licences; and*

h) *a national water policy which excludes caps on water resources held by native title claimants; and*

i) *water resources for Aboriginal peoples under the principles of intergenerational equity.*

Chapter 8 on the Murray-Darling Basin demonstrated that the contextual meaning of Aboriginal water values and Aboriginal property rights in water are not easily translated into Australian values, concepts and frameworks. Australian definitions such as 'cultural, social and spiritual' are inadequate for identifying Aboriginal values because they are derived from Anglo-Australian ontological perspectives. Australian water policy and legislation fails to have due regard for Aboriginal concepts and meanings relating to water.

Australian courts and policy makers struggle to comprehend the complexity of Aboriginal ontology. This book demonstrates how the simplistic use of Australian legal concepts as applied to native title misinterprets Aboriginal concepts.

Recommendation 5: The inseparability of land and water

The Commonwealth, States and Territories should incorporate:

a) *recognition of the Aboriginal concept of the inseparability of land and water within water policy and legislative instruments; and*
b) *Aboriginal ontological concepts of water within definitions used to draft policy and legislation to convey the values and meanings of Aboriginal water use.*

The book has demonstrated that a national focus is required in the development of water policy reform for Aboriginal peoples, so as to significantly improve their participation, access and management of water rights and interests. Australia has historically focused on the allocation of water resources for stakeholders in farming and industry. The allocation of water rights and water ownership between the Commonwealth (under the National Water Commission) and the States has become politicised and controversial. This political melee has disenfranchised Aboriginal peoples within a polarised water rights debate.

The introduction of water reforms for managing Australia's water resources has failed to include dialogue on Aboriginal water rights and interests in the policy development stage. As a consequence Australian water legislation has failed to provide any acceptable level of certainty for Aboriginal communities' access to and use of water. Governments should recognise and incorporate Aboriginal water requirements in water management legislative instruments.

Recommendation 6: Reserved water rights

The Commonwealth, States and Territories, with leadership from Aboriginal communities and representative Aboriginal organisations, should amend legislation to incorporate a national system of Indigenous water rights and interests, so as to provide a permanent range of rights and allocations that are not subject to the water requirements of other stakeholders.

The chapters demonstrate that Aboriginal water concepts cannot be separated from the land because the creation stories have laid the foundations for Aboriginal water values and the cultural use of water for Aboriginal peoples. The lack of formal consultation during the national discussion on reforming water management has resulted in significant gaps in addressing property rights regarding Aboriginal water requirements.

The case study on water rights in Western Australia demonstrated the inconsistent implementation of the national water reforms and significant gaps within the national framework, allowing the Western Australian Government to ignore the recognition and provision of Aboriginal water requirements. In the absence of substantial national water reforms in Western Australia, due to the government's lack of progress in passing the Water Resources Management Bill, the water rights and interests of native title holders and the interests of Aboriginal communities are in limbo. The failure of the Western Australian Government to incorporate Aboriginal water rights and interests such as providing for Reserved Indigenous Water Rights and perpetual water allocations for Aboriginal communities is in stark contrast with the treatment of non-Indigenous water users.

The discretionary nature of the Indigenous Action clauses under the National Water Initiative Agreement limits government's commitment to Indigenous water policy, especially in the absence of compliance mechanisms in the respective jurisdictions. I argue in the book that, to provide certainty for Aboriginal peoples and their unequivocal rights and interests in water a balanced legislative framework which protects First Peoples' water rights is required.

Recommendation 7: Incorporating human rights standards

The Commonwealth, States and Territories, with leadership from Aboriginal communities and representative Aboriginal organisations, should review the national water reform framework and legislative instruments to include:

a) *the recognition of Aboriginal peoples water rights and interests as First Peoples within their jurisdictions; and*

b) *guiding principles to protect and advance Indigenous water management and water planning within their jurisdictions; and*

c) *mandatory actions for Indigenous water rights and interests under the National Water Initiative; and*

d) *biennial reporting to the National Water Commission, measured against international standards of human rights; and*

e) *reserved water allocations for Aboriginal communities outside the consumptive pool within all jurisdictions.*

Chapter 8 identifies the significant social, cultural and environmental impacts resulting from the historic over-allocation of water resources in the Murray-Darling Basin catchments since the introduction of river regulation and irrigation projects. The government emphasis on increasing economic wealth for the pastoral and agricultural industries in Australia stands in stark contrast to the treatment of Aboriginal interests, and this has disenfranchised Aboriginal peoples' access to and use of water in the Murray-Darling catchments.

In 2011 the National Water Commission's third Biennial Assessment of the National Water Initiative[11] reported that Indigenous stakeholders' progress was deficient across all water management jurisdictions.[12] I argue that, in spite of the introduction of national water reforms in Australia and the revised Murray-Darling Basin Plans, the outcomes for Aboriginal communities are negligible.

Chapter 8 demonstrates the impact of the Commonwealth's *Water Act 2007* and *Water Amendment Act 2008* upon the water rights and interests of Aboriginal communities, and identified the gaps in the legislative regime. I argue that the *Water Act 2007* fails to include the necessary recognition and incorporation of Aboriginal water rights and interests in the Murray-Darling Basin, and that the focus is, instead, almost exclusively on the rights and interests of non-Aboriginal stakeholders.

The establishment of environmental flows under the Commonwealth water legislation has resulted in an improvement to the Murray-Darling Basin's ecosystem, but in the absence of legislative recognition of the relationship of Aboriginal communities to the Murray-Darling catchments the environmental river system remains divorced from its spiritual context.

Murray-Darling Aboriginal water rights and interests are understood by their respective river communities in the context of Aboriginal ontological paradigms. Aboriginal water management practices are congruous with Aboriginal water values in their capacity to sensitively nurture the river systems. I argue the protection of Aboriginal water rights is a necessity under human rights standards because Aboriginal peoples' relationship to water is central to Aboriginal identity.

Recommendation 8: Murray-Darling Basin Plan reforms

The Commonwealth and the States under the Murray-Darling Basin Plan, with leadership from Aboriginal communities and representative Aboriginal organisations, should:

  a) *review water policies and strategies, catchment practices, legislative instruments and Indigenous national resource management frameworks, to* incorporate and implement mandatory water requirements for Aboriginal peoples in the Murray-Darling Basin Plan; and

b) apply human rights benchmarks to the national water reform regimes; and

c) review and amend the Water Act 2007 and the Water Amendment Act 2008 (Cth) to enshrine the legal recognition of Indigenous water rights and interests and their cultural obligations in the Murray-Darling river systems; and

d) develop and implement an Indigenous-based methodology to research the impact of Australian water reforms on Indigenous water rights and interests, and identify knowledge gaps in Aboriginal water management in the Murray-Darling region; and

e) review and amend the Water Act 2007 (Cth) to give effect to Indigenous peoples' relationship to and customary knowledge of the Murray-Darling Basin environment, and initiate co-management of the Murray-Darling Basin with Aboriginal communities who are recognized as 'Traditional Owners'; and

f) establish Indigenous water rights under water management legislation as a separate category under the Murray-Darling Basin Plan; and

g) undertake academic research on the Murray-Darling Basin catchments to inform the Basin Plan on the inherent customary and economic water rights of Aboriginal peoples with an association to the Murray-Darling region; and

h) consider an independent inquiry to examine and make recommendations on Aboriginal communities' legal and beneficial rights to use the Basin's water resources.

The book demonstrates that Aboriginal peoples lack historic and contemporary legal recognition of their inherent Aboriginal sovereignty. Commonwealth, State and Territory laws have impacted negatively on Indigenous rights and interests, in spite of clearly articulated international human rights standards.

Recommendation 9: Incorporation of Ethical Principles

The Australian Government should:

a) formulate and implement strategies to advance the protection of Indigenous water rights and interests which incorporate ethical principles and standards in national water management; and

b) implement a framework of ethical principles in national water management, for the independent assessment of commercial projects to determine socially responsible investments.

The inclusion of ethical principles in water resource use would provide the necessary guidance within water policy and water laws. This has the capacity to enhance a policy framework with cultural integrity – and provide the necessary checks and balances to the national water framework. Establishing a benchmark of ethical principles for the management of water resources has the capacity to reconcile the cultural and environmental concerns of Aboriginal peoples – most notably in relation to the high level of water extraction by industry under government-supported projects, especially in cases where the precautionary principle is being ignored – for instance the assessment of development and mining exploration applications.

BIBLIOGRAPHY

Australian Broadcasting Corporation, 'Gunns deal off, boss blames green groups', *ABC News* (Tasmania), 9 March 2012, viewed 13 March 2012, <http://www.abc.net.au/news/2012-03-09/gunns-investor-pulls-out/3879344>.

Australian Broadcasting Corporation, 'Aboriginal intervention on the removal of Aboriginal children in the Northern Territory', October 2007 (Mal Brough).

Aboriginal and Torres Strait Islander Social Justice Commissioner, *Building a sustainable national Indigenous representative body: Issues for consideration*, Issues Paper, Australian Human Rights Commission, Sydney, 2008.

—— 'Draft Native Title Report 2008', Human Rights and Equal Opportunity Commission, Sydney, 2007.

—— *Native Title Report 2005*, Human Rights and Equal Opportunity Commission, Sydney.

Aboriginal and Torres Strait Islander Social Justice Commissioner, *Native Title Report 2006*, Human Rights and Equal Opportunity Commission, Sydney, 2007.

—— *Native Title Report 2007*, Human Rights and Equal Opportunity Commission, Sydney, 2008.

—— *Native Title Report 2008*, Australian Human Rights Commission, Sydney, 2009.

—— *Native Title Report 2010*, Australian Human Rights Commission, Sydney, 2011.

—— *Native Title Report 2011*, Australian Human Rights Commission, Sydney, 2011.

—— *Social Justice Report 2008*, Australian Human Rights Commission, Sydney, 2009.

—— *Social Justice Report 2010*, Australian Human Rights Commission, Sydney, 2011.

—— *Social Justice Report 2011*, Australian Human Rights Commission, Sydney, 2011.

—— *Social Justice and Native Title Report 2015*, Australian Human Rights Commission, Sydney, 2015.

—— & Acting Race Discrimination Commissioner, *Review of the 1994 water report*, Human Rights and Equal Opportunity Commission, Sydney, 2001, p. 2, viewed 5 October 2016, <https://www.humanrights.gov.au/our-work/race-discrimination/publications/review-1994-water-report-2001>.

Aboriginal Victoria, 'Self-determination for Aboriginal people', n.d., viewed 7 October 2016, <http://consult.aboriginalvictoria.vic.gov.au/Open-Meeting>.

—— *Treaty fact sheet*, n.d., viewed 7 October 2016, <http://consult.aboriginalvictoria.vic.gov.au/Open-Meeting/documents/34862/download>.

ACIL Tasman in association with Freehills, *An effective system of defining water property titles*, Australian Government, Department of Agriculture, Fisheries and Forestry and Land and Water Australia, Canberra, 2004.

ALRC (Australian Law Reform Commission), *Aboriginal customary law: A general regime for recognition*, Aboriginal Customary Research Paper No. 8, ALRC, Sydney, 1982, p. 23.

—— *Connection to Country: Review of Native Title Act 1993* (Cth), ALRC Report 126, ALRC, Sydney, 2015.

—— *Family violence and Commonwealth laws: Improving legal frameworks*, Report No. 117, ALRC, Sydney, 2011.

—— *Review of the Uniform Evidence Acts*, ALRC Discussion Paper 69/NSWLRC Discussion Paper 47, ALRC, Sydney, 2005.

—— *The recognition of Aboriginal customary law*, ALRC Report 31, ALRC, Sydney, 1986 (2 vols), viewed 4 October 2016, <http://www.alrc.gov.au/publications/report-31>.

Altman, Jon assisted by V Branchut, *Fresh water in the Maningrida region's hybrid economy: Intercultural contestation over values and property rights*, Centre for Aboriginal Economic Policy Research Working Paper No. 46, Australian National University, Canberra, 2008.

Altman, Jon & William Arthur, *Commercial water and Indigenous Australians: A scoping study of licence allocations*, Working Paper No. 57, Centre for Aboriginal Policy Research, Australian National University, Canberra, 2009.

Anaya, S James, Special Rapporteur, GA Agenda Item 3, 15th sess, UN Doc A/HRC/15/37Add.4 (1 March 2012) <http://dacess-dds-ny.un.org/UNDOC/GEN/G10/138/87/PDF/G1013887.pdf?OpenElement>

Andrews, Gavin 'Negotiating Aboriginal access agreements to culturally significant land, water and natural resources in New South Wales', Working Paper, Department of Natural Resources NSW, Sydney, 2006.

Anon, 'Indian Reserved Water Rights: The Winters of Our Discontent' (1979) 88(8) *Yale Law Journal* 8, pp. 1689-1712.

Anon, 'International law as an interpretative force in federal Indian law (2003) 116(6) *Harvard Law Review* pp. 1751-1773.

Arnold, Craig Anthony, 'The reconstruction of property: Property as a web of interests' (2002) 26 *Harvard International Law Review* pp. 281-4.

ATSIC (Aboriginal and Torres Strait Islander Commission) & Lingiari Foundation, *Onshore, offshore: Indigenous rights to waters report and recommendations*, ATSIC, (Canberra, 2002) <http://atsic.gov.au/issues/Indigenous_Rights/Indigenous_Rights_Waters/Default.asp>.

Australian Government, House of Representatives, *Parliamentary debates*, 18 March 1986, 1475.

Australian Academy of Technological Sciences and Engineering, *Academy symposium: Perception of water in Australian law re-examining rights and responsibilities*, ATSE, Melbourne, 24 September 2004, <http://www.atse.org.au/index.php?sectionid=629>.

Australian Capital Territory Government, *Towards an ACT Human Rights ACT: Report of the ACT Bill of Rights Consultative Committee*, Department of Urban Services, (Canberra, 2003)

Australian Government, *Closing the gap: Prime Minister's report 2016*, Department of the Prime Minister and Cabinet, Canberra, viewed 4 October 2016, <http://closingthegap.dpmc.gov.au/assets/pdfs/closing_the_gap_report_2016.pdf>.

—— *Implementation plan for the National Aboriginal and Torres Strait Islander Health Plan 2013-2023*, Department of Health, Canberra, 2015.

—— *Indigenous Business Australia: Annual report 2004-2005*, Indigenous Business Australia, Woden, ACT, 2005.

—— *Our north, our future: White paper on developing northern Australia*, Commonwealth of Australia, (Canberra, 2015)

—— *Water legislation*, Department of Sustainability, Environment, Water, Population and Communities, Canberra, 2012 <http://www.environment.gov.au/water/australia/water-act/index.html#amendment-2008>.

Australian Human Rights Commission, 'Australian Human Rights Commission submission to the Committee on the Rights of the Child', 2011, viewed 5 October 2016, <http://www.humanrights.gov.au/information-concerning-australia-and-convention-rights-child-0#s3_2>.

—— 'Indigenous property rights', 2016, viewed 4 October 2016, <https://www.humanrights.gov.au/our-work/aboriginal-and-torres-strait-islander-social-justice/projects/indigenous-property-rights>.

Australian Institute of Health and Welfare, *The health and welfare of Australia's Aboriginal and Torres Strait Islander peoples 2015*, Cat. No. IHW 147, AIHW, Canberra, 2015, viewed 4 October 2016, <http://www.aihw.gov.au/WorkArea/DownloadAsset.aspx?id=60129551281>.

Australian Medical Association, *AMA report card on Indigenous health*, AMA, Canberra, 2015, viewed 4 October 2016, <https://ama.com.au/2015-ama-report-card-indigenous-health-closing-gap-indigenous-imprisonment-rates>.

Baalman, John, *Outline of law in Australia*, 2nd ed, Law Book, Sydney, 1955.

Ballardong Natural Resource Management Working Group, Avon Catchment Council, *Ballardong Noongar budjar: 'Healthy country, healthy people'*, Australian Government, 2006.

Bardon, Jane, 'Traditional owners burn Arnhem Land fracking plan', *ABC News*, Sydney, 18 March 2013, viewed 10 October 2016, <http://www.abc.net.au/news/2013-03-18/maningrida-traditional-owners-burn-fracking-plan/4579438>.

Barlow, Maude, *Blue covenant: the global water crisis and the coming battle for the rights to water* Black Inc., Melbourne, 2007.

Barresi, Paul, 'Beyond fairness to future generations: an intragenerational alternative, intergenerational equity in the international environmental arena', *Tulane Environmental Law Journal*, 11 (1) 1997.

Bartlett, Richard, 'Canada: Indigenous land claims and settlements' in Brian Keon-Cohen (ed.), *Native title in the new millennium*, Aboriginal Studies Press, Canberra, 2001.

——*Native title in Australia*, 2nd ed, Lexis Nexis Butterworths, Sydney, 2004.

Basten, John, 'Beyond *Yorta Yorta*', *Land, Rights, Laws: Issues of Native Title*, 2 (24), AIATSIS, Canberra, 2003, p. 5, viewed 6 September 2016, <http://aiatsis.gov.au/sites/default/files/products/issues_paper/basten-ntip-v2n24-beyond-yorta-yorta.pdf>.

Bates, Daisy, *The passing of the Aborigines: a lifetime spent among the natives of Australia* John Murray, London, 1972 (first published 1938).

Batzin, Carlos, 'Panel discussion from South America', speech delivered at the Garma Indigenous Water Knowledge, Indigenous Water Interests Conference, Gove, NT, 7 August 2008.

Beckwith Environmental Planning, *Draft Water Resources Management Bill: Recommended legislative framework*, Water Reform Implementation Committee, Department of Water, WA, May 2007 52.

Beder, Sharon, *Environmental principles and policies: An interdisciplinary approach*, University of New South Wales Press, Sydney, 2006.

Behrendt, Larissa, *Aboriginal dispute resolution: A step towards self-determination and community autonomy*, Federation Press, Leichhardt, NSW, 1995.

—— *Achieving social justice: Indigenous rights and Australia's future*, Federation Press, Sydney, 2003.

Behrendt, Jason & Peter Thompson, 'The recognition and protection of Aboriginal interests in NSW rivers', (2004)3 *Journal of Indigenous Policy*, pp. 37–140.

——& Peter Thompson, *The recognition and protection of Aboriginal interests in NSW rivers*, Occasional Paper No. 1008, Healthy Rivers Commission, NSW, 2003.

Bennett, Mark, 'Indigenous autonomy and justice in North America' (2004) 2 *New Zealand Journal of Public and International Law* pp. 203–58.

Benton, Lauren, *Law and colonial cultures: Legal regimes in world history, 1400–1900*, Cambridge University Press, 2002.

Berndt, Ronald M, 'A profile of good and bad in Australian Aboriginal religion' in Max Charlesworth (ed.), *Religious business: Essays on Australian Aboriginal spirituality*, (Cambridge University Press, Cambridge, 1998), pp. 24-45.

Berndt, RM & CH, *The world of the First Australians*, Rigby, Adelaide, 1985.

Blackshield, Simon. 'Is the United States doctrine of indigenous rights of self-regulation applicable to Australia's common law?' Research paper, n.d.

Blackshield, Tony & George Williams, *Australian constitutional law and theory: Commentary and theory*, 2nd ed, Federation Press, Leichhardt, NSW, 1998.

Blowes, Robert, 'From *terra nullius* to every person's land: A perspective from legal history' in Jim Birckhead, Terry De Lacy & Laurajane Smith (eds), *Aboriginal involvement in parks and protected areas*, Aboriginal Studies Press, Canberra, 1992, pp. 149-57.

Blumer, Mark, 'In search of the common bunyip: A commonsense approach to water property rights in New South Wales'(2000) 17 (4) *Environmental and Planning Law Journal.*

Boast, R, *The foreshore*, Rangahaua Whanui National Theme, Waitangi Tribunal, Wellington, 1996.

Bodkin, Frances, 'Experiencing a cultural landscape: The D'harawal lands of the Yandelora and Wirrimbirra', course information, 1–2 May 2003.

—— & Lorraine Robertson, *D'harawal: Seasons and climatic cycles*, L Robertson & National Heritage Trust, Sydney, 2008.

Boelens, Rutgerd, 'Water law and Indigenous rights: Research, action and debate' (2002) *Wageningen University*, The Netherlands. <http://ww.indigenouswater.org/user/Water%20Workshop%20 Summary.pdf>.

Branson, Catherine, 'Take judges out of human rights process', *The Australian*, 8 May 2009, p. 27.

Brazenor, Clare, *The spatial dimensions of native title* (Master of Geomatics Science, The University of Melbourne, 2000).

Brennan, Sean, Larissa Behrendt, Lisa Strelein & George Williams, *Treaty*, Federation Press, Leichhardt, NSW, 2005.

Brock, Peggy, 'South Australia' in Ann McGrath (ed.), *Contested ground: Australian Aborigines under the British Crown*, Allen & Unwin, St Leonards, NSW, 1995, pp. 208–39.

Brooks, Robert, Sinclair Davidson & Robert Faff, 'Sudden changes in property rights: The case of Australian native title' (2003) 52 *Journal of Economic Behaviour and Organisation*, pp. 427–42.

Broome, Richard, 'Victoria' in Ann McGrath (ed.), *Contested ground: Australian Aborigines under the British Crown*, Allen & Unwin, St Leonards, NSW, 1995, pp. 121–67.

Brown, AJ, *Paradoxes & principles*, Federation Press, Leichhardt, NSW, 2011.

Brown, C Rebecca & James I Reynolds, 'Aboriginal title to sea spaces: A comparative study' (2004) 37 *University of British Columbia Law Review*, pp. 483–91.

Bruns, Bryan, 'Water tenure reform: Developing an extended ladder of participation', paper presented at Politics of the Commons: Articulating Development and Strengthening Local Practices, RCSD Conference, 11–14 July 2003, Chiang Mai, Thailand, viewed 2 September 2016, <http://www.bryanbruns.com/bruns-ladder.pdf>.

Bryan, Bradley, 'Property as ontology: On Aboriginal and English understanding of ownership' (2000) 13(3) *Canadian Journal of Law and Jurisprudence*, pp. 1, 12 <http://au.westlaw.com/ result/documenttext.aspx?RS=WLAU4.09&VR=2.0&SP=Fed...>.

Buergenthal, Thomas, 'International human rights in an historical perspective' in Janusz Symonides (ed.), *Human rights: Concepts and standards* (2000) UNESCO and Ashgate, Aldershot, pp. 3-30.

Burchi, Stefano, 'The interface between customary and statutory water rights: A statutory perspective', paper presented at African Water Laws: Plural Legislative Frameworks for Rural

Water Management in Africa, South Africa, 26–28 January 2005, viewed 6 October 2016, <http://www.fao.org/fileadmin/user_upload/legal/docs/lpo45.pdf>.

Bureau of Meteorology, 'Indigenous weather knowledge: D'harawal calendar', Australian Government, viewed 2 September 2016, <www.bom.gov.au/iwk/dharawal>.

Burnside, Julian, *Watching brief: Reflections on human rights, law and justice*, Scribe, Melbourne, 2007.

Burrows, John, 'Living between water and rocks: First Nations, environmental planning and democracy' (1997) 47 *University of Toronto Law Journal*, pp. 417–68.

Burt, Miles & Russell McVeagh, 'Water securities and the case for an Australian Personal Property Securities Act' (2004) 20(2) *Australian Banking and Finance Law Bulletin*, pp. 17-20.

Burton, J, *Review of reforms in the water industry 1988*, report to the Minister for Natural Resources, Department of Water Resources, NSW June 1988.

Byrnes, Jill, *Aboriginal economic independence: A report on some Canadian initiatives*, Research report, Rural Development Centre, University of New England, 1990.

Callaghan, Bruce, NSW Aboriginal Land Council & Department of Land and NSW Water Conservation, *Report on the Boomanulla Conference for Country*, 5–6 March 2002 Canberra, 2002.

Calma, Tom, 'UN Declaration on the Rights of Indigenous Peoples: Australia should sign', *Koori Mail*, 24 September 2008, p. 27.

Cane, Scott, 'Aboriginal fishing on the New South Wales South coast: A court case' (1998) 48 *Oceania Monograph*, University of Sydney.

——*Aboriginal fishing on the south coast of New South Wales*, report to Blake Dawson and Waldron and the NSW Aboriginal Land Council, Narooma, NSW, July 1992.

Carter, J (ed.), *Native title and land law: The laws of Australia*, Thomson Reuters, Pyrmont, NSW, 2016.

Caruana, W, *Aboriginal art*, Thames and Hudson, London, 1993.

Cawte, John, *The universe of the Warramirri: Art, medicine and religion in Arnhem Land*, New South Wales University Press, Kensington, NSW, 1993.

Centre for the Indigenous History and the Arts, *Ngulak ngarnk nidja boodja: Our mother, this land*, University of Western Australia, Perth, 2000.

Centre for World Indigenous Studies, *A treaty between indigenous nations on the protection of cultural property and traditional resource rights: Asserting indigenous nation sovereignty*, Centre for World Indigenous Studies, <http://www.cwis.org/260fge/260tcptr.html>.

Clark, Ian D & Toby Heydon, *A bend in the Yarra: A history of the Merri Creek Protectorate Station and Merri Creek Aboriginal School 1841–1851*, AIATSIS, Canberra, 2004.

Clark, Manning (ed.), *Select documents in Australian history 1851–1900 Volume 2*, revised ed, Angus and Robertson, Sydney, 1979.

Clifford, H, G Pearson, P Franklin, R Walker & G Zosky, 'Environmental health challenges in remote Aboriginal Australian communities: clean air, clean water and safe housing', (2015) 15(2) *Australian Indigenous Health Bulletin*, viewed 5 October 2016, <http://healthbulletin.org.au/articles/environmental-health-challenges-in-remote-aboriginal-australian-communities-clean-air-clean-water-and-safe-housing/>.

Close the Gap Campaign Steering Committee, *Progress and priorities report 2016*, Oxfam Australia, 2016.

Cockayne, James, '*Members of Yorta Yorta Aboriginal Community v Victoria*: Indigenous and colonial traditions in native title' (2001) 25 *Melbourne University Law Review*.

Collard, David, 'Panel discussion', speech delivered at the Australian Indigenous Water Focus Group, National Water Commission, Adelaide, 18 November 2008.

Collings, Neva & Virginia Falk [Marshall], 'Water: Aboriginal peoples in Australia and their spiritual relationship with waterscapes' in Elliot Johnston, Martin Hinton & Daryle Rigney (eds), *Indigenous Australians and the law*, 2nd ed, Routledge-Cavendish, Abingdon, Oxon, 2008, Chapter 9.

—— 'Water rights and international law' in Lingiari Foundation, *Background Briefing Papers: Indigenous Rights to Waters*, Broome, 2002, pp. 43-64, <http://pandora.nla.gov.au/pan/41033/20060106-0000/ATSIC/issues/Indigenous_Rights/Indigenous_Rights_Waters/docs/layout_papers.pdf>

Collins, Richard B, 'Sacred sites and religious freedom on government land' (2003) 5(2) *Journal of Constitutional Law*, pp. 241-70.

Commonwealth of Australia, *Australia's Constitution*, 2nd ed, Government Printers, Canberra, 1998.

Commonwealth, *Parliamentary debates*, House of Representatives, Native Title Bill 1993, 2 (Paul Keating).

Connell, Daniel, *Water politics in the Murray–Darling Basin*, Federation Press, Annandale, NSW, 2007.

Connor, Michael, *The invention of terra nullius: Historical and legal fictions on the foundation of Australia*, Macleay Press, Paddington, NSW, 2005.

Coombs, HC, 'Towards a new federation' in HC Coombs, *Shame on us! Essays on a future Australia* revised ed, ANU, Centre for Resource and Environmental Studies, Canberra, 1993 (first published 1992).

Cooper, David & Sue Jackson, 'Preliminary study on Indigenous water values and interests in the Katherine region of the Northern Territory', Research report, CSIRO Sustainable Ecosystems, Darwin, 2008.

Cornwall, Amanda, *Restoring identity: Final report of the Moving Forward Consultation Project*, Public Interest Advocacy Centre, Sydney, 2002.

Corpuz, Victoria Tauli, Special Rapporteur, *Report of the Special Rapporteur on the rights of indigenous peoples*, 13th sess, Agenda Item 3, UN Doc A/HRC/30/41 (6 August 2015) < https://documents-dds-ny.un.org/doc/UNDOC/GEN/G15/173/83/PDF/G1517383.pdf? OpenElement >.

Council for Aboriginal Reconciliation, 'Walking together: The first steps, report of the Council for Aboriginal Reconciliation 1991-1994 to Federal Parliament', Australian Government, Canberra, 1994.

Coyne, Darren, 'Now or never: NSW inquiry action tackling Indigenous disadvantage', *Koori Mail*, 26 March 2008.

Craig, Donna, 'Indigenous property rights to water: Environmental flows, cultural values and tradeable property rights' (2005) unpublished essay, Macquarie University.

Craven, Matthew, *The International Covenant on Economic, Social, and Cultural Rights: A perspective on its development*, Clarendon Press, Oxford, 1995.

Crawford, James R, *Aboriginal customary law: A general regime for recognition*, Research Paper No. 8, Australian Law Reform Commission, Sydney, 1982.

Crommelin, Michael, 'Economic analysis of property' in D.J. Galligan (ed.), *Essays in legal theory*, Melbourne University Press, Carlton, 1984.

Crowley, Teresa, 'Culture and common property: Indigenous tenure issues within Western society', paper presented at 15th Annual Colloquium of the Spatial Information Research Centre, University of Otago, New Zealand, 1–3 December 2003.

Culcutt, Lane, 'Video: Barnaby Joyce disagrees with Malcolm Turnbull over Australian 'invasion'', 9news.com.au, 15 June 2016, viewed 11 October 2016, <http://www.9news.com.au/national/2016/06/15/19/59/barnaby-joyce-disagrees-with-malcolm-turnbull-over-australian-invasion>.

Cullen, Mark, 'Rights to offshore resources after Mabo 1992 and the Native Title Act 1993 (Cth)' (1996) 18(2) *Sydney Law Review*.

Cullen, Peter, 'Water: The key to sustainability in a dry land' in Jenny Goldie, Bob Douglas & Bryan Furnass (eds), *In search of sustainability*, CSIRO, Collingwood, Vic., 2005, pp. 79–92.

Daes, Erica Irene A, *Preliminary report on prevention of discrimination and protection of indigenous people: indigenous peoples' permanent sovereignty over natural resources*, E/CN.4/Sub.2/2003/20, UNESCOR, 55th session, Agenda Item 5(b), 21 July 2003.

—— 'Protection of the world's Indigenous peoples and human rights' in Janusz Symonides (ed), *Human rights: concept and standards*, Ashgate and UNESCO, 2000, Aldershot, pp. 301–08.

Dare, HH, *Water conservation in Australia*, University of Queensland & Simmons, Sydney, 1939.

Davis, Megan & Hannah McGlade, *International human rights law and the recognition of Aboriginal customary law*, Background Paper No. 10, Law Reform Commission of Western Australia, March 2005.

Dayton, Leigh, 'Research raises a toxic dust', *The Australian*, 21–22 November 2009, p. 12.

De Santolo, Jason, 'Responses to the "Sealord deal": Fishing for insights' (2004) 4 *Journal of Indigenous Policy*, pp. 49–64.

Denholder, T & G Gishubl, 'First decade of Mabo part 2', paper presented at Australian Mining and Petroleum Law Association, Gold Coast, Queensland, 14–17 August 2002.

Department of Aboriginal Affairs NSW, 'Draft NSW Aboriginal languages policy', 2002, unnumbered.

——*Two ways together report on indicators: The NSW Aboriginal Affairs Plan 2003–2012*, Department of Aboriginal Affairs, Surry Hills, NSW, 2005.

—— *Two ways together, partnerships: A new way of doing business with Aboriginal people, NSW Aboriginal Affairs Plan 2003–2012*, Surry Hills, NSW, 2003.

Department of Land and Water Conservation (NSW), *Guidelines for assessing the impacts of water sharing plans on Aboriginal peoples*, Economic and Social Policy Branch, Department of Land and Water Conservation, 2001.

Department of Natural Resources (NSW), 'Water Management Division business plan 2006–2007', draft, 21 August 2006.

Department of Sustainability and Environment, 'Securing our water future together', Victorian Government White Paper, June 2004, p. 18, <http://www.dse.gov.au>.

Department of Sustainability, Environment, Water, Population and Communities, *Australia's biological diversity conservation strategy*, 2010, viewed 14 November 2011, <http://www.environment.gov.au/biodiversity/publications/strategy-2010-30/pubs/biodiversity-strategy-2010.pdf>.

Department of Water (NSW), *Our water our country: An information manual for Aboriginal people and communities about the water reform process*, 'ch' 2.0, NSW Government, Sydney, 2012.

Department of Water (WA), 'Draft policy for consultation with Aboriginal people', Government of Western Australia, 2008.

—— *Report for the Minister for Water Resources on water services in discrete Indigenous communities*, Government of Western Australia, Perth, 2006.

—— *Western Australia's implementation plan for the National Water Initiative*, Government of Western Australia, Perth, 2007.

Department of Water, Government of Western Australia & Miriuwung-Gajerrong Aboriginal Corporation, 'Interim management plan for Reserve 31165', August 2006.

Diamond, Jared, *Collapse: How societies choose to fail or survive*, revised ed, Penguin, Camberwell, Vic., 2007.

Dicey, A V, *Introduction to the study of the law of the Constitution*, Macmillan, London, 1908 (first published 1885).

Dick, Tim, 'Land rights in limbo', *The Sydney Morning Herald*, 26–28 January 2007, p. 29.

Dorais, L, *Quatag: Modernity and identity in an Inuit community*, University of Toronto, 1997.

Durie, Judge Taihakurei Edward, Richard Boast & Hana O'Regan, 'Ministerial review of the *Foreshore and Seabed Act 2004*', report summary and vols 1-3, New Zealand Government, June 2009.

Dusevic, Tom, 'John Howard: The making of a populist', *Time Magazine* (Sydney), no. 9, 6 March 2006.

Eades, Diana (ed.), *Language in evidence: Issues confronting Aboriginal and multicultural Australia*, UNSW Press, Sydney, 1995.

Egloff, Brian, Nicholas Peterson & Sue Wesson, *Biamanga and Gulaga: Aboriginal cultural association with Biamanga and Gulaga national parks*, Office of the Registrar *Aboriginal Land Rights Act 1983* (NSW), Surry Hills, NSW, 2005.

Expert Panel on Constitutional Recognition of Indigenous Australians, *Recognising Aboriginal and Torres Strait Islander peoples in the Constitution*, 2012, viewed 14 October 2016, <http://www.recognise.org.au/wp-content/uploads/shared/uploads/assets/3446_FaHCSIA_ICR_report_text_Bookmarked_PDF_12_Jan_v4.pdf>.

Falk [Marshall], Virginia, 'Aboriginal water rights and interests: An emerging issue in Australian water law', paper submitted to Lawlab 2010 Water Law Award, Sydney, 17 February 2010.

—— 'Beyond native title: The rights response to social justice and the conceptual problems of resource development', Native Title Conference 2010, <http://www.aiatsis.gov.au/ntru/documents/[Virginia Falk] BeyondNativeTitleAbstract.pdf>.

—— 'Draft Indigenous access to water entitlements in Western Australia', Department of Water, Government of Western Australia, 2008.

—— 'Much ado about Bundy on tap' in Denis Wilson, *Peonyden*, 29 July 2009, <*peonyden.blogspot.com/2009_07_01_archive.htm*>.

—— *Indigenous access to water in Australia*, Department of Water, Western Australia, 2008.

—— 'The rise and fall of ATSIC: A personal opinion' (2004) 8(4) *Australian Indigenous Law Reporter*.

Federal Race Discrimination Commissioner, *Water: A report on the provision of water and sanitation in remote Aboriginal and Torres Strait Islander communities*, Human Rights and Equal Opportunity Commission, Sydney, 1994.

Fenwick, Julie, *Worrying about our land: Conceptualising land rights 1963–1971*, Monash Publications, Clayton, Vic., 2001.

Fitzpatrick, Brian, *The British Empire in Australia: An economic history 1834–1939*, Melbourne University Press, 1941.

Forsyth, Hannah, 'The Barkinji people are losing their "mother", the drying Darling River', *The Conversation*, 4 May 2016.

Friends of the Earth Melbourne, <http://www.melbourne.foe.org.au/?q=bmc/indigenous_justice>.

'From little things big things grow — Kev Carmody and Paul Kelly', *YouTube*, uploaded 25 January 2012, <www.youtube.com/watch?v=tbHR-apIHLU>.

Gardner-Rush, Jelita, 'Judicial treatment of international law in Yarmirr' (2004) 23 *Australian Year Book of International Law*.

Garnett, Stephen & Bev Sithole, *Sustainable northern landscapes and the nexus with Indigenous health: Healthy country healthy people*, Research Report NTU07, Land and Water Australia, Canberra, 2007.

Getzler, Joshua, *A history of water rights at common law*, revised ed, Oxford University Press, 2006.

Giblett, Rod, 'Black and white: cross-cultural colour-coding of the life-blood of the earth body', *University of South Australia*, 14 February 2007, <http://www.unisa.edu.au/waterpolicylaw/documents/water_justice_papers.pdf>.

Gibson, Joel, 'Aboriginal council axed by Macklin', *The Sydney Morning Herald*, 16 January 2008, viewed 5 October 2016, <http://www.smh.com.au/news/national/aboriginal-council-axed-by-macklin/2008/01/15/1200159449363.html>.

—— 'Damming the river of shame', *The Sydney Morning Herald*, 3–4 January 2009, p. 14.

Giddens, Anthony, *Sociology*, revised ed, Polity Press, Cambridge, 1993.

Gillespie, Dan, Peter Cooke & John Taylor, *Improving the capacity of Indigenous people to contribute to the conservation of biodiversity in Australia*, Environment Australia & the Biological Diversity Advisory Council, Canberra, 2001.

Glaskin, Katie, 'Native title and the bundle of rights model: Implications for the recognition of Aboriginal relations to country' (2003) 13(1) *Anthropological Forum*, pp. 67-88.

Goldflam, Russell, 'Silence in court! Problems and prospects in Aboriginal legal interpreting' in Diana Eades (ed.), *Language in evidence: Issues confronting Aboriginal and multicultural Australia*, University of New South Wales Press, Sydney, 1995.

Goldschein, Eric, '15 outrageous facts about the bottled water industry', *Business Insider Australia*, 28 October 2011, viewed 10 October 2016, <http://www.businessinsider.com.au/facts-bottled-water-industry-2011-10?r=US&IR=T#the-first-documented-case-of-selling-bottled-water-was-in-boston-in-the-1760s-1>.

Goodall, Heather, 'New South Wales' in Ann McGrath (ed.), *Contested ground: Australian Aborigines under the British Crown*, Allen & Unwin, St Leonards, NSW, 1995, pp. 55–120.

Goode, Brad, Colin Irvine & Melinda Cockman, *Report on conferences held with the Nyungar community for the South West Water Plan*, Department of Water, Perth, 2007.

Goodman, Ed, 'Protecting habitat for off-reservation tribal hunting and fishing rights: Tribal co-management as a reserved right' (2000) 30 *Environmental Law*, pp. 279–362.

Gover, Kirsty & Natalie Baird, 'Identifying the Maori treaty partner' (2002) 52(1) *University of Toronto Law Journal*.

Grattan, Michelle & Lindsay Murdoch, 'Labor cool on any change to leases', *The Age*, 8 April 2005, p. 4.

Green, Dick in conjunction with the community of Wagga Wagga, *Wiradjuri heritage study for the Wagga Wagga Local Government Area of New South Wales*, revised ed, Wagga Wagga City Council & NSW Heritage Office, Wagga Wagga, NSW, 2003.

Greer, Germaine, 'Whitefella jump up: The shortest way to nationhood' (2003) 11 *Quarterly Essay*, issue.

Bibliography

Han, Esther & Emily Smith, 'Bottled water producer admits consumers paying for plastic not "pure, safe" water', *Sydney Morning Herald*, 17 July 2016, viewed 10 October 2016, <http://www.smh.com.au/business/consumer-affairs/bottled-water-producer-admits-consumers-paying-for-plastic-not-pure-safe-water-20160715-gq6oif.html>.

Hargrove, Eugene C, *Foundations of environmental ethics*, Prentice Hall, 1989.

Harris, JW, *Property and justice*, Clarendon Press, Oxford, 1996.

Hawken, Paul, Amory B Lovins & L Hunter Lovins, *Natural capitalism: The next industrial revolution*, Earthscan, Abingdon, Oxon, 1999.

Hawkins, Scott, 'Caught, hook, line and sinker' (1992) 3 *Journal of Indigenous Policy*.

Hawkesbury Nepean Catchment Management Authority, 'World Wetlands Day: Paddy's River', brochure, 2 February 2009.

Hepburn, Samantha, *Principles of property law*, 3rd revised ed, Routledge-Cavendish, Coogee, NSW, & London, 2006.

Hill, Justice Graham, *Which way to Damascus? A Bill of Rights or Chapter III of the Constitution*, Federal Court Intranet, 30 June 2004, <http://intranet.fedcourt.gov.au/upload_judges/judges/Damascus.htm>.

Hill, R, *Native American expressive culture*, Akwe Kon Press, Ithaca, NY, 1995.

Holzberger, Melissa Kate, 'Access to water resources for mining purposes in South Australia' *University of Dundee* <http://www.dundee.ac.uk/cepmlp/car.html/car7_article10.pdf>.

Horne, Donald, *The lucky country: Australia today*, Penguin, Ringwood, Vic., 1964.

House Standing Committee on Regional Australia, *Of drought and flooding rains: Inquiry into the impact of the Murray-Darling Basin Plan in regional Australia*, Parliament of Australia, Canberra, 2011.

Howlett, M, M Gray & B Hunter, *Unpacking the incomes of Indigenous and non-Indigenous Australians: Wages, government income and other payments*, Working Paper No. 99, Centre for Aboriginal Economic Policy Research, Canberra, 2015.

Huber, Sean, 'The Wellesley Island decision: Offshore native title post *Yarmirr* and *Ward*' (2004) 23 *University of Queensland Law Journal*, pp. 244

Human Rights and Equal Opportunity Commission, *Bringing them home: Report of the National Inquiry into the Separation of Aboriginal and Torres Strait Islander Children from Their Families*, Human Rights and Equal Opportunity Commission, Sydney, 1997.

Imai, Shin, 'Sound science, careful policy analysis, and ongoing relationships: Integrating litigation and negotiation in Aboriginal lands and resources' (2003) 41(4) *Osgoode Hall Law Journal*, pp. 587-627.

Indigenous Business Australia, *Indigenous investment principles*, Majura Park, ACT, 2015, <https://www.google.com.au/?client=firefox-b#q=indigenous+investment+principles&gfe_rd=cr>.

Indigenous Peoples Kyoto Water Declaration, Third World Water Forum, Kyoto, Japan, 2003.

Irvine, Jessica, 'Mineral boom frittered away', *The Sydney Morning Herald*, 8–9 March 2008, p. 13.

Jackson, Sue, 'Compartmentalising culture: The articulation and consideration of Indigenous values in water resource management' (2006) 37(1) *Australian Geographer*.

—— *Indigenous interests and the National Water Initiative: water management, reform and implementation: Report for the IWPG, November 2007*, NAILSMA (North Australian Indigenous land and Sea Management Alliance), Darwin, 2007.

—— 'Indigenous values for water resource management' (2005) 12(3) *Australasian Journal of Environmental Management*, pp. 136-146

—— 'Panel Discussion', speech delivered at the Garma Indigenous Water Knowledge, Indigenous Water Interests Conference, Gove Northern Territory, 7 August 2008).

—— & Joe Morrison, 'Indigenous perspectives in water management, reforms and implementation' in Karen Hussey & Stephen Dovers (eds), *Managing water for Australia: The social and institutional challenges*, CSIRO Publishing, Collingwood, Vic., 2007, pp. 23–42.

—— & Joe Morrison, 'Indigenous perspectives in water management, reforms and implementation', draft manuscript, LWA.NWIx4.doc, 2006.

—— Brad Moggridge & Cathy Robinson, *Effects of changes in water availability on Indigenous people of the Murray–Darling Basin: A scoping study and report to the Murray–Darling Basin Authority*, CSIRO, 2010.

—— Michael Storrs & Joe Morrison, 'Recognition of Aboriginal rights, interests and values in river research and management: Perspectives from northern Australia' (2005) 6(2) *Ecological Management and Restoration*.

Jagger, Ken & Helen Kurz, 'Native title and the tide of history: The *Yorta Yorta* case' December 2002–January 2003 17(6) *Australian Property Law Bulletin*.

Jakeman, Tony, Rebecca Letcher & Serena Chen, 'Integrated assessment of impacts and water allocation changes across social, economic and environmental dimensions' in Karen Hussey & Stephen Dovers (eds), *Managing water for Australia: The social and institutional challenges*, CSIRO Publishing, Collingwood, Vic., 2007, pp. 97–112.

Jebb, Mary Anne, *Blood, sweat and welfare: A history of white bosses and Aboriginal pastoral workers*, University of Western Australia Press, Nedlands, WA, 2002.

Johnston, Elliott, *Royal Commission into Aboriginal Deaths in Custody: National report*, vol. 1, Australian Government, Canberra, 1991.

Jopson, Debra, 'Aborigines demand $250 million over water rights system', *The Sydney Morning Herald*, 3 June 2002, p. 1.

Juleff, Stephanie, 'Budj Bim heritage site to get $8 million upgrade to help UNESCO bid', *ABC News* (Sydney), 24 April 2016, viewed 10 October 2016, <http://www.abc.net.au/news/2016-04-24/government-to-spend-8m-to-improve-budj-bim-heritage-site/7353772>.

Kabaila, Peter Rimas, *Wiradjuri places: The Murrumbidgee River basin*, vol. 1 of *Wiradjuri places*, revised ed, Black Mountain Projects, Canberra, 1998.

Karvelas, Patricia, 'Push for Aboriginal rights over resources', *The Australian*, 11 April 2008, p. 6.

Kauffman, Paul, *Wik, mining and Aborigines*, Allen & Unwin, St Leonards, NSW, 1998.

Keirnan, Tamar, 'Water justice: water as a human right in Israel' in Gidon Bromberg (ed.), *Global Issue Papers No. 15*, Henrich Boll Stiftung, Friends of the Earth, Middle East, March, 2005.

Kelly, Brett, *Collective wisdom: interviews with prominent Australians*, Clown, Strathfield, NSW, 1998.

Kempton, Kate & Olthuis Kleer Townshend, *Bridge over troubled waters: Canadian law on Aboriginal and treaty water rights and the Great Lakes Annex*, Toronto, 2003, p. 13, <http://www.thewaterhole.ca/publications/aboriginal20%water%20rights%20and%20annex%20paper%20finalpdf>.

Kildea, Paul & George Williams, 'The Constitution and the management of water in Australia's rivers' (2010) 32 *Sydney Law Review*, pp. 595–616.

Kimberley Aboriginal Law and Culture Centre, *New legend: A story of law and culture and the fight for self-determination in the Kimberley*, revised ed, Kimberley Aboriginal Law and Culture Centre, Fitzroy Crossing, WA, 2007.

Knight, Peter, 'Land tenure and relationship to place: An essay uniting spatial, political, and spiritual themes in the formulation of a PhD topic', Department of Surveying, University of Otago, <http://www.business.otago.ac.nz/SIRCO5/conferences/2000/14_knight.pdf>.

Lametti, David, 'The concept of property: Relations through objects of social wealth' (2003) 53 *University of Toronto Law Journal*, pp. 325-378.

Land, Approvals and Native Title Unit, 'Noongar Recognition Act 2016', 2016, viewed 10 October 2016, <https://www.dpc.wa.gov.au/lantu/south-west-native-title-settlement/Noongar-Recognition-Act-2016/Pages/default.aspx>.

—— 'Settlement publications', 2016, viewed 10 October 2016, <https://www.dpc.wa.gov.au/lantu/south-west-native-title-settlement/Pages/Settlement-Publications.aspx>.

Langton, Marcia, *An Aboriginal ontology of being and place: The performance of Aboriginal property relations in the Princess Charlotte Bay area of eastern Cape York Peninsula, Australia* (PhD Thesis, Macquarie University, 2005).

—— 'Freshwater' in Lingiari Foundation, *Background Briefing Papers: Indigenous Rights to Waters*, Broome, 2002, pp. 43-64, <http://pandora.nla.gov.au/pan/41033/20060106-0000/ATSIC/issues/Indigenous_Rights/Indigenous_Rights_Waters/docs/layout_papers.pdf>

—— 'Real change for real people', *The Australian*, 26–27 January 2008, p. 31.

Larcombe, FA, *The origin of local government in New South Wales 1831–58*, Sydney University Press, 1973.

Law Institute of Victoria, *Charter impact project report*, Law Institute of Victoria, Melbourne, 2011, viewed 1 January 2012, <http://www.liv.asn.au/News-and-Publications/Victoria-Human-Rights-Charter>.

Lee, Julian, 'Message on a bottle labelled as greenwash', *The Sydney Morning Herald*, 23–24 February 2008, p. 11.

Lennon, Jane, Brian Egloff, Adrian Davey & Ken Taylor, *Conserving the cultural values of natural areas: A discussion paper*, University of Canberra, 1999.

Lewis, Daniel & Marian Wilkinson, 'Licence to spill is a big water fight', *The Sydney Morning Herald*, 30 June–1 July 2007, p. 30.

Lynch, Andrew, 'Judge right on rights', *The Australian*, 20 March 2009, p. 28.

McDonald, Edward, Bryn Coldrick & Linda Villiers, *Study of groundwater-related Aboriginal cultural values on the Gnangara Mound, Western Australia*, Department of Environment Western Australia, 2005.

Macdonald, Gaynor, 'Self-determination or control: Aborigines and land rights legislation in New South Wales' (1998) 24 *Social Analysis*, pp. 34–49.

McFarlane, Bardy, 'The National Water Initiative and acknowledging Indigenous interests in planning' (Paper presented at the National Water Conference, Sydney, 2004) <http://www.nntt.gov.au/news-and-communications/speeches-and-papers/documents/2004/speeches%20national%20water%20initiative%20mcfarlane%20november%202004.pdf>.

McGrath, Ann, 'Tasmania: 1' in Ann McGrath (ed.), *Contested ground: Australian Aborigines under the British Crown* Allen & Unwin, St Leonards, NSW, 1995, pp. 306–37.

McHugh, PG, 'Aboriginal title in New Zealand: A retrospect and prospect' (2004) 2 *New Zealand Journal of Public and International Law*.

McLachlin, Beverley 'Reconciling sovereignty: Canada and Australia's dialogue on Aboriginal rights' (2003) Federal Court, Sydney, p. 3 <http://unicorn.fedcourt.gov.au/uhtbin/cgisirsi/0000/000/38/10/x?user_id=SYD_WEBBpassword=SYD_WEB>.

McNeil, Kent, *Common law Aboriginal title*, Clarendon Press, Oxford, 1989.

—— *The inherent right of self-government: Emerging directions for legal research*, First Nations Governance Centre, November, 2004.

—— 'The vulnerability of Indigenous land rights in Australia and Canada' (2004) 42(2) *Osgoode Hall Law Journal*.

Maddox, Marion, *Indigenous religion in secular Australia*, Research Paper No. 11, Department of the Parliamentary Library, Canberra, 1999–2000.

Maine, Sir Henry Sumner, *Ancient law: Its connection with the early history of society and its relation to modern ideas*, John Murray, London, 1927 (first published 1906).

Marsden, John, 'Water entitlements and property rights: An economic perspective' in *Property: Rights and responsibilities, current Australian thinking*, Land and Water Australia, Canberra, 2002.

Marshall, Lucy & Colleen Hattersley, *Reflections of a Kimberley woman*, Mudjalla, Broome, WA, 2005.

Marshall, Paul (ed.), *Raparapa: Stories from the Fitzroy River drovers*, 2nd ed, Magabala Books, Broome, 2011.

Marshall, Virginia, A web of Aboriginal water rights: Examining the competing Aboriginal claim for water property rights and interests in Australia (PhD thesis, Macquarie University, Sydney, 2014).

—— 'Aboriginal water rights and interests: Constitutional recognition', Symposium, Legal Intersections Research Centre, Faculty of Law, University of Wollongong, NSW, 23 May 2012.

—— 'Indigenous water rights and governance' (Paper presented at the Trade, Intellectual Property and the Knowledge of Indigenous Peoples: The Developmental Frontier Conference, University of Victoria, New Zealand, 7–10 December 2010).

—— 'The progress of Aboriginal water rights & interests in the Murray Darling Basin in NSW: An essential element of culture' (2015) 30(6-7) *Australian Environment Review*.

Martin, Sarah, *Lake Victoria environmental impact statement anthropological report*, Department of Land and Water Conservation (NSW) & Murray-Darling Basin Commission, Canberra, 1997.

—— *The Paakantji claimants Wentworth Native Title Claim NC 95/10: applicants Irene Mitchell and Ray Lawson Snr* (Research report, NSW Aboriginal Land Council, Parramatta, NSW, 1998).

Maxwell, Rudi, '21 Aboriginal nations join water battle', *Koori Mail*, 2 May 2012, p. 35.

Meek, C K, *Land law and custom in the colonies* Oxford University Press, London, 1946.

Meyers, Gary D, 'Aboriginal rights to the profits of the land: The inclusion of traditional fishing and hunting rights in the content of native title' in Richard H Bartlett & Gary D Meyers (eds), *Native title legislation in Australia* University of Western Australia, Nedlands, WA, 1994, pp. 213–30.

—— 'Native title rights in natural resources: A comparative perspective of common law jurisprudence' (2002) 19(4) *Environmental and Planning Law Journal*, pp. 245–57.

Mikaere, Ani, Nin Thomas & Kerensa Johnston, 'Treaty of Waitangi and Māori Land Law' (2003) *New Zealand Land Review*.

Milovanovic, Selma, 'Native title proof may be reversed', *The Age*, 10–11 April 2009, p. 3.

Moodie, Douglas JR, 'Aboriginal maritime title in Nova Scotia: an extravagant and absurd idea?' (2003) 37(1) *University of British Columbia Law Review*, pp. 495–540.

Morgan, Monica, Lisa Strelein & Jessica Weir, *Indigenous rights to water in the Murray–Darling Basin: In support of the Indigenous final report to the Living Murray Initiative*, Research Discussion Paper No. 14, AIATSIS, Canberra, 2004.

Morris, James DK & Jacinta Ruru, 'Giving voice to rivers: Legal personality as a vehicle for recognising Indigenous peoples' relationships to water?' (2010) 14(2) *Australian Indigenous Law Review*, pp. 49–59.

Mountford, Charles P, *The Dreamtime book: Australian Aboriginal myths* (Rigby, Adelaide, revised ed, 1976).

Mueke, Stephen, *Ancient and modern: Time, culture and Indigenous philosophy* (University of New South Wales Press, Sydney, revised ed, 2006).

Murray, Elizabeth, 'Pilbara anger over drowned spring', *Koori Mail*, 6 June 2007, p. 17.

——'Welfare to work legislation criticised', *Koori Mail*, 21 November 2007, p. 13.

Murray-Darling Basin Authority, *Aboriginal partnerships action plan*, Murray-Darling Basin Authority, Canberra, 2015.

——*Delivering a healthy working basin: About the draft Basin Plan*, Discussion paper, Australian Government, Canberra, 2011.

—— *Guide to the proposed Basin Plan: Overview*, volume 1, Australian Government, Canberra, 2010.

—— *Guide to the proposed Basin Plan: Technical background*, volume 2, part 1, Australian Government, Canberra, 2010.

——*Plain English summary of the proposed Basin Plan*, Australian Government, Canberra, 2011.

——*Proposed Basin Plan: A draft for consultation*, Australian Government, Canberra, 2011.

——*The Draft Basin Plan: Catchment by catchment*, Australian Government, Canberra, 2011.

Murray-Darling Basin Commission, 'Final draft: The Murray-Darling Basin Indigenous Action Plan', Murray-Darling Basin Commission, Canberra, 2005, <www.mdbc.gov.au>.

—— *The Murray-Darling Basin Indigenous Action Plan*, Murray-Darling Basin Commission, Canberra, 29 July 2005, <www.mdbc.gov.au>.

Murray-Darling Basin Ministerial Council, *Murray-Darling Basin environmental resources study*, Murray-Darling Basin Ministerial Council, Sydney, 1987.

NAILSMA (North Australian Indigenous Land and Sea Management Alliance), *A policy statement on north Australian Indigenous water rights*, NAILSMA, November 2009, <http://nailsma. org.au/sites/default/files/Water-Policy-Statement-web-view.pdf>.

—— *Garma International Indigenous Water Declaration*, NAILSMA, 2008, viewed 24 May 2012, <http://nailsma.org.au/nailsma/forum/download/Garma-International-Indigenous-Water-Declaration.pdf>.

——'Indigenous Water Policy Group to take an Indigenous position on water to the 2020 Summit', media release, 18 April 2008.

National Human Rights Consultation Committee, *National human rights consultation report*, 2009, Australian Government, Barton, ACT, <http://www.ag.gov.au/RightsAndProtections/HumanRights/TreatyBodyReporting/Documents/NHRCReport.pdf>.

National Human Rights Network, 'Australian non-governmental organisations submission to the Committee on the Elimination of Racial Discrimination', National Association of Community Legal Centres, January 2005.

National Parks and Wildlife NSW, 'D'harawal brochure', NSW Department of Environment and Conservation, 2005.

National Water Commission, Australian Indigenous Water Focus Group, National Water Commission, Adelaide, 18 November 2008.

——*Australian water reform 2009: Second biennial assessment of progress in implementation of the National Water Initiative*, Australian Government, Canberra, 2010.

—— *Intergovernmental agreement on a national water initiative between the Commonwealth of Australia and the governments of New South Wales, Victoria, Queensland, South Australia, the Australian Capital Territory and the Northern Territory*, Australian Government, 2004, viewed

2 September 2016, <http://nwc.gov.au/__data/assets/pdf_file/0008/24749/Intergovernmental-Agreement-on-a-national-water-initiative.pdf>.

—— *National water assessments* <http://www.nwc.gov.au/nwi/biennial-assessments>.

—— *The National Water Initiative: Securing Australia's water future: 2011 assessment*, Australian Government, Canberra.

Neal, Tony, 'The forensic challenge of native title' (1995) *Law Institute Journal*, pp. 880–3.

Neate, Graeme, 'The tidal wave of justice and the tide of history: Ebbs and flows in Indigenous land rights in Australia' (Paper presented at the 5th World Summit of Noble Peace Laureates, Italy, 10 November 2004).

Neidjie, Big Bill, Stephen Davis & Allan Fox, *Australia's Kakadu man Bill Neidjie* (Resource Managers, Darwin, revised ed, 1986).

New South Wales, *Charter of Rights update*, Parl. Paper No.1/09, Gareth Griffith QC, January 2009.

—— *Official record of the debates of the National Australasian Convention*, Sydney, 2 March–9 April 1891.

—— *Parliamentary debates: Water Management Bill*, Legislative Assembly, 9393, 21–22 June 2000 (Second Reading)

—— Government, *Parliamentary Debates*, Legislative Assembly, 14 November 2000, 9855 (George Souris).

New South Wales Aboriginal Community Water and Sewerage Working Group, 'Aboriginal community water supply and sewerage systems', Draft report, Department of Commerce NSW Sustainable Water Solutions, 2006.

—— 'Aboriginal community water supply and sewerage', Final draft report, Department of Commerce (NSW) Sustainable Water Solutions, 2007.

New South Wales Legislative Assembly, *Parliamentary debates*, 14 November 2000, 9855.

New Zealand Government, 'Ngāti Apa and foreshore', Parliamentary Briefing Note No. 12, Parliamentary Library, December 2003.

Niblett, Michael, *Preliminary anthropological report on the Walbanga (Walbunja) Application Area NC 96/29 NSW South Coast*, NSW Aboriginal Land Council, Parramatta, NSW, 2002

Nicholls, Frank G, 'Aboriginal hunting rights and fauna protection legislation: *Yanner v Eaton* [1999] in its political context' (2000) 30(3) *Environmental Policy and Law*, pp. 143–6.

Nicholson, Robert, 'Law and language: The case of native title', Federal Court, 2004 <http://intranet.fedcourt.gov.au/search97cgi_cgi?Action=View&VdkVgwkey=%2>.

—— 'The use of history in proving native title: A judge's perspective', Federal Court, viewed 6 September 2016 <http://intranet.fedcourt.gov.au/search97cgi/s97_cgi?Action=View&VdkVgwKey=%2...>.

Northern Territory Government, 'Office of Township leasing', 17 December 2012, <http://www.otl.gov.au/site/>.

NSW Aboriginal Land Council, 'NSW Native Title Bill: A brief critique by the NSW Aboriginal Land Council', Working Paper, 1993.

—— 'Submission to the Department of Natural Resources (NSW): Draft implementation plan for the National Water Initiative', 8 December 2005.

—— 'United Nations Permanent Forum on Indigenous Issues, Tenth Session, New York, 16–27 May 2011: Agenda item 6: The right to water and indigenous peoples', viewed 20 March 2012, <http://www.hreoc.gov.au/social_justice/international_docs/2011/7_Right_to_Water_NSWALC_FINAL.pdf>.

Bibliography

——& NSW Department of Land and Water Conservation, 'Report on the Boomanulla Conference for Country' (Paper presented at the Boomanulla Conference, Canberra, 5–6 March 2002).

NSW Parliament, 'Inquiry into Crown land' (23 June 2016), viewed 5 October 2016, <https://www.parliament.nsw.gov.au/committees/inquiries/Pages/inquiry-details.aspx?pk=2404>.

Nyikina Mangala Aboriginal Corporation, Draft Mardoowarra Wila Booroo plan, 2010, Nyikina Mangala Aboriginal Corporation, WA.

Nyikina Mangala Community School (Jarlmadangah Community), *Woonyoomboo* (Jarlmadangah Burru Aboriginal Corporation, WA, 2nd ed, 2004).

O'Donnell, Michael, *NAILSMA TRaCK Project 6.2: Indigenous rights in water in northern Australia*, NAILSMA Tropical Rivers and Coastal Knowledge & Australian Government, Darwin, 2011, viewed 11 October 2016, <http://www.nailsma.org.au/nailsma/projects/downloads/TRaCK-6-2-Indigenous-Rights-in-Water-in-Northern-Australia-Final-Report-2.pdf>.

O'Farrell, Barry, 'Media launch', speech delivered at the Goulburn Liberal Party Office, Goulburn, NSW, February 2007.

O'Regan, Tipene, 'Draft declaration and recommendations for Indigenous water knowledge and interests', speech delivered at the Garma Indigenous Water Knowledge, Indigenous Water Interests Conference, Gove, Northern Territory, 8 August 2008.

Olsen, Anna & Ray Lovett, 'Existing knowledge, practice and responses to violence against women in Australian Indigenous communities: State of knowledge paper', Research Paper No. 2, Australia's National Research Organisation for Women's Safety, Sydney, 2016).

Osborne, Katy, Fran Baum & Lynsey Brown, 'What works? A review of actions addressing the social and economic determinants of Indigenous health', Issues Paper No. 7, Closing the Gap Clearinghouse, Canberra, 2013).

Palmer, Kingsley, 'Understanding another ethnography: The use of early texts in native title inquiries' in Toni Bauman (ed.), *Dilemmas in applied native title anthropology in Australia* (AIATSIS, Canberra, 2010) pp. 72-96.

Parke, Erin, 'WA Government urged to fix contaminated water supplies in remote Indigenous communities', *ABC*, 23 May 2016.

Pascoe, Bruce, *Dark emu black seeds: Agriculture or accident?* (Magabala Books, Broome, WA, 2nd revised ed 2014, 2016).

Patton, Paul, 'The translation of Indigenous land into property: The mere analogy of English jurisprudence' (2000) 6(1) *Parallax*, pp. 25–38.

Pearce, Dennis & Robert Geddes, *Statutory interpretation in Australia*, (Lexis Nexis Butterworths, Sydney, 7th ed, 2011).

Pearlman, Jonathon, 'Water will be the next big battleground, says Chief Justice', *The Sydney Morning Herald*, 11 February 2008.

Pearson, Christopher, 'Stanner's Aboriginal essays show their age', *The Australian*, 21–22 March 2009.

Pearson, Noel, *Our right to take responsibility* (Noel Pearson, Cairns, Qld, 2000).

Penner, JE, *The idea of property in law* (Clarendon Press, Oxford, 1997).

Peterson, Nicolas, 'Capitalism, culture and land rights: Aborigines and the state in the Northern Territory' (1985) 18 *Social Analysis*, pp. 85–101.

——& Bruce Rigsby (eds), 'Customary marine tenure in Australia' (1998) *Oceania Monograph* 48, University of Sydney.

Poiner, Gretchen, *The good rule: Gender and other power relationships in a rural community* (Sydney University Press, 1990).

Productivity Commission, *Water rights arrangements in Australia and overseas: Annex A, Murray-Darling Basin*, Productivity Commission, Melbourne, 2003.

Queensland Government, 'Freehold title information for communities', 4 June 2015, viewed 6 September 2016, <https://www.qld.gov.au/atsi/environment-land-use-native-title/freehold-title-communities>.

Radcliffe, Murray, 'International perspective', speech delivered at the Australian Indigenous Water Focus Group, National Water Commission, Adelaide, 18 November 2008.

—— 'National Water Commission introduction and engagement', speech delivered at the Australian Indigenous Water Focus Group, National Water Commission, South Australia, 18 November 2008.

—— 'Strategic development for future Indigenous dialogue and engagement at the national level', speech delivered at the Australian Indigenous Water Forum Focus Group, National Water Commission, Adelaide, 18 November 2008.

Rawls, John, *A Theory of Justice* (Harvard University Press, Cambridge, 1971).

Raymond, James, *The New South Wales calendar and General Post Office directory 1832* The Trustees of the Public Library of New South Wales, first published 1832, 1966 ed.

Read, Peter, 'Northern Territory' in Ann McGrath (ed.), *Contested ground: Australian Aborigines under the British Crown* (Allen & Unwin, St Leonards, NSW, 1995) pp. 269–305.

Reilly, Alex, 'Cartography, property and the aesthetics of place: Mapping native title in Australia' in AT Kenyon & PD Rush (eds), (2004) 34 *Aesthetics of law and culture: Texts, images, screens*, pp. 221–39.

—— & Ann Genovese, 'Claiming the past: Historical understanding in Australian native title jurisprudence' (2004) 3 *Indigenous Law Journal*, pp. 19–42.

Reynolds, Henry, *Frontier: Aborigines, settlers and land* (Allen & Unwin, St Leonards, NSW, 1987).

—— & Dawn May, 'Queensland' in Ann McGrath (ed.), *Contested ground: Australian Aborigines under the British Crown* (Allen & Unwin, St Leonards, NSW, 1995) pp. 168–207.

Richardson, Benjamin, 'The ties that bind: Indigenous peoples and environmental governance' in Benjamin Richardson, Shin Imai & Kent McNeil (eds), *Indigenous peoples and the law: Comparative and critical perspectives* (Hart, Oxford and Portland, Oregon, 2009) pp. 33770.

Ridge, Kathy, 'Water supply' in David Farrier & Paul Stein (eds), *Environmental law handbook* (Redfern Legal Centre, Redfern NSW, 4th ed, 2006).

Ridgeway, Aden, 'Addressing the economic exclusion of Indigenous Australians through native title', Mabo Lecture, Coffs Harbour, NSW, 3 June 2005 <http://www.aiatsis.gov.au/ntru/nativetitleconference/conf2005/papers/RidgewayA.pdf>.

Rigney, Matthew, 'Broad principles on Indigenous engagement on water issues', speech delivered at the Australian Indigenous Water Focus Group, National Water Commission, Adelaide, South Australia, 18 November 2008.

Rimmer, Matthew, 'Blame it on Rio: biodiscovery, native title, and traditional knowledge', (2003) 7 *Southern Cross University Law Review*.

Rintoul, Stuart, 'Dog eat dog in the fight for water', *The Australian*, 12–13 July 2008, p. 8.

Roughley, Alice & Susie Williams, *The engagement of Indigenous Australians in natural resource management: Key findings and outcomes from Land and Water Australia and the broader literature*, Land & Water Australia, 2007, Canberra, viewed 5 October 2016, <www.aiatsis.gov.au/research/publications/Land&Water/pn21610.pdf>.

Rowse, Tim, *Indigenous futures: Choice and development for Aboriginal and Torres Strait Islander Australia* (University of New South Wales Press, Sydney, 2002).

Rural and Regional Affairs and Transport References Committee, *Rural water usage in Australia*, Parliament of Australia, Darwin, 18 November 2003.

Sackville, Ronald, *The 2003 term: the inaccessible constitution*, Federal Court, 30 June 2004, <http://intranet.fedcourt.gov.au/search97cgsi/s97_cgi?Action=View&VdkVgwKey=%2>.

Saggers, S & D Gray, *Aboriginal health and society: The traditional and contemporary Aboriginal struggle for better health* (Allen & Unwin, North Sydney, 1991).

Santa Clara University, 'Common grounds, common waters: Toward a water ethic' (2008) *Santa Clara Journal of International Law Symposium* <http://scjil.wordpress.com/program-description>.

Santoro, Emilio, 'The rule of law and the liberties of the English: The interpretation of Albert Venn Dicey' in Pietro Costa & Danilo Zolo (eds), *The rule of law: history, theory and criticism* (Springer, The Netherlands, 2007).

Scambary, Ben, *Mining and Indigenous values of water: Gulf of Carpentaria case study*, NAILSMA & CSIRO, Darwin, 2007.

Schiveley, Geoffrey Robert, 'Negotiation and native title: Why common law courts are not a proper fora for determining native land title issues' (2000) 33 *Vanderbuilt Journal of Transnational Law*.

Steering Committee for the Review of Government Service Provision, *Overcoming Indigenous disadvantage: Key indicators 2005*, Productivity Commission, Canberra, 2005.

——*Overcoming Indigenous disadvantage: Key indicators 2011*, Productivity Commission, Canberra, 2011, viewed 1 January 2012, <http://www.pc.gov.au/__data/assets/pdf_file/0018/111609/key-indicators-2011-report.pdf>.

Seaman, Paul, 'The negotiation stage' in Gary Meyers (ed.), *In the wake of Wik: Old dilemmas, new directions in native title law* (National Native Title Tribunal, Perth, 1999).

Select Committee on the Murray-Darling Basin Plan, *Refreshing the plan*, Parliament of Australia, Canberra, 2016, viewed 9 October 2016, <http://www.aph.gov.au/Parliamentary_Business/Committees/Senate/Murray_Darling_Basin_Plan/murraydarling/Report>.

Senate Select Committee on the Administration of Indigenous Affairs, *After ATSIC: Life in the mainstream?* Parliament of Australia, Canberra, 2005.

Sharp, Nonie, 'Australian native title and Irish marine rights: An inquiry on the west coast of Ireland' (1998) 16(2) *Law in Context*.

Shaun Berg, 'A fractured landscape: The effect on Aboriginal title to land by the establishment of the Province of South Australia' in Shaun Berg (ed.), *Coming to terms: Aboriginal title in South Australia* (Wakefield Press, Kent Town, SA, 2010) pp. 1–24.

Shestack, Jerome, 'The Philosophical Foundations of Human Rights' in Janusz Symonides (ed.), *Human rights: concepts and standards* (Ashgate and UNESCO, Aldershot, 2000) pp. 31–61.

Simpson, Tony, Submissions re: Domestic dependant nations, unpublished working paper, 2004.

Simpson, Virginia, 'Aboriginal access to water across Australia', Draft report, South Australian Government, Department of Water, Land and Biodiversity Conservation, 2007.

Skelton, Russell, 'One country, two standards', *The Sydney Morning Herald*, 19–20 May 2007, p. 26.

Smith, JC & David N Weisstub, *The Western idea of law* (Butterworths, London, 1983).

Smith, Stewart, *Water reforms in NSW: An up-date: Briefing paper: Briefing Paper No 12/02*, NSW Parliament, Sydney, September 2002 <http://www.parliament.nsw.gov.au/prod/parlment/publications.nsf/0/435D6C31A6EA...>.

—— *Water reforms in NSW: Briefing paper 4/98*, NSW Parliament, Sydney, 6 November 2006, <http://www.parliament.nsw.gov.au/prod/parlment/publications.nsf/0/435D6C31A6EA...>.

Statt, Graham R, 'Tapping into water rights: an exploration of native entitlement in the Treaty 8 Area of Northern Alberta' (2003) 18(1) *Canadian Journal of Law and Society*, pp. 103–29.

Steiner, Henry J & Philip Alston, *International human rights in context: Law, politics, morals* (Oxford University Press, 2nd ed, 2000) p. 77.

Storey, M, 'The black sea' (1996) 3 *Aboriginal Law Bulletin*, pp. 4–8.

Strelein, Lisa, 'A comfortable existence: commercial fishing and the concept of tradition in native title' (2002) 5 *Balayi: Culture, Law and Colonialism*, pp. 94–123.

—— *AIATSIS: An incubator for Indigenous researchers?* AIATSIS, Canberra, 2011, viewed 2 September 2016, <http://aiatsis.gov.au/sites/default/files/products/submission/aiatsis_-_an_incubator_for_indigenous_researchers.pdf>.

——*Compromised jurisprudence: Native title cases since Mabo* (Aboriginal Studies Press, Canberra, 2nd ed, 2009).

Sturgess, Gary & Michael Wright, *Water rights in rural New South Wales: The evolution of a property rights system* (Centre for Independent Studies, St Leonards, NSW, 1993).

Syme, Geoffrey J & Steve Hatfield-Dodds, 'The role of communication and attitudes research in the evolution of effective resource management arrangements' in Karen Hussey & Stephen Dovers (eds), *Managing water for Australia: The social and institutional challenges* (CSIRO Publishing, Collingwood, Vic., 2007) pp. 11–22.

Tan, Poh-Ling, 'An historical introduction to water reform in NSW — 1975 to 1994' (2002) 19 *Environmental and Planning Law Journal*, pp. 445–60.

—— 'Conflict over water resources in Queensland: All eyes on the Lower Balonne' (2000) 17(6) *Environmental and Planning Law Journal* pp. 545–68.

—— 'Irrigators come first: conversion of existing allocations to bulk entitlements in the Goulburn and Murray catchments, Victoria' (2001) 18(2) *Environmental and Planning Law Journal* pp. 154–87.

—— 'Legal issues relating to water use' in *Property: Rights and Responsibilities, current Australian thinking* (Land and Water Australia, Canberra, 2002).

—— 'Water law reform in NSW - 1995 to 1999' (2003) 20 *Environmental Planning Law Journal*.

—— 'Water licences and property rights: the legal principles for compensation in Queensland' (1999) 16(4) *Environmental and Planning Law Journal* pp. 284–89.

Tarrant, Stella, *Biljabu v Western Australia* HCA <http://www.austlii.edu.au/au/journals/AboriginalLB/1994/13.html>.

Taylor, John, *Tracking change in the relative economics status of Indigenous people in New South Wales*, Discussion Paper No. 277, Australian National University, Canberra, 2005.

Taylor, Rebe, *Unearthed: the Aboriginal Tasmanians of Kangaroo Island* (Wakefield Press, Kent Town, SA, 2002).

Tehan, Maureen, 'Report for the Attention of Members of the Committee on the Elimination of Racial Discrimination, A Hope Disillusioned, an Opportunity Lost? Reflections on Common Law Native Title and Ten Years of the *Native Title Act*' (Report, Foundation for Aboriginal and Islander Research Action, February 2005).

The Australian, 'Bundanoon in world-first ban on bottled water', 26 September 2009, viewed 10 October 2016, <http://www.theaustralian.com.au/news/nation/bundanoon-in-world-first-ban-on-bottled-water/story-e6frg6nf-1225779878437>.

Throsby, Margaret, interview with Geoffrey Robertson, radio interview, 95.70 FM, 1 April 2009.

Tjamiwa, Tony, 'Tjunguringkula waakaripai: Joint management of Uluru National Park' in Jim Birckhead, Terry De Lacy & Laurajane Smith (eds), *Aboriginal involvement in parks and protected areas* (Aboriginal Studies Press, Canberra, 1992) pp. 7–11.

Bibliography

Tobias, Terry N, *Chief Kerry's moose: A guidebook to land use and occupancy mapping, research design and data collection* (Union of British Columbia Indian Chiefs & Ecotrust Canada, Vancouver, 2000).

Toohey, Paul , 'Fishing for votes ends as a dream becomes reality', *The Australian*, 6 August 2008.

Toussaint, Sandy, 'Western Australia' in Ann McGrath (ed.), *Contested ground: Australian Aborigines under the British Crown* (Allen & Unwin, St Leonards, NSW, 1995) pp. 240–68.

Transcript of proceedings, *Harrington-Smith on behalf of the Wongatha People v Western Australia* (Federal Court, No. 9, Lindgren J, July 2002).

Transcript of proceedings, *Jango v Northern Territory* [2004] FCA 1539 (Federal Court, Weiner J).

UNESCO, *Water: A shared responsibility: The United Nations World Water Development Report 2*, UNESCO, Paris, 2006, viewed 1 September 2016, <http://www.unesco.org/new/en/natural-sciences/environment/water/wwap/wwdr/wwdr2-2006/downloads-wwdr2/>.

United Nations, *United Nations Declaration on the Rights of Indigenous Peoples*, viewed 1 July 2011, <http://www.un.org/esa/socdev/unpfii/documents/DRIPS_en.pdf>.

United Nations University Institute of Advanced Studies, 'Water Discussion Paper for the United Nations Permanent Forum on Indigenous Issues, New York 2007', pp. 1–8, <https://www.ias.unu.edu/default.aspx>.

University of Technology Sydney & North West Local Land Services, *Recognising and protecting Aboriginal knowledge associated with natural resource management*, White Paper to the NSW Office of the Environment, UTS, 2014, viewed 9 October, 2016, <https://www.ipaustralia.gov.au/sites/g/files/net856/f/uts_-_recognising_and_protecting_aboriginal_knowledge.pdf>.

UTS News, 'Research aimed at safeguarding Indigenous knowledge receives ARC grant', 7 June 2016, viewed 10 October 2016, <https://www.uts.edu.au/about/faculty-law/news/research-aimed-safeguarding-indigenous-knowledge-receives-arc-grant>.

Verran, Helen, 'Re-imagining land ownership in Australia' (1998) 1(2) *Postcolonial Studies* pp. 237–54.

Victorian Government, *Building the economic base: The Victorian Government's Indigenous Business Development Strategy 2005–2007*, Koori Business Network, Department of Innovation, Industry and Regional, Melbourne, 2007.

Warren, Matthew, 'Rain changes debate', *The Australian*, 23–24 February 2008, p. 1.

Waste Streams, *Trading in the future of water*, 27 September 2006,

Water Reform Implementation Committee, *A blueprint for water reform in Western Australia: Final advice to the Western Australian Government*, Government of Western Australia, December 2006.

Wentworth, William Charles, *Statistical, historical, and political description of the colony of New South Wales and its dependent settlements in Van Diemen's Land: A particular enumeration of the advantages which these colonies offer for emigration, and their superiority in many respects over those possessed by the United States of America* (Griffen Press, London, 1978, first published 1819).

Western Australian Government, *Delivering essential services to remote Aboriginal communities*, Report No. 8, Office of the Auditor General Western Australia, Perth, 2015, viewed 5 October 2016, <https://audit.wa.gov.au/wp-content/uploads/2015/05/report2015_08-AbServices.pdf>.

Western Australian Legislative Assembly, Education and Health Standing Committee, *A successful initiative: Family income management*, Parliament of Western Australia, Perth, 2007.

Westpac Bank, 'The Equator Principles', November 2006, <https://www.westpac.com.au/about-westpac/sustainability/the-way-we-work/commitments-and-partnerships-equator-principles/>.

Whitlam, Gough, *Abiding interests* (University of Queensland Press, St Lucia, Qld, 1997).

Wilcox, Justice Murray, *Should Australia have a Bill of Rights?* Federal Court, 30 June 2004, <http://intranet.fedcourt.gov.au/search97cgi/s97_cgi?Action=View&VdkVgwKey=%2>.

Williams, Chris, *Old land, new landscapes: A story of farmers, conservation and the Landcare movement* (Melbourne University Press, 2004).

Williams, George, 'A court short on answers', *The Australian*, 26–27 January 2008, p. 29.

—— 'Racist premise of our constitution remains', *The Sydney Morning Herald*, 7 April 2009, p. 11.

Williams, Ruth, 'Mining rites', *The Age*, 17 May 2008, p. 5.

Wilson, Deborah, *Different white people: Radical activism for Aboriginal rights 1946–1972* (University of Western Australia Press, Nedlands, WA, 2015).

Windle, Jill & John Rolfe, *Natural resource management and the protection of Aboriginal cultural heritage*, Occasional Paper No. 5, Institute for Sustainable Regional Development, Queensland Government, 2002.

Wolf, Aaron T, *Transboundary waters: Sharing benefits, lessons learned*, International Conference on Freshwater, Bonn 1, 27 March 2007, <http://www.water-2001.de/co_doc/transboundary_waters.pdf>.

Working Group for Advancing Indigenous Reconciliation in Primary Industries and Natural Resource Management, *Indigenous reconciliation in primary industries and natural resource management: Annual report 2006–2007*, Natural Resource Management and Primary Industries Ministerial Councils, 2007.

—— 'Key issues: Indigenous employment and engagement in natural resources management and primary industries', draft report, 2008.

Yamatji Marlpa Barna Maaja Aboriginal Corporation, *Annual Report 2007*, WA, 2007.

Yothu Yindi Foundation, 'Garma Festival Program 2008', <http://yyf.com.au/>

Ziff, Bruce, *Principles of property law* (Carswell, Thomson Reuters, Toronto, 5th ed, 2010).

NOTES

Foreword

1   Justice of the High Court of Australia (1996–2009); Australian Human Rights Medal, 1991; Gruber Justice Prize, 2010.

2   Ch. 4 citing UNESCO, *Water: a shared responsibility: The United Nations World Water Development Report 2*, UNESCO, Paris, 2006, 47, viewed 1 September 2016, <http://www.unesco.org/new/en/natural-sciences/environment/water/wwap/wwdr/wwdr2-2006/downloads-wwdr2/>.

3   *Attorney-General (NSW) v Brown* (1847) 2 SCR (NSW) (app) 30, applied *Milirrpum v Nabalco Pty Ltd (Gove Land Rights Case)* (1971) 17 FLR 141, per Blackburn J.

4   *Brown* (1847) 2 SCR (NSW) (APP) 30 at 33 per Stephen CJ.

5   Ibid 34–5.

6   Mason CJ, Brennan, Deane, Toohey, Gaudron and McHugh JJ; Dawson J dissenting.

7   (1992) 175 CLR 1.

8   Ibid. at 58, per Brennan J (Mason CJ and McHugh J concurring).

9   Ibid. at 42, per Brennan J.

10 Ibid. at 42, per Brennan J.

11 (1996) 187 CLR 1.

12 *Mason v Tritton* (1994) 34 NSWLR 572 at 579–582, per Kirby P. See also Mark Cullen, 'Rights to offshore resources after Mabo 1992 and the Native Title Act 1993 (Cth)', *Sydney Law Review*, vol. 18, no. 2, 1996, p. 124. Cf. M Storey, 'The black sea', *Aboriginal Law Bulletin*, vol. 3, 1996, p. 4, and J Carter (ed.), *Native title and land law: the laws of Australia*, Thomson Reuters, Pyrmont, NSW, 2016, pp. 24–5. See also at 104 [1.3.1250] with references to the *Native Title Act 1993* (Cth), section 17 (2) subsection 17 (3) states that if the entitlement arises only because one, but not both of paras (a) and (b) of subsection (2) is satisfied, the entitlement relates only to the effect of the native title in relation to the onshore place or the offshore place.

13 Toohey, Gaudron, Gummow and Kirby JJ; Brennan CJ, Dawson and McHugh JJ dissenting.

14 *Wik v Queensland* (1996) 187 CLR 1 at 126–127, 130–131 per Toohey J, 221–226, per Kirby J; also at 85 per Brennan CJ (diss). See now *Queensland v Congoo* (2015) 89 ALJR 528; [2015] HCA 17 [34], per French CJ and Keane J. Contrast at [60]–[66] per Hayne J; [87]–[89] per Kiefel J; and [130]–[131] per Bell J. Also [156]–[159] per Gageler J.

15 ALRC, *Connection to Country: Review of Native Title Act 1993* (Cth), ALRC Report 126, ALRC, Sydney, 2015.

16 The recommendations are contained in Ch. 12 *infra*.

17 ALRC, *The Recognition of Aboriginal Customary Law*, ALRC Report 31, ALRC, Sydney, 1986 (2 vols).

18 Australian Government, House of Representatives, *Parliamentary debates*, 18 March 1986, 1475 (Hon. Clyde Holding MP).

19 *Australian Constitution*, s 51 (xxi), amended by Act No. 55 1967.

20 ALRC, *The recognition of Aboriginal customary law*.

Chapter 1 Introduction — the web of water rights

1   Nyikina Mangala Community School, Jarlmadangah Community (WA), *Woonyoomboo* (Jarlmadangah Burru Aboriginal Corporation, 2nd ed, 2004) 26.

2   Ibid. 26. See also Paul Marshall (ed), *Raparapa: Stories from the Fitzroy River drovers* (Magabala Books, 2nd ed, 2011).

3   Neva Collings and Virginia Falk [Marshall], 'Aboriginal peoples in Australia and their spiritual relationship with waterscapes' in Elliot Johnston, Martin Hinton and Daryle Rigney (eds), *Indigenous Australians and the Law* (Routledge-Cavendish, 2nd ed, 2008) 131.

4   Ben Scambary, *Mining and Indigenous Values of Water: Gulf of Carpentaria Case Study* (NAILSMA, CSIRO, Darwin, 2007) 1-2.

5   Ibid.

6   Ibid. 6.

7   Nyikina Mangala Aboriginal Corporation, Draft Mardoowarra Wila Booroo plan (2010) 8. See generally that the word 'country' broadly means the Aboriginal land and waters recognized by Aboriginal peoples to establish the particular boundaries or shared 'country'.

8   The word 'belong' broadly means that a person holds kinship under Nyikina law and the exercise of use, obligation to and rights on land, waters and resources.

9   Nyikina Mangala Aboriginal Corporation, 'Draft Mardoowarra Wila Booroo plan' (2010) 3-7. The meaning of 'wila booroo' is the living water of Nyikina 'country' and 'country' means the land, the water and all tangible and intangible things that exists within the Nyikina boundaries under Nyikina law.

10   Ibid.14.

11   David Cooper and Sue Jackson, 'Preliminary Study on Indigenous Water Values and Interests in the Katherine Region of the Northern Territory', Research Report, CSIRO, Sustainable Ecosystems, March 2008, 26.

12   Generally 'Aboriginal mythology' is defined as 'the totality of the mythology which consists of beliefs, values, traditions etc. of a society or culture or group'. See also 'mythos' 799 and 'logos' 706 in the *Macquarie Concise Dictionary* (Macquarie Library, 4th revised ed, 2006).

13   Kimberley Aboriginal Law and Culture Centre, *New Legend: A Story of Law and Culture and the Fight for Self-determination in the Kimberley* (Kimberley Aboriginal Law and Culture Centre, revised ed, 2007) 16.

14   Charles P Mountford, *The Dreamtime Book: Australian Aboriginal Myths* (Rigby, revised ed, 1976) 36. Mountford was an amateur ethnographic writer around the 1940s to 1960s.

15   Kingsley Palmer, 'Understanding Another Ethnography: the use of Early Texts in Native Title Inquiries' in Toni Bauman (ed), *Dilemmas in Applied Native Title Anthropology in Australia* (Australian Institute of Aboriginal and Torres Strait Islander Studies, 2010) 72-73.

16   *Yorta Yorta Community v Victoria* (2001) 180 ALR 655

17   Graham R Statt, 'Tapping into Water Rights: an Exploration of Native Entitlement in the Treaty 8 Area of Northern Alberta' (2003) 18 *Canadian Journal of Law and Society* 1.

18   ALRC, 'Aboriginal Customary Law: a General Regime for Recognition, Aboriginal Customary Research Papers', Research Paper No 8, (1982) 23.

19   Sue Jackson, Michael Storrs and Joe Morrison, 'Recognition of Aboriginal Rights, Interests and Values in River Research and Management: Perspectives from Northern Australia' (2005) 6(2) *Ecological management and restoration* 107.

20   Jackie Huggins quoted in Stephen Mueke, *Ancient and Modern: Time, Culture and Indigenous Philosophy*, University of New South Wales Press, revised ed, (2006) 104-105.

21   Christopher Pearson, 'Stanner's Aboriginal essays show their age', *The Australian* (Sydney), 21-22 March 2009, 24.

22   Ibid.

23   Bruce Pascoe, *Dark Emu Black Seeds: Agriculture or Accident?* (Magabala, reprinted 2016).

24   Peter Rimas Kabaila, '*Wiradjuri Places: The Murrumbidgee River Basin Volume 1 and Ngunawal*' (Black Mountain Projects, revised ed, 1998) 11.

25   John Borrows, 'Living between Water and Rocks: First Nations, Environmental Planning and Democracy' (1997) 47 *University of Toronto Law Journal* 4.

26   Craig Anthony Tony Arnold, 'The Reconstruction of Property: Property as a Web of Interests' (2002) 26 *Harvard International Law Review* 281-284.

27   Gretchen Poiner, *The Good Rule: Gender and Other Power Relationships in a Rural Community* (Sydney University Press, 1990) 77.

28   Gary D Meyers, 'Aboriginal Rights to the Profits of the Land: The Inclusion of Traditional Fishing and Hunting Rights in the Content of Native Title' in Richard H Bartlett and Gary D Meyers (eds), *Native Title Legislation in Australia* (University of Western Australia, 1994) 221-222.

29   Gleeson C.J., Quoted in Jonathon Pearlman, 'Water Will be the Next Big Battleground, says Chief Justice', *The Sydney Morning Herald*, (Sydney), 11 February 2008.

30   New South Wales Government, *Parliamentary Debates*, Legislative Assembly, 14 November 2000, 9855 (George Souris).

31   Dr Virginia Marshall, 'The progress of Aboriginal water rights & interests in the Murray Darling Basin in NSW: An essential element of culture' (2015) 30 *Australian Environment Review* 158.

32   (1992) 175 CLR 1.

33   Kent McNeil, *Common Law Aboriginal Title* (Clarendon Press, 1989) 298-306. McNeil published his Oxford research thesis which is a comprehensive examination on how English law would bestow title on Indigenous people where they occupied their lands at the time of settlement, and under the doctrine of tenure could the British have legally claimed Indigenous territories. In his conclusion McNeil argues that the Crown would have had international recognition to claim Indigenous land because of the Crown's prerogative and deny Indigenous peoples sovereignty. However McNeil submits that at the municipal level the Crown could not ignore that Indigenous peoples occupied their land or the presumptive title which is held by Indigenous peoples as tenants at the point of the Crown acquiring title. The scope of this book does not allow a deeper analysis of McNeil's research.

34   Valerie Cooms, quoted inLisa Strelein, *AIATSIS: An incubator for Indigenous Researchers?* Australian Institute of Aboriginal and Torres Strait Islander Studies <http://aiatsis.gov.au/sites/default/files/products/submission/aiatsis_-_an_incubator_for_indigenous_researchers.pdf.

Chapter 2 'We belong to water' — Aboriginal identity and cultural authority

1   Big Bill Neidjie, Stephen Davis and Allan Fox, *Australia's Kakadu Man Bill Neidjie* (Resource Managers, revised ed, 1986) 52.

2   Sue Jackson and Joe Morrison, 'Indigenous Perspectives in Water Management, Reforms and Implementation' in Karen Hussey and Stephen Dovers (eds), *Managing Water for Australia:*

The Social and Institutional Challenges (Commonwealth Scientific and Industrial Research Organisation, 2007) 28.

3   National Parks and Wildlife NSW 'D'harawal Brochure', NSW Department of Environment and Conservation, 2005. The information in the brochure was informed by several recognised D'harawal knowledge holders which explains the traditional boundaries and the recognition of bitterwater, freshwater and saltwater Aboriginal people within D'harawal communities.

4   Virginia Falk [Marshall], personal communication with D'harawal peoples, Frances Bodkin and Gavin Andrews, 2006.

5   Virginia Falk, personal communication with Lionel Mongta.

6   Marcia Langton, *An Aboriginal Ontology of Being and Place: The Performance of Aboriginal Property Relations in the Princess Charlotte Bay Area of Eastern Cape York Peninsula*, Australia (PhD Thesis, Macquarie University, 2005) 377.

7   Ibid.

8   S Saggers and D Gray, *Aboriginal Health and Society: The Traditional and Contemporary Aboriginal Struggle for Better Health* (Allen and Unwin, 1991) 44.

9   John Cawte, *The Universe of the Warramirri: Art, Medicine and Religion in Arnhem Land* (UNSW Press, 1993) 12.

10 Ibid.

11 Bruns, Bryan, 'Water tenure reform: Developing an extended ladder of participation', paper presented at Politics of the Commons: Articulating Development and Strengthening Local Practices, RCSD Conference, 11–14 July 2003, Chiang Mai, Thailand, viewed 2 September 2016, <http://www.bryanbruns.com/bruns-ladder.pdf>.

12 David Cooper and Sue Jackson, 'Preliminary Study on Indigenous Water Values and Interests in the Katherine Region of the Northern Territory' ('Research Report', Commonwealth Scientific and Industrial Research Organisation, Sustainable Ecosystems, March 2008) 4.

13 Working Group for Advancing Indigenous Reconciliation in Primary Industries and Natural Resource Management, 'Key Issues: Indigenous Employment and Engagement in Natural Resources Management and Primary Industries' ('Draft Report', 2008) 4.

14 Ibid. 14.

15 Chris Williams, *Old Land, New Landscapes: A Story of Farmers, Conservation and the Landcare Movement* (Melbourne University Press, 2004) 30.

16 Fran Bodkin and Lorraine Robertson, *D'harawal: Seasons and Climatic Cycles* (L Robertson and National Heritage Trust, 2008) 100.

17 Ibid.

18 Hawkesbury Nepean Catchment Management Authority, *World Wetlands Day: Paddys River* ('Brochure', 2 February 2009) 4.

19 Bureau of Meteorology *Indigenous Weather Knowledge: D'harawal Calendar* <http://www.bom.gov.au/iwk/dharawal/>.

20 Ballardong Natural Resource Management Working Group, Avon Catchment Council, *Ballardong Noongar Budjar: Healthy Country, Healthy People* ('Project Study', Australian Government 2006) 7.

21 Ibid. 8.

22 Frances Bodkin, 'Experiencing a Cultural Landscape: The D'harawal Lands of the Yandelora and Wirrimbirra' ('Course Information', 1-2 May 2003). See the section on 'Climatic cycles'.

23 Donna Craig, 'Indigenous Property Rights to Water: Environmental Flows, Cultural Values and Tradeable Property Rights' (2005) *Macquarie University* ('Unpublished essay') 14.

24 Teresa Crowley, 'Culture and Common Property: Indigenous Tenure Issues within Western Society' (Paper presented at 15th Annual Colloquium of the Spatial Information Research Centre, University of Otago, New Zealand, 1-3 December 2003) 2, quoting W Caruana, *Aboriginal Art* (Thames and Hudson, 1993); R Hill, *Native American Expressive Culture* (Akwe Kon Press, 1995) and L Dorais, *Quatag: Modernity and Identity in an Inuit Community* (University of Toronto, 1997).

25 Matthew Rigney, 'Broad Principles on Indigenous Engagement on Water Issues' (Speech delivered at the Australian Indigenous Water Focus Group, National Water Commission, Adelaide, South Australia, 18 November 2008).

26 Jon Altman assisted by V Branchut, 'Fresh Water in the Maningrida Region's Hybrid Economy: Intercultural Contestation over Values and Property Rights' ('Working Paper', No 46, Australian National University, 2008) 27.

27 Katie Glaskin, 'Native Title and the Bundle of Rights Model: Implications for the Recognition of Aboriginal Relations to Country' (2003) 13(1) *Anthropological Forum* 78.

28 Virginia Falk, (2008) personal communication between Aboriginal knowledge holders and the author during Aboriginal site consultation and Aboriginal artefact recovery.

29 Personal communication with Leela Watson (Jarlmadangah Burru Community, Western Australia, July 2016).

30 Ibid.

31 *Bennell v Western Australia* [2006] 153 FCR 120.

32 Ibid. 165. Witness evidence given by Dorothy Gartlett.

33 Virginia Falk, personal communication with D'harawal people, Frances Bodkin and Gavin Andrews during my cultural mentoring, 2006-2007.

34 Ibid.

35 Lucy Marshall and Colleen Hattersley, *Reflections of a Kimberley Woman* (Mudjalla, 2005) 94.

36 Ibid. 13.

37 Ibid. 32.

38 Nyikina Mangala Community School, Jarlmadangah Community (WA), *Woonyoomboo* (Jarlmadangah Burru Aboriginal Corporation, 2nd ed, 2004) 26. John Watson, Senior Lawman of the Nyikina Mangala peoples has cultural responsibility for the story about the mudjala and Woonyoomboo, the creator of the 'mardoowarra' used the 'mudjala' tree.

39 *Milirrpum v Nabalco* (1971) 17 FLR 141 ('*Gove Land Rights Case*') 146.

40 Ibid. 150.

41 Ibid.

42 Ibid. 151.

43 Ibid. 146.

44 (1971) 17 FLR 141.

45 Ibid. 267.

46 Rebe Taylor, *Unearthed: The Aboriginal Tasmanians of Kangaroo Island* (Wakefield Press, 2002) 20.

47 Big Bill Neidjie, Stephen Davis and Allan Fox, *Australia's Kakadu Man Bill Neidjie* (Resource Managers, revised ed, 1986) 31.

48   Sarah Martin, 'The Paakantji Claimants Wentworth Native Title Claim NC 95/10: Applicants Irene Mitchell and Ray Lawson Snr' ('Research Report', NSW Aboriginal Land Council, December 1998) 92.

49   Kimberley Aboriginal Law and Culture Centre, *New Legend: A Story of Law and Culture and the Fight for Self-Determination in the Kimberley* (Kimberley Aboriginal Law and Culture Centre, revised ed, 2007) 16, 38–39.

50   Tony Tjamiwa, *Tjunguringkula waakaripai: Joint Management of Uluru National Park*, (1992) Australian Institute of Aboriginal and Torres Strait Islander Studies Report Series, Jim Birckhead, Terry De Lacy and Laurajane Smith (eds), (Paper presented at Aboriginal Involvement in Parks and Protected Areas, Albury NSW, 22-24 July 1991) 7–11.

51   Ibid. 11.

52   Ibid.

53   Big Bill Neidjie, Stephen Davis and Allan Fox, *Australia's Kakadu Man Bill Neidjie* (Resource Managers, revised ed, 1986) 24.

54   Ibid. 39.

55   Ibid. 54.

56   Ibid. 14.

57   Ronald M Berndt, 'A Profile of Good and Bad in Australian Aboriginal Religion' in *Religious Business: Essays on Australian Aboriginal Spirituality*, Max Charlesworth (ed), (Cambridge University Press, 1998) 42-43.

58   See Chapter 8 on Opinion Rules and Chapter 5 on Examination and Cross-Examination of Witnesses in the ALRC, the NSW Law Reform Commission and the Victorian Law Reform Commission, *Review of the Uniform Evidence Acts*, Discussion Paper No (ALRC) 69 and (NSWLRC) 47 (2005). See also Diana Eades (ed), *Language in Evidence: Issues Confronting Aboriginal and Multicultural Australia* (UNSW Press, 1995).

59   See *Native Title Act 1993* (Cth) s 82(1).

60   [2001] 208 CLR 1.

61   Aboriginal and Torres Strait Islander Social Justice Commissioner, 'Native Title Report 2007' (Human Rights and Equal Opportunity Commission, 2008) 217.

62   Ibid.

63   Transcript of Proceedings, *Harrington-Smith on behalf of the Wongatha People v Western Australia* (Federal Court, No 9, Lindgren J, July 2002) (Harvey Murray during witness evidence for 'Autobiographical and Claims to Country') 5. Transcript states 'Ngurra' means 'country' which one belongs to by birth and skin group.

64   *Jango v Northern Territory* [2004] FCA 1539.

65   Transcript of Proceedings, *Jango v Northern Territory* [2004] FCA 1539 (Federal Court, Weiner J) (Johnny Jango during evidence-in-chief by D Parsons SC *in situ* in November 2003) 21. Transcript provides 'evidence of country'.

66   Ibid.

67   Transcript of Proceedings, *Harrington-Smith on behalf of the Wongatha People v Western Australia* (Federal Court, No 9, Lindgren J, July 2002) (Hudson Westlake during witness evidence for 'Autobiographical and Claims to Country') 14. Note, Mr Murray is a 'wati', initiated man and that his father was also a 'wati', 14; Waitku is men's law, 15.

68   Transcript of Proceedings, *Jango v Northern Territory* [2004] FCA 1539 (Federal Court, Weiner J), (examination-in-chief of Reggie Uluru by D Parsons SC *in situ* in November 2003) 45.

69   Ibid.

70   Ibid. 39.

71   Ibid. 18.

72   *De Rose v South Australia [No. 1]* (2003) FCAFC 286.

73   Ibid See Westlaw, *Case Law* (11 November 2004) <http://au.westlaw.com/result/documenttext.aspx?RS=WLAU4.09&VR=2.0&SP=Fed>

74   Ibid.

75   *Bennell v Western Australia* [2006] 153 FCR 120.

76   Ibid. 232.

77   Ibid. 176.

78   Ibid. 178.

79   141 FCR 457.

80   Ibid. 16.

81   Ibid. 81.

82   Ibid.

83   Ibid.

84   Thomas Mitchell, quoted in Sarah Martin, 'The Paakantji Claimants Wentworth Native Title Claim NC 95/10: Applicants Irene Mitchell and Ray Lawson Snr' ('Research Report', NSW Aboriginal Land Council, December 1998) 60.

85   British Parliament, 'British Parliamentary Records 1841', Papers Relate to the Aborigines Australian Colonies of New South Wales', No 41, 151.

86   Samuel Beckett, quoted in Sarah Martin, 'The Paakantji Claimants Wentworth Native Title Claim NC 95/10: Applicants Irene Mitchell and Ray Lawson Snr' ('Research Report', NSW Aboriginal Land Council, December 1998) 58.

87   In Clark and Heydon (2004). Ian D Clark, and Toby Heydon, *A Bend in the Yarra: A History of the Merri Creek Protectorate Station and Merri Creek Aboriginal School 1841-1851* ('Report Series', Australian Institute of Aboriginal and Torres Strait Islander Studies, 2004).

88   Ibid. 10.

89   Sarah Martin, 'Lake Victoria Environmental Impact Statement Anthropological Report' ('Research Report', Department of Land and Water Conservation (NSW) and Murray-Darling Basin Commission, June 1997) 19-20.

90   Ibid. 20.

91   Ibid. 68.

92   Edward McDonald, Bryn Coldrick and Linda Villiers, 'Study of Groundwater-related Aboriginal Cultural Values on the Gnangara Mound, Western Australia' ('Research Report', Department of Environment Western Australia, October 2005) 37.

93   Ibid As quoted by Edward McDonald et al in 'Study of Groundwater-related Aboriginal Cultural Values on the Gnangara Mound, Western Australia' and citing L Strawbridge, 'Aboriginal Sites in the Perth Metropolitan Area: A Management Scheme', Report to the Department of Aboriginal Affairs, Western Australian Museum, 1988.

94   Ballardong Natural Resource Management Working Group, Avon Catchment Council, 'Ballardong Noongar Budjar: Healthy Country, Healthy People' ('Project Study', Australian Government, 2006) 5.

95   Dick Green in conjunction with the Community of Wagga Wagga, 'Wiradjuri Heritage Study-For the Wagga Wagga Local Government Area of New South Wales' ('Research Report', Wagga Wagga City Council and NSW Heritage Office, revised ed, 2003) 1.

96   Ibid. 58-59

97   Ibid. 59.

98   Ibid. 150.

99   Gavin Andrews, 'Negotiating Aboriginal Access Agreements to Culturally Significant Land, Water and Natural Resources in New South Wales' ('Working Paper', Department of Natural Resources NSW, 2006) 2.

100 Peter Rimas Kabaila, 'Wiradjuri Places: The Murrumbidgee River Basin Volume 1 and Ngunawal' (Black Mountain Projects, revised ed, 1998) 8.

101 Centre for the Indigenous History and the Arts, 'Ngulak Ngarnk Nidja Boodja: Our Mother, This Land' ('Research Project', University of Western Australia, 2000) 62.

102 Brian Egloff, Nicholas Peterson and Sue Wesson, 'Biamanga and Gulaga: Aboriginal Cultural Association with Biamanga and Gulaga National Parks' ('Research Report', Office of the Registrar *Aboriginal Land Rights Act 1983* (NSW) (2005) 59.

103 Dick Green in conjunction with the Community of Wagga Wagga, 'Wiradjuri Heritage Study: For the Wagga Wagga Local Government Area of New South Wales' ('Research Report', Wagga Wagga City Council and NSW Heritage Office, revised ed, 2003) 1.

104 Ibid. 23.

105 Ibid. 20-23.

106 Brett Kelly, *Collective Wisdom: Interviews with Prominent Australians* (Clown, 1998) 142.

107 Germaine Greer, 'Whitefella Jump Up: The Shortest Way to Nationhood' (2003) 11 *Quarterly Essay*, 17.

108 Ibid.

109 *Members of the Yorta Yorta Aboriginal Community v Victoria* [1998] 4 ALIR 91.

110 Ken Jagger and Helen Kurz, 'Native title and the Tide of History: The *Yorta Yorta* Case', December 2002-January 2003 17(6) *Australian Property Law Bulletin* 42.

111 Ibid.

112 *Members of the Yorta Yorta Aboriginal Community v Victoria* [2001] 180 ALR 655.

113 James Cockayne, '*Members of Yorta Yorta Aboriginal Community v Victoria*: Indigenous and Colonial Traditions in Native Title' (2001) 25 *Melbourne University Law Review* 794. See the Macquarie Dictionary definition of 'tradition' in the ordinary meaning of the word quoted by Black CJ in *Members of the Yorta Yorta Aboriginal Community v Victoria* [2001] 180 ALR 655.

114 Ibid.

115 David Lametti, 'The Concept of Property: Relations through Objects of Social Wealth' (2003) 53 *University of Toronto Law Journal* 328.

116 Ibid.

117 Tom Dusevic, 'John Howard: The Making of a Populist' *Time Magazine* (Sydney) 6 March 2006 (9) 22.

118 John Basten, *Beyond Yorta Yorta'*, *Land, Rights, Laws: Issues of Native Title* (October 2003) 2(24) Australian Institute of Aboriginal and Torres Strait Islander Studies 4, 5 <http://www.aiatsis.gov. au/ntru/docs/publications/issues/ip03v2n24.pdf>.

119 Robert Blowes, 'From *terra nullius* to Every Person's Land: A Perspective from Legal History' Australian Institute of Aboriginal and Torres Strait Islander Studies Report Series, Jim Birckhead, Terry De Lacy and Laurajane Smith (eds), (Paper presented at Aboriginal Involvement in Parks and Protected Areas, Albury NSW, 22-24 July 1991) 149.

120 Ibid.

121   See Queensland Government <https://www.qld.gov.au/atsi/environment-land-use-native-title/ freehold-title-communities/> and the Northern Territory Government <http://www.otl.gov.au/ site/about.html>.

122   Rod Giblett, 'Black and White: Cross-Cultural Colour-Coding of the Life-Blood of the Earth Body' (14 February 2007) *University of South Australia* 64 <http://www.unisa.edu.au/ waterpolicylaw/documents/water_justice_papers.pdf>.

123   Gary D Meyers, 'Aboriginal Rights to the Profits of the Land: The Inclusion of Traditional Fishing and Hunting Rights in the Content of Native Title' in Richard H Bartlett and Gary D Meyers (eds), *Native Title Legislation in Australia* (University of Western Australia, 1994) 221-222.

124   Sean Brennan, Larissa Behrendt, Lisa Strelein and George Williams, *Treaty* (Federation Press, 2005) 32.

125   Commonwealth, Royal Commission into Aboriginal Deaths in Custody, *National Report: Overview and Recommendations* (1991) vol 1 [1.10] <http://www.austlii.edu.au/au/other/ IndigLRes/rciadic/national/vol1/ >.

126   Ibid.

127   Education and Health Standing Committee, Western Australian Legislative Assembly, *A Successful Initiative: Family Income Management* ('Report', 2007) [5].

128   Noel Pearson, *Our Right to Take Responsibility* (Noel Pearson, 2000) 27.

129   Marcia Langton, 'Real Change for Real People' *The Australian* (Sydney), 26-27 January 2008, 31.

130   I participated at the Garma Indigenous Water Knowledge, Indigenous Water Interests Conference Festival, Gove, Northern Territory, on the panel 'Identifying Commonalities: Development of Draft Observations and Recommendations', with Dr Marcia Langton, Renee Gurneau and Steven Ross.

131   Yothu Yindi Foundation, 'Garma Festival Program 2008', 9 <http://www.yyf.com.au/>.

132   United Nations University -Institute of Advanced Studies, Information delegate letter for 'Indigenous Water Knowledge, Indigenous Water Interests Conference', Garma Festival, Northern Territory 7-8 August 2008.

133   Ibid.

134   Ibid.

135   Carlos Batzin, 'Panel Discussion from South America' (Speech delivered at the Garma Indigenous Water Knowledge, Indigenous Water Interests Conference, Gove, Northern Territory, 7 August 2008).

136   Sir Tipene O'Regan, 'Draft Declaration and Recommendations for Indigenous Water Knowledge and Interests', speech delivered at the Garma Indigenous Water Knowledge, Indigenous Water Interests Conference, Gove, Northern Territory, 8 August 2008.

Chapter 3   Aboriginal property and Western values — concepts of ownership

1   Transcript of Proceedings, *Harrington Smith on behalf of the Wongatha People v Western Australia* (Federal Court, No 9, Lindgren J, 28 November 2002) (Cyril Simms during witness evidence for 'Autobiographical and Claims to Country') 1.

2   Jane Lennon, Brian Egloff, Adrian Davey and Ken Taylor, 'Conserving the Cultural Values of Natural Areas' ('Discussion Paper', University of Canberra, August 1999) 4.

3   Gary D Meyers, 'Aboriginal Rights to the Profits of the Land: The Inclusion of Traditional Fishing and Hunting Rights in the Context of Native Title' in Richard H Bartlett and Gary D Meyers (eds), *Native Title Legislation in Australia* (1994) 213-219. See Meyer (1994) footnote 216 where Meyers cites the work of R M Behrendt on 'Traditional Concepts of Aboriginal Land'.

4   Sandy Toussaint, 'Western Australia' Ann McGrath (ed), in *Contested Ground: Australian Aborigines under the British Crown* (Allen and Unwin, 1995) 244.

5   Marcia Langton, *An Aboriginal Ontology of Being and Place: The Performance of Aboriginal Property Relations in the Princess Charlotte Bay Area of Eastern Cape York Peninsula, Australia* (D Phil Thesis, Macquarie University, 2005) 434.

6   Robert Brooks, Sinclair Davidson and Robert Faff, 'Sudden Changes in Property Rights: The Case of Australian Native Title' (2003) 52 *Journal of Economic Behaviour and Organisation* 429.

7   Neva Collings and Virginia Falk [Marshall], 'Water: Aboriginal peoples in Australia and their Spiritual Relationship with Waterscapes' in Elliott Johnston, Martin Hinton and Daryle Rigney (eds), *Indigenous Australians and the Law* (Routledge-Cavendish, 2nd ed, 2008) 141.

8   Justice Robert Nicholson, 'The Use of History in Proving Native Title: A Judge's Perspective' *Federal Court Intranet* <http://intranet.fedcourt.gov.au/search97cgi/s97_cgi?Action=View&VdkVgwKey=%2...>

9   Jared Diamond, *Collapse: How Societies Choose to Fail or Survive* (Penguin, revised ed, 2007) 409.

10   Michael Niblett, 'Preliminary Anthropological Report on the Walbanga (Walbunja) Application Area NC 96/29 NSW South Coast' ('Research Report', NSW Aboriginal Land Council, 2002) 67.

11   Ibid.

12   Brian Fitzpatrick, *The British Empire in Australia: An Economic History 1834-1939* (Melbourne University Press, 1941) 106.

13   Ibid.

14   Ibid. 107.

15   Ibid.

16   F A Larcombe, The Origin of Local Government in New South Wales 1831-58 (Sydney University Press, 1973) 24.

17   H H Dare, Water Conservation in Australia (University of Queensland and Simmons, 1939) 14, 15.

18   Ibid. 107.

19   Virginia Falk in personal communication with D'harawal peoples, Frances Bodkin and Gavin Andrews during my cultural teaching on D'harawal history (2006).

20   Brian Fitzpatrick, The British Empire in Australia: An Economic History 1834-1939 (Melbourne University Press, 1941) 220.

21   Ibid. 219-220.

22   Miles Burt and Russell McVeagh, 'Water Securities and the Case for an Australian Personal Property Securities Act' (2004) 20(2) Australian Banking and Finance Law Bulletin 17. The PPS Act regulates personal property securities transactions including security interests registered against water rights. Note, the national water reforms establish statutory environmental water benchmarks and water licences to enable the trading of water to third parties who do not have to be land-owners.

23   Clare Brazenor, The Spatial Dimensions of Native Title (Master of Geomatics Science, University of Melbourne, August 2000) 2. Brazenor cites Kaufmann and Steudler (1998) 'Cadastre 2014: A Vision for Future Cadastre Systems'; Kaufman and Steudler (1998) explain that the Western concept of land and resources is opposed to the Indigenous concept of 'country'.

24   Brian Fitzpatrick, *The British Empire in Australia: An Economic History 1834-1939* (Melbourne University Press, 1941) 87.

25   Ibid. 88-89.

26   Ibid. 89.

27   Heather Goodall, 'New South Wales' Ann McGrath (ed), in *Contested Ground: Australian Aborigines under the British Crown* (Allen and Unwin, 1995) 64.

28   Richard Broome, 'Victoria' Ann McGrath (ed), in *Contested Ground: Australian Aborigines under the British Crown* (Allen and Unwin, 1995) 129.

29   Henry Reynolds and Dawn May, 'Queensland' Ann McGrath (ed), in *Contested Ground: Australian Aborigines under the British Crown* (Allen and Unwin, 1995) 172.

30   Ibid.

31   Ann McGrath (ed), 'Tasmania' in *Contested Ground: Australian Aborigines under the British Crown* (Allen and Unwin, 1995) 307.

32   Ibid.

33   Ibid. 315.

34   Ibid.

35   Henry Reynolds and Dawn May, 'Queensland' Ann McGrath (ed), in *Contested Ground: Australian Aborigines under the British Crown* (Allen and Unwin, 1995) 172.

36   Ibid. 180.

37   Eugene Bargo, personal communication, Brisbane June 2015.

38   Peggy Brock, 'South Australia' Ann McGrath (ed), in *Contested Ground: Australian Aborigines under the British Crown* (Allen and Unwin, 1995) 213-215.

39   Ibid. 213.

40   Shaun Berg, 'A Fractured Landscape: The Effect on Aboriginal Title to Land by the Establishment of the Province of South Australia' in Shaun Berg (ed), *Coming to Terms: Aboriginal Title in South Australia* (Wakefield Press, 2010) 1.

41   Ibid. Cited in the first page of the foreword by Geoffrey Robertson QC.

42   Ibid. 215.

43   Sandy Toussaint, 'Western Australia' Ann McGrath (ed), in *Contested Ground: Australian Aborigines under the British Crown* (Allen and Unwin, 1995) 242.

44   Ibid. 243-244.

45   Mary Anne Jebb, *Blood, Sweat and Welfare: A History of White Bosses and Aboriginal Pastoral Workers* (University of Western Australia Press, 2002) 64.

46   Ibid.

47   Ibid.

48   Peter Read, 'Northern Territory' Ann McGrath (ed), in *Contested Ground: Australian Aborigines under the British Crown* (Allen and Unwin, 1995) 273-274.

49   Ibid. 271.

50   Deborah Wilson. *Different White People: Radical Activism for Aboriginal Rights 1946-1972* (University of Western Australia Press, 2015) 254.

51   Songwriters Kev Carmody and Paul Kelly wrote a song about the Wave Hill 'Gurindji' strike and released it in 1993, 'From little things big things grow'. See <https://www.youtube.com/watch?v=6_ndC07C2qw> and <https://www.google.com.au/?client=firefox-b#q=little+things+grow+kevin+carmody&gfe_rd=cr>.

52   Deborah Wilson, *Different white people: radical activism for Aboriginal rights 1946-1972* (The University of Western Australia Press, Nedlands, WA, 2015) 256.

53   Manning Clark, (ed) *Select Documents in Australian History 1851-1900 Volume 2* (Angus and Robertson, revised ed, 1979) 98.

54   Ibid. 113.

55   New South Wales, *Official Report of the National Australasian Convention Debates*, Sydney 2 March-9 April 1891, 220 (John Forrest).

56   New South Wales, *Official Report of the National Australasian Convention Debates*, Sydney, 2March–9 April 1891, 24 (Henry Parkes).

57   Ani Mikaere, Nin Thomas and Kerensa Johnston, 'Treaty of Waitangi and Māori Land Law' (2003) *New Zealand Land Review* 480. See also James D K Morris and Jacinta Ruru, 'Giving Voice to Rivers: Legal Personality as a Vehicle for Recognising Indigenous Peoples' Relationships to Water?' (2010) 14(2) *Australian Indigenous Law Review* 49-59. Morris and Ruru (2010) examine a 'new legal framework that would recognise the legal personality of a river whereby a river would have *locus standi* to protect its river system from harm and recognise Māori tribes in relationship with the river as beneficiaries.' In October 2012 I attended the World Indigenous Lawyers Conference at University of Waikato, New Zealand, where it was announced that a legal agreement had recognised the Whanganui River with legal standing and personhood.

58   Ibid

59   Michael Connor, *The Invention of Terra Nullius: Historical and Legal Fictions on the Foundation of Australia* (Macleay Press, 2005) 310.

60   Ibid. 14-15.

61   Elliott Johnston, 'National Report, Overview and Recommendations: Royal Commission into Aboriginal Deaths in Custody' (Australian Government, 1991) 7.

62   Larissa Behrendt, *Achieving Social Justice: Indigenous Rights and Australia's Future* (Federation Press, 2003) 36.

63   Ibid.

64   Anthony Giddens, *Sociology* (Polity Press, revised ed, 1993) 722.

65   H H Dare, *Water Conservation in Australia* (University of Queensland and Simmons, September 1939) 15-16.

66   Joshua Getzler, *A History of Water Rights at Common Law* (Oxford University Press, revised ed, 2006) 1.

67   Ibid.

68   Ibid. 45.

69   Ibid. 65.

70   Ibid. 67.

71   Ibid. 1. See J Locke, *Second Treatise of Government* ss. 29 and 33, in *Two Treatises of Government*, Peter Laslett (ed), (Cambridge, Cambridge University Press, 1970).

72   Ibid. 175.

73   Ibid.

74   Quoted in Sir Henry Sumner Maine, *Ancient Law: Its Connection with the Early History of Society and its Relation to Modern Ideas* (John Murray, first published 1906, 1927 ed) 264-265.

75   Joshua Getzler, *A History of Water Rights at Common Law* (Oxford University Press, revised ed, 2006) 37.

76   Michael Duffy, 'A Good Land Right is a Good Deed', *The Sydney Morning Herald* (Sydney), 9 April 2005, 41.

77   Marion Maddox, *Indigenous Religion in Secular Australia* ('Research Paper', No 11, Parliamentary Library, 1999-2000) 6.

78   Terry N Tobias, 'Chief Kerry's Moose: A Guide to Land Use and Occupancy Mapping, Research Design and Data Collection' ('Research Report', Union of British Columbia Indian Chiefs and Ecotrust Canada, 2000) 16.

79   Kate Kempton and Olthuis Kleer Townshend, *Bridge over Troubled Waters: Canadian Law on Aboriginal and Treaty Water Rights and the Great Lakes Annex* (2003) 13 <http://www.thewaterhole.ca/publications/aboriginal20%water%20rights%20and%20annex%20paper%20finalpdf>.

80   Ibid. 13.

81   William Collins and Sons, *Collins Concise Dictionary of the English Language* Wilkes and Krebs (eds) (Collins, 2nd ed, 1988) 273.

82   Nicolas Peterson and Bruce Rigsby (eds), 'Customary Marine Tenure in Australia' (1998) 48 *Oceania Monograph University of Sydney* 2.

83   Ibid. 10.

84   R Boast, 'Report, The Foreshore, Theme Q', Waitangi Tribunal, November 1996). See Ninety Mile Beach (1957) 85 Northern MB 126 before the Māori Land Court. See also Fenton J in *Kauwaerunga* 1870 Native Land Court decision on foreshore and seabed ownership.

85   See *Attorney-General v Ngati Apa [2002]* 2 NZLR 661 (HC). The judgements in the Court of Appeal reversed the decision of the High Court in *Attorney-General v Ngati Apa.*

86   See *In re Application for Investigation of Title to the Ninety Mile Beach (Wharo Oneroa a Tohe)* [1960] NZLR 673.

87   [2003] NZCA 117. See NZ Government, 'Ngati Apa and Foreshore' ('Parliamentary Briefing Note', No 12, Parliamentary Library, December 2003) 1-22.

88   Judge Taihakurei Edward Durie, Richard Boast and Hana O'Regan, 'Ministerial Review of the *Foreshore and Seabed Act 2004*' (Report Summary, NZ Government, June 2009). See also Durie, Boast and O'Regan, 'Ministerial Review of the *Foreshore and Seabed Act 2004*' (Volumes 1-3, NZ Government, June 2009).

89   *Te Ture Whenua Maori Act 1993* (NZ) s 129(2)(a).

90   C Rebecca Brown and James I Reynolds, 'Aboriginal Title to Sea Spaces: A Comparative Study' (2004) 37(1) *University of British Columbia Law Review* 483-491. See *Attorney General v Ngati Apa* (2003) 3 NZLR 643 *('Ngati Apa Appeal')* ('*Marlborough Sounds Case*'). The *Foreshore and Seabed Act 2004* (NZ) extinguished all Aboriginal title; the NZ parliament rejected the High Court decision to recognise Māori water rights. The *Foreshore and Seabed Act 2004* (NZ) was repealed in 2011 and replaced with the *Marine and Coastal Areas (Takutai Moana) Act 2011* (NZ) (*'Takutai Moana Act'*) to increase recognition of customary rights. See also ALRC, *Connection to Country: Review of the Native Title Act 1993* (Cth), 'Final Report' No 126 (2015) 283-286.

91   Ibid. 487-490. See *In Re Ninety-Mile Beach* (1963) NZLR 461 (CA).

92   Ibid. 481-483.

93   [1996] HCA 40.

94   See Australian Government, 'Our North, Our Future: White Paper on Developing Northern Australia' (Commonwealth of Australia, 2015) 4.

95   Tim Dick, 'Land Rights in Limbo', *The Sydney Morning Herald* (Sydney), 26-28 January 2007, 29.

96   Brian Donovan, 'The evolution and present status of common law Aboriginal title in Canada: the laws crooked path and hollow promise of *Delgamuukw* (2001-2002) 35 *University of British Columbia Law Review* 88.

Chapter 4   Health, wealth and water rights

1   Close the Gap Campaign Steering Committee, 'Progress and Priorities Report 2016' ('Report', Oxfam Australia, February 2016).

2	Australian Government, 'Implementation plan for the National Aboriginal and Torres Strait Islander Health Plan 2013-2023' ('Policy Plan', Department of Health, 2015).

3	Ruth Williams, 'Mining Rites', *The Age* (Melbourne), 17 May 2008, 5.

4	Katy Osborne, Fran Baum and Lynsey Brown, 'What works? A review of actions addressing the social and economic determinants of Indigenous health' ('Issues Paper' No 7, Closing the Gap Clearinghouse, December 2013) 11.

5	Ibid. 10. See also the World Health Organisation reports.

6	Australian Medical Association, 'AMA Report Card on Indigenous Health' ('Report', AMA, 2015) 4.

7	Ibid. 3.

8	Ibid. 5.

9	William Jonas, 'Review of the 1994 Water Report' ('Research Report', Human Rights and Equal Opportunity Commission, 2001) 2 Human Rights and Equal Opportunity Commission <http://www.hreoc.gov.au/racial_discrimination/water_report/index.html>.

10	Ibid

11	Federal Race Discrimination Commissioner, 'Water: A Report on the Provision of Water and Sanitation in Remote Aboriginal and Torres Strait Islander Communities' ('Final Report', Human Rights and Equal Opportunity Commission, 1994).

12	Ibid. 2.

13	Ibid.

14	Ibid See the case studies section in the report for further information.

15	Australian Medical Association, *2015 AMA Report Card on Indigenous Health* Australian Medical Association <https://ama.com.au/2015-ama-report-card-indigenous-health-closing-gap-indigenous-imprisonment-rates>. See also Australian Institute of Health and Welfare for the 2015 report on the health and welfare of Indigenous peoples in Australia <http://www.aihw.gov.au/WorkArea/DownloadAsset.aspx?id=60129551281>.

16	Dr A Olsen and Dr R Lovett, 'Existing Knowledge, Practice and Responses to Violence against Women in Australian Indigenous Communities: State of knowledge Paper' ('Research Paper', No 2, Australia's National Research Organisation for Women's Safety: To Reduce Violence against Women and their Children, 2016) 10.

Ibid. 13. The Report cites F Al-Yaman, M Van Doeland and M Wallis (2006) 'Family Violence among Aboriginal and Torres Strait Islander Peoples', Australian Institute of Health and Welfare.

17	Ibid. 58.

18	Aden Ridgeway, 'Addressing the Economic Exclusion of Indigenous Australians through Native Title' (the Mabo Lecture, Coffs Harbour, 3 June 2005) 8 <http://www.aiatsis.gov.au/ntru/nativetitleconference/conf2005/papers/RidgewayA.pdf>.

19	C K Meek, *Land Law and Custom in the Colonies* (Oxford University Press, 1946).

20	Ibid. 6.

21	Ibid. 7.

22	Ibid. 27.

23	Jon Altman quoted in Patricia Karvelas, 'Push for Aboriginal Rights over Resources', *The Australian*, 11 April 2008, 6.

24	Australian Institute of Health and Welfare, *The Health and Welfare of Australia's Aboriginal and Torres Strait Islander peoples 2015* Australian Institute of Health and Welfare <http://www.aihw.gov.au/WorkArea/DownloadAsset.aspx?id=60129551281>

25   Australian Government, Department of the Prime Minister and Cabinet *Closing the Gap Prime Minister's Report 2016* <http://closingthegap.dpmc.gov.au/assets/pdfs/closing_the_gap_report_2016.pdf>

26   Indigenous Business Australia, *Indigenous Investment Principles* (2015) <https://www.google.com.au/?client=firefox-b#q=indigenous+investment+principles&gfe_rd=cr>. See page 12.

27   I am a member of the Australian Human Rights Commission Indigenous Property Rights Roundtable which is to progress and recommend sustainable opportunities for Indigenous peoples to access and benefit from their native title rights, in land, water and resources. See <https://www.humanrights.gov.au/our-work/aboriginal-and-torres-strait-islander-social-justice/projects/indigenous-property-rights>

28   Department Aboriginal Affairs NSW, 'Two Ways Together Report on Indicators: The NSW Aboriginal Affairs Plan 2003-2012' ('Report', June 2005) 7.

29   Ibid.

30   M Howlett, M Gray and B Hunter, 'Unpacking the Incomes of Indigenous and non-Indigenous Australians: Wages, Government Income and other Payments' ('Working Paper' No 99, Centre for Aboriginal Economic Policy Research, January 2015) 4.

31   Elizabeth Murray, 'Welfare to Work Legislation Criticised' *Koori Mail* (NSW) 21 November 2007, 13.

32   John Taylor, 'Tracking Change in the Relative Economics Status of Indigenous People in New South Wales' ('Discussion Paper', No 277, Australian National University, 2005) 30.

33   Brad Goode, Colin Irvine and Melinda Cockman, 'Report on Conferences held with the Nyungar Community for the South West Water Plan ('Research Report', Department of Water, Western Australia, June 2007).

34   Ibid. 32.

35   Ibid. 1-48.

36   Sue Jackson and Joe Morrison, 'Indigenous Perspectives in Water Management, Reforms and Implementation' (Draft Manuscript, LWA.NWIx4.doc, 2006) 3.

37   Nicolas Peterson, 'Capitalism, Culture and Land Rights: Aborigines and the State in the Northern Territory' 18 (December 1985) *Social Analysis* 97.

38   Ibid.

39   Monica Morgan, Lisa Strelein and Jessica Weir, 'Indigenous Rights to Water in the Murray-Darling Basin' ('Research Discussion Paper' No 14, Australian Institute of Aboriginal and Torres Strait Islander Studies, Canberra, 2004) 6.

40   Senate Select Committee on the Administration of Indigenous Affairs, Parliament of Australia, *After ATSIC: Life in the Mainstream?* (March 2005) [2.23].

41   Ibid.

42   Human Rights and Equal Opportunity Commission, 'Bringing Them Home: Report of the National Inquiry into the Separation of Aboriginal and Torres Strait Islander Children from Their Families' ('Report', Human Rights and Equal Opportunity Commission, April 1997) 319.

43   Ibid.

44   Mark Bennett, 'Indigenous Autonomy and Justice in North America' (2004) 2 *New Zealand Journal of Public and International Law* 207.

45   Kirsty Gover and Natalie Baird, 'Identifying the Maori Treaty Partner' (2002) *University of Toronto Law Journal* 2. Citing Mason Durie.

46   Shin Imai, 'Sound Science, Careful Policy Analysis, and Ongoing Relationships: Integrating Litigation and Negotiation in Aboriginal Lands and Resources' (2003) 41 *Osgoode Hall Law Journal* 7.

47   Ibid.

48   McLachlin, Beverley CJ, 'Reconciling Sovereignty: Canada and Australia's Dialogue on Aboriginal Rights' (2003) High Court Centenary Conference, Canberra, 3 <http://unicorn.fedcourt.gov.au/uhtbin/cgisirsi/0000/000/38/10/x?user_id=SYD_WEBBpassword=SYD_WEB>

49   (2006) 230 ALR 603 [791].

50   Aboriginal and Torres Strait Islander Social Justice Commissioner, 'Native Title Report 2007' (Human Rights and Equal Opportunity Commission, 2008) 148.

51   Tim Rowse quoted in Alice Roughley and Susie Williams, 'The Engagement of Indigenous Australians in Natural Resource Management: Key Findings and Outcomes from Land and Water Australia and the Broader Literature' ('Research Report', Land and Water Australia, November 2007) 28 <www.aiatsis.gov.au/research/publications/Land&Water/pn21610.pdf>. See also T Rowse (2002) 'Indigenous Futures: Choice and Development for Aboriginal and Torres Strait Islander Australia' University of New South Wales Press, Sydney.

52   Gaynor Macdonald, 'Self-Determination or Control: Aborigines and Land Rights Legislation in New South Wales' (1988) 24 *Social Analysis* 37.

53   Dr James R Crawford, 'Aboriginal Customary Law: A General Regime for Recognition' ('Research Paper' No 8, Australian Law Reform Commission, December 1982) 10.

54   ALRC, 'Chapter 10', The Recognition of Aboriginal Customary Law, ALRC Report 31, ALRC, Sydney, 1986 (2 vols), viewed 4 October 2016, <http://www.alrc.gov.au/publications report-31>

55   Larissa Behrendt, *Aboriginal Dispute Resolution: A Step Towards Self-Determination and Community Autonomy* (Federation Press, 1995) 39.

56   Alice Roughley and Susie Williams, 'The Engagement of Indigenous Australians in Natural Resource Management: Key Findings and Outcomes from Land and Water Australia and the Broader Literature' ('Research Report', Land and Water Australia, November 2007) 18, 23 <www.aiatsis.gov.au/research/publications/Land&Water/pn21610.pdf>.

57   Ibid. 23.

58   Working Group for Advancing Indigenous Reconciliation in Primary Industries and Natural Resource Management, 'Key Issues: Indigenous Employment and Engagement in Natural Resource Management and Primary Industries' ('Draft Report', 2008) 1.

59   Email from Primary Industries Ministerial Council and the Natural Resource Management Ministerial Council to Virginia Falk [Marshall], April 2006; general email.

60   Yamatji Marlpa Barna Maaja Aboriginal Corporation, 'Annual Report 2007' ('Report', 15 October 2007) 22.

61   Peter Cullen, 'Water: The Key to Sustainability in a Dry Land' in Jenny Goldie, Bob Douglas and Bryan Furnass (eds), *In Search of Sustainability* (Commonwealth Scientific and Industrial Research Organisation, 2005) 85.

62   Aboriginal and Torres Strait Islander Social Justice Commissioner, 'Native Title Report 2007' (Human Rights and Equal Opportunity Commission, Sydney, 2008) 218.

63   Aden Ridgeway, 'Addressing the Economic Exclusion of Indigenous Australians through Native Title' (The Mabo Lecture, Coffs Harbour, 3 June 2005) 8 <http://www.aiatsis.gov.au/ntru/nativetitleconference/conf2005/papers/RidgewayA.pdf>.

64   Ibid. 5.

65   Alice Roughley and Susie Williams, 'The Engagement of Indigenous Australians in Natural Resource Management: Key Findings and Outcomes from Land and Water Australia and the Broader Literature' ('Research Report', Land and Water Australia, November 2007) 29 <www.aiatsis.gov.au/research/publications/Land&Water/pn21610.pdf>.

66   Email from David Collard to Virginia Falk, the Minister for Indigenous Affairs to the Cabinet Standing Committee on Social Policy (WA), 2004.

67   Ed Goodman, 'Protecting Habitat for Off-Reservation Tribal Hunting and Fishing Rights: Tribal Co-management as a Reserved Right' (2000) 30 *Environmental Law* 284.

68   Jill Byrnes, 'Aboriginal Economic Independence: A Report on some Canadian Initiatives' ('Research Report', Rural Development Centre, University of New England, 1990) 6.

69   Bruce Callaghan, NSW Aboriginal Land Council and the Department of Land and NSW Water Conservation, *Report on the Boomanulla Conference for Country 5-6 March 2002 Canberra* (2002) 4.

70   Senate Select Committee on the Administration of Indigenous Affairs, Parliament of Australia, *After ATSIC: Life in the Mainstream?* (2005) [2.2].

71   Ibid.

72   Virginia Falk, 'The Rise and Fall of ATSIC: A Personal Opinion' (2004) 8(4) *Australian Indigenous Law Reporter* 17.

73   Ibid.

74   Ibid.

75   See Joel Gibson, 'Aboriginal Council axed by Macklin', *The Sydney Morning Herald* (online) 16 January 2008 <http://www.smh.com.au/news/national/aboriginal-council-axed-by-mackl in/2008/01/15/1200159449363.html>.

76   The Abbott Federal Government set up an Indigenous Advisory Committee, by Ministerial appointment, which was restructured by the Turnbull Federal Government into Indigenous Advisory Council including non-Indigenous members; again selected by Ministerial appointment.

77   Gough Whitlam, *Abiding Interests* (University of Queensland Press, 1997) 92-93.

78   H C Coombs, 'Towards a New Federation' in Essays of H C Coombs *Shame on Us! Essays on a Future Australia* (first published 1992, revised ed 1993) 32.

79   Noel Pearson, *Our Right to Take Responsibility* (Noel Pearson, 2000) 29-30.

80   See other treaties ratified by Australia such as the *International Covenant on Civil and Political Rights* (ICCPR), the *International Covenant on Economic Social and Cultural Rights* (ICESCR), *Convention on the Elimination of All Forms of Discrimination Against Women* (CEDAW), the *Convention on the Elimination of All Forms of Racial Discrimination* (CERD).

81   Australian Human Rights Commission, Submission to the Committee on the rights of the child, August 2011 <http://www.humanrights.gov.au/information-concerning-australia-and-convention-rights-child-0#s3_2>.

82   Gretchen Poiner, *The Good Rule: Gender and Other Power Relationships in a Rural Community* (Sydney University Press, 1990) 77.

83   Robert Blowes, Jim Birckhead, Terry De Lacy and Laurajane Smith (eds), 'From *terra nullius* to Every Person's Land: A Perspective from Legal History' (Australian Studies Press, 1992).

84   UNESCO, Water: A shared responsibility: The United Nations World Water Development Report 2, UNESCO, Paris, 2006, viewed 1 September 2016, <http://www.unesco.org/new/en/natural-sciences/environment/water/wwap/wwdr/wwdr2-2006/downloads-wwdr2/>.

85   See for example Hannah Forsyth, 'The Barkinji People are losing their 'mother', the drying Darling River' (*The Conversation*, 4 May 2016, 1-3 < http://theconversation.com/the-barkindji-people-are-

losing-their-mother-the-drying-darling-river-57884>; Erin Parke, 'WA Government urged to fix contaminated water supplies in remote Indigenous communities' (*ABC*, 23 May 2016), 1 <http://www.abc.net.au/news/2016-05-22/wa-communities-grow-impatient-over-lack-of-drinking-water/7435474>

86   New South Wales Aboriginal Community Water and Sewerage Working Group, 'Aboriginal Community Water Supply and Sewerage Systems' ('Draft Report', Department of Commerce NSW Sustainable Water Solutions, 2006) 5.

87   Ibid. 23.

88   National Water Commission, 'Intergovernmental Agreement on a National Water Initiative between the Commonwealth of Australia and the Governments of New South Wales, Victoria, Queensland, South Australia, the Australian Capital Territory and the Northern Territory' (2004)   Australian   Government   <http://nwc.gov.au/__data/assets/pdf_file/0008/24749/Intergovernmental-Agreement-on-a-national-water-initiative.pdf>

89   New South Wales Aboriginal Community Water and Sewerage Working Group, 'Aboriginal Community Water Supply and Sewerage Systems' ('Draft Report', Department of Commerce NSW Sustainable Water Solutions, 2006) 4.

90   Ibid. 5.

91   NSW Aboriginal Community Water and Sewerage Working Group, 'Aboriginal Community Water Supply and Sewerage' ('Final Draft Report', Department of Commerce (NSW) Sustainable Water Solutions, 2007) 57. See also Department of Aboriginal Affairs (NSW), 'Two Ways Together Report on Indicators: The NSW Aboriginal Affairs Plan 2003-2012' ('Report', June 2005).

92   Ibid. 8. I represented the Department of Natural Resources (NSW) on the Aboriginal Working Group in my capacity as Executive Officer of the NSW Aboriginal Water Trust.

93   Ibid. 10.

94   Darren Coyne, 'Now or Never: NSW Inquiry Action Tackling Indigenous Disadvantage', *Koori Mail* (NSW), 26 March 2008, 10.

95   Ibid. 4.

96   Department of Land and Water Conservation (NSW), 'Guidelines for Assessing the Impacts of Water Sharing Plans on Aboriginal Peoples' (Economic and Social Policy Branch, Department of Land and Water Conservation, August 2001) 18.

97   Ibid. 8.

98   New South Wales Aboriginal Community Water and Sewerage Working Group, 'Aboriginal Community Water Supply and Sewerage Systems' ('Draft Report', Department of Commerce (NSW) Sustainable Water Solutions, 2006) 10.

99   Department of Water (WA), Government of Western Australia, 'Draft Policy for Consultation with Aboriginal People' (2008) 31.

100   Ibid.

101   Ibid. 36.

102   Department of Water, Government of Western Australia, 'Report for the Minister for Water Resources on Water Services in Discrete Indigenous Communities' (December 2006) 5.

103   Ibid. 6.

104   Email from David Collard to Virginia Falk on Primary Industries Ministerial Council and the Natural Resource Management Ministerial Council to The Author, April 2006.

105   Department of Water, 'Western Australia's Implementation Plan for the National Water Initiative' ('Report', Government of Western Australia, April 2007).

106   Ibid. 25.

107 Ibid.

108 Ibid.

109 Department of Water, Government of Western Australia, 'Report for the Minister for Water Resources on Water Services in Discrete Indigenous Communities' (December 2006).

110 Ibid. 49, 78.

111 Western Australian Government, 'Delivering Essential Services to Remote Aboriginal Communities' ('Report' No 8, Western Australian Auditor General, May 2015) 8 <https://audit.wa.gov.au/wp-content/uploads/2015/05/report2015_08-AbServices.pdf>. See H Clifford, G Pearson, P Franklin, R Walker and G Zosky, *Environmental health challenges in remote Aboriginal Australian Communities: clean air, clean water and safe housing* (2015) Australian Indigenous Health Bulletin <http://healthbulletin.org.au/articles/environmental-health-challenges-in-remote-aboriginal-australian-communities-clean-air-clean-water-and-safe-housing/>.

112 Neva Collings, *Water Rights and International Law: Background Briefing Papers Lingiari Report Indigenous Rights to Water Report and Recommendations* Aboriginal and Torres Strait Islander Commission <http://atsic.gov.au/issues/Indigenous_Rights/Indigenous_Rights_Waters/Default.asp>

113 Aboriginal and Torres Strait Islander Social Justice Commissioner, 'Social Justice Report 2010', (Australian Human Rights Commission, 2011) ix, xii.

114 Australian Human Rights Commission, *Native Title Report* (2008) <https://www.humanrights.gov.au/our-work/aboriginal-and-torres-strait-islander-social-justice/publications/native-title-report-2008>. See 'ch' 6 for Indigenous water rights issues.

115 Ibid. 2-3.

116 Ibid. 4.

117 Australian Human Rights Commission, *Review of the 1994 Water Report* <https://www.humanrights.gov.au/our-work/race-discrimination/publications/review-1994-water-report-2001>.

118 Ibid.

119 Ibid. 9.

120 Ibid. 38.

121 Ibid See 'ch' 5 Conclusions.

122 Aboriginal and Torres Strait Islander Social Justice Commissioner, 'Social Justice Report 2008' (Australian Human Rights Commission, 2009) 284.

123 Ibid.

124 Ibid. 283.

125 Amanda Cornwall, 'Restoring Identity: Final Report of the Moving Forward Consultation Project' ('Research Report', Public Interest Advocacy Centre, August 2002) 23.

126 *Council for Aboriginal Reconciliation Act 1991* (Cth).

127 Council for Aboriginal Reconciliation, 'Walking Together: The First Steps, Report of the Council for Aboriginal Reconciliation 1991-1994 to Federal Parliament' (Australian Government, Canberra, 1994) 14.

128 Ibid. 14-15.

129 Aboriginal and Torres Strait Islander Social Justice Commissioner, 'Native Title Report 2006' (Human Rights and Equal Opportunity Commission) 22.

130 Aboriginal and Torres Strait Islander Commissioner, 'Native Title Report 2007' (Human Rights and Equal Opportunity Commission, 2008) 9.

131   Aboriginal and Torres Strait Islander Commissioner, 'Native Title Report 2008' (Human Rights Commission, 2009) 169.

132   Ibid. 179. See also interview with Virginia Falk on 16 December 2008 in the Native Title Report (2008).

133   Email from David Collard to Virginia Falk, State Solicitor's Office, Western Australia, 'National Water Initiative: Indigenous Access and Entitlement Rights', 12 December 2007, 5.

134   Ibid As held in *Ngalpil v Western Australia* [2001] FCA 1140 (Tjurabalan People), *Nangkiriny v Western Australia* [2002] FCA 660 (Karajarri Determination Area A), *Brown v Western Australia* [2001] FCA 1462 (Kiwirrkurra People) and *James v Western Australia* [2002] FCA 1208 (Martu People). See Email from David Collard to Virginia Falk, State Solicitor's Western Australia, 'National Water Initiative: Indigenous Access and Entitlement Rights', 12 December 2007, 5.

135   'Native Title report 2009' quoted in Ibid.. As held in Ngalpilv Western Australia..

136   Aboriginal and Torres Strait Islander Social Justice Commissioner', 'Native Title Report 2008' (Human Rights and Equal Opportunity Commission, 2009) 27. See Chapter six of 'Indigenous peoples and Water' in the 'Native Title Report 2008'.

137   Ibid See *Native Title Act 1993* (Cth) s 24HA.

138   Ibid.

139   Aboriginal and Torres Strait Islander Social Justice Commissioner', 'Native Title Report 2010' (Australian Human Rights Commission, 2011) 12-13.

140   See ALRC, *Connection to Country: Review of the Native Title Act 1993* (Cth), Final Report No 126 (2015). [8.97]; which discusses water rights and interests.

141   Aboriginal and Torres Strait Islander Social Justice Commissioner, 'Native Title Report 2011' (Australian Human Rights Commission, 2011) 36-37.

Chapter 5 'Little more than a sense of justice': Mabo and native title

1   Kent McNeil, *Common Law Aboriginal Title*, (Clarendon Press, 1989) 298-306.

2   Aboriginal and Torres Strait Islander Social Justice Commissioner, 'Native Title Report 2007' (Human Rights and Equal Opportunity Commission, 2008) 217

3   (1992) 175 CLR 1.

4   Ibid. 127.

5   Michael Connor, *The Invention of Terra Nullius: Historical and Legal Fictions on the Foundation of Australia* (Macleay Press, 2005) 15.

6   (1992) 175 CLR 1.

7   (1971) 17 FLR 141.

8   Quoted in Paul Patton, 'The Translation of Indigenous Land into Property: The Mere Analogy of English Jurisprudence' (2000) 6(1) *Parallax* 34-35.

9   Quoted in Geoffrey Robert Schiveley, 'Negotiation and Native Title: Why Common Law Courts are not a Proper Fora for Determining Native Land Title Issues' (2000) 33 *Vanderbuilt Journal of Transnational Law* 464-465.

10   (1992) 175 CLR 1.

11   Ibid. 128.

12   Ibid.

13   A J Brown, *Paradoxes & Principles* (Federation Press, 2011) 239.

14   Alex Reilly, 'Cartography, Property and the Aesthetics of Place: Mapping Native Title in Australia' (2004) in Kenyon and Rush (eds), 34 *Aesthetics of Law and Culture: Texts, Images, Screens* 230.

15   Commonwealth, *Parliamentary Debates*, House of Representatives, Native Title Bill 1993 2 (Paul Keating). Advice from Dennis Rose QC to the Australian Government in 23 December 1993 'confirmed the validity of special laws being made by the Commonwealth on behalf of Aboriginal and Torres Strait Islander peoples'.

16   Ibid.

17   Richard Bartlett, *Native Title in Australia* (Lexis Nexis, 2nd ed, 2004) 15.

18   Commonwealth, *Parliamentary Debates*, House of Representatives, 16 November 1993, 2878 (Paul Keating, Prime Minister of Australia)

19   Aboriginal and Torres Strait Islander Commissioner, 'Native Title Report 2008' (Human Rights Commission, 2009) 192. See *Native Title Act 1993* (Cth) ss 223 and 253.

20   Commonwealth, *Parliamentary Debates*, House of Representatives, Native Title Bill 1993 2 (Paul Keating) 95.

21   Ibid. 27. See also *Native Title Act* 1993 (Cth) ss 221 and 212.

22   *Native Title Act 1993* (Cth).

23   Lisa Strelein, *Compromised Jurisprudence: Native Title Cases Since Mabo* (Aboriginal Studies Press, 2nd ed, 2009) 117.

24   Ibid. 118.

25   Ibid.148-149.

26   Ibid. 149.

27   Ibid.

28   *Commonwealth v Yarmirr* (2001) 208 CLR 1.

29   Ibid. (292).

30   Jelita Gardner-Rush, 'Judicial Treatment of International Law in Yarmirr' (2004) 23 *Australian Year Book of International Law* 192.

31   166 CLR 186. The High Court in a majority of 4-3 held that the *Queensland Coast Islands Declaratory Act* was invalid as the Act was inconsistent with the *Racial Discrimination Act 1975* (Cth).

32   (1992) 175 CLR 1.

33   (1971) 17 FLR 141.

34   Paul Patton, 'The Translation of Indigenous Land into Property: The Mere Analogy of English Jurisprudence' (2000) 6(1) *Parallax* 33.

35   [2002] 191 ALR 1.

36   Ibid. 821.

37   Tony Blackshield and George Williams, *Australian Constitutional Law and Theory: Commentary and Theory* (Federation Press, 2nd ed, 1998) 20.

38   Ibid

39   [2002] 191 ALR 1.

40   Tony Blackshield and George Williams, *Australian Constitutional Law and Theory: Commentary and Theory* (Federation Press, 2nd, 1998) 21.

41   Scott Hawkins, 'Caught, Hook, Line and Sinker' (1992) 3 *Journal of Indigenous Policy* 4.

42   Paul Toohey, 'Fishing for Votes Ends as a Dream becomes Reality', *The Australian*, 6 August 2008.

43   (1992) 175 CLR 1.

44   Stella Tarrant, *Biljabu v Western Australia* HCA <http://www.austlii.edu.au/au/journals/AboriginalLawB/1994/13.html>.

45   *Western Australia v Commonwealth* (1995) 187 CLR 373. *Wororra Peoples v Western Australia* and *Biljabu v Western Australia* joined the Commonwealth against the Western Australia Government.

46   Stella Tarrant, *Biljabu v Western Australia* <http://www.austlii.edu.au/au/journals/AboriginalLawBulletin/1994/13.html>.

47   Ibid.

48   Megan Davis and Hannah McGlade, 'International Human Rights Law and the Recognition of Aboriginal Customary Law' ('Background Paper' No 10, Law Reform Commission of Western Australia, March 2005) 21.

49   Ibid.

50   (1992) 175 CLR 1.

51   Ibid. 193.

52   (2002) 213 CLR 401.

53   Ibid. [126].

54   Paul Patton, 'The Translation of Indigenous Land into Property: The Mere Analogy of English Jurisprudence' (2000) 6(1) *Parallax* 28.

55   Ibid. 28-29.

56   Ibid. 29.

57   Lauren Benton, *Law and Colonial Cultures: Legal Regimes in World History, 1400–1900* (Cambridge University Press, 2002) 2.

58   Ibid. 23.

59   Ibid. 184.

60   Lisa Strelein, 'A Comfortable Existence: Commercial Fishing and the Concept of Tradition in Native Title' (2002) 5 *Balayi: Culture, Law and Colonialism* 123.

61   Ibid. 100.

62   (1992) 175 CLR 1.

63   *Commonwealth v Yarmirr* [1999] FCA 1668. See *Mabo v Queensland* [No 2] (1992) 175 CLR 1(Toohey J) 207.

64   Aboriginal and Torres Strait Islander Social Justice Commissioner, 'Native Title Report 2006' (Human Rights and Equal Opportunity Commission, 2007) 43.

65   ALRC, *Connection to Country: Review of the Native Title Act 1993* (Cth), 'Final Report' No 126 (2015) 137.

66   (2002) 213 CLR 1 [76] (Gleeson CJ, Gummow and Hayne JJ).

67   Paul Seaman, 'The Negotiation Stage' in Gary Meyers (ed), *In the Wake of Wik: Old dilemmas, New Directions in Native Title Law* (National Native Title Tribunal, May 1999) 382.

68   (1992) 175 CLR 1.

69   Tony Simpson, pers.comm. 2004 2.

70   (1992) 175 CLR 1.

71   Tony Simpson, Pers. comm. 34-38.

72   (1992) 175 CLR 1.

73   (1971) FLR 141.

74   (1996) 187 CLR 1.

75   Ibid. at 206.

76   Ibid.

77   [1993] 175 CLR 1.

78   (1996) 187 CLR 1.

79   Evidence to Senate Legal and Constitutional Committees, Parliament of Australia, Canberra, July-December (1997) vol 3, 34 (Michael Kirby).

80   Ibid See *Thorpe v Commonwealth* (No 3) (1997) 144 ALR 677, 687.

81   [2002] 191 ALR 1, 161-162.

82   Matthew Rimmer, 'Blame it on Rio: Biodiscovery, Native Title, and Traditional Knowledge' (2003) 7 *Southern Cross University Law Review* 30.

83   Ibid.

84   [1998] 156 ALR 370.

85   Nonie Sharp, 'Australian Native Title and Irish Marine Rights: An Inquiry on the West Coast of Ireland' (1998) 16(2) *Law in Context* 35. See *Lardil Peoples v Queensland* [2004] FCA 298 ('*The Wellesley Sea Case*').

86   Ibid. 36.

87   [1999] FCA 1668.

88   *Commonwealth v Yarmirr* [1999] FCA 1668 (Olney J) 576.

89   Nicolas Peterson and Bruce Rigsby (eds), 'Customary Marine Tenure in Australia' (1998) 48 *Oceania Monograph University of Sydney* 11.

90   Julie Fenwick, *Worrying about Our Land: Conceptualising Land Rights 1963-1971* (Monash Publications, 2001) 31.

91   Ibid. 34.

92   Quoted in P G McHugh, 'Aboriginal Title in New Zealand: A Retrospect and Prospect' (2004) 2 *New Zealand Journal of Public and International Law* 179. See *Western Australia v Ward* (2002) 191 ALR 1.

93   Ibid.

94   Gary D Meyers, 'Native Title Rights in Natural Resources: A Comparative Perspective of Common Law Jurisprudence' (2002) 19(4) *Environmental and Planning Law Journal* 257.

95   *Yorta Yorta Aboriginal Community v Victoria* (2002) 194 ALR 538.

96   Alex Reilly and Ann Genovese, 'Claiming the Past: Historical Understanding in Australian Native Title Jurisprudence' (2004) 3 *Indigenous Law Journal* 35.

97   Ibid. 29.

98   (2002) 213 CLR 1.

99   Ibid. [567].

100   Ibid. 213.

101   Aboriginal and Torres Strait Islander Social Justice Commissioner, 'Native Title Report 2006' (Human Rights and Equal Opportunity Commission, 2007) 49.

102   Email from David Collard to Virginia Falk, State Solicitor's Office Western Australia, 'National Water Initiative: Indigenous Access and Entitlement Rights' (12 December 2007) 5.

103   *Smirke on behalf of the Jurruru Peoples Part A v WA* [2015] FCA 939. See also a recent decision handed down in South Australia on rights over settled areas including fishing, pastoral leases, mining and Crown land in *Croft on behalf of Barngarla Peoples* (No 2) v SA [2016] FCA 724.

104   *Graham on behalf of the Ngadju Peoples v WA* [2014] FCA 1247.

105   Australian Law Reform Commission, *Connection to Country: Review of the Native Title Act 1993 (Cth)*, 'Final Report' No 126 (2015) 248 [8.97].

106   Ibid. 249 [8.105].

107   [2013] HCA 33. See also *Akiba v Queensland [No 3]*(2010) 204 FCR 1 and *Commonwealth v Akiba* (2012) 204 FCR 260.

108   Ibid

109   [2001] FCA 1140.

110   Email from David Collard to Virginia Falk [Marshall], State Solicitor's Office Western Australia, 'National Water Initiative: Indigenous Access and Entitlement Rights' (12 December 2007) 5.

111   [2002] FCA 660.

112 Email from David Collard to Virginia Falk, State Solicitor's Office Western Australia, 'National Water Initiative: Indigenous Access and Entitlement Rights' (12 December 2007) 5.

113 [2006] FCA 459.

114 Email from David Collard to Virginia Falk, State Solicitor's Office Western Australia, 'National Water Initiative: Indigenous Access and Entitlement Rights' (12 December 2007) 6.

115 [2005] FCA 1716.

116 Email from David Collard to Virginia Falk, State Solicitor's Office Western Australia, 'National Water Initiative: Indigenous Access and Entitlement Rights' (12 December 2007) 6.

117 Sean Huber, 'The Wellesley Island Decision: Offshore Native Title Post *Yarmirr* and *Ward*' (2004) 23 *University of Queensland Law Journal* 242. See *Lardil Peoples v Queensland* [2004] FCA 298.

118 Ibid. 242.

119 Ibid. 248.

120 [2004] FCA 298.

121 Sean Huber, 'The Wellesley Island Decision: Offshore Native Title Post *Yarmirr* and *Ward*' (2004) 23 *University of Queensland Law Journal* 244.

122 Ibid. 245.

123 Ibid.

124 Ibid.

125 Ibid.

126 Rrumburriya Borroloola Claim Group v Northern Territory [2016] FCA 776.

127 Nicolas Peterson and Bruce Rigsby (eds), 'Customary Marine Tenure in Australia: Introduction' (1998) 48 *Oceania Monograph University of Sydney* 1.

128 (1992) 175 CLR 1.

129 Nicolas Peterson and Bruce Rigsby (eds), 'Customary Marine Tenure in Australia: Introduction' (1998) 48 *Oceania Monograph University of Sydney* 1.

130 Ibid. 2.

131 Ibid. 6.

132 Ibid. 9.

133 Scott Cane, 'Aboriginal Fishing on the New South Wales South Coast: A Court Case' (1998) 48 *Oceania Monograph University of Sydney* 66-83. Kevin Mason and other Aboriginal defendants were arrested and charged under the *Fisheries and Oyster Farms Act 1935* (NSW) with possession of various abalone above the statutory quota. The proceedings were heard in the local court and on appeal to the Court of Appeal from 1992 to 1994. The author was the instructing solicitor in defended hearings for Legal Aid NSW in 2004 for defendants connected with the Mason case. See also Scott Cane, Aboriginal Fishing on the South Coast of New South Wales, Report to Blake Dawson and Waldron and the NSW Aboriginal Land Council (Narooma, NSW, July 1992).

134 Nicolas Peterson and Bruce Rigsby (eds), 'Customary Marine Tenure in Australia: Introduction' (1998) 48 *Oceania Monograph University of Sydney* 10.

135 Lisa Strelein, 'A Comfortable Existence: Commercial Fishing and the Concept of Tradition in Native Title' (2002) 5 *Balayi: Culture, Law and Colonialism* 119. Strelein (2002) cites Western Australia v Ward [2002] HCA 28 [241].

136 Ibid.

137 [2013] HCA 47. The originating proceedings were heard in the Magistrates Court of South Australia and the defendants were found not guilty of possessing undersized abalone. An appeal heard in the Supreme Court of South Australia overturned the Magistrates decision. Special leave to the High Court of Australia was granted.

138 Working Group for Advancing Indigenous Reconciliation in Primary Industries and Natural Resource Management, 'Indigenous Reconciliation in Primary Industries and Natural Resource Management: Annual Report 2006-2007' ('Report', Natural Resource Management and Primary Industries Ministerial Councils, November 2007) 23.

139 Ibid. 12.

140 Bronwyn de Satge on behalf of the *Butchulla Peoples (No 2) v Queensland* [2014] FCA 1132.

141 *Djabagay People v Queensland* [2004] FCA 1652.

142 Ibid.

143 NSW Aboriginal Land Council, 'NSW Native Title Bill: A Brief Critique by the NSW Aboriginal Land Council' ('Working Paper', 1993) 14.

144 See *Quandamooka Peoples v Queensland [No 1] v Queensland* [2011] <http://www.atns.net.au/agreement.asp?EntityID=5569> and Quandamooka Peoples [No 2] v Queensland [2011] <http://www.atns.net.au/agreement.asp?EntityID=5570>.

145 Aboriginal and Torres Strait Islander Social Justice Commissioner, 'Native Title Report 2006' (Human Rights and Equal Opportunity Commission, 2006) 43.

146 Ibid.

147 Stephen Mueke, Ancient and Modern: Time, Culture and Indigenous Philosophy, (University of New South Wales Press, revised ed, 2006) 14-15.

148 Selma Milovanovic, 'Native Title Proof may be Reversed', *The Age* (Melbourne), 10-11 April 2009, 3.

149 (1996) 187 CLR 1.

150 Katie Glaskin, 'Native title and the Bundle of Rights Model: Implications for the Recognition of Aboriginal Relations to Country' (2003) 13(1) *Anthropological Forum* 69-70.

151 New South Wales Aboriginal Land Council, 'Submission to the Department of Natural Resources (NSW): Draft Implementation Plan for the National Water Initiative' (8 December 2005) 6.

152 Ibid. 1.

153 Frank G Nicholls, 'Aboriginal Hunting Rights and Fauna Protection Legislation: *Yanner v Eaton* [1999] in its Political Context' (2000) 30(3) *Environmental Policy and Law* 146.

154 Richard B Collins, 'Sacred Sites and Religious Freedom on Government Land' (2003) 5(2) *Journal of Constitutional Law* 250.

155 Melissa Kate Holzberger, 'Access to Water Resources for Mining Purposes in South Australia' *University of Dundee* <http://www.dundee.ac.uk/cepmlp/car.html/car7_article10.pdf>. See *Western Australia v Ward* [2002] 191 ALR 1. See *Western Australian v Brown* [2014] HCA 8 where the Court was 'unanimous in its decision that a Pilbara mining lease granted in the 1960s did not extinguish the Ngarlga Peoples native title rights to exercise hunting and gathering', recognising co-existence of both mining and native title rights.

156 Ibid. 11-12. Holzberger quotes T Denholder and G Gishubl, 'First Decade of Mabo Part 2' (Paper presented at Australian Mining and Petroleum Law Association, Gold Coast, Queensland, 14-17 August 2002) 470.

157 Maureen Tehan, 'Report for the Attention of Members of the Committee on the Elimination of Racial Discrimination, A Hope Disillusioned, an Opportunity Lost? Reflections on Common Law Native Title and Ten Years of the *Native Title Act*' ('Report', Foundation for Aboriginal and Islander Research Action, February 2005) 14.

Chapter 6 Polarised paradigms — Western and Aboriginal conceptions

1   ACIL Tasman in association with Freehills, 'An Effective System of Defining Water Property Titles' ('Research Report', Australian Government, Department of Agriculture, Fisheries and Forestry and Land and Water Australia, Canberra, March 2004) 17.

2   Craig Anthony Tony Arnold, 'The Reconstruction of Property: Property as a Web of Interests' (2002) 26 *Harvard International Law Review* 281-284.

3   Ibid. 282.

4   Ibid. 283-284.

5   Ibid. 318-319. As quoted by Arnold 'cultural ontology' means the nature of being and the principles and categories which represent the cultural embodiment of a group of people.

6   Bradley Bryan, 'Property as Ontology: On Aboriginal and English Understanding of Ownership' (2000) 13(3) *Canadian Journal of Law and Jurisprudence* 1, 12 <http://au.westlaw.com/result/documenttext.aspx?RS=WLAU4.09&VR=2.0&SP=Fed...>

7   Ibid. 1-23.

8   Ibid. 1-3.

9   Ibid. 2.

10   Ibid.

11   Ibid. 7.

12   Ibid. 8.

13   *De Rose v South Australia [No 1]* (2003) 133 FCR 325.

14   Alex Reilly, 'Cartography, Property and the Aesthetics of Place: Mapping Native Title in Australia' (2004) in Andrew Kenyon and Peter Rush (eds), *Aesthetics of Law and Culture: Texts, Images and Screens* 227- 228. Reilly cites Helen Verran's (1998) 'Re-imagining Land Ownership in Australia' 1(2) *Postcolonial Studies* 237-254 which examines Indigenous relationships to land as highly developed epistemic and ontic relationships.

15   Centre for World Indigenous Studies, *A Treaty between Indigenous Nations on the Protection of Cultural Property and Traditional Resource Rights: Asserting Indigenous Nation Sovereignty* Centre for World Indigenous Studies <http://www.cwis.org/260fge/260tcptr.html>.

16   Ibid.

17   Dan Gillespie, Peter Cooke and John Taylor, 'Improving the Capacity of Indigenous People to Contribute to the Conservation of Biodiversity in Australia' ('Research Report', Environment Australia and the Biological Diversity Advisory Council, 2001) 57. See also Department of Sustainability, Environment, Water, Population and Communities, *Australia's Biological Diversity Conservation Strategy* (14 November 2011) <http://www.environment.gov.au/biodiversity/publications/strategy-2010-30/pubs/biodiversity-strategy-2010.pdf>

18   Stefano Burchi, 'The Interface between Customary and Statutory Water Rights: A Statutory Perspective' (Paper presented at the African Water Laws: Plural Legislative Frameworks for Rural Water Management in Africa, South Africa, 26-28 January 2005) 32:1 <http://www.fao.org/fileadmin/user_upload/legal/docs/lpo45.pdf>. Burchi (2005) cites Nowlan (2004) on western and northern Canadian water rights.

19   Email from Waubin Richard Aken to Virginia Falk [Marshall], 13 November 2008.

20   Eugene C Hargrove, *Foundations of Environmental Ethics* (Prentice Hall, 1989) 25.

21   Ibid.

22   Ibid.

23   Ibid.

24   Justice Robert Nicholson, 'Law and Language: The Case of Native Title' *Federal Court Intranet*
      <http://intranet.fedcourt.gov.au/search97cgi_cgi?Action=View&VdkVgwkey=%2>.

25   Ibid.

26   Ibid.

27   Ibid.

28   Francis Bennion, 'Introduction'Statutory Interpretation: A Code 4th Ed, (Butterworths: 2002).
      p.5

29   William Collins and Sons, *Collins Concise Dictionary of the English Language* Wilkes and Krebs
      (eds) (Collins, London, 2nd ed, 1988) 794.

30   Ibid. 273.

31   Lauren Benton, *Law and Colonial Cultures: Legal Regimes in World History, 1400 to 1900*
      (Cambridge University Press, 2002) 10.

32   NSW Aboriginal Land Council and the NSW Department of Land and Water Conservation,
      'Report on the Boomanulla Conference for Country' (Paper presented at the Boomanulla
      Conference, Canberra, 5-6 March 2002) 6.

33   Russell Goldflam, 'Silence in Court! Problems and Prospects in Aboriginal Legal Interpreting'
      in Diana Eades (ed), *Language in Evidence: Issues Confronting Aboriginal and Multicultural
      Australia*, (University of New South Wales Press, 1995) 38.

34   Neva Collings and Virginia Falk, 'Water: Aboriginal Peoples in Australia and their Spiritual
      Relationship with Waterscapes' in Elliott Johnston, Martin Hinton and Daryle Rigney (eds),
      Indigenous Australians and the Law (Routledge-Cavendish, 2nd ed, 2008) 144.

35   *Water Management Act 2000* (NSW).

36   Ibid.

37   Big Bill Neidjie, Stephen Davis and Allan Fox, *Australia's Kakadu Man Bill* Neidjie (Resource
      Managers, revised ed, 1986) 47.

38   Craig Anthony Tony Arnold, 'The Reconstruction of Property: Property as a Web of Interests'
      (2002) 26 *Harvard Environmental Law Review* 281.

39   Ibid.

40   Mark Blumer, 'In Search of the Common Bunyip: A Commonsense Approach to Water Property
      Rights in New South Wales' (August 2000) 17(4) *Environmental and Planning Journal* 336.

41   Ibid.

42   David Lametti, 'The Concept of Property: Relations through Objects of Social Wealth' (2003) 53
      University of Toronto Law Journal 328.

43   Ibid.

44   Ibid.

45   Ibid.

46   A V Dicey, *Introduction to the Study of the Law of the Constitution* (Macmillan, first published
      1885, 1908) 61.

47   J W Harris, *Property and Justice* (Clarendon Press, 1996) 68-69.

48   Ibid. 74-75.

49   Ibid.

50   David Lametti, 'The Concept of Property: Relations through Objects of Social Wealth' (2003) 53
      University of Toronto Law Journal 14.

51   Ibid.

52   Bruce Ziff, *Principles of Property Law* (Carswell, Thomson Reuters, 5th ed 2010) 2.

53 Craig Anthony Tony Arnold, 'The Reconstruction of Property: Property as a Web of Interests' (2002) 26 *Harvard Environmental Law Review* 281.

54 Ibid.

55 Ibid. 282.

56 Ibid. 283.

57 Ibid. 282, 296

58 Ibid.

59 Ibid. 283

60 Lisa Strelein, *Compromised Jurisprudence: Native Title Cases Since Mabo* (Aboriginal Studies Press, 2nd ed 2009) 121.

61 213 CLR 1.

62 Ibid. 117.

63 Ibid. 121.

64 Katie Glaskin, 'Native Title and the Bundle of Rights Model: Implications for the Recognition of Aboriginal Relations to County' (2003) 13(1) *Anthropological Forum* 67.

65 Ibid. 68.

66 Craig Anthony Tony Arnold, 'The Reconstruction of Property: Property as a Web of Interests' (2002) 26 *Harvard Environmental Law Review* 283.

67 J E Penner, *The Idea of Property in Law* (Clarendon Press, 1997) 1.

68 Samantha Hepburn, *Principles of Property Law* (Routledge-Cavendish, 3rd revised ed 2006) 3.

69 Craig Anthony Tony Arnold, 'The Reconstruction of Property: Property as a Web of Interests' (2002) 26 *Harvard Environmental Law Review* 287.

70 Samantha Hepburn, *Principles of Property Law* (Routledge-Cavendish, 3rd revised ed 2006) 7.

71 J C Smith and David N Weisstub, *The Western Idea of Law* (Butterworths, 1983) 384-387.

72 Ibid. 1.

73 Kent McNeil, *Common Law Aboriginal Title* (Clarendon Press, 1989) 11.

74 Samantha Hepburn, *Principles of Property Law* (Routledge-Cavendish, 3rd revised ed 2006) 15-16.

75 Craig Anthony Tony Arnold, 'The Reconstruction of Property: Property as a Web of Interests' (2002) 26 *Harvard Environmental Law Review* 284.

76 Ibid. 295.

77 Ibid.

78 Ibid.

79 Ibid.

80 Michelle Grattan and Lindsay Murdoch, 'Labor Cool on any Change to Leases', *The Age* (Melbourne), 8 April 2005, 4.

81 David Cooper and Sue Jackson, 'Preliminary Study on Indigenous Water Values and Interests in the Katherine Region of the Northern Territory' ('Research Report', Commonwealth Scientific and Industrial Research Organisation Sustainable Ecosystems, March 2008) 54. The Report quotes a Senior Elder of Katherine in the Northern Territory.

82 David Lametti, 'The Concept of Property: Relations through Objects of Social Wealth' (2003) 53 *University of Toronto Law Journal* 11.

83 *Milirrpum v Nabalco* (1971) FLR 141, 259. This section refers to the colony being settled in South Australia in 1840.

84 David Lametti, 'The Concept of Property: Relations through Objects of Social Wealth' (2003) 53 *University of Toronto Law Journal* 22.

85 Ibid. 14.

86   Ibid. 53-55.

87   Ibid. 54-55.

88   Craig Anthony Tony Arnold, 'The Reconstruction of Property: Property as a Web of Interests' (2002) 26 *Harvard Environmental Law Review* 281.

89   Ibid.

90   Bradley Bryan, 'Property as Ontology: On Aboriginal and English Understandings of Ownership' (2000) 13(3) *Canadian Journal of Law and Jurisprudence* 23-24. Bryan argues that centralising the meaning of Aboriginal definitions such as *sui generis*, expresses Aboriginal concepts by a universality approach and fails to interpret these values through their own cultural concepts.

91   See Bradley Bryan, 'Property as Ontology: On Aboriginal and English Understanding of Ownership' (2000) 13(3) *Canadian Journal of Law and Jurisprudence*.

92   For a more thorough examination of Western property theories, see Virginia Marshall, *A Web of Aboriginal Water Rights: Examining the Competing Aboriginal claim for Water Property Rights and Interests in Australia* (PhD Thesis, Macquarie University, 2014).

Chapter 7 'A fluid element' — water in Australian policy

1   Bryan Bruns, 'Water Tenure Reform: Developing an Extended Ladder of Participation' (2003) *University of South Australia* 2 <http://unisa.edu.au/waterpolicylaw/documents/water_justice_papers.pdf>.

2   Stephen and Bev Sithole 'Sustainable Northern Landscapes and the Nexus with Indigenous Health: Healthy Country Healthy People' ('Research Report', NTU07, Land and Water Australia, 2007) 35.

3   David Pannell, University of Western Australia, 'Thinking like an Economist 20: Challenges for Policy Economists' <http://www.pannelldiscussions.net/2005/05/52-thinking-like-an-economist-16-weaknesses-of-economists/>.

4   Ibid.

5   Virginia Falk [Marshall] personal communication with Frances Bodkin, 2006. During cultural education about the preparation of Aboriginal medicines of the D'harawal peoples.

6   Sue Jackson and Joe Morrison, 'Indigenous Perspectives in Water Management, Reforms and Implementation' in Karen Hussey and Stephen Dovers (eds), *Managing Water for Australia: The Social and Institutional Challenges* (Commonwealth Scientific and Industrial Research Organisation, 2007) 25.

7   Poh-Ling Tan, 'Water Law Reform in NSW — 1995 to 1999' (2003) 20 *Environmental Planning Law Journal* 166.

8   Matthew Warren, 'Rain Changes Debate', *The Australian* , 23-24 February 2008, 1.

9   Marcia Langton quoted in Sue Jackson, Michael Storrs and Joe Morrison, 'Recognition of Aboriginal Rights, Interests and Values in River Research and Management: Perspectives from Northern Australia' (2005) 6(2) *Ecological Management and Restoration* 106.

10   Geoffrey J Syme and Steve Hatfield-Dodds, 'The Role of Communication and Attitudes Research in the Evolution of Effective Resource Management Arrangements' in Karen Hussey and Stephen Dovers (eds), *Managing Water for Australia: The Social and Institutional Challenges* (Commonwealth Scientific and Industrial Research Organisation, 2007) 11-18.

11   Ibid.

12   Ibid. 11-12.

13   Ibid.

14   Sue Jackson, Michael Storrs and Joe Morrison, 'Recognition of Aboriginal Rights, Interests and Values in River Research and Management: Perspectives from Northern Australia' (2005) 6(2) *Ecological Management and Restoration* 106-107.

15   Working Group for Advancing Indigenous Reconciliation in Primary Industries and Natural Resource Management, 'Key Issues: Indigenous Employment and Engagement in Natural Resource Management and Primary Industries' ('Draft Report', 2008) 2.

16   Gleeson CJ quoted in Jonathon Pearlman, 'Water Will be the Next Big Battleground, says Chief Justice', *The Sydney Morning Herald*, (Sydney), 11 February 2008.

17   Ibid.

18   Bardy McFarlane, 'The National Water Initiative and Acknowledging Indigenous Interests in Planning' (2004) <http://www.nntt.gov.au/news-and-communications/speeches-and-papers/documents/2004/speeches%20national%20water%20initiative%20mcfarlane%20november%202004.pdf>. Paper presented at the National Water Conference, Sydney.

19   National Water Commission, 'Australian Water Reform 2009: Second Biennial Assessment of Progress in Implementation of the National Water Initiative' ('Report', Australian Government, 2010) 104.

20   Ibid.

21   Ibid. 108.

22   Poh-Ling Tan, 'Irrigators Come First: Conversion of Existing Allocations to Bulk Entitlements in the Goulburn and Murray Catchments, Victoria' (2001) 18(2) *Environmental and Planning Law Journal* 164.

23   Ibid. 187.

24   Ibid. 182.

25   Bardy McFarlane, 'The National Water Initiative and Acknowledging Indigenous Interests in Planning' (2004) <http://www.nntt.gov.au/news-and-communications/speeches-and-papers/documents/2004/speeches%20national%20water%20initiative%20mcfarlane%20november%202004.pdf>. Paper presented at the National Water Conference, Sydney.

26   National Water Commission, 'Intergovernmental Agreement on a National Water Initiative between the Commonwealth of Australia and the Governments of New South Wales, Victoria, Queensland, South Australia, the Australian Capital Territory and the Northern Territory' (2004) National Water Commission <http://nwc.gov.au/__data/assets/pdf_file/0008/24749/Intergovernmental-Agreement-on-a-national-water-initiative.pdf>.

27   Ibid.

28   Ibid.

29   Bardy McFarlane, 'The National Water Initiative and Acknowledging Indigenous Interests in Planning' (2004) <http://www.nntt.gov.au/news-and-communications/speeches-and-papers/documents/2004/speeches%20national%20water%20initiative%20mcfarlane%20november%202004.pdf>. Paper presented at the National Water Conference, Sydney.

30   Emilio Santoro, 'The Rule of Law and the Liberties of the English: The Interpretation of Albert Venn Dicey' in Pietro Costa and Danilo Zolo (eds), *The Rule of Law: History, Theory and Criticism* (Springer, The Netherlands, 2007) 155-156.

31   Letter from Geoff Clark to Bob Carr, 2 April 2004. A letter from the Aboriginal and Torres Strait Islander Commission, Canberra.

32   Virginia Falk [Marshall], personal communication with Jennifer Whitmore, Senior Officer, Cabinet Taskforce, Water Reform Policy, NSW Government, 2006. Communication took place at the Department of Natural Resources (NSW) Parramatta.

33   Ibid.

34 Virginia Falk, participation in the State Water Sharing Workshops, Department of Natural Resources (NSW), 2006-2007. I attended the state workshops as the Executive Officer of the NSW Aboriginal Water Trust.

35 Ibid.

36 Jill Windle and John Rolfe, 'Natural Resource Management and the Protection of Aboriginal Cultural Heritage' ('Occasional Paper', No 5, Institute for Sustainable Regional Development, Queensland Government, 2002) 6.

37 Sue Jackson, 'Panel Discussion' (Speech delivered at the Garma Indigenous Water Knowledge, Indigenous Water Interests Conference, Gove Northern Territory, 7 August 2008).

38 Ibid.

39 Murray Radcliffe, 'Strategic Development for Future Indigenous Dialogue and Engagement at the National Level' (Speech delivered at the Australian Indigenous Water Forum Focus Group, National Water Commission, Adelaide South Australia, 18 November 2008).

40 Poh-Ling Tan, 'An Historical Introduction to Water Reform in NSW — 1975 to 1994' (2002) 19 *Environmental and Planning Law Journal* 451.

41 Sue Jackson and Joe Morrison, 'Indigenous Perspectives in Water Management, Reforms and Implementation' in Karen Hussey and Stephen Dovers (eds), *Managing Water for Australia: The Social and Institutional Challenges* (Commonwealth Scientific and Industrial Research Organisation, 2007) 3.

42 National Water Commission, Australian Indigenous Water Focus Group, National Water Commission, Adelaide, South Australia, 18 November 2008.

43 Ibid. 2.

44 Peter Knight, *Land Tenure and Relationship to Place: An Essay Uniting Spatial, Political, and Spiritual Themes in the Formulation of a PhD Topic* Department of Surveying, University of Otago <http://www.business.otago.ac.nz/SIRCO5/conferences/2000/14_knight.pdf>.

45 Murray Radcliffe, 'National Water Commission Introduction and Engagement' (Speech delivered at the Australian Indigenous Water Focus Group, National Water Commission, South Australia, 18 November 2008). I attended the meeting as an Indigenous delegate with the Indigenous Water Focus Group.

46 National Water Commission, *National Water Assessments* <http://www.nwc.gov.au/nwi/biennial-assessments>.

47 National Water Commission, 'The National Water Initiative: Securing Australia's Water Future' ('Report', Australian Government, 2011 Assessment). See also National Water Commission, 'Australian Water Reform: Second Biennial Assessment of Progress in Implementation of the National Water Initiative' ('Report', Australian Government, 2009).

48 National Water Commission, 'The National Water Initiative: Securing Australia's Water Future' ('Report', Australian Government, 2011 Assessment) 57.

49 National Water Commission, 'Australian Water Reform: Second Biennial Assessment of Progress in Implementation of the National Water Initiative' ('Report', Australian Government, 2009) 27.

50 National Water Commission, 'The National Water Initiative: Securing Australia's Water Future' ('Report', Australian Government, 2011) 44.

51 National Water Commission, Intergovernmental Agreement on a National Water Initiative between the Jurisdictions (2004) <http://nwc.gov.au/__data/assets/pdf_file/0008/24749/Intergovernmental-Agreement-on-a-national-water-initiative.pdf>.

52 National Water Commission, 'The National Water Initiative: Securing Australia's Water Future' ('Report', Australian Government, 2011) 104.

53   National Water Commission, 'Australian Water Reform: Second Biennial Assessment of Progress in Implementation of the National Water Initiative' ('Report', Australian Government, 2009) 27.

54   National Water Commission, 'The National Water Initiative: Securing Australia's Water Future' ('Report', Australian Government, 2011) 45.

55   Ibid Note: the National Water Commission was abolished in 2014 by the Federal Government.

56   National Water Commission, 'The National Water Initiative: Securing Australia's Water Future' ('Report', Australian Government, 2011).

57   Ibid

58   National Water Commission, Australian Government, 'The National Water Initiative: Securing Australia's Water Future' ('Report', Australian Government, 2011) iii. The Biennial Assessment of the National Water Initiative is regulated under s 7 of the *National Water Commission Act 2004* (Cth). Commencing from 200 in app B the report has a summary on the progress of National Water Initiative Actions under the jurisdictions.

59   Ibid. 44.

60   Ibid. 222.

61   Ibid.

62   Ibid.

63   Ibid. 211.

64   Ibid.

65   Ibid. 251.

66   Ibid.Ibid. 265.

67   Ibid. 294.

68   Ibid.

69   Friends of the Earth, *Melbourne* <http://www.melbourne.foe.org.au/?q=bmc/indigenous_justice>

70   National Water Commission, Australian Government, 'The National Water Initiative: Securing Australia's Water Future' ('Report', Australian Government, 2011) 294.

71   Ibid.

72   Ibid. 44.

73   Ibid.

74   National Water Commission, Australian Government, 'The National Water Initiative: Securing Australia's Water Future' ('Report', Australian Government, 2011).45.

75   Ibid. 46.

76   Ibid.

77   David Collard, personal communication to Virginia Falk February 2009. The appointment of representatives at the Indigenous Focus Group Conference, Adelaide, South Australia on 17-19 February 2009 was confirmed during the conference.

78   Rutgerd Boelens, 'Water Law and Indigenous Rights: Research, Action and Debate' (2002) Wageningen University <http://ww.indigenouswater.org/user/Water%20Workshop%20Summary.pdf>.

79   Sue Jackson and Joe Morrison, 'Indigenous Perspectives in Water Management, Reforms and Implementation' in Karen Hussey and Stephen Dovers (eds), *Managing Water for Australia: The Social and Institutional Challenges* (Commonwealth Scientific and Industrial Research Organisation, 2007) 7.

80   Poh-Ling Tan, 'An Historical Introduction to Water Reform in NSW — 1975 to 1994' (December 2002) 19(6) *Environmental and Planning Law Journal* 445-446.

81   Ibid.

82   Ibid. 448.

83   Ibid. 449.

84   *Latta v Klinberg* [1977] NSWSC (1 July 1977) Lee J.

85   Poh-Ling Tan, 'An Historical Introduction to Water Reform in NSW — 1975 to 1994' (December 2002) 19(6) *Environmental and Planning Law Journal* 450.

86   Email from David Collard to Virginia Falk, State Solicitor's Office, Western Australia, 'Water Resources Bill, Water Entitlements and their Administration', Reference 1851-08, 18 April 2008, 27.

87   Poh-Ling Tan, 'An Historical Introduction to Water Reform in NSW — 1975 to 1994' (2002) 19(6) *Environmental and Planning Law Journal* 453. Tan explains 'licence stacking' as a practice of purchasing land to gain increased water supply, where a person would buy parcels of land and transfer the licence/s between the land holdings. See also Gary Sturgess and Michael Wright, *Water Rights in Rural New South Wales: The Evolution of a Property Rights System* (Centre for Independent Studies, 1993); Poh-Ling Tan, 'Water Law Reform in NSW — 1995 to 1999' (2003) 20 *Environmental and Planning Law Journal*.

88   Ibid. 454. See also J Burton, *Review of Reforms in the Water Industry 1988*, Report to the Minister for Natural Resources (June 1988).

89   Stewart Smith, *Water Reforms in NSW: Briefing Paper* 4/98 (6 November 2006) NSW Parliament <http://www.parliament.nsw.gov.au/prod/parlment/publications.nsf/0/435D6C31A6EA...>.

90   Poh-Ling Tan, 'Conflict over Water Resources in Queensland: All Eyes on the Lower Balonne' (December 2000) 17(6) *Environmental and Planning Law Journal* 567.

91   Ibid. 566.

92   Ibid. 567.

93   Email from David Collard to Virginia Falk on Virginia Simpson, 13 November 2007.

94   Poh-Ling Tan, 'Water Licences and Property Rights: The Legal Principles for Compensation in Queensland' (1999) 16(4) *Environmental and Planning Law Journal* 179.

95   Ibid. 289.

96   Ibid. 284.

97   Ibid. 288.

98   Poh-Ling Tan, 'Irrigators Come First: Conversion of Existing Allocations to Bulk Entitlements in the Goulburn and Murray Catchments, Victoria' (April 2001) 18(2) *Environmental and Planning Law Journal* 172.

99   Ibid. 163-165. Tan (2001) comments that the *Water Act 1989* (Vic) introduced a recognition of property rights over private water rights, where a Bulk Entitlement was used to allocate water for public interests, environment and for authorities to divert or sell on water to individuals.

100   Ibid. 180.

101   Ibid. 182.

102   Department of Sustainability and Environment, *Securing Our Water Future Together* (June 2004) 18 <http://www.dse.gov.au>.

103   Ibid. 19.

104   See Victorian Government, *Aboriginal Victoria: Self-determination for Aboriginal people* <http://consult.aboriginalvictoria.vic.gov.au/Open-Meeting>.

105   Ibid See *Aboriginal Treaty Fact Sheet* <http://consult.aboriginalvictoria.vic.gov.au/Open-Meeting>. See also *Traditional Owner Settlement Act 2010* (Vic).

106   Ibid. 187.

107   Henry Reynolds, *Frontier: Aborigines, Settlers and Land* (Allen and Unwin, 1987) 127.

108 Sue Jackson, 'Compartmentalising Culture: The Articulation and Consideration of Indigenous Values in Water Resource Management' (March 2006) 37(1) *Australian Geographer* 19.

109 Ibid. 20.

110 Sue Jackson, 'Compartmentalising Culture: The Articulation and Consideration of Indigenous Values in Water Resource Management' (2006) 37(1) *Australian Geographer* 21.

111 Ibid. 24.

112 Ibid. 26.

113 Tony Neal, 'The Forensic Challenge of Native Title' (September 1995) *Law Institute Journal* 880, 883.

114 Sue Jackson and Joe Morrison, 'Indigenous Perspectives in Water Management, Reforms and Implementation' in Karen Hussey and Stephen Dovers (eds), *Managing Water for Australia: The Social and Institutional Challenges* (Commonwealth Scientific and Industrial Research Organisation, 2007) 23.

115 Ibid.

116 Ibid. 29, 35.

117 Ibid. 32.

118 Ibid. 33.

119 Ibid. 34.

120 Ibid. 35.

121 Australian Broadcasting Corporation, 'Aboriginal intervention on the removal of Aboriginal children in the Northern Territory' October 2007 (Mal Brough).

122 Barry O'Farrell, 'Media Launch' (Speech delivered at the Goulburn Liberal Party Office, Goulburn NSW, February 2007).

123 Sharon Beder, *Environmental Principles and Policies: An Interdisciplinary Approach* (University of New South Wales Press, 2006) 71-90.

124 Ibid.

125 Virginia Falk, 'The Rise and Fall of ATSIC: A Personal Opinion' (2004) 8(4) *Australian Indigenous Law Reporter* 18.

126 Senate Select Committee on the Administration of Indigenous Affairs, Parliament of Australia, *After ATSIC: Life in the Mainstream?* (March 2005) [1.3].

127 ATSIC (Aboriginal and Torres Strait Islander Commission) and the Lingiari Foundation, *Onshore, Offshore: Indigenous Rights to Waters Report and Recommendations* ATSIC, Canberra, 2002 <http://atsic.gov.au/issues/Indigenous_Rights/Indigenous_Rights_Waters/Default.asp>. See Virginia Falk, 'The Rise and Fall of ATSIC: A Personal Opinion' (2004) 8(4) *Australian Indigenous Law Reporter*.

128 Ibid.

129 Ibid See *Offshore, Onshore: Indigenous Rights to Water Report and Recommendations* in chapter 1 'Project Background and Existing Government Policy Environment.

130 Ibid. See *Offshore, Onshore: Indigenous Rights to Water Report and Recommendations* in 'National Water Quality Management Strategy'.

131 Ibid. See *Offshore, Onshore: Indigenous Rights to Water Report and Recommendations* in 'Indigenous Rights to Waters in Australia'.

132 Ibid. See *Offshore, Onshore: Indigenous Rights to Water Report and Recommendations* in chapter 5 in recommendations 6, 29, 36.

133 Aboriginal Torres Strait Islander Commissioner, 'Social Justice and Native Title Report 2015' (Australian Human Rights Commission, 2015) 24. See also Australian Government 'Closing the Gap Report 2016'.

Chapter 8 The Murray-Darling Basin and the Commonwealth Water Act

1   Murray-Darling Basin Authority, *Guide to the Proposed Basin Plan: Volume 2 Part 1* (Australian Government, 2010) 10.

2   Ibid.

3   Ibid. 16.

4   Ibid. 21.

5   Monica Morgan, Lisa Strelein and Jessica Weir, 'Indigenous Rights to Water in the Murray-Darling Basin' ('Research Discussion Paper' No 14, Australian Institute of Aboriginal and Torres Strait Islander Studies, Canberra, 2004) 7.

6   Gretchen Poiner, *The Good Rule: Gender and Other Power Relationships in a Rural Community* (Sydney University Press, 1990) 35.

7   New South Wales Aboriginal Land Council and the Department of Land and Water (NSW) (Paper presented at the Boomanulla Conference for Country, Canberra, 5-6 March 2002) 11.

8   New South Wales Aboriginal Land Council, *Tenth Session, Agenda Item 6: The Right to Water and Indigenous Peoples* (20 March 2012) United Nations Permanent Forum on Indigenous Issues, Tenth Session, 16-27 May 2011, New York <http://www.hreoc.gov.au/social_justice/international_docs/2011/7_Right_to_Water_NSWALC_FINAL.pdf>.

9   See Select Committee on the Murray –Darling Basin Plan and Recommendations <http://www.aph.gov.au/Parliamentary_Business/Committees/Senate/Murray_Darling_Basin_Plan/murraydarling/Report>.

10   Stuart Rintoul, 'Dog Eat Dog in the Fight for Water', *The Australian* (Sydney), 12-13 July 2008, 8.

11   Manning Clark (ed), *Select Documents in Australian History 1851-1900 Volume 2* (Angus and Robertson, revised ed, 1979) 164-165.

12   Murray-Darling Basin Ministerial Council, 'Murray-Darling Basin Environmental Resources Study' ('Research Report', Murray-Darling Basin Ministerial Council, July 1987) 145.

13   Daniel Lewis and Marian Wilkinson, 'Licence to Spill is a Big Water Fight', *The Sydney Morning Herald* (Sydney), 30 June-1 July 2007, 30.

14   ATSIC (Aboriginal and Torres Strait Islander Commission) and the Lingiari Foundation, *Onshore, Offshore: Indigenous Rights to Water Report and Recommendations* ATSIC, <http://atsic.gov.au/issues/Indigenous_Rights/Indigenous_Rights_Waters/Default.asp>.

15   Stuart Rintoul, 'Dog Eat Dog in the Fight for Water', *The Australian*, 12-13 July 2008, 8.

16   Stewart Smith, *Water Reforms in NSW: An Update: Briefing Paper* NSW Parliament <http://www.parliament.nsw.gov.au/prod/parlment/publications.nsf/0/435D6C31A6EA...>

17   Ibid.

18   Poh-Ling Tan, 'Conflict over Water Resources in Queensland: All Eyes on the Lower Balonne' (2000) 17(6) *Environmental and Planning Law Journal* 545.

19   Ibid.

20   Paul Kildea and George Williams, 'The Constitution and the Management of Water in Australia's Rivers' (2010) 32 *Sydney Law Review* 595.

21   Ibid. 596.

22   Ibid. 605.

23   Ibid. 598-599.

24   Ibid. 598.

25   Productivity Commission, *Water Rights Arrangements in Australia and Overseas: Annex A, Murray-Darling Basin* ('Research Paper', 2003) 4.

26 Kathy Ridge, 'Water Supply' in David Farrier and Paul Stein (eds), *Environmental Law Handbook* (Redfern Legal Centre, 4th ed, 2006) 517.

27 Murray-Darling Basin Authority, *Guide to the Proposed Basin Plan: Volume 2 Part 1*, 75.

28 Productivity Commission, *Water Rights Arrangements in Australia and Overseas: Annex A, Murray-Darling Basin* ('Research Paper', 2003) 11-12.

29 Department of Sustainability, Environment, Water, Population and Communities, *Water Legislation* (2012) <http://www.environment.gov.au/water/australia/water-act/index.html#amendment-2008>.

30 Ibid.

31 Ibid.

32 Murray-Darling Basin Authority, *Guide to the Proposed Basin Plan: Overview Volume 1*, (2010) 4-5.

33 The *Water Amendment Act 2008* (Cth) sch 4 had two amendments to ss 10 and 11 of the *Water Act 2007*; s 202(3)(b) to insert at subsection (c) 'an Indigenous water Subcommittee, to guide the consideration of Indigenous matters relevant to the Basin's water resources' and s 202(5) to add at subsection (c) 'an individual with expertise in Indigenous matters relevant to the Basin's water resources'.

34 Murray-Darling Basin Authority, *Guide to the Proposed Basin Plan: Overview Volume 1*, 5-6.

35 Murray-Darling Basin Authority, *Guide to the Proposed Basin Plan: Volume 2 Part 1*, 67.

36 Australian Government, *Water Legislation* (2012) Department of Sustainability, Environment, Water, Population and Communities <http://www.environment.gov.au/water/australia/water-act/index.html#amendment-2008>.

37 Ibid.

38 Ibid.

39 *Water Amendment Act 2008* (Cth). See sub-div B.

40 Ibid See sub-divs D, E and F.

41 Ibid See div 4c135.

42 Ibid See sch B pt VII.

43 Ibid See sch D app 2.

44 The referral of powers from the States to the Commonwealth is for specific matters dealing with the Basin States, and does not interfere with the operation of ss 99 and 100 of the *Australian Constitution*. See also the reading down provision s 11 of the *Water Act 2007* (Cth).

45 Murray-Darling Basin Authority, *Guide to the Proposed Basin Plan: Overview Volume 1*, 4-5.

46 Ibid *Water Act 2007* (Cth) app D and s 21(1).

47 Murray-Darling Basin Authority, *Plain English Summary of the Proposed Basin Plan* (Australian Government, 2011) iv.

48 Murray-Darling Basin Authority, Australian Government, 'Delivering a Healthy Working Basin: About the Draft Basin Plan' ('Discussion Paper', November 2011) foreword.

49 Ibid. 161.

50 House Standing Committee on Regional Australia, Parliament of Australia, *Inquiry into the Impact of the Murray-Darling Basin Plan in Regional Australia* (2 June 2011) 1, 23. See also Rural and Regional Affairs and Transport References Committee, Parliament of Australia, Darwin, *Rural Water Usage in Australia* (18 November 2003), 448-453 (Sue Jackson). See New South Wales, *Parliamentary Debates: Water Management Bill*, Legislative Assembly, 9393 21-22 June 2000 (Second Reading).

51 Ibid.

52 Ibid. 5.

53   Ibid. 9.

54   Ibid. 2.58.

55   Ibid. 2.74, 2.76.

56   Ibid. 2.59.

57   Ibid. 4.24.

58   Ibid. 4.19.

59   Ibid. 1, 23. See also Rural and Regional Affairs and Transport References Committee, Parliament of Australia, Darwin, *Rural Water Usage in Australia* (18 November 2003), 448-453 (Sue Jackson). See New South Wales, *Parliamentary Debates: Water Management Bill*, Legislative Assembly, 9393 21-22 June 2000 (Second Reading).77.

60   Ibid. 78.

61   Ibid. 81.

62   Ibid. 89.

63   Ibid. 93.

64   Murray-Darling Basin Authority, 'Delivering a Healthy Working Basin: About the Draft Basin Plan' ('Discussion Paper', Australian Government, November 2011) 5. See also Murray-Darling Basin Authority, 'Guide to the Proposed Basin Plan: Overview Volume 1' ('Public Consultation Guide', Australian Government, 2010) and Murray-Darling Basin Authority, 'Guide to the Proposed Basin Plan: Technical Background Volume 2, Part 1 of 3' ('Public Consultation Guide', Australian Government, 2010).

65   Murray-Darling Basin Authority, *The Draft Basin Plan: Catchment by Catchment*, (Australian Government, 2011) 3.

66   Ibid.

67   Ibid .

68   Murray-Darling Basin Authority, 'Plain English Summary of the Proposed Basin Plan: Including Explanatory Notes' (Australian Government, November 2011) Explanatory Note.

69   Ibid. 52-53.

70   Ibid.

71   Murray-Darling Basin Authority, *Plain English Summary of the Proposed Basin Plan* (Australian Government, 2011) iii.

72   See Part 14 titled 'Indigenous Values and Uses' in the Murray-Darling Basin Authority, 'Proposed Basin Plan: A Draft for Consultation,' (Australian Government, November 2011) 83.

73   Ibid. 84. See clause 9.59 in the 'Proposed Basin Plan: A Draft for Consultation,' (November 2011).

74   Ibid See clause 9.58 in the 'Proposed Basin Plan: A Draft for Consultation,' (November 2011).

75   Ibid.

76   Virginia Marshall, Symposium, 'Aboriginal Water Rights and Interests: Constitutional Recognition' (23 May 2012) Legal Intersections Research Centre, Faculty of Law, University of Wollongong. See Virginia Falk, 'Beyond Native Title: The Rights Response to Social Justice and the Conceptual Problems of Resource Development' Development (2010) Native Title Conference <http://www.aiatsis.gov.au/ntru/documents/[Virginia Falk] BeyondNativeTitleAbstract.pdf>. See Virginia Marshall, 'Indigenous Water rights and Governance' (Paper presented at the Trade, Intellectual Property and the Knowledge of Indigenous Peoples: The Developmental Frontier Conference, University of Victoria, New Zealand, 7-10 December 2010). See also Virginia Falk, 'Aboriginal Water Rights and Interests: An Emerging Issue in Australian Water Law' (Paper submitted to Lawlab 2010 Water Law Award, Sydney, 17 February 2010); Virginia Marshall quoted in R. Maxwell, '21 Aboriginal nations join water battle', Koori Mail, 2 May 2012, 35.

77   Murray-Darling Basin Commission, 'Final Draft: The Murray-Darling Basin Indigenous Action Plan' (2006) Murray-Darling Basin Commission, Canberra, <www.mdbc.gov.au>.

78   Ibid.

79   Ibid.

80   Murray-Darling Basin Authority, *Guide to the Proposed Basin Plan: Volume 2 Part 1*, 27.

81   Ibid. 25. Represented by the following Aboriginal groups, Barkindji, Barunggam, Bidjara, Bigambul, Budjiti, Euahlayi, Gamilaroi, Githabul, Gunggari, Gwamu (Kooma), Jarowair, Kunja, Kwiambul, Malangapa, Mandandanji, Mardigan, Murrawarri, Ngemba, Ngiyampaa, Wailwan and Wakka Wakka.

82   Ibid. 25. Represented by the following Aboriginal groups, Barapa, Latji Latji, Mutti Mutti, Ngarrindjeri, Taungurung, Wadi Wadi, Wamba Wamba, Wergaia Wiradjuri and Yorta Yorta.

83   Ibid.

84   Murray-Darling Basin Commission, *The Murray-Darling Basin Indigenous Action Plan* (29 July 2005) Murray-Darling Indigenous Action Plan <www.mdbc.gov.au>.

85   Murray-Darling Basin Authority, *Guide to the Proposed Basin Plan: Volume 2 Part 1*, 26.

86   Murray-Darling Basin Commission, 'Final Draft: The Murray-Darling Basin Indigenous Action Plan' (29 July 2005) Murray-Darling Basin Commission, Canberra, iii-20 <www.mdbc.gov.au>.

87   Ibid.

88   Ibid.

89   Ibid.

90   See Murray-Darling Basin Authority, *Aboriginal Partnerships Action Plan* (April 2015).

91   Sue Jackson and Joe Morrison, 'Indigenous Perspectives in Water Management, Reforms and Implementation' in Karen Hussey and Stephen Dovers (eds), *Managing Water for Australia: The Social and Institutional Challenges* (Commonwealth Scientific and Industrial Research Organisation, 2007) 23-41.

92   Ibid.

93   Ibid.

94   Dennis Pearce and Robert Geddes, *Statutory Interpretation in Australia* (Lexis Nexis Butterworths, 7th ed, 2011) 30-31. Authors cite Spigelman CJ.

95   Ibid.

96   Sue Jackson, 'Compartmentalising Culture: The Articulation and Consideration of Indigenous Values in Water Resource Management' (2006) 35 *Australian Geographer* 28-29.

97   Ibid.

98   New South Wales Government, Department of Water (NSW) *Our Water Our Country: An Information Manual for Aboriginal People and Communities about the Water Reform Process* (NSW Government, Sydney, 2012) [2:4].

99   Murray-Darling Basin Authority, 'Proposed Basin Plan: A Draft for Consultation' (Australian Government, November 2011) 83.

100   Ibid.

101   Ibid.

102   Ibid.

103   Ibid.

104   Daniel Connell, *Water Politics in the Murray-Darling Basin* (Federation Press, 2007) 44-45.

105   Neva Collings and Virginia Falk, 'Water: Aboriginal peoples in Australia and their Spiritual Relationship with Waterscapes' in Elliott Johnston, Martin Hinton and Daryle Rigney (eds), *Indigenous Australians and the Law* (Routledge-Cavendish, 2nd ed, 2008) 141.

106 Aboriginal and Torres Strait Islander Commission and the Lingiari Foundation, *Indigenous Rights to Water Report and Recommendations* (15 November 2004) Aboriginal and Torres Strait Islander Commission <http://astic.gov.au/issues/Indigenous_Rights/Indigenous_Rights_Waters/Default.asp>.

107 Letter from Tim Fisher to Andrew Chalk, 8 March 1996.

108 *Water Amendment Act 2008* (Cth) s 18H. The Living Murray Initiative was a federal and state government investment to improve the environmental health of the Murray River.

109 Ibid Section 21(4) of the Act confirms the relevance of social and economic factors the Minister must, in exercising their powers and performing their functions under this division, including under (v) social, cultural, Indigenous and other public benefit issues.

110 Marcia Langton, 'Freshwater' in Lingiari Foundation, *Background Briefing Papers: Indigenous Rights to Waters*, Broome (2002) <http://www.atsic.gov.au/issues/Indigenous_Rights/Indigenous_Rights_Waters/Default.asp>.

111 Ibid. 134.

112 Ibid.

113 Ibid.

114 Sue Jackson, Brad Moggridge and Cathy Robinson, *Effects of Changes in Water Availability on Indigenous People of the Murray-Darling Basin: A Scoping Study and Report to the Murray-Darling Basin Authority* (2010) Commonwealth Scientific and Industrial Research Organisation <http://www.csiro.au/Organisation-Structure/Flagships/Water-for-a-Healthy-Country-Flagship/Sustainable-Yields-Projects/MDBSY/MDBSY-indigenous-water-report.aspx>.

115 Ibid.

116 Ibid.

117 University Technology Sydney and North West Local Land Services, 'Recognising and Protecting Aboriginal Knowledge Associated with Natural Resource Management' ('White Paper' to the NSW Office of the Environment, UTS, 30 September 2014) <https://www.ipaustralia.gov.au/sites/g/files/net856/f/uts_-_recognising_and_protecting_aboriginal_knowledge.pdf>. I was a committee member of the Working Party, the Indigenous Knowledge Forum Advisory Board and the UTS research team. In 2016 we received three year funding from the Australian Research Council Linkages Grant to further develop this research and I am a Partner Investigator on the project. See UTS News (7 June 2016) <https://www.uts.edu.au/about/faculty-law/news/research-aimed-safeguarding-indigenous-knowledge-receives-arc-grant>.

118 See Sue Jackson, Brad Moggridge & Cathy Robinson, *Effects of changes in water availability on Indigenous people of the Murray–Darling Basin: A scoping study and report to the Murray–Darling Basin Authority* (2010) CSIRO.

119 Ibid.

120 Murray-Darling Basin Ministerial Council, 'Murray-Darling Basin Environmental Resources Study' ('Research Report', Murray-Darling Basin Ministerial Council, July 1987) preface. The Report includes in the preface the creation story for the 'Ngurunderi' recounted by an initiated man, and cites R M and C H Berndt, *The World of the First Australians* (Rigby, Adelaide, 1985).

121 Ibid. xxiv.

122 Ibid. 3.

123 Ibid. 17, 18.

124 Murray-Darling Basin Ministerial Council, 'Murray-Darling Basin Environmental Resources Study' ('Research Report', Murray-Darling Basin Ministerial Council, July 1987) 18-19.

125 Ibid. 21-22.

126 Ibid. 73-101.

127   Ibid. 353-375.
128   Poh-Ling Tan, 'Conflict over Water Resources in Queensland: All Eyes on the Lower Balonne'
       (2000) 17(6) *Environmental and Planning Law Journal* 567.
129   Monica Morgan, Lisa Strelein and Jessica Weir, 'Indigenous Rights to Water in the Murray-
       Darling Basin: In Support of the Indigenous Final Report to the Living Murray Initiative'
       ('Research Discussion Paper', No 14, Australian Institute of Aboriginal and Torres Strait Islander
       Studies, 2004) 3.
130   Ibid.
131   Ibid. 5. See also Rudi Maxwell, '21 Aboriginal Nations Join Water Battle', *Koori Mail* (Lismore),
       2 May 2012, 35. This article highlights the claim for 100 per cent of the environmental flows by
       the Northern Murray-Darling Basin Aboriginal Nations in the Northern Murray-Darling Basin;
       in the article I am quoted in 'calling for an inquiry into Indigenous water entitlements in the
       Murray-Darling Basin'.
132   Ibid. 5-6.

Chapter 9 Water Rights — for economic independence

1   Gretchen Poiner, *The Good Rule: Gender and Other Power Relationships in a Rural Community*
       (Sydney University Press, 1990) 124.
2   Neva Collings and Virginia Falk [Marshall], 'Water: Aboriginal Peoples in Australia and their
       Spiritual Relationship with Waterscapes' in Elliott Johnston and Martin Hinton and Daryle
       Rigney (eds), *Indigenous Australians and the Law* (Routledge-Cavendish, 2nd ed, 2008) 132.
3   Ibid. 139.
4   Sue Jackson and Joe Morrison, 'Indigenous Perspectives in Water Management, Reforms and
       Implementation' in Karen Hussey and Stephen Dovers (eds), *Managing Water for Australia:
       The Social and Institutional Challenges* (Commonwealth Scientific and Industrial Research
       Organisation, 2007) 23-41.
5   Michael Crommelin, 'Economic Analysis of Property' in D J Galligan (ed) *Essays in Legal Theory*
       (1984) 74-78.
6   Evidence to Senate Rural and Regional Affairs and Transport Reference Committee, Parliament
       of Australia, Canberra, 18 November 2003, 389 (Bill Heffernan, Deputy Chair).
7   Email from David Collard to Virginia Falk on Virginia Simpson, 13 November 2007.
8   Virginia Falk [Marshall], personal communication with John Gillespie Project Advisor for the
       Commonwealth Indigenous Land Corporation (2 July 2006, Cowra NSW). See also email from
       John Gillespie to Virginia Falk, 17 July 2007.
9   William Charles Wentworth, *Statistical, Historical, and Political Description of The Colony of New
       South Wales and its Dependent Settlements in Van Diemen's Land: A Particular Enumeration of
       the Advantages which these Colonies Offer for Emigration, and their Superiority in many Respects
       over those Possessed by the United States of America* (Griffen Press, first published 1819, 1978
       ed) 78.
10   John Baalman, *Outline of Law in Australia* (Law Book, 2nd ed, 1955) 112-114.
11   Ibid.
12   Ibid.
13   Department of Aboriginal Affairs NSW 'Two Ways Together, Partnerships: A New Way of
       Doing Business with Aboriginal People, NSW Aboriginal Affairs Plan 2003-2012' (2003) 7.
14   ACIL Tasman in association with Freehills, 'An Effective System of Defining Water Property
       Titles' ('Research Report', Australian Government, Department of Agriculture, Fisheries and
       Forestry and Land and Water Australia, March 2004) 13.

15 *Wik Peoples v Queensland* (1996) 141 ALR 129, 190.

16 Ibid.

17 Richard Bartlett, *Native Title in Australia* (Lexis Nexis Butterworths, Australia, 2nd ed, 2004) 378. Note, the 1998 amendments were also referred to as the 'Ten Point Plan', whereby the Federal Government reaction was to diminish the Traditional Owners native title rights determined in *Wik Peoples v Queensland* (1996) 187 CLR 1.

18 NSW Parliament, Inquiry into Crown Land (23 June 2016) <https://www.parliament.nsw.gov.au/committees/inquiries/Pages/inquiry-details.aspx?pk=2404>.

19 Donald Horne, *The Lucky Country: Australia Today* (Penguin, 1964) 117.

20 Ibid. 117-118.

21 Quoted in Russell Skelton, 'One Country, Two Standards' *The Sydney Morning Herald* (Sydney), 19-20 May 2007, 26.

22 Ibid.

23 Ibid.

24 Aboriginal and Torres Strait Islander Social Justice Commissioner, 'Social Justice Report 2011' (Australian Human Rights Commission, 2011) 76.

25 Jon Altman and William Arthur, 'Commercial Water and Indigenous Australians: A Scoping Study of Licence Allocations', ('Working Paper' No 57, Centre for Aboriginal Policy Research, Australian National University, 2009).

26 Ibid. 3, 9.

27 Ibid In NSW the water licences were identified as 13,341 megalitres for General Security Licences; 3,030 megalitres for High Security Licences and 7,366 megalitres for Irrigation Licences.

28 Ibid. 8.

29 Ibid.

30 New South Wales Government, Department of Water (NSW) *Our Water Our Country: An Information Manual for Aboriginal People and Communities about the Water Reform Process* (NSW Government, Sydney, 2012) 1:7.

31 Ibid.

32 Paul Barresi, 'Beyond Fairness to Future Generations: An Intragenerational Alternative, Intergenerational Equity in the International Environmental Arena' (1997) 11(1) *Tulane Environmental Law Journal* 60.

33 Quoted in Ibid.

34 Sharon Beder, *Environmental Principles and Policies: An Interdisciplinary Approach* (University of New South Wales Press, 2006) 71.

35 Tony Simpson, pers.comm., 2004. See *Cherokee Nation v State of Georgia* (1831) 30 US 515, 181.

36 Ibid. See *Worcester v State of Georgia* (1831) US 178, 559; *Worcester v State of Georgia* 6 Peter 515 (USSC 1832).

37 Ibid. See *United States v Wheeler* (1978) 435 US 313, 323.

38 Ibid. See *Oliphant v Schlie* (1976) 544 F.2d 1007, 1009.

39 Kent McNeil, 'The Inherent Right of Self-Government: Emerging Directions for Legal Research' ('Research Report', First Nations Governance Centre, November 2004) 22.

40 [1993] 68 ALJR 110.

41 Simon Blackshield, 'Is the United States Doctrine of Indigenous Rights of Self-Regulation Applicable to Australia's Common Law' ('Working Paper', no date) 3.

42 Ibid.

43   Australian Academy of Technological Sciences and Engineering, *Academy Symposium: Perception of Water in Australian Law Re-Examining Rights and Responsibilities* (2004) 1 <http://www.atse.org.au/index.php?sectionid=629>.

44   Ibid. 2.

45   Australian Government, 'Indigenous Business Australia: Annual Report 2004-2005', (Indigenous Business Australia, 2005) 9.

46   Ibid. 40.

47   Victorian Government, 'Building the Economic Base: The Victorian Government's Indigenous Business Development Strategy 2005-2007' (Koori Business Network, Department of Innovation, Industry and Regional, 2007) 5.

48   Ibid.

49   Quoted in John Taylor, 'Tracking Change in the Relative Economic Status of Indigenous People in New South Wales' ('Discussion Paper' No 277, Australian National University, 2005) 18.

50   Aboriginal and Torres Strait Islander Commissioner, 'Native Title Report 2011' (Australian Human Rights Commission, 2011) 126.

51   National Water Commission, 'Australian Water Reform 2009: Second Biennial Assessment of Progress in Implementation of the National Water Initiative' ('Report', Australian Government, 2009) x.

52   Office of Water (NSW), 'Our Water Our Country: An Information Manual for Aboriginal People and Communities about the Water Reform Process' (Department of Primary Industries NSW, 2nd ed, February 2012) 6.3-6.4.

53   Productivity Commission, *Overcoming Indigenous Disadvantage: Key Indicators 2011* (1 January 2012) Steering Committee for the Review of Government Service Provision <http://www.pc.gov.au/__data/assets/pdf_file/0018/111609/key-indicators-2011-report.pdf>.

54   Ibid. 8.1.

55   Ibid. 8.8, 8.9.

56   Ibid.

57   John Taylor, 'Tracking Change in the Relative Economic Status of Indigenous People in New South Wales' ('Discussion Paper' No 277, Australian National University, 2005) 8.19. See Altman 2001; McDermott et al 1998; Rowley et al 2008.

58   Graeme Neate, 'The Tidal Wave of Justice and the Tide of History: Ebbs and Flows in Indigenous Land Rights in Australia' (Paper presented at the 5th World Summit of Noble Peace Laureates, Italy, 10 November 2004) 26.

59   Productivity Commission, Steering Committee for the Review of Government Service Provision 2011, *Overcoming Indigenous Disadvantage: Key Indicators 2011* (1 January 2012) <http://www.pc.gov.au/__data/assets/pdf_file/0018/111609/key-indicators-2011-report.pdf> 8.22.

60   Working Group for Advancing Indigenous Reconciliation in Primary Industries and Natural Resource Management, 'Indigenous Reconciliation in Primary Industries and Natural Resource Management: Annual Report 2006-2007' ('Report', Natural Resource Management and Primary Industries Ministerial Councils, November, 2007) 12.

61   Daniel Connell, *Water Politics in the Murray-Darling Basin* (Federation Press, 2007) 205.

62   Tony Jakeman, Rebecca Letcher and Serena Chen, 'Integrated Assessment of Impacts and Water Allocation Changes across Social, Economic and Environmental Dimensions' in Karen Hussey and Stephen Dovers (eds), *Managing Water for Australia: The Social and Institutional Challenges* (Commonwealth Scientific and Industrial Research Organisation, 2007) 97-98.

63   Ibid.

64   Poh-Ling Tan, 'Water Law Reform in NSW — 1995 to 1999' (2003) 20 *Environmental Planning Law Journal* 175.

65   Sharon Beder, *Environmental Principles and Policies: An Interdisciplinary Approach* (University of New South Wales Press, 2006) 19.

66   National Water Commission, 'Intergovernmental Agreement on a National Water Initiative between the Commonwealth of Australia and the Governments of New South Wales, Victoria, Queensland, South Australia, the Australian Capital Territory and the Northern Territory' (2004) National Water Commission <http://nwc.gov.au/__data/assets/pdf_file/0008/24749/Intergovernmental-Agreement-on-a-national-water-initiative.pdf>.

67   Australian Academy of Technological Sciences and Engineering, *Academy Symposium: Perception of Water in Australian Law Re-examining Rights and Responsibilities* (24 September 2004) <http://www.atse.org.au/index.php?sectionid=629>.

68   Virginia Simpson, 'Aboriginal Access to Water Across Australia' ('Draft Report', South Australian Government, Department of Water, Land and Biodiversity Conservation, 2007) 23-24.

69   Ibid.

70   Ibid. 27.

71   Race Discrimination Commissioner, 'Review of the 1994 Water Report' ('Research Report', Human Rights and Equal Opportunity Commission, 2001) 2 Human Rights and Equal Opportunity Commission <http://www.hreoc.gov.au/racial_discrimination/water_report/index.html>.

72   Productivity Commission, Steering Committee for the Review of Government Service Provision 2011, *Overcoming Indigenous Disadvantage: Key Indicators 2011* (1 January 2012) <http://www.pc.gov.au/__data/assets/pdf_file/0018/111609/key-indicators-2011-report.pdf>.

73   Aboriginal and Torres Strait Islander Social Justice Commissioner, 'Building a Sustainable National Indigenous Representative Body: Issues for Consideration' ('Issues Paper', Australian Human Rights Commission, 2008) 8.

74   Sandy Toussaint, 'Western Australia' Ann McGrath (ed), in *Contested Ground: Australian Aborigines under the British Crown* (Allen and Unwin, 1995) 240.

75   Jane Bardon, 'Traditional Owners burn Arnhem Land Fracking Plan' *ABC* (Sydney), 18 March 2013. See <http://www.abc.net.au/news/2013-03-18/maningrida-traditional-owners-burn-fracking-plan/4579438>.

76   National Water Commission, 'The National Water Initiative, Securing Australia's Water Future: 2011 Assessment' ('Report', Australian Government, 2011) 41.

77   Paul Kauffman, *Wik, Mining and Aborigines* (Allen and Unwin, 1998) 3.

78   See <http://www.smh.com.au/business/consumer-affairs/bottled-water-producer-admits-consumers-paying-for-plastic-not-pure-safe-water-20160715-gq6oif.html>. See also <http://www.businessinsider.com.au/facts-bottled-water-industry-2011-10?r=US&IR=T#the-first-documented-case-of-selling-bottled-water-was-in-boston-in-the-1760s-1>.

79   NAILSMA, *A Policy Statement on North Australian Indigenous Water Rights* (2009) Northern Australian Indigenous Land and Sea Management Alliance <http://nailsma.org.au/sites/default/files/Water-Policy-Statement-web-view.pdf>.

80   'Bundanoon in World-First Ban on Bottled Water', *The Australian* (26 September 2009) <http://www.theaustralian.com.au/news/nation/bundanoon-in-world-first-ban-on-bottled-water/story-e6frg6nf-1225779878437>.

81   Ibid.

82   Virginia Falk, 'Much ado about Bundy on Tap' on Denis Wilson *Peonyden* (29 July 2009) <*peonyden.blogspot.com/2009_07_01_archive.htm*>.

83   Julian Lee, 'Message on a Bottle Labelled as Greenwash', *The Sydney Morning Herald* (Sydney), 23-24 February 2008, 11.

84   Paul Hawken, Amory B Lovins and L Hunter Lovins, *Natural Capitalism: The Next Industrial Revolution* (Earthscan, 1999) 48.

85   Ibid.

86   James Raymond, *The New South Wales Calendar and General Post Office Directory 1832* (The Trustees of the Public Library of New South Wales, first published 1832, 1966 ed) 155-156.

87   Ibid. 156.

88   Waste Streams, *Trading in the Future of Water* (27 September 2006) <http://wastestreams.com. au/ws/white_papers/paper_032006b.asp>.

89   Ibid.

90   Beckwith Environmental Planning, 'Draft Water Resources Management Bill: Recommended Legislative Framework' (Water Reform Implementation Committee, Department of Water, Western Australia, May 2007) 52.

91   Elizabeth Murray, 'Pilbara Anger over Drowned Spring', *Koori Mail* (NSW), 6 June 2007, 17.

92   Bardy McFarlane, 'The National Water Initiative and Acknowledging Indigenous Interests in Planning' (Paper presented at the National Water Conference, Sydney, 29 November 2004) 14 <http://www.nntt.gov.au/news-and-communications/speeches-and-papers/documents/2004/ speeches%20national%20water%20initiative%20mcfarlane%20november%202004.pdf>.

93   Ibid.

94   Leigh Dayton, 'Research Raises a Toxic Dust', *The Australian* (Sydney), 21-22 November 2009, 12.

95   Ibid.

96   Ibid.

97   Aboriginal and Torres Strait Islander Social Justice Commissioner, 'Social Justice Report 2008' (Human Rights Commission, 2009) 24.

98   Email from David Collard to Virginia Falk, 17 February 2009.

99   Ibid.

100   Department of Water, Government of Western Australia and Miriuwung-Gajerrong Aboriginal Corporation, 'Interim Management Plan for Reserve 31165' (August 2006) 14.

101   Ibid.

102   Ibid.

103   Ibid.

104   Ibid.

105   Edward McDonald, Bryn Coldrick and Linda Villiers, 'Study of Groundwater-Related Aboriginal Cultural Values on the Gnangara Mound, Western Australia' ('Research Report', Department of Environment Western Australia, October 2005) 79.

106   Ibid. 59.

107   Ibid.

108   Ibid. 58.

109   Ibid. 70.

110   Ibid.

111   Ibid. 74.

112   Ibid.

113 I undertook regularly internet searches on 'Google' to ascertain any water conference in Australia which represents Aboriginal water use and the representation of Aboriginal people and such references to date are uncommon. Key words used on 'Google' were water conference+ Aboriginal; water conference + Aboriginal 2008; water conference + Aboriginal Australia. For example: the 2008 Water Summit in Sydney did not include Aboriginal presenters, Aboriginal communities, Aboriginal organisations or Aboriginal experts.

Chapter 10 Aboriginal water values in Australian policy and law

1   William Charles Wentworth, *Statistical, Historical, and Political Description of The Colony of New South Wales and its Dependent Settlements in Van Diemen's Land: A Particular Enumeration of the Advantages which these Colonies Offer for Emigration, and their Superiority in many Respects over those Possessed by the United States of America*, (Griffen Press, first published 1819, 1978 ed) 78.

2   Paul Kildea and George Williams, 'The Constitution and the Management of Water in Australia's rivers' (2010) 32(4) *Sydney Law Review* 596-597.

3   Ibid. 597.

4   Ibid.

5   Commonwealth of Australia, *Australia's Constitution* (Government Printers, 2nd ed, 1998) 39.

6   John Marsden, 'Water Entitlements and Property Rights: An Economic Perspective' (2002) in *Property: Rights and Responsibilities, Current Australian Thinking* (Land and Water Australia, 2002) 43.

7   National Water Commission, 'Intergovernmental Agreement on a National Water Initiative between the Commonwealth of Australia and the Governments of New South Wales, Victoria, Queensland, South Australia, the Australian Capital Territory and the Northern Territory' (2004) National Water Commission <http://nwc.gov.au/__data/assets/pdf_file/0008/24749/Intergovernmental-Agreement-on-a-national-water-initiative.pdf>.

8   Poh-Ling Tan, 'Legal Issues Relating to Water Use' (2002) *Property: Rights and Responsibilities, Current Australian Thinking* (Land and Water Australia, 2002) 35.

9   Ibid.

10   Ibid.

11   Joshua Getzler, *A History of Water Rights at Common Law* (Oxford University Press, revised ed, 2006) 43.

12   Poh-Ling Tan, 'Legal Issues Relating to Water Use' (2002) *Property: Rights and Responsibilities, Current Australian Thinking* (Land and Water Australia, 2002) 35.

13   Sue Jackson, Michael Storrs and Joe Morrison, 'Recognition of Aboriginal Rights, Interests and Values in River Research and Management: Perspectives from Northern Australia' (2005) 6(2) *Ecological Management and Restoration* 106.

14   Jason Behrendt and Peter Thompson, 'The Recognition and Protection of Aboriginal Interests in NSW Rivers' (2004) 3 *Journal of Indigenous Policy* 37.

15   Ibid

16   Ibid. 124-125.

17   Murray Radcliffe, 'The National Water Commission Introduction and Engagement' (Speech delivered at the Australian Indigenous Water Focus Group, National Water Commission, Adelaide, South Australia, 18 November 2008). The author was invited to participate as an Indigenous delegate for the Indigenous Water Focus Group in Adelaide.

18   Ibid.

19   David Collard, personal communication with Virginia Falk [Marshall], February 2009.

20   Ibid

21   The nominal consideration of a $1 is referred to in contract law as a 'peppercorn rent' or 'price of a peppercorn'.

22   Email from Dave Miller to Virginia Falk, December 2006.

23   Email from Dave Miller to Virginia Falk, 25 May 2006, 3.

24   Ibid. 4.

25   Dave Miller, personal communication with Virginia Falk, December 2006. Virginia Falk, as the then Executive Officer of the NSW Aboriginal Water Trust, delivered a paper at the Aboriginal Consultation Water Sharing Workshop for Department of Environment and Climate Change (NSW) at Murra Mittagar Penrith, 26 May 2006.

26   Department of Natural Resources (NSW) 'Workshop to Discuss Developing Culturally Appropriate Aboriginal Consultation for Macro Water Sharing Plans', held by the Department of Natural Resources (NSW) (26 May 2006). See also email from Dave Miller to Virginia Falk, December 2006.

27   Ibid.

28   Ibid.

29   Office of Water (NSW), 'Our Water Our Country: An Information Manual for Aboriginal People and Communities about the Water Reform Process' (Department of Primary Industries (NSW), 2nd ed, February 2012) 6.4.

30   Email from Dave Miller to Virginia Falk, 25 May 2006.

31   Ibid.

32   Ibid.

33   Ibid.

34   Ibid.

35   Ibid.

36   *Donna Craig*, pers. comm.,'Indigenous Property Rights to Water: Environmental Flows, Cultural Values and Tradeable Property Rights' (2005) *Macquarie University* ('Unpublished essay') 14, quoting Jason Behrendt and Peter Thompson, 'The Recognition and Protection of Aboriginal Interests in NSW Rivers ('Occasional Paper', No 1008, Healthy Rivers Commission NSW, November 2003) 59-60.

37   Department of Aboriginal Affairs (NSW) 'Two Ways Together, Partnerships: A New Way of Doing Business with Aboriginal People, NSW Aboriginal Affairs Plan 2003-2012' (2003) 4.

38   Email from the Department of Natural Resources (NSW) to Virginia Falk, April 2006.

39   Ibid.

40   Email from Meera Rajagopalan to Virginia Falk, 10 March 2006, 2.

41   Ibid.

42   Ibid.

43   Daniel Connell, *Water Politics in the Murray-Darling Basin* (Federation Press, 2007) 44.

44   Ibid. 44-45.

45   Productivity Commission, *Overcoming Indigenous Disadvantage: Key Indicators 2011* (1 January 2012) Productivity Commission <http//www.pc.gov.au/__data/assets/pdf_file/0018/111609/key-indicators-2011-report.pdf>.

46   Ibid.

47   Virginia Simpson, 'Aboriginal Access to Water across Australia' Draft Report, South Australian Government, Adelaide, Department of Water, Land and Biodiversity Conservation, 2007.

48   Email from David Collard to Virginia Falk on Virginia Simpson, 13 November 2007.

49   Ibid.

50   Poh-Ling Tan, 'Conflict over Water Resources in Queensland: All Eyes on the Lower Balonne' (2000) 17(6) *Environmental and Planning Law Journal* 549-550.

51   Ibid. 546.

52   Email from David Collard to Virginia Falk on Virginia Simpson, 13 November 2007.

53   Ibid.

54   Ibid.

55   Department of Sustainability and Environment Victoria, *Securing Our Water Future Together* (7 June 2007) Victorian Government <www.dse.vic.gov.au>.

56   *Water Act 1989* (Vic).

57   Aboriginal and Torres Strait Islander Commissioner, 'Draft Native Title Report 2008' (Human Rights and Equal Opportunity Commission, 2007) 26.

58   Aboriginal and Torres Strait Islander Social Justice Commissioner, 'Native Title Report 2007' (Human Rights and Equal Opportunity Commission, 2008) 225. See also Stephanie Juleff 'Budj Bim Heritage Site to get $8 million upgrade to help UNESCO bid' *ABC News* (Sydney) 24 April 2016   <http://www.abc.net.au/news/2016-04-24/government-to-spend-8m-to-improve-budj-bim-heritage-site/7353772>.

59   Ibid.

60   Jon Altman assisted by V Branchut, 'Fresh Water in the Maningrida Region's Hybrid Economy: Intercultural Contestation over Values and Property Rights' ('Working Paper' No 46, Australian National University, 2008) 30.

61   Ibid. 31.

62   Ibid. 12.

63   Ibid. 13

64   Ibid See *Wurridjal v Commonwealth* (2009) 237 CLR 309, which is a determination on the compulsory acquisition of Aboriginal owned lands in Maningrida by the Commonwealth to implement policies under the Northern Territory Emergency Response legislation.

65   Email from Peter Sutherland to Virginia Falk, 8 December 2005.

66   Ibid.

67   Ibid.

68   Debra Jopson, 'Aborigines Demand $250 million over Water Rights System', *The Sydney Morning Herald* (Sydney), 3 June 2002, 1.

69   Ibid.

70   Ibid.

71   Ibid.Email from Kim Wagstaff to Virginia Falk, 4 September 2006. The email was in relation to advice provided by me on a key performance indicator for the Department of Natural Resources (NSW) as to the 'volume of water purchased through the Aboriginal Water Trust'.

72   Jon Altman and William Arthur, 'Commercial Water and Indigenous Australians: A Scoping Study of Licence Allocations' ('Working Paper' No 57, Centre for Aboriginal Policy Research, Australian National University, 2009) 7.

73   Virginia Falk, Executive Officer of the NSW Aboriginal Water Trust.

74   Ibid. 5.

75   Ibid.

76   See also Department of Land and Water Conservation (NSW), 'Guidelines for Assessing the Impacts of Water Sharing Plans for Aboriginal Peoples' (Economic and Social Policy Branch, Department of Land and Water Conservation, August 2001) 13. The guidelines state that 'literature reviews can be used to generate and review information that exists about Aboriginal peoples, in respect to water use and values in local and regional contexts'.

77   Email from John Gillespie to Virginia Falk, 17 July 2007, 1.

78   Gavin Andrews, personal communication with Virginia Falk, 29 March 2009. Discussion at Tharawal Aboriginal Land Council for a Land Council community meeting.

79   Cliff Daylight, personal communication with Virginia Falk, 2008. Cliff Daylight held the Acting Executive Officer of the Aboriginal Water Trust (NSW) after my resignation.

80   I held the position of Executive Officer of the NSW Aboriginal Water Trust.

81   Ibid.

82   Virginia Falk, personal communication with Department of Natural Resources (NSW), 2007.

83   Ibid.

84   Department of Natural Resources (NSW), Draft 'Water Management Division Business Plan 2006-2007' (21 August 2006) 11.

85   Virginia Falk, 'Workshop to Discuss Developing Culturally Appropriate Aboriginal Consultation for Macro Water Sharing Plans', held by the Department of Natural Resources (NSW) (26 May 2006). I was invited to present on my involvement of the Aboriginal Water Trust and Indigenous Community Engagement NSW.

86   Ibid.

87   *Water Management Act 2000* (NSW) pt 1 div 1.

88   *Water Management Act 2000* (NSW) s 3.

89   Ibid.

90   Ibid.

91   Ibid. 86.

92   Jason Behrendt and Peter Thompson, 'The Recognition and Protection of Aboriginal Interests in NSW Rivers' ('Occasional Paper', No 1008, Healthy Rivers Commission of NSW, November 2003) 5. See also Behrendt and Thompson, 'The Recognition and Protection of Aboriginal Interests in NSW Rivers' (2004) 3 *Journal of Indigenous Policy* 37.

93   Ibid.

94   Virginia Falk, personal communication with the Department of Water (WA), November 2007.

95   Email from David Collard to Virginia Falk, State Solicitor's Office (WA), 'Water Resources Management Bill and Water Entitlements and their Administration', 18 April 2008, 16.

96   Ibid. 9.

97   Ibid. 16.

98   Ibid.

99   Email from David Collard to Virginia Falk on Vic Fazakerley, David Collard and Paul Rosair, 26 August 2008.

100 Email from David Collard to Virginia Falk, State Solicitor's Office (WA), 'Water Resources Management Bill and Water Entitlement and their Administration', 18 April 2008, 1.

101 Ibid.

102 NAILSMA, 'Indigenous Water Policy Group to take an Indigenous Position on Water to the 2020 Summit' (Media Release, 18 April 2008) 1.

103 Email from David Collard to Virginia Falk, State Solicitor's Office (WA), 'Water Resources Management Bill and Water Entitlements', 18 April 2008, 16.

104 Email from David Collard to Virginia Falk, State Solicitor's Office (WA), 'National Water Initiative: Indigenous Access and Entitlement Rights' 12 December 2007, 9.

105 Ibid.

106 Email from David Collard to Virginia Falk, State Solicitor's Office (WA), 'Water Resources Management Bill and Water Entitlements', 18 April 2008, 16.

107 Ibid. 9-16.

108 Ibid. 8.

109 *Western Australia v Ward* [2002] 213 CLR 1, 263 (Gleeson CJ, Gaudron, Gummow and Hayne JJ)

110 Email from David Collard to Virginia Falk, State Solicitor's Office (WA), 'National Water Initiative: Indigenous Access and Entitlement Rights', 12 December 2007, 8.

111 Email from David Collard to Virginia Falk, 7 January 2009.

112 Email from David Collard to Virginia Falk, State Solicitor's Office (WA), 'Water Resources Management Bill and Water Entitlements', 18 April 2008, 38.

113 Ibid. 29.

114 Ibid. 9.

115 David Collard, personal communication with Virginia Falk, December 2008.

116 Ibid.

117 Memorandum from David Collard to Virginia Falk, 5 June 2008. The communication was in relation to a briefing by Virginia Falk (Marshall) to Department of Water (WA) on Indigenous interests in the water reform process with respect to the Water Resources Management Bill.

118 Email from David Collard to Virginia Falk, 17 February 2009. The email was in relation to a briefing by me to the Department of Water (WA) on Indigenous interests in the water reform process with respect to the Water Resources Management Bill.

119 Ibid The expression *'in situ'* was confirmed by David Collard with the Department of Water (WA). The email was in relation to a briefing by me to Department of Water (WA) on Indigenous interests in the water reform process with respect to the Water Resources Management Bill.

120 David Collard, 'Panel Discussion' (Speech delivered at the Australian Indigenous Water Focus Group, National Water Commission, Adelaide South Australia, 18 November 2008).

121 David Collard, personal communication with Virginia Falk, 17 February 2009.

122 Ibid.

123 Ibid.

124 Email from David Collard to Virginia Falk, State Solicitor's Office (WA), 'Department of Water, Western Australia, Water Resources Management Bill and Water Entitlements', 18 April 2008, 32.

125 Ibid.

126 Email from David Collard to Virginia Falk on Virginia Simpson, 13 November 2007.

127 Ibid.

128 Virginia Simpson, 'Aboriginal Access to Water in Australia' ('Draft Report', 2007).

129 Virginia Falk, 'Indigenous Access to Water in Australia' ('Report', Department of Water, Western Australia, 2008).

130 Email David Collard to Virginia Falk on Virginia Simpson, 13 November 2007.

131 Ibid.

132 Sue Jackson, 'Compartmentalising Culture: The Articulation and Consideration of Indigenous Values in Water Resource Management (2006) 37(1) *Australian Geographer* 21.

133 Memorandum from the Department of Water (WA) from David Collard to Virginia Falk, 7 January 2009.

134 Ibid.
135 Email from David Collard to Virginia Falk, 17 December 2008. See also Virginia Falk, 'Draft Indigenous Access to Water Entitlements in Western Australia' (Department of Water, Government of Western Australia, 2008).
136 Beckwith Environmental Planning, 'Draft Water Resources Management Bill: Recommended Legislative Framework' (Water Reform Implementation Committee, Department of Water, Western Australia, May 2007).
137 Virginia Falk, 'Draft Indigenous Access to Water Entitlements in Western Australia' (Department of Water, Government of Western Australia, 2008) at Recommendation 4.
138 Ibid. Recommendation 5.
139 Ibid. Recommendation 13.
140 Ibid. Recommendation 59.
141 Email from David Collard to Virginia Falk, 17 December 2008 See also the Author, 'Draft Indigenous Access to Water Entitlements in Western Australia' (Department of Water, Government of Western Australia, 2008).
142 Department of Water, 'Western Australia's Implementation Plan for the National Water Initiative' ('Report', Government of Western Australia, April 2007) 5.
143 Ibid. 6.
144 Ibid. 33-34.
145 Ibid. 33.
146 Email from David Collard to Virginia Falk, State Solicitor's Office Western Australia, 'Water Resources Management Bill, Water Entitlements and their Administration', 18 April 2008, 27.
147 Ibid.
148 Department of Water, 'Western Australia's Implementation Plan for the National Water Initiative' ('Report', Government of Western Australia, April 2007) 1.
149 Ibid. 33.
150 Virginia Falk, 'Draft Indigenous Access to Water Entitlements in Western Australia' ('Report', Department of Water, Government of Western Australia, 2008).
151 Department of Water, 'Western Australia's Implementation Plan for the National Water Initiative' ('Report', Government of Western Australia, April 2007) 144. See also Water Reform Implementation Committee, 'A Blueprint for Water Reform in Western Australia: Final Advice to the Western Australian Government' ('Report', Government of Western Australia, December 2006).
152 Department of Water, Government of Western Australia, 'Report for the Minister for Water Resources on Water Services in Discrete Indigenous Communities' (2006) 31.
153 Ibid. 17.
154 Working Group for Advancing Indigenous Reconciliation in Primary Industries and Natural Resource Management, 'Indigenous Reconciliation in Primary Industries and Natural Resource Management: Annual Report 2006-2007' ('Report', Natural Resource Management and Primary Industries Ministerial Councils, November, 2007) 3.
155 Ibid. 14.
156 Ibid. 39.
157 The Western Australian Government and six Noongar clans have negotiated the South West Native Title Settlement in 2015, which includes formal legal recognition by the Western Australian Parliament with the Noongar Recognition Bill. On the 6 June 2016 the Noongar (Koorah, Nitja, Boordahwan) Recognition Act was proclaimed. See <https://www.dpc.wa.gov.au/lantu/south-west-native-title-settlement/Noongar-Recognition-Act-2016/Pages/default.

aspx>. The Settlement provides a range of benefits to resolve the native title claim by Yued, Gnaala Karla Boodja, South West Boojarah, Wagyl Kaip, Ballardong and Whadjuk. See also information on the Settlement <https://www.dpc.wa.gov.au/lantu/south-west-native-title-settlement/Pages/Settlement-Publications.aspx>.

158 Email from David Collard to Virginia Falk on Glen Kelly, 28 February 2008.

159 Ibid.

160 Edward McDonald, Bryn Coldrick and Linda Villiers, 'Study of Groundwater-Related Aboriginal Cultural Values on the Gnangara Mound, Western Australia' ('Research Report', Department of Environment Western Australia, October 2005) 22.

161 Daisy Bates, *The Passing of the Aborigines: A Lifetime Spent among the Natives of Australia* (John Murray, first published 1938, 1972) 30.

162 Brad Goode, Colin Irvine and Melinda Cockman, 'Report on Conferences held with the Nyungar Community for the South West Water Plan' ('Research Report', Department of Water, Western Australia, June 2007) 3-4.

163 Ibid. 4.

164 Ibid.

165 Department of Water Western Australia, 'Report for the Minister for Water Resources on Water Services in Discrete Indigenous Communities' (December 2006).

166 Ibid. 22.

167 Ibid. 6. Page 51 identifies the policy advisor employed 'at the executive level of government'.

168 Ibid. 17.

169 Ibid. 50.

170 Ibid. 52. Page 78 states that governments are to abide by Art. 25 of the *United Nations Universal Declaration of Human Rights 1948* expresses, 'everyone has the right to a standard of living adequate for the health and well-being of himself and of his family including food, clothing, housing and medical care and necessary social services'. See UN General Assembly, *Universal Declaration of Human Rights* (10 December 1948).

171 Jessica Irvine, 'Mineral Boom Frittered Away', *The Sydney Morning Herald* (Sydney), 8-9 March 2008, 13.

172 David Collard, personal communication with Virginia Falk on 18 November 2008.

173 Margaret Throsby, Interview with Geoffrey Robertson (Radio Interview 95.70 FM, 1 April 2009).

Chapter 11 Human Rights — incorporating Aboriginal water rights

1 Joel Gibson, 'Damming the River of Shame', *The Sydney Morning Herald* (Sydney), 3-4 January 2009 14.

2 Michael O'Donnell, *NAILSMA TRaCK Project 6.2: Indigenous Rights in Water in Northern Australia* (11 August 2011) NAILSMA Tropical Rivers and Coastal Knowledge and Australian Government <http://www.nailsma.org.au/nailsma/projects/downloads/TRaCK-6-2-Indigenous-Rights-in-Water-in-Northern-Australia-Final-Report-2.pdf>.

3 Ibid

4 Matthew Rigney, 'Broad Principles on Indigenous Engagement on Water Issues' (Speech delivered at the Australian Indigenous Water Focus Group, National Water Commission, National Water Commission, Adelaide South Australia, 18 November 2008).

5 Matthew Craven, *The International Covenant on Economic, Social, and Cultural Rights: A Perspective on its Development* (Clarendon Press, 1995) 6-7.

6 Ibid. 352.

7   Thomas Buergenthal, 'International Human Rights in an Historical Perspective' in Janusz Symonides (ed), *Human Rights: Concepts and Standards* (UNESCO, 2000) 3-5, 31.

8   Jerome Shestack, in Thomas Buergenthal, 'International Human Rights in an Historical Perspective' in Janusz Symonides (ed), *Human Rights: Concepts and Standards*, (UNESCO, 2000) 31-6. Shestack examines John Rawls's two principles of justice: the first principle on the position of 'rights and liberties', and the second principle on the conception of 'distributive justice'.

9   Erica Irene A Daes, 'Protection of the World's Indigenous Peoples and Human Rights' in Janusz Symonides (ed), *Human Rights: Concept and Standards*, (UNESCO, 2000) 301-308.

10   Matthew Craven, *The International Covenant on Economic, Social, and Cultural Rights: A Perspective on its Development* (Clarendon Press, 1995) 25.

11   Douglas J R Moodie, Aboriginal Maritime Title in Nova Scotia: An Extravagant and Absurd Idea? (2003) 37(1) *University of British Columbia Law Review* 495, 497.

12   Angie Shuter, 'Scoping Paper for Te Puni Kokori: A Review of the Experiences Other States in the Development of *sui generis* Mechanisms for Protecting Traditional Knowledge' ('Scoping Paper', Te Puni Kokori, February 2002) 15.

13   Murray Radcliffe, 'International Perspective' (Speech delivered at the Australian Indigenous Water Focus Group, National Water Commission, Adelaide, South Australia, 18 November 2008).

14   United Nations, *United Nations Declaration on the Rights of Indigenous Peoples* (1 July 2011) United Nations <www.un.org/esa/socdev/unpfii/documents/DRIPS_en.pdf>.

15   Ibid.

16   Ibid.

17   Ibid.

18   *United Nations Declaration on the Rights of Indigenous Peoples* (1 July 2011) United Nations <www.un.org/esa/socdev/unpfii/documents/DRIPS_en.pdf>. Article 25 of the *United Nations Declaration on the Rights of Indigenous Peoples.*

19   James Anaya, Special Rapporteur, 'The situation of indigenous peoples in Australia' *Report by the Special Rapporteur on the situation of human rights and fundamental freedoms of indigenous people,* Agenda Item 3, 15th sess, UN Doc A/HRC/15/37Add.4 (1 March 2012) 29 <http://dacess-dds-ny.un.org/UNDOC/GEN/G10/138/87/PDF/G1013887.pdf?OpenElement>.

20   Victoria Tauli Corpuz, Special Rapporteur, *Report of the Special Rapporteur on the rights of indigenous peoples,* 13th sess, Agenda Item 3, UN Doc A/HRC/30/41 (6 August 2015) <https://documents-dds-ny.un.org/doc/UNDOC/GEN/G15/173/83/PDF/G1517383.pdf?OpenElement>.

21   NAILSMA, *A Policy Statement on North Australian Indigenous Water Rights* (November 2009) Northern Australian Indigenous Land and Sea Management Alliance 1 <http://nailsma.org.au/sites/default/files/Water-Policy-Statement-web-view.pdf>.

22   *United Nations Declaration on the Rights of Indigenous Peoples* (1 July 2011) United Nations <www.un.org/esa/socdev/unpfii/documents/DRIPS_en.pdf>. See Article 25 of the *Declaration.*

23   Ibid.

24   Letter from Tim Fisher to Andrew Chalk, 8 March 1996.

25   Tom Calma, 'UN Declaration on the Rights of Indigenous Peoples: Australia Should Sign', *Koori Mail* (Lismore), 24 September 2008, 27.

26   Tamar Keirnan, 'Water Justice: Water as a Human Right in Israel' Gidon Bromberg (ed), ('Working Paper', No 15, Henrich Boll Stiftung, Friends of the Earth, Middle East March 2005), 1.

27   Erica Irene A Daes, *Preliminary Report on Prevention of Discrimination and Protection of Indigenous People: Indigenous Peoples' Permanent Sovereignty over Natural Resources*, E/CN.4/Sub.2/2003/20, 'UNESCOR', 55th sess. 'Agenda Item 5(b)', 21 July 2003, 5.

28   Ibid.

29   Stephen Garnett and Bev Sithole, 'Sustainable Northern Landscapes and the Nexus with Indigenous Health: Healthy Country Healthy People' ('Research Report', NTU07, Land and Water Australia, 2007) 35.

30   'Indigenous Peoples Kyoto Water Declaration' Third World Water Forum, Kyoto Japan, March 2003, 2.

31   Ibid. 1-2.

32   See also Henry J Steiner and Philip Alston, *International Human Rights in Context: Law, Politics, Morals* (Oxford University Press, 2nd ed, 2000) 77. The authors discuss the rule of *jus cogens*, an early principle of international law, where a treaty could not override natural law. The modern revival of *jus cogens* means that states are not allowed to contract out of the 'peremptory norms of general international law'.

33   Anon, 'International Law as an Interpretive Force in Federal Indian Law' (2003) 116(6) *Harvard Law Review* 1751-1773.

34   (2002) 191 ALR 1.

35   Cited in Matthew Rimmer, 'Blame it on Rio: Biodiscovery, Native Title, and Traditional Knowledge' (2003) 7 *Southern Cross University Law Review* 28.

36   Ibid.

37   National Human Rights Network, 'Australian Non-governmental Organisations Submission to the Committee on the Elimination of Racial Discrimination' (National Association of Community Legal Centres, January 2005) 14.

38   George Williams, 'Racist Premise of our Constitution Remains', *The Sydney Morning Herald* (Sydney), 7 April 2009, 11.

39   Ibid.

40   Kent McNeil, 'The Vulnerability of Indigenous Land Rights in Australia and Canada' (2004) 42(2) *Osgoode Hall Law Journal* 289.

41   Ibid. 294.

42   See the recognition of Indigenous peoples in *Constitution Act 1975* (Vic) s 1A; *Constitution (Preamble) Amendment Act 2010* (Qld) s 4; *Constitution Act 1902* (NSW) s 2; *Constitution Act 1934* (SA) s 2; *Constitution Act 1889* (WA) preamble. The Tasmanian Government has called for submissions to amend the *Constitution Act 1934* (Tas) and insert recognition in the preamble of the *Act*.

43   Expert Panel report on Recognising Aboriginal and Torres Strait Islander Peoples in the Constitution   (2012)   <http://www.recognise.org.au/wp-content/uploads/shared/uploads/assets/3446_FaHCSIA_ICR_report_text_Bookmarked_PDF_12_Jan_v4.pdf>.

44   Justice Graham Hill, *Which Way to Damascus? A Bill of Rights or Chapter III of the Constitution* (30 June 2004) Federal Court Intranet <http://intranet.fedcourt.gov.au/upload_judges/judges/Damascus.htm>.

45   A V Dicey, *Introduction to the Study of the Law of the Constitution* (Macmillan, London, first published 1885, 1908) 122-127.

46   Ibid.

47   Quoted in Justice Ronald Sackville, *The 2003 Term: The Inaccessible Constitution* (30 June 2004) Federal Court Intranet <http://intranet.fedcourt.gov.au/search97cgsi/s97_cgi?Action=View&VdkVgwKey=%2>.

48   New South Wales, *Charter of Rights Update*, Parl Paper No1/09 Gareth Griffith QC (January 2009) 1.

49   Ibid.

50   Ibid.

51   Andrew Lynch, 'Judge Right on Rights', *The Australian* (Sydney), 20 March 2009, 28.

52   National Human Rights Consultation Committee, 'National Human Rights Consultation Report' <http://www.ag.gov.au/RightsAndProtections/Human Rights/TreatyBodyReporting/Documents/NHRCReport.pdf>.

53   Ibid.

54   See ALRC, *Family Violence and Commonwealth Laws: Improving Legal Frameworks*, Report No 117 (November 2011). In Chapter 10 of this report I provide a detailed analysis of these impacts upon Indigenous peoples.

55   Aaron T Wolf, *Transboundary Waters: Sharing Benefits, Lessons Learned* (27 March 2007) International Conference on Freshwater, Bonn 1 <http://www.water-2001.de/co_doc/transboundary_waters.pdf>.

56   Aboriginal and Torres Strait Islander Commissioner, 'Native Title Report 2008' (Human Rights Commission, 2009) 69.

57   *Risk v Northern Territory* [2006] FCA 404.

58   Justice Murray Wilcox, *Should Australia have a Bill of Rights?* (30 June 2004) Federal Court Intranet<http://intranet.fedcourt.gov.au/search97cgi/s97_cgi?Action=View&VdkVgwKey=%2>.

59   Ibid

60   Julian Burnside, *Watching Brief: Reflections on Human Rights, Law and Justice* (Scribe, 2007) 173.

61   Ibid.

62   Ibid. 94.

63   Ibid.

64   Jason De Santolo, 'Responses to the 'Sealord Deal': Fishing for Insights' (2004) 4 *Journal of Indigenous Policy* 64.

65   Richard Bartlett, 'Canada: Indigenous Land Claims and Settlements' in Brian Keon-Cohen (ed), *Native Title in the New Millennium* (Aboriginal Studies Press, 2001) 362.

66   Catherine Branson, 'Take Judges out of Human Rights Process', *The Australian* (Sydney), 8 May 2009, 27.

67   National Human Rights Network, 'Australian Non-governmental Organisations Submission to the Committee on the Elimination of Racial Discrimination' (National Association of Community Legal Centres, January 2005) 13.

68   Australian Capital Territory Government, 'Towards an ACT *Human Rights Act*: Report of the ACT Bill of Rights Consultative Committee' (May 2003) 105.

69   *Human Rights Act 2004* (ACT) s 27.

70   New South Wales, *Charter of Rights* Update, Parliamentary Paper No1/09 Gareth Griffith QC (January 2009) 2.

71　Law Institute of Victoria, *Charter Impact Project Report: Colmar Brunton Findings* (1 January 2012) Law Institute of Victoria <http://www.liv.asn.au/News-and-Publications/Victoria-Human-Rights-Charter>.

72　Ibid.

73　Aboriginal and Torres Strait Islander Social Justice Commissioner, 'Native Title Report 2008' (Human Rights Commission, 2009) 69.

74　George Williams, 'A Court Short on Answers', *The Australian* (Sydney), 26-27 January 2008, 29.

75　See *The Australian* <http://www.9news.com.au/national/2016/06/15/19/59/barnaby-joyce-disagrees-with-malcolm-turnbull-over-australian-invasion>.

76　NAILSMA, *Garma International Indigenous Water Declaration* (24 May 2012) NAILSMA <http://nailsma.org.au/nailsma/forum/download/Garma-International-Indigenous-Water-Declaration.pdf>. The author contributed to the drafting of this Declaration.

77　Ibid.

78　Neva Collings and Virginia Falk, 'Water: Aboriginal Peoples in Australia and their Spiritual Relationship with Waterscapes' in Elliott Johnston, Martin Hinton and Daryle Rigney (eds), *Indigenous Australians and the Law* (Routledge-Cavendish, 2nd ed, 2008) 141.

79　Email from Lorrae McArthur to Virginia Falk [Marshall], 12 November 2008.

80　Ibid.

81　Email from Lorrae McArthur to Virginia Falk, 7 April 2009.

82　Ibid.

83　Benjamin Richardson, 'The Ties that Bind: Indigenous Peoples and Environmental Governance' in Benjamin Richardson, Shin Imai and Kent McNeil (eds), *Indigenous Peoples and the Law: Comparative and Critical Perspectives* (Hart, 2009) 337, 367.

84　Westpac Bank, 'The Equator Principles' (November 2006) <everygeneration.com.au>.

85　Ibid.

86　The Greens Tasmania, *The Tasmanian Pulp Mill News* (18 September 2006) 1-4.

87　Westpac Bank, 'The Equator Principles' (November 2006) <everygeneration.com.au>.

88　'Gunns Deal Off, Boss Blames Green Groups' (13 March 2012) *ABC News* (Tasmania) <http://www.abc.net.au/news/2012-03-09/gunns-investor-pulls-out/3879344>.

89　Ibid.

90　Santa Clara University, *Common Grounds, Common Waters: Toward a Water Ethic* (19 February 2008) Santa Clara Journal of International Law Symposium <http://scjil.wordpress.com/program-description>.

Conclusion — Securing Aboriginal water rights

1　Aboriginal and Torres Strait Islander Social Justice Commissioner, 'Native Title Report 2008' (Human Rights Commission, 2009) 69.

2　Ibid. 171.

3　Sue Jackson, 'Compartmentalising Culture: The Articulation and Consideration of Indigenous Values in Water Resources Management' (2006) 37(1) *Australian Geographer* 29.

4　Ibid.

5　David Lametti, 'The Concept of Property: Relations through Objects of Social Wealth' (2003) 53 *University of Toronto Law Journal* 328.

6　United Nations University Institute of Advanced Studies, 'Water Discussion Paper for the United Nations Permanent Forum on Indigenous Issues, New York 2007' 1-8 <https://www.ias.unu.edu/default.aspx>.

7   *United Nations Declaration on the Rights of Indigenous Peoples* United Nations <www.un.org/esa/socdev/unpfii/documents/DRIPS_en.pdf>. See Article 25 of the *Declaration*.

8   Department of Aboriginal Affairs (NSW), 'Draft NSW Aboriginal Languages Policy' (2002) unnumbered.

9   Patricia Karvelas, 'Push for Aboriginal Rights over Resources', *The Australian*, 11 April 2008, 6.

10   Ibid.

11   National Water Commission, *The National Water Initiative: Securing Australia's Water Future*, (Australian Government, 2011) iii. The Biennial Assessment of the National Water Initiative is regulated under s 7 of the *National Water Commission Act 2004* (Cth).

12   Ibid Commencing from 200 at app B on the progress of the National Water Initiative Actions.

INDEX

Index

AILR (ALIR (sic))	Australian Indigenous Law Review
ALR	Australian Law Reports
ALRC	Australian Law Reform Commission
CLR	Commonwealth Law Reports
FCA	Federal Court of Australia
FCAFC	" " " " — Full Cour
FCR	Federal Court Reports
FLR	Federal Law Reports
HCA	High Court of Australia
NSWLR	NSW Law Reports
NSWLRC	NSW Law Reform Commission
NSWSC	Supreme Court of NSW (includes Full C
SC	Supreme Court
SCR	Supreme Court Reports

Some are medium neutral citations (see AGLC 3.2.